New Developments in UK and EU Competition Policy

New Developments in UK and EU Competition Policy

Edited by

Roger Clarke
Cardiff University, UK

Eleanor J. Morgan
University of Bath, UK

Edward Elgar
Cheltenham UK • Northampton, MA, USA

Published by
Edward Elgar Publishing Limited
Glensanda House
Montpellier Parade
Cheltenham
Glos GL50 1UA
UK

Edward Elgar Publishing, Inc.
William Pratt House
9 Dewey Court
Northampton
Massachusetts 01060
USA

A catalogue record for this book
is available from the British Library

Library of Congress Cataloguing in Publication Data

New developments in UK and EU competition policy / edited by Roger Clarke,
Eleanor J. Morgan.
        p. cm.
Includes bibliographical references and index.
1.   Competition–Great Britain. 2. Competition–European Union countries.
2.   Antitrust law–Great Britain. 4. Antitrust law–European Union
Countries. I. Clarke, Roger, 1949- II. Morgan, Eleanor J.
    HD41.N398 2007
    338.6048094–dc22

                                    2006015845

ISBN-13: 978 1 84542 122 9
ISBN-10: 1 84542 122 1

Printed and bound in Great Britain by MPG Books Ltd, Bodmin, Cornwall

Contents

Figures

vi

Tables

Contributors

Roger Clarke is Professor of Microeconomics at Cardiff University. He previously held positions at the National Institute of Economic and Social Research, Reading University, Sheffield University, Tulane University, New Orleans and George Washington University, Washington DC. His main areas of research are in industrial economics, in particular market structure, conduct and performance, and applied microeconomics, and he has written a number of books and articles in these areas. He is also the author of a well known textbook on industrial economics.

Claude Crampes is Professor of Economics at Université de Toulouse and member of Groupe de Recherche en Economie Quantitative (Gremaq) and Institut D'Economie Industrielle (IDEI). His research field includes R&D and the economics of networks. In the network industries, he has worked mainly on electricity, water distribution and cable TV. In the field of R&D, he has worked on the innovation process, intellectual property rights (mainly patents), and the biotechnology and software industries.

John Cubbin is Professor of Economics at City University. He previously held positions at National Economic Research Associates (NERA), University of Manchester Institute of Science and Technology (UMIST), Queen Mary University of London and Warwick University. His main areas of research are in industrial economics, in recent years focusing on the regulation of natural monopolies, in particular the measurement of their economic performance. He is a member of the UK Competition Commission.

Paul W. Dobson is Professor of Competition Economics at Loughborough University Business School. He has held academic posts previously at the University of Nottingham and the University of St Andrews. His publications cover industrial economics and competition policy, with particular regard to the economic analysis of retailing, vertical agreements, mergers and market power. He has acted as an adviser and consultant to a wide range of competition authorities, international organisations, industry associations and individual companies. He is an advisory board member of the American Antitrust Institute.

David Encaoua is Professor of Economics at the Université Paris 1 Panthéon Sorbonne. He is also a member of the CNRS research team EUREQua. He previously held positions at OECD and the Ministry of Finance (Direction de la Prévision). His main areas of research include game theory, industrial economics and the economics of innovation. He has written a number of articles and books in these areas, including editing the book *The Economics and Econometrics of Innovation* (Kluwer Academic Press, 2000). He is currently a member of the Economic Advisory Board of the European Patent Office in Munich. He is also the co-author of a recent report on Competition Policy for the French Prime Minister.

Abraham Hollander is Professor of Economics at the University of Montreal. He has held a position at the World Bank and was T.D. MacDonald Chair at the Bureau of Competition Policy in Ottawa in 1996-97. His main fields of interest are in industrial economics, the economics of copyrights and international trade policy. He has published in these areas and is a co-author of a graduate textbook on international trade.

Peter Maunder is Senior Lecturer in Economics at Loughborough University. Between 1997 and 2004 he was Associate Dean (Teaching) of the Faculty of Social Sciences and Humanities. While on sabbatical leave in 1991-92, he was an advisor in the OFT identifying possible cartel activity. Between 1992 and 1994 he took leave of absence from Loughborough to act as an economic advisor at the Monopolies and Mergers Commission. He has written extensively on competition policy matters.

Eleanor J. Morgan is Senior Lecturer in Business Economics in the School of Management, University of Bath. Her recent research has two main strands – the economics of innovation, particularly the problems smaller European firms face in the innovation process, and the effect of government policy on investment decisions, especially as regards the operation and effects of EU merger policy. She has published extensively in these areas. She is Founder Editor (since 1994) of the *International Journal of the Economics of Business*.

Fiona Wishlade is Associate Director of the European Policies Research Centre at the University of Strathclyde. She has led a number of projects in the field of State aid control on behalf of the European Commission, the OECD, most EU15 governments and a number of other public and private organisations. She has also been a short-term pre-accession expert on State aid issues in many of the new Member States and was appointed Arbitrator under the WTO Subsidies Agreement in 1999. She has published a monograph on regional State aid and competition policy in the EU as well as a number of articles and book chapters.

Preface

In the last decade, competition policy has become increasingly prominent and active. This book focuses on the substantial changes in competition policy that have taken place in recent years both in the UK and in the EU. These include new legislation as well as other developments which have had a significant effect on institutional structures, substantive assessment and procedures. There has also been an important change in the responsibilities for specific aspects of competition policy between the EU and Member States, including the UK.

In the UK, major changes have been introduced in the 1998 Competition Act and the 2002 Enterprise Act which have led to substantial reform of almost all aspects of competition policy, replacing earlier legislation in this area, namely the 1973 Fair Trading Act and the 1976 Restrictive Trade Practices Act. Amongst the changes, two new prohibitions have been introduced, one covering dominant firms and the other covering agreements between firms; there has been a new appraisal test in merger policy to focus explicitly on a 'substantial lessening of competition'; a leniency programme has been introduced in cartel cases, while criminal penalties have also been introduced in the case of hard core cartels. At the same time, there have also been significant changes in the powers of various competition authorities with the Secretary of State being removed from active participation in most competition cases and an increase in the responsibilities of the Office of Fair Trading and the Competition Commission. Parallel powers have been given to the sector regulators to investigate, in particular, dominant firms. In total, these changes have introduced a radically reformed competition policy in the UK which is the focus, in part, of this book.

At the same time, important changes have taken place in competition policy at EU level. Of these, perhaps the most important has been the introduction of the new 'Modernization Regulation' which provides the first major reform of procedures in EU antitrust policy since the provisions implementing the original EC Treaty. Amongst other things, this Regulation introduces a new 'legal exception' regime in dealing with Article 81(3); provides for a greater role for national competition authorities in Article 81 and 82 cases and for greater coordination of policy within the EU. In addition, a new merger regulation and horizontal merger guidelines were introduced in 2004 which seek to widen and clarify EU policy on mergers; a new block exemption regulation concerning vertical restraints was adopted in 1999, and active consideration is now being given to reforming policy in the areas of dominant firms and State aids. These developments are in themselves wide-ranging and are also the focus of this book.

In producing this book, our main aim has been to provide an account and assessment of the new policies that have been introduced in many of the key areas discussed above. To this end, each of the contributing authors was asked to discuss the changes that have taken place in the area covered by their chapter and to assess economic and other issues surrounding these developments. It is, of course, true that many of these developments are quite new and so there is limited evidence of their effectiveness at the present time. Nevertheless, it is clearly important to identify the main issues that are likely to arise from the changes, and also to consider possible further developments in these fields. In this way, it is hoped that the examination of developments in competition policy in the UK and EU provided here will be of value to specialists in this area, as well as to non-specialists, including teachers and students of Industrial Economics and Law interested in the new developments that have taken place in this increasingly important area of policy.

The editors would like to thank Luke Adams and Nep Elverd of Edward Elgar for their advice and support in the preparation of this book and the contributing authors for their respective chapters. Finally, we would like to thank a number of colleagues and others who have read individual chapters and provided many useful comments.

Roger Clarke
Eleanor J. Morgan

May 2006

1. Introduction

Roger Clarke and Eleanor J. Morgan

There have been considerable changes in competition policy over the last few years in both the UK and EU. The aim of this book is to examine the recent developments in this important and lively policy area. In the UK, the 1998 Competition Act introduced major changes in legislation that moved it away from the long established framework (based on the 1973 Fair Trading Act and the 1976 Restrictive Trade Practices Act) towards a policy more closely in line with the EU's competition regime. Further significant changes were introduced in the 2002 Enterprise Act, dealing with merger policy, market investigation references and cartels. At the same time, additional legislation has been transforming the structure of regulation of the utility industries in the UK, moves which have also affected the work of the competition authorities. This book includes an account of these recent changes that, together, have substantially altered the UK competition policy regime and examines their implications.

Significant new developments in competition policy have also been occurring in the EU. Potentially, the most important of these at the procedural level has been the adoption of the new Modernization Regulation[1] which introduces substantial reform in the way policy towards monopolies and restrictive practices is dealt with compared with previous arrangements (based on the founding EC Treaty). This regulation amongst other things abolishes the notification system in relation to Article 81(3) of the Treaty, provides for more decentralized application of Articles 81 and 82 and for increased coordination of competition policy within the EU. In addition, the EU has adopted significant changes in other areas. In the case of merger policy, a new Merger Regulation[2] was introduced in 2004. This aims to ensure that the effects of mergers on competition, rather than their structural effects, are the focus of policy and to widen the scope of merger control. Policy on vertical restraints, one of the more difficult areas in competition policy, has also been changed with the adoption of a new Block Exemption Regulation[3] whilst important changes have also been made in policy on the most serious types of cartels, including a new leniency policy introduced in 2002. Together these and other legislative developments[4] have led to significant changes in the framework of EU competition policy and its operation that are an important focus of this study.

1

Competition policy is intertwined with other areas of policy and important new initiatives in industrial policy have affected policies to protect competition. In particular, there have been important steps at EU level towards liberalising the utility industries resulting in some convergence between competition policy and utility regulation that has affected the work of NCAs. The control of State aids is also a key component of EU competition policy and provision for centralised control was established under the founding EC Treaty. Recent changes have aimed to allow 'less and better targeted' aid and ensure competition is not unduly distorted in the attempt to achieve other policy objectives. Similarly, there are also potential tensions between the law regarding intellectual property rights (IPRs), which gives firms incentives to develop new products and new technologies, and the protection of competition in the market. Recent developments here include major Court judgements that clarify EU policy. Developments in these areas of competition policy are examined within the later chapters of the book.

One theme underlying recent changes in competition policy, particularly in the UK, has been the attempt to introduce greater harmonization of policy within the enlarging EU. In addition, there has also been an increased recognition that the degree of competition is a major determinant of the effectiveness of the market in bringing about economic efficiency and of its importance in providing benefits for consumers (for example, through lower prices, greater choice and better quality products). This belief has been reflected at the UK level in measures such as the substantial increase in powers given to the Office of Fair Trading (OFT) and the Competition Commission (CC) and also in policy underlying the progressive privatization of regulated industries where the aim has been to introduce competition into the market whenever possible, relying increasingly on market forces (overseen as part of competition policy) rather than sector specific regulation to ensure satisfactory performance. There have also been changes in procedures under the EU Modernization Regulation, as noted above, which envisage a larger role for NCAs in dealing with dominant firms and restrictive practices. These are expected also to give the Competition Directorate-General (DG Competition) more time to concentrate on the serious competition cases and to allow more effective policing of State aids as well as encouraging further progress with the liberalisation of the utilities.

The next two sections of this chapter provide a brief overview of the developments in the key elements of competition policy in the UK and EU in recent years. We begin with developments in the UK and, in particular, the two most recent major pieces of competition legislation– the 1998 Competition Act and the 2002 Enterprise Act. This is followed by a discussion of EU competition policy, including Articles 81 and 82 of the EC Treaty, as well as other areas of policy reform.[5] The final section of this chapter then provides an outline of the rest of the book.

DEVELOPMENTS IN UK POLICY: AN OVERVIEW

The developments in UK competition policy, as noted above, stem from the 1998 Competition Act and the 2002 Enterprise Act (see Figure 1.1). In the first of these, attention focused on horizontal and vertical agreements between firms and on dominant firms. In the second, a number of further important policy changes relating to cartels, market investigation references and mergers were introduced, accompanied by some significant procedural reforms. Together these changes have led to a substantial reform in UK policy in many of the key areas usually considered important in competition policy. This section reviews these developments.

Policy Reform: the Competition Act 1998

The primary aim of the 1998 Competition Act has been to bring UK competition policy more into line with policy in the EU (see Utton, 2000b).[6] As is well known, the Act introduced two important new prohibitions into UK law: the Chapter I prohibition which deals with cartels and restrictive practices, and is closely modelled on Article 81 of the EC Treaty, and the Chapter II prohibition which deals with monopoly problems in the form of dominant firms and is closely modelled on Article 82 of the Treaty.

In a little more detail, under Chapter I

> . . . agreements between undertakings, decisions by associations of undertakings or concerted practices which
>   (a) may affect trade within the United Kingdom, and
>   (b) have as their object or effect the prevention, restriction or distortion of competition within the United Kingdom,
> are prohibited unless they are exempt in accordance with the provisions of this Part (Competition Act, 1998, Section 2(1)).

The wording of this test moved UK policy from an emphasis on the particular form of agreement to an 'effects based' policy that matches Article 81 of the EC Treaty (which applies to trade between Member States).

Similarly, in line with EU policy, the Act identifies a number of types of agreement that might infringe this effects based prohibition. Agreements may be prohibited if they:

(a)   directly or indirectly fix purchase or selling prices or any other trading conditions;
(b)   limit or control production, markets, technical development or investment;
(c)   share markets or sources of supply;
(d)   apply dissimilar conditions to equivalent transactions with other trading parties, thereby placing them at a competitive disadvantage;

(e)   make the conclusion of contracts subject to acceptance by the other parties of supplementary obligations which, by their nature or according to commercial usage, have no connection with the subject of such contracts (Competition Act, Chapter I, section 2(2)).

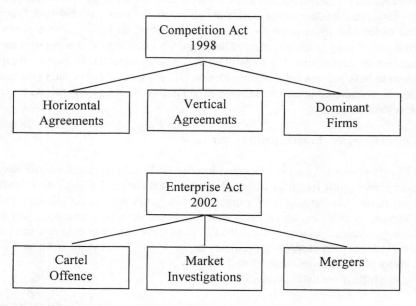

Figure 1.1 Recent UK competition policy

This list of types of agreement is not meant to be exhaustive, however, and other types of agreement may also be prohibited depending on their effects. The Act relates to both horizontal and vertical restraints. The strongest policy is toward horizontal agreements and, in particular, hard core cartels, such as agreements which fix prices, limit production, share markets or rig bids, which may act to prevent, restrict or distort competition and these are, typically, prohibited under the Act. In the case of vertical agreements, the view is generally held in the UK (as in the EU) that such agreements are unlikely to have undesirable effects if markets are competitive, although they may do where market shares are high.

The Act allows for several exemptions to the prohibition, again in line with EU policy. First, an agreement can be subject to an 'individual exemption' if the firms can show that the agreement contributes to improving production or distribution, or promoting technical or economic progress, and it also allows a fair share of the benefits to consumers. In this case, the agreement must be limited to only matters strictly necessary to achieve these benefit(s) and must not involve eliminating competition from a substantial part of the market.[7] Second, agreements may be subject to a 'block exemption', where a class of agreement is exempted from the prohibition. This was applied, initially, to all non-price vertical agreements following the 1998 Act, although subsequently this block exemption has been removed in favour of the EU's effects based approach.[8] Third, an agreement can obtain a 'parallel exemption' in the UK if it already has an individual or block exemption at EU level and this provides for greater harmonization of UK policy with the EU.

There are two further exemptions to the prohibition on agreements which prevent, restrict or distort competition worth noting. First, under the Act, an 'appreciable effect test' is applied in line with EU policy whereby, in the case of a horizontal agreement, an agreement will not be found to have appreciable effect on competition if the combined market share of the firms involved is less than 10 per cent.[9] However, this does not apply to agreements between firms which fix prices or market shares, limit production or set resale prices (in hard core cartels) where no market share limit is set. The Act also gives immunity from financial penalties for 'small agreements' where the combined turnover of the firms is less than £20 million.[10] This is provided to protect small firms from possible bankruptcy (or, at least, financial difficulty) if a large fine were to be imposed. Again, the protection does not apply to agreements involving price-fixing or limiting supply or production, market sharing or bid-rigging.

The Competition Act also brought in significant changes in UK policy on monopolies/dominant firms. In this case, the Chapter II prohibition states that

> any conduct on the part of one or more undertakings which amounts to the abuse of a dominant position in a market is prohibited if it may affect trade within the United Kingdom (Competition Act, 1998, Section 18(1)).

As with the Chapter I prohibition, the Act gives examples of conduct that could constitute an abuse which are in line with EU policy. These include setting unfair prices and other trading conditions, limiting production, applying dissimilar conditions to equivalent transactions or using tie-in sales. Again, these are to be treated as examples and are not meant to be exhaustive.

The prohibition focuses on two issues: the idea of dominance and the abuse of a dominant position. As noted later in this chapter, EU policy as applied by the European Commission normally treats a market share above 50 per cent as evidence of dominance, although other factors, such as competition from other firms and new entrants, will also be taken into account. The OFT has indicated that evidence of dominance will not normally be found if a market share is below 40 per cent although again this can depend on other factors.[11] The Chapter II prohibition also applies to an *abuse* of a dominant position and hence does not apply to cases where a firm has a dominant position, but is not found to be abusing that position. This is in line with EU policy, and similarly with policy in the US.[12]

Procedures under the prohibitions are similar under Chapter I and Chapter II. The OFT[13] is required to keep markets under review and to undertake an investigation if an infringement of a prohibition is thought to exist. If the OFT finds evidence of an infringement, it will, initially, issue a 'provisional decision' following which firms affected are allowed to make a response. If it still believes an infringement exists, the OFT can then make an 'infringement decision' and also impose fines. Currently, the maximum fine for an infringement is 10 per cent of the worldwide turnover of the firms involved (usually calculated in the previous financial year), in line with EU policy. In contrast to earlier policy, however, firms can appeal the OFT's decision to the Competition Appeal Tribunal (CAT) (previously known as the Competition Commission Appeal Tribunal (CCAT))[14] which can refer the case back for review or vary the amount of a fine. The Act also allows for appeals to the Court of Appeal (or the Court of Session in Scotland) but only on points of law or the level of fines imposed.

The new policy strengthens earlier policies in a number of different ways. First, the Act gives wide powers to the OFT to investigate cases where an infringement of the prohibition is suspected and, if necessary, it can conduct 'dawn raids' on premises to collect information. This contrasts with the relatively weak powers it had to collect information under the earlier legislation. Second, the OFT has the power to reach decisions in restrictive practice and dominance cases and to impose fines. This compares with earlier policy on monopoly, in particular, where the Secretary of State had the power to make decisions and impose remedies. Decisions on restrictive practices were previously made separately by the Restrictive Practices Court. The provision for fines is also new. As well as strengthening the OFT's powers in these ways the Act gives a right of appeal to the OFT's decisions and this compares with very limited rights of appeal in earlier policy.

Following the introduction of the 1998 Act, the UK government, initially, chose to retain some parts of the 1973 Fair Trading Act (FTA), in addition to the Chapter II prohibition.[15] The main aim here was to ensure that there was no weakening of the law in this area. First, it took the view that while the new prohibition might be used against single dominant firms, experience at EU level suggested that it was less clear that it could be used to deal with collective dominance, where several firms might be involved. In light of this, it retained the 'complex monopoly' provisions of the FTA, which related to cases where several firms had a combined market share of 25 per cent or more. Second, it also decided that some positions of dominance might not be dealt with effectively with fines and, in particular, that structural remedies might be required. It, therefore, retained the 'scale monopoly' provisions of the FTA to deal with such cases.[16] These powers were, however, repealed and replaced under the provisions of the 2002 Enterprise Act.

Policy Reform: the Enterprise Act 2002

Further significant changes were introduced in the 2002 Enterprise Act. First, the Act tightened policy on restrictive agreements, in particular, to allow criminal penalties against individuals found to be involved in hard core cartels. Second, the Act introduced a revised policy on mergers updating the earlier policy under the FTA. Finally, the Act also introduced a new policy of 'market investigation references' which replaced the earlier monopoly provisions of the FTA.[17]

In the case of cartels, the Act strengthened policy in two areas. First, it provided for much wider powers of investigation in cases of hard core cartels. In addition to its powers to make 'dawn raids' under the 1998 Act, the OFT now has the power to engage in directed and covert surveillance, including the use of bugging devices, use of hidden cameras and so on. This reflects the stronger line being taken on hard core cartels in the UK (and, more generally, in the EU and US). Second, the Act created a new offence, 'the cartel offence', which introduces criminal penalties for individuals involved in hard core cartel cases. Under this provision[18] of the Act, which is similar to policy in the US, individuals (rather than firms) can be held liable for engaging in hard core cartels. The maximum penalty for this offence is an unlimited fine and/or imprisonment for five years. Cases will, typically, be dealt with by the Serious Fraud Office, although the OFT also has concurrent powers. This criminalisation of cartel activity, as noted above, is in line with US policy, but not with EU policy where no criminal penalties exist. This marks a significant difference between EU and UK policy.

The Act has also introduced a new merger policy replacing the earlier policy based on the 1973 FTA and resulting in several changes. First, responsibility for merger cases has been transferred to the OFT and the Competition Commission (CC), and the role of government ministers has been reduced in all but a very few cases.[19] Under the new policy, the OFT makes references to the CC as before but the CC now has the power to make decisions whether or not a merger is allowed to go ahead. This reflects a general move away from government intervention in competition policy in recent years. Second, the OFT and the CC are required to be more transparent in their decision-making, with the OFT, in particular, now being required to publish reasons for its decisions. Following this, both the OFT and the CC have published guidelines on how they will conduct merger investigations which are similar to the guidelines that have operated for a long period in the US. Third, there is a new right of appeal to the CAT which is able to review merger decisions and refer them back to the CC if necessary. Finally, the Act has also introduced a new competition test – the substantial lessening of competition (SLC) test – in merger cases. This test focuses directly on how the merger affects competition rather than on the broader 'public interest' test included in the earlier legislation. This is in line with practice as it had developed in the UK and was already formalised in legislation elsewhere, particularly in the US.

New 'market investigation references' were introduced under the Enterprise Act to replace the statutory monopoly provisions of the FTA. This policy change gives the OFT power to refer cases to the CC if it believes that competition is not working effectively in a particular market. There are three conditions for the policy to be applied: first, the OFT must be sure that the case cannot be dealt with more effectively under the Chapter I and II prohibitions; second, the problem must be important enough to require a reference to the CC and third, it must be likely that a satisfactory remedy can be found.[20] The CC undertakes an investigation (which may take up to two years) and can impose remedies on the firm(s) involved. The firm(s) can appeal the CC's decision to the CAT in the same way as in Chapter I, Chapter II and merger decisions.

The new policy differs from policy under the 1973 FTA in a number of ways. In contrast to the FTA, there is no explicit requirement that a statutory monopoly exists in a market investigation reference. This enables the CC to focus on the question of competition rather than ancillary requirements such as whether a certain market share test is met or not. The CC also has the power to impose remedies in market investigation cases in a similar way to merger policy so government ministers no longer play a significant role in policy in this area. As with merger policy, firms can appeal decisions of the CC to the CAT which has the power to refer cases back to the CC. This again contrasts with the earlier position where the Secretary of State had strong powers to impose remedies in FTA cases and there was no right of appeal, other than on points of law.

Finally, it should be noted that following the Modernization Regulation discussed in the next section, the OFT has been given powers by the UK Government to investigate infringements of Articles 81 and 82 of the EC Treaty, in addition to the Chapter I and II prohibitions, thereby significantly widening its powers to consider infringements which affect trade between Member States as well as trade within the UK.

DEVELOPMENTS IN EU POLICY: AN OVERVIEW

The main features of EU competition policy are summarised in Figure 1.2. The basis of EU policy as originally enacted is given in Articles 81 and 82 of the EC Treaty which deal with agreements between firms and abuse of a dominant position respectively. The key features of EU policy in each of these areas are now outlined in turn. This is followed by a discussion of the developments in four areas of EU competition policy – the Modernization Regulation, merger policy, vertical restraints and State aid.

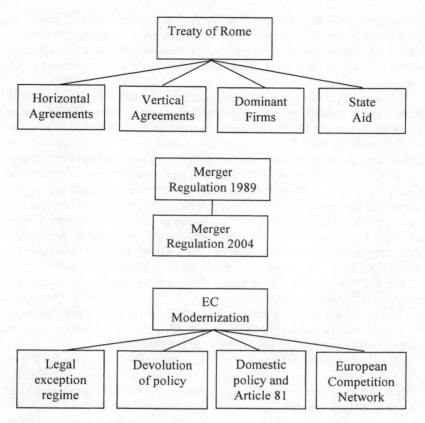

Figure 1.2 EU competition policy

Articles 81 and 82

Agreements between firms are prohibited under Article 81 of the Treaty if they have the effect of preventing, restricting or distorting competition within the EU. Thus, in Article 81(1)

> The following shall be prohibited as incompatible with the common market: all agreements between undertakings, decisions by associations of undertakings and concerted practices which may affect trade between Member States and which have as their object or effect the prevention, restriction or distortion of competition within the common market (EC Treaty, Article 81(1)).

Article 81(2) declares such agreements to be void. Article 81(3), however, provides for exemptions from the Article 81(1) prohibition. These exemptions, as noted for the UK, can arise if an agreement has the effect of improving production or distribution, or of promoting technical or economic progress, as long as it is necessary to achieve the benefits, does not eliminate competition in a substantial part of the market in question and also provides a fair share of the benefits to consumers.

EU policy like that in the UK covers both vertical and horizontal agreements. In the case of vertical agreements ('vertical restraints'), a number of important block exemptions had been introduced over time including some key forms of vertical restraint such as exclusive distribution, exclusive purchasing and franchising, but these have been replaced[21] by a new block exemption regulation which we discuss further below. The general view on vertical restraints, as in the UK, is that they are unlikely to be harmful if competition is relatively strong in a market but they can be so if competition is already weak, in particular if one or more firms has a high market share. In the case of horizontal agreements, most attention has focused on hard core cartels which are seen as particularly damaging to consumer welfare. This has led to a number of significant cases in which firms have been found to be restricting competition and fined.[22]

The EU has recently had considerable success in introducing a leniency programme[23] following earlier success of such a policy in the US. This policy has had a dramatic effect on the operation of EU policy with a large increase in the number of cartels successfully prosecuted in recent years.[24] Further revisions to the leniency programme were introduced in 2002.[25]

EU policy on dominant firms is dealt with under Article 82 of the EC Treaty which focuses on abuse of a dominant position in one or more markets affecting trade within the common market. In line with policy in the UK, dominance is not held to be an infringement of Article 82 but rather any conduct which amounts to an abuse of a dominant position may be dealt with under this provision. In terms of US policy this implies the EU uses a 'rule of reason' approach rather than a *per se* prohibition in this case.[26]

Article 82 states that

> any abuse by one or more undertakings of a dominant position within the common market or in a substantial part of it shall be prohibited as incompatible with the common market in so far as it may affect trade between Member States.

The Article goes on to list forms of abuse of a dominant position as

(a)   directly or indirectly imposing unfair purchase or selling prices or other unfair trading conditions;

(b)   limiting production, markets or technical developments to the prejudice of consumers;

(c)   applying dissimilar conditions to equivalent transactions with other trading parties, thereby placing them at a competitive disadvantage;

(d)   making the conclusion of contracts subject to acceptance by the other parties of supplementary obligations which, by their nature or according to commercial usage, have no connection with the subject of such contracts (EC Treaty, Article 82).

This list of possible forms of abuse is not meant to be exhaustive and other forms of abuse can arise.

Although Article 82 does not define a dominant position, the European Court provided a generally accepted definition in a relatively early decision:

[a] dominant position . . . relates to a position of economic strength enjoyed by an undertaking which enables it to prevent effective competition being maintained on the relevant market by affording it the power to behave to an appreciable extent independently of its competitors, its customers and ultimately of the consumers (*Hoffman-La Roche*, 1979).[27]

As discussed in the previous section, the European Commission has adopted the view that a market share of 50 per cent or more will normally be seen as evidence of dominance, although other factors such as the strength of existing competitors and potential entry will also be taken into account. In addition, the Commission has stated that

dominance is more likely to be found in the market share range of 40 per cent to 50 per cent than below 40 per cent, although also undertakings with market shares below 40 per cent could be considered to be in a dominant position. However, undertakings with market shares of no more than 25 per cent are not likely to enjoy a (single) dominant position on the market concerned (DG Competition, 'The application of Article 82 of the Treaty to exclusionary abuses,' Discussion paper, December 2005, p. 11).

In practice, however, it appears that the market share test of 50 per cent is most often used.

Recent Developments in EU Policy

There have been a number of important changes in EU policy in recent years and four of these developments are considered here.[28] The adoption of the 'Modernization Regulation', which came into effect on 1 May 2004, was the most significant development from a procedural point of view and is discussed first. The other changes highlighted are the new policy on mergers, the new vertical restraints block exemption and the changing approach to State aid.

The new Modernization Regulation has made four important changes to the operation of EU competition policy compared with Regulation 17/62[29] which previously regulated procedures. First, under the Regulation the earlier system of notification of agreements under Article 81(3) of the EC Treaty has been replaced by a 'legal exception' regime. Under the earlier policy, firms were required to notify agreements to the Commission if they wished to gain exemption under Article 81(3) and this led to many, often innocuous, agreements being notified. Under the new Regulation, this policy no longer operates and firms are responsible themselves for ensuring that an agreement satisfies the conditions for exemption under Article 81(3). While this may increase costs for firms to some extent (in so far as they may need to take legal advice in considering whether an agreement satisfies Article 81(3)), it will also substantially reduce the workload of the Commission, allowing it to focus on cases where a more significant restriction on competition is thought to exist.

Second, the Regulation seeks to decentralize the application of Articles 81 and 82 to NCAs and courts within Member States. While the power to apply parts of Article 81, and all of Article 82, already existed under the earlier Regulation, national courts were hampered in this in relation to Article 81 in that the Commission alone could determine whether an individual exemption would apply. Under the new Regulation, Articles 81 and 82 apply in their entirety and hence, in particular, Article 81 cases can be dealt with fully by national courts. In addition, while NCAs could play a role in Article 81 and 82 cases under the earlier Regulation, this required national law to empower them to do so and in practice investigations were primarily the responsibility of the Commission. Under the new Regulation, NCAs are required to apply Articles 81 and 82 when domestic competition law is employed and trade between Member States is affected in relation to restrictive agreements and the abuse of a dominant position. It is envisaged that as a result of these changes, a significant proportion of cases under Article 81 and 82 will now be dealt with by NCAs and national courts rather than at EU level. The Commission will, however, take responsibility for cases with a significant Community-wide dimension or where potential important precedents may arise.

Third, Member States are required to implement domestic policies on restrictive agreements in line with EU policy. More specifically, they are required not to prohibit an agreement between firms at national level which would not be prohibited under Article 81. A similar requirement in relation to the abuse of a dominant position, however, does not apply.

Finally, the new Regulation creates a European Competition Network (ECN) comprising the European Commission and NCAs to coordinate competition policy within the EU. This is primarily concerned with the allocation of cases between the Commission and the NCAs and aims to use the most appropriate jurisdiction in any particular case.

Although these changes are procedural they are nevertheless important. In particular, the decentralization of powers is expected to lead to a major change in the way Articles 81 and 82 are applied while the reform of policy on Article 81(3) will eliminate wasteful examination of innocuous agreements. The other measures will also lead to greater coordination and harmonization of policies within the EU although less so as far as Article 82 is concerned.

The next recent development considered here is the introduction of a new Merger Regulation (ECMR) (in 2004)[30] to replace the earlier regulation adopted in 1989.[31] This marked the most radical change in EU merger control since the 1989 merger regulation was first adopted. The new regulation introduces an important substantive change in merger policy as well as changes to the division of jurisdiction in merger control, and was accompanied by important procedural and organisational reforms.

Turning to the substantive change first, the new regulation sought to deal with important problems under the earlier ECMR. Under the original regulation, the appraisal test was based on the creation or strengthening of a 'dominant position' in a market using a concept of 'dominance' drawn from the case law under Article 82. Although the interpretation of dominance had been widened in the course of applying the ECMR to bring mergers which might lead to oligopolistic coordination within its scope ('collective dominance'), there were concerns both that the wording of the test put too much emphasis on market structure and that it excluded oligopolistic behaviour which was not coordinated but might still be anti-competitive. The new regulation sought to improve this situation by introducing a new appraisal test. While dominance is still noted in the new test as a particular case, the test is primarily based on whether the merger creates a significant impediment to effective competition (SIEC):

> A concentration which would significantly impede effective competition in the common market or in a substantial part of it, in particular as a result of the creation or strengthening of a dominant position, shall be declared incompatible with the common market (ECMR, 2004, Article 2 (3)).

The Commission has also published horizontal merger guidelines[32] for the first time which, together with the preamble to the ECMR, make it clear that the new SIEC test is expected to bring non-coordinated effects among oligopolists within the scope of the regulation, so extending the scope of the regulation beyond the threshold at which collective dominance could be found. The guidelines also clarify how the effects of mergers on efficiency are to be treated under the new regulation as well as outlining the approach the Commission expects to adopt in appraising horizontal mergers. These have considerable similarities to the approach adopted in the US, and indicate a further convergence of EU merger policy towards the US merger regime.

As regards jurisdiction, the EU merger control was designed from the outset to provide a 'one stop shop', with the allocation of responsibility for scrutinising mergers between the Commission and NCAs being based on turnover thresholds (with limited exceptions involving referrals to or from Member States at the Commission's discretion). These thresholds were intended to ensure that significant mergers with a 'Community-wide dimension' were subject to centralised control. Supplementary thresholds were introduced in 1998 to try to include mergers within the ECMR that would otherwise be likely to involve multiple filings in three or more Member States and minor adjustments were made to the provisions for referrals.[33]

While the thresholds determining jurisdiction remained unchanged in 2004, further changes were made to the referral provisions. Most notably, these allowed referrals to be requested earlier than previously (before the merger is formally notified) and these requests can now be made by the firms involved rather than the NCAs in order to improve case allocation and streamline policy.

A third development is in the treatment of vertical restraints by the EU. This relates to the new Block Exemption Regulation adopted in 1999.[34] Under this regulation, the Commission has moved away from a policy based on the particular form of an agreement towards an 'effects-based' approach. Under the new regulation, vertical agreements between firms are assumed *not* to have anti-competitive effects if the combined market share of the firms involved is less than 30 per cent. On the other hand, if their share is above 30 per cent anti-competitive effects may, but cannot be presumed, to arise. The regulation, however, identifies certain hard core restraints (relating to resale price maintenance and a number of types of exclusivity agreement) where the 30 per cent cut-off point does not apply. The new regulation simplifies the operation of the policy in this area and allows the Commission to focus on cases where concerns over vertical restraints are most likely to exist.

Finally, there are continuing changes in State aid policy, which has been an integral part of EU competition policy since the founding Treaty of Rome but has received increased attention since the early 1990s as trade barriers were further dismantled under the Single Market programme. Article 87 of the EC Treaty prohibits any aid granted by a Member State that distorts or threatens to distort competition by favouring certain firms or the production of certain goods in so far as trade between Member States is affected. The Treaty explicitly allows for exceptions to the ban where the proposed aid scheme may have a beneficial impact overall, and does not distort intra-Community competition and trade to an extent which is against the common interest.

The Commission has made a number of changes in recent years with the aim of focusing attention on the most distortionary types of aid, encouraging less and better targeted aid and making policy more predictable. These piecemeal changes have resulted in a very complex system of control and a comprehensive reform of State aid policy is currently under discussion. The reform plan has been prompted by the recent enlargement of the EU which has underlined the need to prioritise action and make choices more transparently, as well as to introduce better governance to ensure more effective control of State aid.[35]

OUTLINE OF THE BOOK

The rest of the book is organised as follows. In Chapter 2, Roger Clarke discusses developments in policy on dominant firms and monopoly in the UK and EU. In the UK, the main changes that have been introduced are the Chapter II prohibition of the 1998 Competition Act which brought UK policy more closely into line with policy in the EU and the introduction of market investigation references under the 2002 Enterprise Act. The former policy represents a shift in emphasis in UK policy towards abuse of dominance in line with EU policy, but the latter provides additional powers not available at the EU level to deal with markets where competition appears not to be working effectively but which cannot be dealt with under the Chapter II (or Chapter I) prohibitions. The latter provides wider scope for UK policy in this area than in EU policy. However, some potential weaknesses of this policy are the relatively long time periods between the start of investigations and the time when remedies are likely to put in place (including time for possible appeals) and whether the CC is best placed to implement the remedies that it proposes.

The chapter also discusses EU policy on dominant firms under Article 82 of the EC Treaty together with the new Modernization Regulation. This policy has not changed dramatically in the last few years although there has been some reform under the Modernization Regulation. The chapter reviews a selection of recent high profile cases, notably *Microsoft* and *Coca Cola*, and assesses the effectiveness of policy in these examples. The chapter concludes by considering the proposed reforms of Article 82 policy recently put forward by the European Commission in its 2005 discussion paper. These include the introduction of a new test in cases where exclusionary behaviour may exist based on an 'as-efficient competitor', whereby behaviour would be judged on whether it would exclude or weaken an equally efficient competitor, and the use of an efficiency defence in Article 82 cases. The chapter discusses some problems with the first of these proposed reforms and it remains to be seen whether (and in what form) the test will be developed.

In Chapter 3, Peter Maunder examines the operation of the new UK merger control regime that was introduced in June 2003. This chapter highlights the major reform of the structural framework for merger control which transferred decision-making authority in all but very exceptional merger cases from government ministers to the OFT and CC. Although, in practice, ministerial involvement had become fairly limited, he shows that some of the residual uncertainty surrounding merger control has been removed by taking merger control almost entirely from the political arena.

The chapter discusses both the new appraisal provisions, under which the 'public interest' test has been replaced by a purely competition-based test, and the introduction of new detailed guidelines, demonstrating that these largely formalise and sharpen existing policy. It assesses the procedural changes which were designed to increase the accountability and transparency of the newly independent competition authorities and to speed merger decisions. The combined effect of the requirement that the OFT publish all decisions on mergers and the new right to apply for a review of OFT and CC decisions to the CAT, which has already made its mark in merger policy, are seen as providing a significant check on the OFT's and CC's new powers and as likely to encourage sounder decisions. Overall, the evidence in this chapter shows that the new developments in UK merger policy do not amount to a radical change of direction but usefully build on and strengthen a regime that has been evolving, and continues to evolve, over time.

Eleanor Morgan examines new developments in the EU system of merger control, especially those relating to horizontal mergers, in Chapter 4. The breadth of the recent reform package was partly due to a series of high profile Court judgements against the Commission which highlighted serious inadequacies in the previous system and facilitated change. The revised wording of the appraisal test introduced by the new Merger Regulation in May 2004, together with the new horizontal guidelines, should reduce the emphasis on structure *per se* in horizontal merger decisions even though reference to dominance has been retained.

The new provisions relating to unilateral ('non-coordinated') effects by oligopolists are the only area in which the scope of merger control has apparently been enlarged although the practical significance of this development, which has yet to be tested in the Courts, is questioned. In general, the substantive changes are shown to bring the treatment of horizontal mergers more closely into line with the US regime. The changes to the Commission's internal working methods and organization are seen as the most significant of the new developments and it is argued that the increased emphasis on economic expertise, slight relaxation of time limits and enhanced provision for checks and balances, should help to improve the quality of merger decisions. The chapter concludes that it will take time to see if these reforms will restore the credibility of the merger control system or whether more far reaching changes to the EU's administrative system of merger control are required.

In Chapter 5, Roger Clarke and Eleanor Morgan consider developments in restrictive trade practices policy/policy on horizontal agreements in the UK and EU. Such policy has undergone a number of important changes in recent years in both jurisdictions. One part of this has been the recognition in both the UK and EU that 'hard core' cartels – those relating to price-fixing, limiting supply or production, market sharing and bid-rigging, in particular – almost always restrict or distort competition and should be effectively prohibited in both the EU and UK. In addition, the UK has adopted a stronger policy than the EU by introducing criminal penalties in hard core cartel cases. This represents a major change in policy in the UK although how effective this policy will be remains to be seen.

Also of major importance are the leniency programmes introduced in the UK and EU following earlier success with such measures in the US. These programmes, at least in the EU (it is too early to evaluate the success or otherwise of UK policy) have led to a substantial increase in prosecutions in cartel cases. It is argued that these measures, more than any others, have strengthened policy in this area, although some weaknesses in EU policy, in particular, are also discussed. The chapter ends by considering possible further developments in policy in this area. Topics discussed include greater cooperation between countries in dealing with international cartels, further reform of leniency policies in the UK and EU and the targeting of sectors and industries in dealing with cartel cases.

In Chapter 6, Paul Dobson considers developments in the EU and UK in policy on vertical restraints. These restraints involve restrictions on the freedom of action of firms at different stages of production and distribution and the effects these may have in restricting, preventing or distorting competition. In contrast to horizontal agreements, vertical restraints generally have an ambiguous effect on economic welfare: on the one hand, possibly restricting competition (for example by affecting intra- or inter-brand competition) and on the other, by increasing economic efficiency. As far as the EU is concerned, the chapter focuses, in particular, on the new Block Exemption Regulation (BER) adopted in 1999. The new BER replaces the earlier 'form-based' approach with an 'effects-based' approach concentrating on the anti-competitive effects of a restraint rather than the particular form of the restraint. It is argued that this provides a better method for dealing with vertical restraints, given the different forms of vertical restraint that exist, and their combination, which can have similar economic effects. The policy also introduces a market share test to deal with non-hard core vertical restraints.

The chapter also considers UK policy on vertical restraints which came into force in May 2005. The chapter provides a general appraisal of the reforms and argues that whilst the move to an 'effects-based' approach is desirable, other weaknesses remain. Nevertheless, the new policy is a useful step forward in the treatment of vertical restraints.

In Chapter 7, John Cubbin shows how the process of liberalisation of selective industries has been assisted by using the competition policy provisions of national and European law, including those relating to the abuse of dominance, anti-competitive practices, merger control and EU policy on State aids. Such controls have, however, not in themselves been sufficient to guarantee effective competition in the utilities and this chapter places them in context by looking more broadly at the various measures which may be used to try to increase competition – in the market, for the market, for corporate control and for inputs – and at regulation which may attempt to mimic the behaviour of markets where competition in the market is not feasible.

In the UK, these mechanisms have been most fully and successfully applied in energy markets and the evidence in this chapter suggests that direct competition in the market facilitated by vertical ownership separation has been the most effective of all the measures. The UK approach, with its successes and failures, has had an important influence on EU policy. The chapter discusses EU policy towards telecommunications and energy where the main focus to date has been on encouraging the development of competition in the market through opening access to networks rather than vertical separation. It highlights difficulties in securing reform of the utility industries through EU level initiatives and shows the variation in the extent to which EU Directives have currently been adopted by Member States, although some encouraging signs of progress are identified.

In Chapter 8, Claude Crampes, David Encaoua and Abraham Hollander discuss competition and intellectual property rights (IPRs) and the tensions that exist between them. While competition policy is concerned to protect competition in markets for goods and services, intellectual property rights exist to give incentives for firms to develop new products and new technologies. As the authors stress, the important thing here is to provide *ex ante* incentives to invest in innovations rather than adopt an *ex post* reward approach often favoured by lawyers. In an *ex post* approach, the focus is on competition after the investment has been made and this ignores the incentives to undertake the research in the first place.

The authors consider three areas of tension between competition policy and IPRs. First, in the area of parallel imports, the ECJ has taken the view that attempts to segment markets within the EU contravene the EC Treaty and hence are typically not allowed. Attempts to bring in parallel imports from outside the EU are often blocked, however, thereby providing a protectionist element in EU policy. The second issue concerns refusals to licence technical know-how, or products protected by patents and copyrights. While IPRs give firms the right to decide whether licensing should take place, competition policy may be affected if these rights relate, in particular, to an essential input. In this case, refusal to license an input indispensable in the production of another good or service may contravene Article 82 of the EC Treaty. In practice, the ECJ has dealt with this on a case-by-case basis deciding in some cases (notably the *Magill* case) that compulsory licensing is required. Finally, the chapter considers collectives and highlights the potential conflicts which arise in the monopolization of rights by collectives. A 'rule of reason' approach has been used in this area recognising the need to protect the property rights of individuals on the one hand and giving incentives to parties to minimise costs on the other.

In Chapter 9, Fiona Wishlade provides an overview of the current position and future directions in EU State aid control policy. Although enshrined in the

Treaty from the outset, EU State aid control was long regarded as the Cinderella of the EU competition rules. Initially, the Commission's use of its extensive powers was rather tentative, but, since the 1990s, policy has evolved rapidly. The Commission has been increasingly willing to take decisions against Member States and the scope of policy to control State aid has been broadened.

The chapter begins by setting out the context for State aid control – notably in terms of expenditure on State aid and the role of the Commission – before discussing what constitutes State aid. This is a difficult but crucial question since the powers of the Commission over other national measures that distort competition tend to be limited. In principle, State aids are banned under the Treaty, but certain exceptions are provided for and the interpretation of these exceptions is the prerogative of the Commission. The Commission's interpretation of the exceptions from the State aid prohibition has spawned a massive body of 'soft' law and, increasingly, 'hard' law and the chapter shows how the Commission has exercised its discretion in key policy areas. Last, the main themes underpinning recent developments in State aid policy are discussed. The chapter reviews the conceptual, technical and political challenges ahead as the Commission attempts to refocus State aid control to take account of the effects of enlargement and the priorities of the Lisbon Agenda.

Finally, in Chapter 10, the editors draw together some of the elements discussed in the preceding chapters and consider possible future directions for competition policy in the UK and EU. Clearly, a number of major changes have taken place in competition policy in these jurisdictions and a case can be made for a period of consolidation to allow the effects of the various changes to be considered. Nevertheless, there are areas of current policy concern.

As regards UK policy, it is not clear how effective market investigation references will be in dealing with market power issues as discussed in Chapter 2. Also, while important changes have taken place in policy on hard core cartels, including the introduction of the new leniency programme and the criminal cartel offence, it remains to be seen whether the provisions will be effective in dealing, in particular, with large cartel cases.

At the EU level, another such area is the new Merger Regulation, discussed in Chapter 4, where an eventual compromise was reached in the wording of the regulation; it is not clear whether this has ensured that dominance *per se* will not matter in future and whether unilateral effects among oligopolists will be dealt with satisfactorily. This will ultimately depend on the interpretation of the Regulation in the European Court of Justice. Major changes have also been introduced to deal with vertical restraints; this is a relatively difficult area of competition policy and it remains to be seen whether this new policy will prove satisfactory. EU policies on dominant firms and State aids are areas where there may be scope for substantial reform in future and possible changes to policy in these two areas are currently under consideration.

The chapter also considers further developments in the competition policy field. This discussion highlights internal developments including moves to improve the transparency of the new policies, the increased use of economic analysis in dealing with policy problems and the issue of ensuring accountability. These matters are all important in the operation of future competition policy. The chapter concludes with a discussion of external developments, including the need to harmonize competition policy at the extra-EU level, and looks at some of the limited moves to date in this area.

NOTES

1. Council Regulation (EC) No 1/2003 of 16 December 2002 on the implementation of the rules laid down in Articles 81 and 82 of the Treaty, OJ L1, 4 January 2003.
2. Council Regulation (EC) No 139/2004 of 20 January 2004 on the control of concentrations between undertakings, OJ L24, 29 January 2004.
3. Council Regulation (EC) No. 2790/1999 of 22 December 1999 on the application of Article 81(3) of the Treaty to categories of vertical agreements and concerted practices (the EC Block Exemption Regulation), OJ L336, 29 December 1999.
4. At time of writing, the European Commission is also reviewing dominant firm (Article 82) policy. For a discussion of this development see Chapter 2.
5. These include: merger policy, the revised policy on vertical restraints and developing policy on State aids. For brevity, policies on the liberalisation of regulated industries and intellectual property rights are not considered further in this overview. For developments in these areas see Chapters 7 and 8 respectively.
6. UK policy differs from EU policy in a number of key areas, however. For discussion of these see further below.
7. Office of Fair Trading, The Competition Act 1998: the major provisions, OFT 400, March 1999, p. 5.
8. The block exemption came into force under the Competition Act 1998 (Land and Vertical Agreements) Order 2000 (SI 2000 No. 310). It was removed from 1 May 2005 when the UK adopted a policy in line with EU policy in this area.
9. Office of Fair Trading, Agreements and concerted practices, OFT Competition Law Guideline, December 2004, pp. 10-12.
10. Office of Fair Trading, Agreements and concerted practices, ibid., pp. 34-5.
11. See Office of Fair Trading, Abuse of a dominant position, OFT Competition Law Guideline, 2004, pp. 14-15.
12. US policy differs from UK and EU policy, among other things, in that exploitative behaviour is not viewed as an 'abuse' under Section 2 of the Sherman Act while it can be seen as an abuse under UK and EU policy. See Chapter 2 for a discussion.
13. Some sector regulators also have concurrent powers to apply the Competition Act. They are: OFGEM in energy markets, OFWAT in water, OFCOM in telecommunications, ORR in railway services, the CAA in air traffic control and OFREQ in gas and electricity in N. Ireland.
14. The CCAT was originally part of the Competition Commission under the 1998 Act. It was replaced by the CAT on 1 April 2003.
15. See Office of Fair Trading, The Competition Act 1998: the major provisions, op cit., p. 20.
16. A 'scale monopoly' is defined such that a single firm has at least a 25 per cent market share. Under the FTA, the Secretary of State had wide powers to impose remedies in monopoly cases including breaking up companies, imposing price controls and requiring termination of practices found to be against the public interest.
17. The Act also introduced some institutional changes. In particular, the OFT was given a statutory basis as a corporate body under the Act having earlier been just a support body to the Director

General of Fair Trading. This is in line with the extension of the OFT's powers under the 1998 and 2002 Acts.

18. The offence is introduced under section 188 of the Enterprise Act.
19. The Secretary of State only maintains powers to intervene in merger cases under a public interest criterion (currently relating only to national security) or for mergers in the newspaper and water industries. This compares with earlier policy where, in particular, the Secretary of State had wide powers to implement remedies in merger (and monopoly) cases.
20. See Office of Fair Trading, Market investigation references, OFT Guidance, 2003.
21. The new block exemption replaces most of the earlier block exemption regulations in this area – the notable exception being the motor vehicle Block Exemption Regulation. For details see Chapter 6.
22. For details see Chapter 5.
23. Commission Notice on the non-imposition or reduction of fines in cartel cases, OJ C207, 18 July 1996. The UK also introduced a leniency programme in 2001.
24. As an example, in its first full year of operation, in 2001, the Commission reached 10 successful decisions in cartel cases compared to only nine in the preceding 14 years.
25. Commission Notice on immunity from fines and reduction of fines in cartel cases, OJ C45, 19 February 2002.
26. For a discussion of US policy see Scherer and Ross (1990, Chapter 12).
27. Case 85/76 [1979] ECR 461, 520: 3 CLMR 211, 274. See also the *United Brands* case one year before: Case 27/76 [1978] ECR 207:1 CMLR 429.
28. Other developments are discussed in the relevant chapters below. They include, in particular, recent consideration of reforms in policy on Article 82 together with developments in the areas of the regulation of industries and IPRs.
29. Council Regulation (EEC) No 17/62 of 6 February 1962, first regulation implementing Articles 85 and 86 (now 81 and 82) of the Treaty, OJ 13, 12 February 1962.
30. Council Regulation (EC) No 139/2004 of 20 January 2004 on the control of concentrations between undertakings, OJ L24, 29 January 2004.
31. Council Regulation (EC) No. 4064/1989 of 21 December 1989 on the control of concentrations between undertakings, OJ L395, 30 December 1989.
32. Guidelines on the assessment of horizontal mergers under the Council Regulation on the control of concentrations between undertakings, OJ C31, 5 February 2004.
33. Council Regulation (EC) No. 1310/97 of 30 June 1997 amending Regulation (EEC) No 4064/89 on the control of concentrations between undertakings, OJ L180, 9 July 1997.
34. See note 3.
35. The text of the Action Plan can be found on DG Competition's web site: http://europa.eu.int/comm/competition/state_aid/others/action_plan/.

2. Dominant Firms and Monopoly Policy in the UK and EU

Roger Clarke

INTRODUCTION[1]

Recent developments in competition policy have seen important changes in the operation of policy at both the UK and EU levels. In the UK, the 1998 Competition Act introduced major changes in UK policy designed to move it more into line with policy in the EU. These changes affect the operation of UK policy on both horizontal agreements and dominant firms. In addition, at the EU level, the 'Modernization Regulation' has introduced significant changes to the policy process including the devolution of responsibility for investigating cases to individual Member States and setting up a new European Competition Network (ECN). Also at EU level, a major review of policy on dominant firms is currently underway which may presage further changes in the operation of EU policy. These developments may also produce significant changes in the operation of the policy at the EU level in the next few years.

In the light of these changes, this chapter focuses on recent developments in competition policy in relation to dominant firms and monopoly. In the UK, in contrast to earlier legislation based on the 1973 Fair Trading Act (FTA), the 1998 Competition Act has involved a change of emphasis in policy away from the investigation of monopolies to a greater emphasis on dominant firms. At a more specific level, this implies that cases that might have been dealt with as 'scale' or 'complex' monopolies under the FTA may fail to be investigated as part of the Chapter II prohibition of the 1998 Act.[2] This would suggest a weakening of policy in this area.

At the same time, and partly for this reason, the UK has maintained further powers to deal with monopoly cases which are not available at EU level. Initially, at the time of the 1998 Act, this was done by retaining the provisions of the FTA to deal with cases where firms might fail the test of dominance and where remedies put in place under the 1998 Act might fail to deal adequately with an abuse of a dominant position. Subsequently, the provisions of the FTA have been replaced in the 2002 Enterprise Act by 'market investigation references'. These have the advantage that they can be used in any market where competition appears not to be working effectively and do not require a specific market share test. Hence, potentially, they can deal with situations of both 'scale' and 'complex' monopoly dealt with under the earlier Act. There are, however, some weaknesses in this policy which may or may not be important in its development and these are discussed briefly further below.

At the EU level, policy on dominant firms is dealt with under Article 82 of the EC Treaty and the Modernization Regulation. In the former, the basic principle of EU policy is embodied in the prohibition of the abuse of a dominant position and 'Modernization' has introduced procedural modifications in EU policy (relating both to the treatment of dominant firms and agreements between firms). Also, over a long period of time, case evidence has built up on dominant firms which provides some guide to conduct that might be seen as an abuse of a dominant position. However, this is an area where simple rules do not always apply, and where the effect of conduct on the operation of a market will often depend on the circumstances of a particular case.

In light of this, the European Commission is now conducting a review of policy under Article 82 to consider whether rules can be developed in some fields to identify areas of abuse and to provide greater legal certainty for firms that might be involved. In particular, the Commission is considering introducing an 'as-efficient competitor' test in Article 82 cases whereby evidence that conduct by a dominant firm would not exclude an equally efficient competitor from the market would be evidence that conduct was not abusive ('safe harbour'). There are, however, problems with this test, in particular that the test may not provide a necessary condition for the abuse of a dominant position, and this and other issues are considered later in this chapter.

The rest of this chapter is organized as follows. The next section provides a brief overview of the problem of monopoly abuse and provides some examples of the abuses that can arise. The next section considers developments in policy in the UK focusing, in particular, on the new Chapter II prohibition and market investigation references. It also considers briefly market studies undertaken by the OFT. The following section discusses EU policy under Article 82 of the EC Treaty and the Modernization Regulation and also reviews some key recent cases. This is followed by a discussion of the current review of Article 82 policy and a final section concludes.

EXAMPLES OF MONOPOLY ABUSE

As in the US under Section 2 of the Sherman Act of 1890, the aim of EU and UK policy in the area of monopoly or abuse of a dominant position is to support competition in the market and to limit the extent of market power. Towards this end, EU and UK policy focuses on two areas dealing with exclusionary and exploitative behaviour. In the first, which is also the key area in the US, the aim is to protect competition from the activities of a monopolist or dominant firm which have the effect of weakening competition on the market, where such weakening may involve weakening the position of existing competitors or new entrants. This area of policy, therefore, deals with the possibility of market foreclosure[3] and, as described below, may include many different forms of behaviour by monopolists or dominant firms. Second, and differing from the US, EU and UK policy also cover exploitative behaviour (such as setting high prices) whereby monopolists or dominant firms seek to exploit their dominant market position. This is an area not covered in US policy (see, for example, Gal (2004) but is viewed as an important feature of EU and UK policy.

It is worthwhile pausing to consider the thinking behind this area of policy, specifically in relation to exclusionary and exploitative behaviour. Clearly the aim in all jurisdictions is to protect the consumer from the abuse of market power, and to bring about a more efficient allocation of resources. In focusing on exclusionary behaviour, the policies aim to protect competition in markets as far as possible to ensure that they work effectively in bringing about these aims. It is important to stress that the aim is to support *competition*, not *competitors*, and hence dominant firms or monopolies should not be penalised, for example, if they produce better quality products or they are more efficient firms. Rather the aim is to ensure that policies are in place which prevent market foreclosure, while allowing all firms to compete on the market.

In the case of exploitative behaviour, it is the view in the UK and EU, but not the US, that measures should also be in place to prevent monopolies or dominant firms exploiting their position by setting prices and so on which harm their customers, and ultimately consumers. This reflects a different underlying approach in the UK and EU compared to the US, whereby the latter's policy makers believe that competition will itself deal with the problem of monopoly abuse and that further intervention is not required. In the UK and EU, the view is that in some situations (for example, where barriers to entry are high) competition might not be able to deal with the problems that arise and further measures are required to deal with these situations as well.

In practice, there are a large number of practices which might be seen as exclusionary or exploitative, and it's worthwhile to consider some of the key ones here. As developed in EU policy (and now adopted in the UK) the aim is to show that conduct by monopolies or dominant firms has an effect in disadvantaging rivals or new entrants, or exploiting customers, to the appropriate legal degree. It is not required to show intent in such policies although evidence of intent may be helpful in determining the existence of an abuse (Vickers, 2005, p. F246). Both price and non-price based policies exist, and price based policies are considered first followed by non-price activities:[4]

- *predatory pricing* involves setting prices low (or adopting other predatory tactics) in the short run in order to weaken or eliminate competitors, and to raise prices in the long run.
- *selective price-cutting* involves setting low prices strategically for some products or markets to weaken competition in those markets. This is distinguished from predatory pricing in that it may not require reducing prices below average total costs, while predatory pricing in EU (and UK) law requires pricing below average total costs.
- *margin squeezes* involve setting prices such that competitors' margins are insufficient to enable them to make a profit or break even. A typical case would involve an upstream firm which sets a high price for downstream firms, including its own (downstream) firm. By setting price at a high level, it squeezes downstream margins so that rival firms are not able to compete.
- *discounts and rebates*. These involve payments to firms, for example, for loyalty to a supplier's products or for exclusive purchasing from that supplier. They are often seen as borderline anti-competitive practices, however, in that discounts and rebates can also be seen as a form of price competition and reasonably strong evidence that they are exclusionary (when practiced by a monopoly or dominant firm) is typically required.
- *excessive pricing* is an exploitative abuse which arises if a firm has a monopoly or a dominant position and is able to exploit its customers, and ultimately consumers. This, in turn, requires that rivals are weak and/or entry barriers are high, which, in turn, may be due to exclusionary behaviour by the monopoly or dominant firm.
- *price discrimination* involves setting different prices to different customers or markets, or using non-linear tariffs. It can be seen as exploitative if it enables a firm to set high prices in markets where competition is weak and lower prices where competition is strong, and it can be exclusionary if it leads, for example, to selective price cutting or predatory pricing.

Turning to non-price activities:

- *single branding or exclusive purchasing* is an exclusionary tactic whereby a monopoly or dominant firm requires its customers to stock only its own products. This policy stops other firms from competing on a level playing field with the firm concerned.
- *exclusive distribution*. This practice typically involves a contract given to a firm to be the sole provider of good or service in an area (such as a car dealership). In comparison with single branding, it commonly gives rise to a restriction on intra-brand rather than inter-brand competition.[5]

- *tying and bundling*. This involves requiring customers to take, or giving them incentives to take, other products that a firm supplies, or bundles of its products. This can result in foreclosing the market to rival firms.
- *refusal to supply* involves not supplying a product to rival firms and is a basic exclusionary device. It must be treated with care, however, since an objective reason for such a refusal may exist, such as health and safety concerns, a poor credit rating and so on.
- *essential facilities*. A variant on refusal to supply is in the supply of an essential facility whereby a facility or some form of infrastructure (such as a port), required for operation in a particular market, is withheld from competitors or supplied only on disadvantageous terms. Again the issue is one of exclusion and, again, this can be justified objectively in some cases.

UK POLICY: THE CHAPTER II PROHIBITION, MARKET INVESTIGATIONS AND MARKET STUDIES

The Chapter II Prohibition

UK legislation on dominant firms is based on the 1998 Competition Act which came into force on 1 March 2000. Under Section 18(1) of this Act conduct on the part of a firm or firms which amounts to an abuse a dominant position in the UK or part of it is prohibited (the Chapter II prohibition). The Act states that:

> ... any conduct on the part of one or more undertakings which amounts to the abuse of a dominant position in a market is prohibited if it may affect trade within the United Kingdom (Competition Act, 1998, Section 18(1)).

The Act also gives examples of conduct that might constitute an abuse in line with Article 82 of the EC Treaty:

(a) directly or indirectly imposing unfair purchase or selling prices or other unfair trading conditions;
(b) limiting production, markets or technical development to the prejudice of consumers;
(c) applying dissimilar conditions to equivalent transactions with other trading parties, thereby placing them at a competitive disadvantage;
(d) making the conclusion of contracts subject to acceptance by the other parties of supplementary obligations which, by their nature or according to commercial usage, have no connection with the subject of the contracts (Competition Act, 1998, Section 18(2)).

This list, however, is not exhaustive and any form of conduct which amounts to an abuse of a dominant position can be caught under the Act.[6]

The Chapter II prohibition is closely modelled on Article 82 of the EC Treaty. In addition, under the Act, the competition authorities are required to reach decisions in Chapter II (and Chapter I) cases in line with policy at the EU level. Thus, Section 60(1) of the Act states:

> The purpose of this section is to ensure that so far as is possible (having regard to any relevant differences between the provisions concerned), questions arising under this Part in relation to competition within the United Kingdom are dealt with in a manner which is consistent with the treatment of corresponding questions arising in Community law in relation to competition within the Community (Competition Act, 1998, Section 60(1)).

In particular, this implies that the Office of Fair Trading (OFT) must act in line with decisions reached by the European Commission, and ultimately the European courts. As such the UK is bound by past decisions made at EU level in the way this aspect of its policy is run. This compares with other areas of UK policy discussed below which are not so bound.

The Act gives powers for the Office of Fair Trading (OFT) (or the sector regulators)[7] to investigate cases where an abuse of a dominant position is suspected. The OFT has wide powers to collect information including the power to undertake 'dawn raids' on firms if necessary (with or without a warrant). Following this, the OFT undertakes an investigation and provides an opportunity for a firm (or firms) to present their views in a case. The OFT can then issue an 'infringement decision' whereby the conduct of the firm, or firms, is found to be an abuse of a dominant position. If this is the case, the OFT can impose fines which, in line with EU policy, can be up to 10 per cent of the worldwide turnover of the firm, or firms, involved.

More recently (in 2004), the OFT has also been given the power to accept commitments from firms in place of an infringement decision.[8] In this case, the OFT is required to consult on these commitments but can then accept them and close the case. The advantage of this, in particular, is that it removes the adversarial approach in reaching decisions in cases where fines may not be appropriate, as well as potentially reducing the time involved in investigating cases.

Several features of the Act can be noted briefly here. First, in line with EU policy, the OFT uses a market share test in dealing with Chapter II cases. As discussed later in this chapter, the European Commission has taken the view that a market share higher than 50 per cent would normally be evidence that a firm has a dominant position, although subject to other factors that might be relevant in a particular case. These factors are discussed in more detail later in this chapter. Similarly, in the UK, the OFT has stated that a market share below 40 per cent would not normally be taken as evidence of a dominant position, although again other factors would need to be taken into account.[9] As noted in the introduction to this chapter, this change would suggest a weakening of UK policy compared to the earlier FTA, where a 25 per cent market share test was applied, although other measures have been put in place to deal with this particular issue.

In line with EU policy, the Chapter II prohibition also covers collective dominance, whereby several firms together may act to abuse a dominant position. In principle, this allows for the investigation of 'oligopoly' cases which cannot be dealt with in terms of single firm dominance. However, this is not an area where EU policy has been widely used and it seems likely that it will not be used widely within the UK.[10]

The Act also provides for appeals of the OFT's decision. Under the Act, firms can appeal to the Competition Appeal Tribunal (CAT) (previously the Competition Commission Appeal Tribunal (CCAT)) which can refer cases back to the OFT and/or change the level of the fine imposed. The CAT does not have the power, however, to investigate cases itself. Firms can also subsequently appeal to the Court of Appeal (or the Court of Session in Scotland) but only on points of law, or the level of the fine imposed. This change compares to earlier policy under the FTA where the Secretary of State had wide powers to implement remedies with no right of appeal, apart from on points of law.

It is useful to consider some of the early cases under the prohibition to see how effective the policy has been so far. Over the period between 1 March 2000 when the Competition Act came into force and the end of 2005, the OFT had considered 19 cases (including four reinvestigations) under Chapter II of the Act (see Table 2.1).[11] Perhaps surprisingly, it found of these evidence of abuse of a dominant position in only three separate cases, and in one further case (*London-wide newspaper distribution* (2005)) it accepted commitments in lieu of an infringement decision. Of the remaining cases, the OFT found that no dominant firm was involved in six cases and in nine cases there was no evidence of an abuse (in two of these cases, there was *both* no evidence of dominance and no evidence of abuse). Also, in one further case (*N&W Belfast Health Trust* (2002, 2003)), the trust involved was held not to be an 'undertaking' as defined under the Act. All cases involved a single dominant firm.

The four early cases where an abuse of a dominant position has been found, or a commitment has been accepted, give some idea of the likely application of the new legislation.

Napp (2001)[12]

In the first case, Napp Pharmaceuticals Ltd. was found to be the dominant supplier of the sustained-release morphine product MST and to have abused its dominant position by charging patients higher prices for its product in the community than it charged in hospitals. Napp's prices in the community, in particular, were typically more than ten times higher than in its hospital contracts. The aim of this strategy was to dominate the hospital market and, at the same time, given the reluctance of GPs to change a patient's medication, the community market as well. The OFT found that this pricing structure was an abuse of its dominant position because it prevented rival firms from competing in the hospital market, and hence in the community market, thereby enabling Napp to charge very high prices in the community market.

In this case, Napp was required to reduce its prices to the community and to reduce the difference between its prices in the two markets. In addition, it was fined £3.2 million (although this was reduced to £2.2 million on appeal).

In this case, both exclusionary and exploitative practices were considered. The price discrimination was exclusionary because it prevented rivals competing in either market, and it was exploitative because of the high prices charged in the community market. In particular, exploitative factors were involved in the costs of the practice to the National Health Service and the estimated cost savings to the NHS were thought to be about £2 million a year.[13]

Genzyme (2003)[14]

In this case, Genzyme Ltd was a monopoly supplier of a drug called Cerezyme which was at the time the only effective treatment for the rare, inherited Gaucher disease. The case was concerned with Genzyme's practice of charging the National Health Service for both the drug and home care services (bundling), and for setting its price to other possible service providers at too high a level for them to compete (margin squeeze).

The OFT found that this behaviour was exclusionary and required Genzyme to supply the drug to the National Health Service at a stand-alone price and to supply the drug to other service providers at no price higher than this. Genzyme was also fined a total of £6.8 million (although this was reduced to £3 million on appeal).

In this case, Genzyme appealed the remedies ordered by the OFT but the OFT's decision was substantially upheld in a subsequent CAT decision.[15]

Aberdeen Journals (2001, 2002)[16]

In the *Aberdeen Journals* case, Aberdeen Journals was found to have a dominant position in the market for advertising space in the Aberdeen region of Scotland and to have abused its position by offering advertising space below cost in its free newspaper, the Aberdeen Herald and Post. The OFT found this pricing to be predatory against its rival, the Aberdeen and District Independent, a free newspaper which had entered the market in 1996.

In this case, the CCAT referred the OFT's initial decision back to the OFT on the grounds that insufficient attention had been given to market definition. However, the OFT reached essentially the same decision following a review and this was upheld by the CAT in June 2003. Aberdeen Journals was fined £1.3 million (reduced to £1 million on appeal).

Table 2.1 Chapter II cases investigated by the OFT, 2000-2005[a]

Case	Date on Register	Outcome	Fine (£m)	Reason for decision[e]	Main Problem
Napp Pharmaceutical Holdings	05/04/01	X	3.2[b]	-	Price discrimination/predatory pricing
DSG/Compaq/Packard Bell	18/04/01	√	-	ND	Exclusive distribution
Consignia/PPS Ltd.	15/06/01	√	-	NA	Exclusive distribution
Aberdeen Journals (I)	16/07/01	X	1.3	-	Predatory pricing
ICL/Synstar	26/07/01	√	-	ND	Tying contracts
N&W Belfast Health Trust (I)	30/04/02	√	-	NU	Unfair prices/terms and conditions
Harwood Park Crematorium (I)	06/08/02	√	-	ND	Refusal to supply
Aberdeen Journals (II)	25/09/02	X	1.3[c]	-	Predatory pricing
Companies House	25/10/02	√	-	NA	Unfair prices/predatory pricing
ABTA/British Airways	12/12/02	√	-	NA	Unfair prices
BSkyB (I)	30/01/03	√	-	NA	Unfair prices/mixed bundling

BSkyB (II)	12/08/03	√	-	NA	Unfair prices/mixed bundling
Genzyme Ltd.	27/03/03	X	6.8^d	-	Bundling/margin squeeze
du Pont de Nemours/Op. Graphics	22/09/03	√	-	NA	Refusal to supply
N&W Belfast Health Trust (II)	23/12/03	√	-	NA	Unfair prices/terms and conditions
First Edinburgh/Lothian	09/06/04	√	-	NA/ND	Predatory pricing/ predatory tactics
Harwood Park Crematorium (II)	12/08/04	√	-	ND/NA	Refusal to supply
TM /MacDonald Dettwiler	29/09/04	√	-	ND	Predatory pricing/unfair prices
London-wide newspaper distribution	07/04/05^f	-	-	COM	Exclusive contracts

Notes

a This table relates only to cases investigated by the OFT.
b Fine reduced to £2.2 million on appeal to the CAT.
c Fine reduced to £1.0 million on (second) appeal to the CAT.
d Fine reduced to £3.0 million on appeal to the CAT.
e Reasons for decision: ND (not dominant), NA (not abuse), NU (the case did not involve an undertaking and hence was outside the scope of the 1998 Act) and COM (commitment accepted).
f Date of announcement of commitment.

Source: Competition Act Public Register, OFT website.

London-wide newspaper distribution (2005)[17]

Finally, in this case, Northern & Shell (N&L), publisher of the Daily Express, made a complaint (in 2003) that it was prevented from introducing a free afternoon and evening newspaper in London because of exclusivity agreements between Associated Newspapers Limited (ANL) and the London Underground, Network Rail and some train operating companies which gave ANL 24 hour exclusive rights to sell its newspapers in stations in and around London. It sold its free newspaper *Metro* in the mornings and its other newspaper, the *Evening Standard*, in the afternoons and evenings. N&L argued that these agreements prevented it from entering the market because of the superior cost effectiveness of selling newspapers at tube and railway stations.

The OFT concluded that these agreements were restrictive and hence were likely to infringe both Chapter I and Chapter II. In contrast to the decisions above, however, it decided to accept a binding commitment[18] from ANL to give up its rights to exclusive distribution at these stations in the afternoon and evening, and to give third parties access to, and space on, its distribution racks. In return, the OFT agreed to close the case.[19]

The case is interesting because it shows that it is possible to use a negotiated, non-adversarial approach in some cases where a fine is not necessarily required, and it may be that this kind of approach will be used increasingly in future cases.

The evidence so far shows that there has been a relatively small proportion of cases in which an abuse of a dominant position has been found. This is due, in part, to the nature of the process under the Act whereby firms are able to make complaints and, after some initial checks, the OFT may undertake an investigation if it believes there is a *possible* infringement of the prohibition. In quite a few cases, the evidence showed that there was no real case to answer (either because a firm was not dominant or there was no evidence of an abuse) and the case was closed relatively quickly. In addition, however, the OFT has taken a reasonably firm line in considering an abuse (for example in *ABTA/British Airways* (2002)[20] and *First Edinburgh/Lothian* (2004)[21]) and it is clear that it will not simply support a claim of an abuse without firm evidence.

The evidence also raises some concern that the OFT is concentrating on relatively small cases, at least in cases where an abuse has been found, and this was a feature, to some extent, of earlier policy under the FTA.[22] It is clearly important for the OFT to identify more significant cases if the policy is to be successful in dealing with abuses in this area.

Market Investigations and Market Studies

In addition to the Chapter II prohibition, the UK has retained additional powers to deal with monopoly and oligopoly problems which are not available at EU level. At the time of the 1998 Act, powers were retained under the 1973 FTA to deal with cases that might not be dealt with effectively under the new prohibition. The aim was twofold.[23] First, in cases where an abuse under the Chapter II prohibition had been found and the OFT believed that there was a real prospect of further abuse in the future, cases could be referred to the CC under the 'scale' monopoly provisions of the FTA. These applied if a single firm had a market share of 25 per cent or more and, in these cases, the CC had powers, in particular, to recommend structural changes to remedy a problem. Second, in cases not caught by either the Chapter I or Chapter II prohibitions where, in particular, there was no single dominant firm, could be referred to the CC under the 'complex' monopoly provisions of the FTA. These applied if several firms jointly held a market share of at least 25 per cent and acted to restrict competition. In these cases, the CC had powers to suggest remedies, although the actual decisions were taken by the Secretary of State.

These policies were replaced, however, in the 2002 Enterprise Act which introduced 'market investigation references' to deal with cases not dealt with under the Chapter II prohibition. In the case of market investigation references, the OFT has powers to refer cases to the CC if it believes that competition is not working effectively in a particular market. In doing this, it must consider whether it would be more appropriate to use either the Chapter I or Chapter II prohibitions of the Competition Act; whether the problem is of enough significance to warrant a reference to the CC; whether it is likely that an effective remedy can be found and whether it would be appropriate to accept a commitment rather than make a reference.[24] If the criteria are met, the CC then undertakes an investigation to decide whether there is evidence of a restriction or distortion of competition in the relevant market, and, if so, what remedies can be used. The Commission also has powers to accept undertakings or to make an order on the firm, or firms, involved. As under the Competition Act, firms can appeal the Commission's decision to the CAT which has the power to return the case to the Commission for further consideration.[25]

The new law makes several important changes to earlier policy. First, in contrast to the FTA, there is no explicit requirement that the CC show that a statutory monopoly exists in a market investigation case. This means that the Commission can focus directly on the issue of competition rather than on applying a specific market share test. Second, the Commission itself has been given the power to implement remedies under the 2002 Act.[26] This is a major change from earlier policy whereby the Secretary of State held powers to decide what remedies to put in place. As in other areas of UK policy,[27] the aim is to reduce the role played by government ministers in making competition policy decisions. Finally, the decisions of the CC can be appealed to the CAT, which has the power to send back cases for further consideration by the Commission. This is also a major change from earlier policy where the Secretary of State had wide powers to impose orders or accept undertakings from firms with no specific rights of appeal, except on points of law.

In maintaining these additional provisions, the government has taken the view that the powers under Chapter II of the Competition Act (and, by implication, Article 82) are not sufficient to deal with monopoly and oligopoly cases. In particular, whilst the Chapter II prohibition allows for the possibility of collective as well as single firm dominance, the view has been that this policy has not been used effectively at EU level, and that consequently cases that fail to satisfy the single firm dominance test, will not be covered (adequately) under Chapter II at UK level. The evidence in early cases, noted above, indicates that the OFT proposes to consider primarily single firm dominance cases under the Competition Act. Market investigation references, therefore, are designed to fill a gap in the legislation, in particular, as far as oligopoly cases are concerned, and also in cases where structural changes in the market may be required.

At time of writing, five market investigation cases have been referred to the CC (see Table 2.2) but no decisions have yet been reached.[28] It therefore remains to be seen how effective this policy will be.

Table 2.2 Market investigation references

Reference	Date referred
Store cards	18 March 2004
Supply of liquefied petroleum gas	5 July 2004
Home collected credit	20 December 2004
Classified directory advertising services	5 April 2005
Northern Ireland banking	26 May 2005

Source: OFT website.

There are some reservations with the policy. First, the CC has given an undertaking to complete market investigations within a period of two years. However, given the time required to implement remedies, as well as the time likely to be taken up in appeals to the CAT, the actual timeframe in such cases could easily be three or four years (or more). This raises concern over the likely effectiveness of the policy which was also an issue under the scale and complex monopoly provisions of the FTA. There could be a case for shortening the time period of some investigations (and, at the same time, shortening the scale of reports traditionally produced by the CC in this type of case) in the interests of increasing the efficacy of the policy. Second, it is not clear at present whether the CC will be best placed to implement the remedies proposed in market investigation cases, given its earlier focus on investigations and the limited resources that it has. This, again, remains to be seen.

In addition to market investigation references, the OFT also has powers to undertake market studies and to deal with so-called 'super-complaints' (see further below). Market studies are undertaken by the Markets and Policy Initiatives branch of the OFT and cover different issues including both consumer and competition concerns. They can lead to a market investigation reference (or a commitment in place of a reference) and the OFT also has powers to publish advice to consumers and make recommendations to Government or sector regulators, and to enforce consumer and competition law.[29] These studies can, therefore, lead to other action in a number of different directions.

In these studies the OFT typically conducts an analysis under Section 5(1) of the 2002 Enterprise Act.[30] It normally undertakes one of two types of study: a short study which can be instigated by the Director of the OFT's Markets and Policy Initiatives branch and typically takes three to six months, and a full study which is initiated by the Board of the OFT and takes about a year.[31] The OFT publishes both types of report, typically under Section 4(4) of the Act.

The early evidence suggests market studies can be useful in promoting competition although overall the picture is mixed. In the case of *Extended warranties for electrical goods* (2002),[32] for example, it found that consumers had insufficient information when making decisions to buy extended electrical warranties and that retailers used their point-of-sale advantage to sell their own warranties, often at very high prices. In this case, the study led to a reference to the CC under the FTA (in July 2002),[33] the result of which was an order requiring retailers to provide more information on their warranties, and to allow consumers a 'cooling-off' period in which they could cancel their policies.[34]

A similar case was *Store cards* (2004)[35] where the OFT found that stores provided insufficient information for consumers on the costs of store cards, that very high interest rates prevailed and that competition was not working effectively on the supply side of the market. In particular, the APRs on store cards were, typically, more than 10 percentage points higher than those on credit cards. In this case, the study led to a reference to the CC (in March 2004), although this case is still under review.[36]

In contrast, in the case of *New car warranties* (2003)[37] the OFT considered the restriction in many new car warranties which required customers to have their cars serviced in manufacturers' dealerships. This practice was believed to apply to about 50 per cent of all new car warranties at the time of the study. The OFT found that this tie restricted competition in the service market and threatened to send the case to the European Commission (under Article 81 of the EC Treaty) if changes were not introduced. As a result of this all the leading manufacturers in the UK agreed by negotiation to remove this condition from their warranties (in 2004), and further action was not required.[38] The OFT also conducted a consumer awareness campaign (in March 2004) to let consumers know of their rights.[39]

Finally, in the *Pharmacies* (2003)[40] case, the OFT considered regulations which gave local health authorities the right to control the number of pharmacies able to dispense NHS medications in their areas on the basis of what they saw as necessary and desirable to provide an adequate service. The OFT argued in this case that this regulation limited the number of outlets selling NHS medications, and, in some cases, over-the-counter medicines as well. This, in turn, meant that consumers had less choice in terms of location and hours of opening, as well as being charged possibly higher prices on over-the-counter medicines. In this case, however, the government chose not to follow the OFT's advice, and, instead, only moderate relaxation of the regulations was introduced.[41]

Clearly there are some limitations on the effectiveness of market studies and in some cases, notably the *Pharmacies* case, they have not met with success. On the other hand, they can be a useful way of 'flagging up' areas of concern, which can also lead to further action, as in several areas so far.

Finally, it should be noted that under Section 11 of the 2002 Enterprise Act the OFT (and the sector regulators) are required to deal with 'super-complaints' brought by designated consumer bodies.[42] These complaints lead to a 'fast track' procedure in that the OFT (and the sector regulators) are required to respond within 90 days once a complaint has been lodged. Three such complaints so far have given rise to market studies in non-competition fields (*Private dentistry, Doorstep selling* and *Care homes*) and in one case (*Mail consolidation*) the case was passed to the regulator Postcomm. In two further cases (*Home collected credit* and *Northern Ireland banking*, in December 2004 and May 2005 respectively) complaints have led to a market investigation reference.

EU POLICY: ARTICLE 82 AND THE MODERNIZATION REGULATION

EU policy on dominant firms is based on Article 82 of the EC Treaty together with the Modernization Regulation. Article 82 states that:

> Any abuse by one or more undertakings of a dominant position within the common market or in a substantial part of it shall be prohibited as incompatible with the common market in so far as it may affect trade between Member States (EC Treaty, Article 82).

The article also lays down certain examples of such abuses which are the same as noted above in the UK case. As in the UK, these examples are not exhaustive and other possible abuses can arise.

Under Article 82, several features are important in determining an abuse of a dominant position. In particular, it is necessary to define what is meant by dominance in a *market*, and how to identify a position of *dominance*. These issues have been discussed at length in the literature but, nevertheless, are worth considering briefly here.

One important issue, of course, is how to define a market. If it is assumed that dominance means 'a position of strength in a relevant market',[43] it is necessary to establish what the 'relevant market' is. The EU, along with most other competition regimes, uses the SSNIP test to determine the relevant market. In the EU, the test is applied as follows.[44] First, a single firm (or a small group of firms) is considered and the question is asked: what would happen if the firm(s) introduced a Small but Significant Non-transitory Increase in Price of their products? If the effect of this would be that it was unprofitable for the firm(s), either because consumers could switch to alternative products or they could obtain their supplies from other geographic regions, the market is not defined widely enough and it is necessary to include other products and suppliers in the definition. Again, the question is asked whether these firms acting together as a monopolist could profitably increase their prices by a small non-transitory amount. When, at some stage, the answer is eventually 'yes', the limits of the market have been reached, and this is the relevant market in this case. In the EU a 'small but significant non-transitory increase in price' is usually held to be about 5-10 per cent.

Clearly, this approach has intuitive appeal, but it also suffers from certain weaknesses (as is well known in the literature).[45] First, ideally, the test should be applied to markets where prices are at the competitive level, thereby avoiding the 'cellophane fallacy'.[46] Thus, most appropriately, the question should be whether the firm(s) can increase their price profitably by 5-10 per cent from the competitive price. In Article 82 cases, however, dominant firms are already likely to have price significantly above the competitive level and hence the test could be misleading. It may well be that a firm is unable to raise its price profitably by 5-10 per cent above its existing level but this will understate its market power. The end result will be that the market will tend to be defined more widely than it actually should be.

A second problem with the test is that it is hypothetical; that is, it asks the question what would happen if a monopolist increased its market price by 5-10 per cent in the absence (typically) of any actual price increase. This makes it necessary to apply judgement in dealing with the test. Nevertheless, it provides an important means of identifying rival products and firms in practical situations and hence it remains a key policy instrument in this area (as elsewhere). In practice, the Commission also uses other measures to identify markets such as product characteristics, evidence of price movements using historical data, consumer surveys and so on.

In addition to market definition, the question of defining dominance needs to be considered. This has been established in a number of judgements in the European courts, and, in particular, in the case of *United Brands* (1978).[47] In practice, the Commission uses a market share of 50 per cent in determining dominance, although firms can still be dominant under some conditions at lower market shares:

this [a finding of dominance] would be the case where an undertaking holds 50 per cent or more of the market, provided that rivals hold a much smaller share of the market. In the case, of lower market shares, dominance is more likely to be found in the market share range of 40 per cent to 50 per cent than below 40 per cent, although also undertakings with market shares below 40 per cent could be considered to be in a dominant position. However, undertakings with market shares of no more than 25 per cent are not likely to enjoy a (single) dominant position on the market concerned (DG Competition, 'The application of Article 82 of the Treaty to exclusionary abuses,' Discussion paper, December 2005, p. 11).

In practice, the Commission also considers other factors in determining dominance including size and number of competitors, the persistence of market shares, entry barriers and possibly off-setting buyer power.

Article 82, in principle, also applies if several firms operate together to prevent, restrict or distort competition although in practice this has been used much less widely than single firm dominance in the EU. Collective dominance can arise from an agreement or concerted practice (which would also be infringements of Article 81)[48] and also if firms adopt exclusionary and/or parallel behaviour with no evidence of actual contact between firms. In this latter case:

> Undertakings in oligopolistic markets may sometimes be able to raise prices substantially above the competitive level without having recourse to any explicit agreement or concerted practice. Coordination is more likely to emerge in markets where it is relatively simple to reach a common understanding on the terms of coordination. The simpler and more stable the economic environment, the easier it is for undertakings to reach a common understanding (DG Competition, 'The application of Article 82 of the Treaty to exclusionary abuses,' op cit., p. 16).

The main problem in this area, however, is to show that collective dominance exists in a market; that is, that firms together operate collectively to exclude competitors and/or exploit their dominant position. Clearly, evidence that firms are setting high prices or engaging in exclusionary price discrimination can be used although in practice it can be difficult to distinguish simply weak competition from collective dominance. This is less of a problem if there is evidence of an explicit agreement or a concerted practice and this is illustrated in an example further below.

While collective dominance may be difficult to establish in practice, three conditions are usually[49] held to be necessary for it to exist. First, firms must be able to monitor the actions of their rivals so that it is not possible for rivals to renege on the agreement or understanding. Second, there must be penalties available to 'punish' firms that renege. And finally, it must be possible to 'monopolize' the market; that is, there is sufficient scope for the firms to raise prices, or limit production, without attracting new entrants to the market. These conditions are typically applied by the Commission in considering whether evidence of collective dominance exists.[50]

The new Modernization Regulation[51] which came into force on 1 May 2004 introduces four major changes in the way competition policy operates within the EU[52] of which two, in particular, are relevant here. First, the policy aims to decentralize the application of Articles 81 and 82 to national competition authorities (NCAs) and courts within Member States. While the power to apply Article 82 had existed prior to the introduction of the new Regulation under Regulation 17/62,[53] in practice many NCAs did not exercise this power with the implication that the Commission was primarily responsible for the application of Articles 81 and 82. Under the new Regulation, NCAs are *required* to apply Articles 81 and 82 at the same time as the apply domestic competition policy in the areas of restrictive agreements and abuse of a dominant position. As a result, it is envisaged that many more cases will be dealt with by NCAs and national courts and that the Commission will focus on larger cases with a more Community-wide dimension. This change should lead to more efficiency in the application of policy as NCAs are able to examine cases where Articles 81 and 82 apply both domestically and on a wider scale.

Under the new policy, it is envisaged that NCAs will conduct investigations where the abuse of a dominant position is mainly focused on one particular Member State and this will involve some cooperation between Member States.[54] In cases where the abuse affects a number of Member States but is nevertheless limited, two or three Member States may cooperate in investigating a case. Where a wider effect is involved, the Commission itself will undertake an investigation. It is also envisaged that the Commission will investigate cases where potential precedents are likely to be involved and may investigate cases in parts of the Community where enforcement of competition policy is weak.[55]

The Modernization Regulation also established a European Competition Network (ECN) consisting of NCAs and the European Commission with the aim of coordinating policy between Member States and the Commission. The aim here is to establish, in particular, the allocation of cases between Member States and to enhance cooperation in a number of different areas.

Several other points of relevance to Article 82 can be mentioned here. First, a new remedy has been introduced in Article 7 of the Modernization Regulation to break up companies or require them to divest their assets under some conditions. This is available only in cases where a behavioural remedy is not thought to be sufficient to deal with a particular abuse, or it would be judged more burdensome on firms concerned than a structural remedy. This, therefore, brings EU policy more into line with policy already in operation in the UK under the Enterprise Act. Second, the regulation gives new powers to the Commission to adopt interim measures (Article 8) or to accept commitments from firms involved in Article 81 and 82 cases (Article 9).[56] These commitments are binding on firms and the Commission has the power to re-open cases if there is a material change in the facts, or if firms fail to keep to their commitments or if information previously provided by firms turns out to be incomplete or incorrect. These commitments, if widely applied, are likely to speed the process of investigation and reduce the costs (on both sides) in Article 81 and 82 cases.

There have obviously been a large number of investigations under Article 82 since the EC Treaty was first put in place and which cannot be covered in a chapter such as this. In what follows, consideration is given to some important cases in recent years and the lessons that can be learned.

It is useful to begin with to consider EU policy on collective dominance under Article 82. This has been a relatively little used power, as noted earlier, although some application of the provision has occurred more recently. An example of this is the *TACA* case.

TACA (1998)[57]

This case concerned a network of agreements and rules operated by the Trans-Atlantic Conference Agreement (TACA), a group of shipping companies who provided container freight transport services between northern EU ports and the US. In this case, TACA was involved in setting prices both internally within the EU and on trade between northern Europe and the US. Transatlantic shipping services, however, were exempted from Article 81(1) of the EC Treaty under a block exemption for maritime transport introduced in 1987. In its investigation the Commission found that TACA was involved in a number of agreements which potentially infringed Article 81. These included, in particular, the fixing of prices for transatlantic shipping services and also transport services within the EU. Given the block exemption, however, it opted to use Article 82 rather than 81 of the Treaty

In its investigation, the Commission found that TACA members accounted for over 60 per cent of trade in the transatlantic market and hence would satisfy the requirement for (collective) dominance. In addition, TACA restricted the ability of its members to enter into service contracts with shippers which might have led to closer ties between individual shippers and shipping companies and it also encouraged potential new competitors to join TACA rather than act as independent firms. The Commission argued that these policies violated the Article 82 prohibition and imposed fines, in total, of 273 million euros.

The importance of this case was that the Commission was able to use the collective dominance provisions of Article 82 when its way was blocked under Article 81. In other cases where Article 81 is available, however, this is usually the preferred route.

Turning now to single firm dominance, a number of interesting cases have been investigated recently under Article 82.

Wanadoo (2003)[58]

This case concerned Wanadoo Interactive (a subsidiary of France Telecom) which was alleged to have engaged in predatory pricing in the retail market for ADSL-based internet access services in France. In its investigation, the Commission argued that Wanadoo had adopted a conscious policy of setting low prices in order to prevent entry from taking place and, therefore, increase its market share in this fast growing market. In particular, in the period from March to August 2001, Wanadoo had set its prices well below average variable cost while from August 2001 to October 2002 it had its set prices on a par with average variable cost but significantly below average total cost. Evidence for predatory pricing was found in large losses that Wanadoo made in internet access services. In addition, Wanadoo had been able to increase its share of the market from 46 per cent in January 2001 to 72 per cent in September 2002, and a significant competitor (Mangoosta) had been forced out of the market (in August 2001). The abuse ended in October 2002 when France Telecom (as the wholesale supplier of ADSL services) reduced its prices by 30 per cent. Following this, Wanadoo stopped setting prices below average cost and this allowed other suppliers to provide more effective competition in the market. Wanadoo was fined 10.4 million euros for its abuse of its dominant position.

This case is interesting because it relates to the particular problem whereby dominant firms seek to prevent entry or restrict competition as new markets are developed in IT, and in other areas as well. In such areas, it is clearly important to protect competition in the market with the benefits that this will involve.

Clearstream (2004)[59]

This case concerned Clearstream Banking's refusal to supply cross-border securities clearing and settlement services and the setting of discriminatory prices. The case involved a refusal by Clearstream (a subsidiary of Clearstream International) to supply clearing and settlement services to Euroclear Bank for registered securities issued under German law. Given that Clearstream was effectively the only depository of such securities, this restricted the operation of Euroclear's cross-border clearing and settlement service. The refusal of supply operated for a two year period up to November 2001. In addition, the Commission found that Clearstream had charged Euroclear higher prices for its services than it charged other securities depositories outside Germany in the period January 1997 to January 2002, and that this difference did not reflect a difference in costs. The Commission found, on both counts, that Clearstream had abused its dominant position in the market for cross-border clearing and settlement services. Perhaps surprisingly, no fine was imposed in this case partly because Euroclear obtained clearing and settlement services from Clearstream in November 2001 and the price discrimination was brought to an end in January 2002. In addition, the Commission found that it was not clear where the rights and responsibilities lay in clearing and settlement services and so it was not appropriate to fine Clearstream for its actions in this case.

Microsoft (2004)[60]

This important case concerned the alleged abuse of a dominant position by Microsoft, the leading US software company. Two problems were considered. First, it was alleged that Microsoft had used its dominance in the PC operating system market to leverage itself into a dominant position in the market for work group servers by not allowing rivals full access to the code required for efficient inter-operability with the Windows system. Given the dominance of Windows in the PC operating system market, rival work group server suppliers operated at a competitive disadvantage to Microsoft because of this. Second, it was alleged that Microsoft had leveraged itself into the market for media players by bundling its Windows Media Player free with Windows. In this case, rival suppliers were put at a competitive disadvantage which enabled Microsoft to attain a high market share.

In its decision of 24 March 2004, the Commission concluded that Microsoft had abused its dominant position in both of these areas. It, therefore, ordered Microsoft, first, to make available, within 120 days, the code required to allow full inter-operability in the work group server market. Second, it required Microsoft, within 90 days, to make available copies of Windows which did not include the Windows Media Player. This would provide a level playing field for other firms in this market. Finally, in light of the seriousness of the case, the Commission fined Microsoft 497 million euros.

The interest in this case is in the difficulty there is in applying measures when a large multinational company is involved. Microsoft appealed to the European courts although eventually it was not successful in overturning the decision. In addition, it has also been slow to comply with the decision, in particular, in the work group server market. As a result, the Commission has had to issue fines to get it to comply with the decision, and, at time of writing, significant problems appear to remain.

Coca Cola (2004)[61]

Finally, the *Coca Cola* case involved a number of exclusivity conditions and rebate schemes operated by Coca Cola in the market for carbonated soft drinks. Amongst other things, it was found that Coca Cola used exclusive purchasing conditions in outlets it supplied and that it provided free chilled cabinets to outlets on condition that they only stock its products (that is, partial exclusive purchasing). In addition, it operated a system of rebates which had the effect of excluding other carbonated soft drink suppliers from the market.

Following a five year investigation the Commission found these practices were an abuse of a dominant position. In this context, however, it accepted commitments[62] from Coca Cola aimed at increasing competition and consumer choice rather than imposing a fine. These commitments were:

1. Coca Cola agreed not to impose exclusive purchasing conditions on its customers;
2. it agreed not to pay retrospective rebates to customers who continued to buy the same amount or more of its products;
3. it agreed not to require ties-ins of other products to the main products it supplied and not to offer rebates encouraging such ties; and
4. finally, it agreed to allow retailers to stock other soft drinks in its chiller cabinets to at least 20 per cent of their capacity, if no other cabinets were available in an outlet.

Clearly these commitments provide strong evidence of the Commission's ability to obtain significant results, thereby increasing competition and consumer choice. As in the UK, use of commitments may be a better way to deal with problems, at least in some cases, rather than applying a more adversarial approach.

THE CURRENT REVIEW OF POLICY UNDER ARTICLE 82

Most recently, the European Commission (in the form of DG Competition) has initiated a review of policy under Article 82. The main aims of this review are to introduce more transparency into EU policy and to develop, if possible, clearer rules that can be applied in Article 82 cases. In particular, DG Competition has published a Discussion Paper on the treatment of exclusionary abuses under Article 82 (in December 2005) and this section considers some of the issues reviewed in this paper.[63]

As noted earlier in this chapter, abuse of a dominant position can take a variety of forms ranging from price-based abuses such as predatory pricing, price discounts and rebates and margin squeezes, to non-price abuses, such as tying and bundling, exclusive purchasing and refusal to supply. As also noted, these can be divided into exclusionary abuses, which aim to weaken or eliminate competitors or new entrants, and exploitative abuses, which directly harm customers, and ultimately consumers. The focus of the review is primarily on exclusionary abuses, and, in particular, price-based exclusionary abuses.[64]

More specifically, the Discussion Paper considers two main areas where there may be scope for reform: the use of a test for an exclusionary abuse based on an 'as-efficient competitor' and the introduction of an efficiency defence in Article 82 cases. In the first, it suggests that the Commission could adopt a test based on whether the conduct of a dominant firm would weaken or eliminate an 'as-efficient' or more efficient competitor and hence, by implication, the dominant firm itself.[65] The logic of this test is that it will not, in general, be desirable to eliminate an equally efficient firm from the market, and hence this would be a useful standard to apply in Article 82 cases.[66] Under the policy, as suggested, evidence that an 'as-efficient competitor' could compete given the behaviour of a dominant firm would be evidence that there is no abuse of a dominant position ('safe harbour'), while evidence that an 'as-efficient competitor' could *not* compete would suggest a 'capability' of abuse, and the likely impact of the behaviour would need to be considered further (Discussion Paper, para. 66, pp. 20-1). Under this approach, but subject to provisos discussed below, the test could provide a dividing line above which, in particular, there would no evidence of an abuse.[67]

The test could be applied in a number of different areas as the Discussion Paper makes clear. For example, in the case of predatory pricing, pricing above average cost by a dominant firm (and, hence, an 'as-efficient competitor') would not be seen as evidence of an abuse (at least in the form noted above) while pricing below average cost could be seen as an abuse and further evidence would need to be examined. This is in line with current practice, depending on the definition of 'average cost',[68] where price below 'average cost' is seen as possible evidence of abuse and pricing below average variable cost is seen as firm evidence of an abuse (following the initial work of Areeda and Turner (1974/5)). Similarly, in a margin squeeze, if there is evidence that an upstream supplier is setting prices so high that an 'as-efficient downstream firm' could not compete with the firm's own downstream producer, there would be evidence of the capability of an abuse. The test would effectively involve considering whether the supplier's own downstream firm could compete effectively with these prices. And again, in the case of selective price cutting, a test would involve determining whether the firm involved is itself selling below average cost in the market where the selective price cuts take place. These arguments would also apply to other areas, such as discounts and rebates, providing a basis for reviewing a number of exclusionary forms of behaviour using a cost-based test.

However, a number of problems arise with this test, as presently conceived, some of which are noted in the Discussion Paper. At a practical level, there are a number of issues involved in determining the appropriate standard in calculating costs. For example,[69] in the case of multi-product firms, there is the problem of allocating common costs between different products. One solution is to allocate common costs *pro rata* with turnover (or using some other defensible method) to derive a measure of average total cost (ATC) although an alternative is just to ignore common costs and calculate long run average incremental cost (LAIC). Again, if only fixed costs used to support the supposed exclusionary behaviour are considered, an appropriate measure would be average avoidable costs (AAC). Typically, AAC will be lower than LAIC because not all fixed costs are included in calculating AAC while LAIC will be lower than ATC because the

LAIC does not include common costs. Second, there might be a problem in obtaining reliable evidence on the appropriate level of its costs from the dominant firm although in this case it is argued that a test based on hypothetical costs of an 'apparently efficient competitor' could be used (Discussion Paper, para. 67, p. 21). Also, the Commission may need to take a wider view of revenues and costs, rather than focusing on just one product or market. This would be the case, for example, if the dominant firm's behaviour affects its revenues in other markets or where several successive markets are involved (Discussion Paper, para. 67, p. 21).

There are also some theory-based reservations with the test. First, in using an 'as efficient competitor' dividing line, the test is implicitly assuming (at least in the strong form outlined above) that behaviour that would weaken or eliminate a *less* efficient firm would not be seen as an abuse. As is clear from standard theory (see Vickers, 2005, p. F256), however, this ignores the fact that competition from a less efficient firm is, nevertheless, competition, which is likely to benefit consumers by reducing prices.[70] In general,[71] for a marginally inefficient competitor, there will be a trade-off between lower prices for consumers and less efficient production, which over some range of possibilities implies an overall gain from protecting competition.[72] This suggests that, in its strong form at least (that is, in providing a *sufficient* condition for not finding evidence of an abuse) the test would fail to protect economic (and consumer) welfare.

Second, as noted in the Discussion Paper, a problem also arises if competitors are not as efficient as a dominant firm but may become so later; for example, because of learning effects, or economies of scale or scope, or first-mover advantages initially enjoyed by dominant firms (Discussion Paper, para. 67, p. 21). In response to this, the Discussion Paper argues that, of necessity, the policy would need to be applied in a 'specific market context' where such issues would be considered. Hence, the test would not apply absolutely. Both points, however, argue against a strong form of the test in finding that behaviour is *not* abusive if an 'as-efficient competitor' could compete.

The Discussion Paper also considers possible defences against a finding of abuse under Article 82, and, in particular, the introduction of an efficiency defence.[73] Under Article 82, there is no explicit reference to efficiency and this means that the Article is out of line with other areas of EU policy, in particular in relation to agreements between firms (Article 81) and mergers. The Discussion Paper, therefore, proposes that an efficiency defence be introduced in Article 82 cases along similar lines to those elsewhere. Four conditions are proposed:

(i) that efficiencies are realised or likely to be realised as a result of the conduct concerned;
(ii) that the conduct concerned is indispensable to realise these efficiencies;
(iii) that the efficiencies benefit consumers;

(iv) that competition in respect of a substantial part of the products concerned is not eliminated (Discussion Paper, para. 84, p. 26).

The first condition is to be interpreted widely (as under Article 81(3)) to cover conduct which contributes to the improvement of production or distribution, or the promotion of technical or economic progress, including, for example, producing better quality products as well as making cost savings. Firms are required to produce evidence to show that their conduct produces such beneficial effects. Second, it must be shown that the conduct is indispensable to obtain those benefits although the Discussion Paper does not suggest that firms need to consider all possible hypothetical circumstances in showing this to be true. Rather it is necessary for them to show that realistic alternatives which could be put in place would not produce similar gains (or similar levels of gains).

Third, as under Article 81(3), it is necessary to show that there are real benefits to consumers as a result of these efficiencies, although in this case it is not clear whether this implies only direct consumer gains or more general gains associated with a more efficient allocation of resources.[74] The Discussion Paper notes that it is less likely that competition will be effective if a firm already has a position close to a monopoly, and hence an efficiency defence is less likely to succeed in such a case. Similarly, if there is a very inelastic demand (so that a dominant firm has substantial market power) it is less likely that the defence could succeed. Finally, and directly, it argues that efficiencies are *not* likely to be accepted as a defence if competition is restricted in a large part of the market, again reflecting policy under Article 81. Interestingly, it suggests that if a firm has a market position approaching that of a monopoly where its market share is above 75 per cent, competition in the rest of the market is weak and there are substantial barriers to entry, it is *highly unlikely* that an efficiency defence could succeed. This is so because of the basic principle underlying the policy that restriction of competition should be avoided over-rides other considerations in such cases.

The changes in relation to efficiencies have the merit that they bring Article 82 more closely into line with other areas of competition policy (notably Article 81) in that they offer the possibility that a firm can claim efficiencies (and other benefits) from their behaviour as part of their defence in Article 82 cases. Given that it is still unlikely that exclusionary behaviour could be justified by an efficiency defence, especially where a dominant firm has a very high market share, it seems likely that this change will not have a major effect on the operation of policy if adopted in the future.

CONCLUSIONS

This chapter has shown that there have been significant changes in UK (and, to some extent, EU) policies on monopolies and dominant firms in recent years. In the UK, the 1998 Competition Act has brought UK policy more into line with policy in the EU, based on Article 82 of the EC Treaty. In addition, and in contrast, the 2002 Enterprise Act has retained further powers to deal with monopoly problems in the UK. Early cases considered under the Competition Act suggest that it can be an effective way of dealing with dominant firms, although only a limited number of cases have been dealt with so far and these have been relatively minor cases. It is too early, therefore, to assess how effective the policy is likely to be. In the case of market investigation references no cases have so far been determined by the CC[75] although the chapter noted some possible weaknesses in the current policy in the long time periods required for a CC investigation and likely to be taken up in appeals to the CAT. It also raised the issue whether the CC is best placed to implement the remedies it proposes given its earlier focus on investigations and its limited resources. In addition, investigations by the OFT (market studies) offer some scope for reviewing markets in which competition appears not to be operating effectively, although results so far in dealing with these cases have been mixed.

The chapter also considered EU policy on dominant firms under Article 82 of the EC Treaty and the new Modernization Regulation. In this area, there has been some reform although changes introduced have not been great. Considerable case evidence has grown up over the years and the Commission continues to consider some high profile cases, notably *Microsoft* (2004) and *Coca Cola* (2004) in recent years. The use of commitments rather than final decisions, brought in under the Modernization Regulation, seems also to have been effective in the *Coca Cola* case, and it may be that it will be more widely used in the future. Most recently, a review of EU policy under Article 82 has suggested significant reforms – in particular, that an 'as-efficient competitor' test be used to consider exclusionary behaviour and that an efficiency defence be introduced in Article 82 cases. Some problems exist with the first of these proposed reforms and it remains to be seen whether (and in what form) this test is developed in the future.

NOTES

1. My thanks to Eleanor Morgan for her comments on this chapter.
2. The key point as emphasised below is that the market share test used in dominance cases is significantly higher than that used under the FTA. In principle, this can be overcome by using the provision on collective dominance under the 1998 Act, but, following EU experience, the government

of the day believed that this power was insufficient to deal with 'oligopoly' cases covered under the FTA.

3. Market foreclosure means that the monopoly or dominant firm adopts policies which limit the ability of rivals or new entrants to compete in the market. Examples, as discussed below, include predatory pricing, exclusive purchasing and margin squeezes.

4. It is not possible in the limited space in this chapter to discuss all policies that could be used, or discuss policies in detail. For further discussion see Whish (2003, Chapters 17 and 18) or Goyder (2003, Chapter 15).

5. Intra-brand competition relates to competition between downstream firms in the sale of a particular manufacturer's goods or services. Inter-brand competition relates to competition between the goods and services of different manufacturers at the downstream level.

6. See Office of Fair Trading, Abuse of a dominant position, OFT Competition Law Guideline, 2004. This is also the case with Chapter I cases concerning agreements between firms which are discussed in Chapter 5.

7. A number of sector regulators have concurrent powers with the OFT to undertake Chapter II investigations. For reasons of space, cases brought by sector regulators are not discussed in this chapter.

8. This power was introduced in the Competition Act 1998 and Other Enactments (Amendment) Regulations 2004, which came into force on 1 May 2004.

9. See Office of Fair Trading, Abuse of a dominant position, op cit., pp. 14-15.

10. For a brief discussion of collective dominance at the EU level, see later in this chapter. Cases under the Competition Act so far (see Table 2.1) have all involved single firm dominance.

11. In some cases, for example *London-wide newspaper distribution* (2005), the Chapter I prohibition was also involved. Note also, that there have been a large number of Chapter II investigations by sector regulators although these are not discussed in this chapter. It appears that, in most (or possibly all) of these cases, no evidence of abuse was found.

12. Office of Fair Trading, *Napp Pharmaceutical Holdings*, CA/98/2/01, Decision of 30 March 2001.

13. See OFT press release, 15 January 2002.

14. Office of Fair Trading , *Exclusionary behaviour by Genzyme Ltd.*, CA/98/3/03, Decision of 27 March 2003.

15. See OFT press release, 29 September 2005.

16. Office of Fair Trading, *Predation by Aberdeen Journals Ltd.*, CA/98/5/01, Decision of 16 July 2001 and Office of Fair Trading, *Predation by Aberdeen Journals Ltd.*, CA/98/14/02, Decision of 16 December 2002.

17. The decision in this case was put out for consultation in April 2005; see OFT press release, 7 April 2005.

18. As noted earlier, the possibility of using a binding commitment to deal with Competition Act cases was introduced on 1 May 2004.

19. The actual decision to close the case was made in early March 2006 as this book was going to press.

20. Office of Fair Trading, *The Association of British Travel Agents and British Airways plc*, CA/98/19/02, Decision of 11 December 2002.

21. Office of Fair Trading, *First Edinburgh/Lothian*, CA/98/5/04, Decision of 29 April 2004.

22. See Clarke, Davies and Driffield (1998). Some cases were larger, notably *ABTA/British Airways* (2002).

23. Office of Fair Trading, The Competition Act: the major provisions, OFT 400, March 1999.

24. See Office of Fair Trading, Market investigation references, OFT Guidance, 2003, p. 5.

25. See Office of Fair Trading, Overview of the Enterprise Act, OFT Guidance, 2002, p. 15.

26. The Secretary of State retains some powers to intervene in market investigations, for example in public interest cases (at present defined to include only national security issues).

27. The CC also has powers to implement remedies in most merger cases, as discussed in Chapter 3. Policy under the Chapter I and II prohibitions is, in most cases, dealt with independently of ministerial intervention.

28. At a late stage in the preparation of this book the CC reported on its first case: see Competition Commission, *Store cards market investigation*, final report, 7 March 2006. This report found evidence of over-charging on store cards compared to other forms of credit and suggested a number

of reforms related to improving consumer awareness which at time of writing had not yet been put in place.

29. See Office of Fair Trading, Market studies, OFT Guidance, November 2004.
30. The OFT has a general duty to keep markets under review and has conducted its own studies over a long period, initially under Section 2 of the FTA. It began publishing these studies, however, only in 2003 and they are now published under the Enterprise Act.
31. See Office of Fair Trading, Market studies, op cit., p. 10.
32. Office of Fair Trading, *Extended warranties on domestic electrical goods*, OFT 387, July 2002.
33. See Competition Commission, *Extended warranties on domestic electrical goods*, Cm 6089, December 2003.
34. The Supply of Extended Warranties on Domestic Electrical Goods Order, 2005. The Order came into force on 6 April 2005.
35. Office of Fair Trading, *Store cards*, OFT 706, March 2004.
36. The CC has now reported in this case: see note 28.
37. Office of Fair Trading, *New car warranties*, OFT 683, December 2003.
38. See OFT press release, 14 May 2004.
39. An interesting feature of this case was that many consumers believed that such ties applied to their warranties even if they did not. Whether the consumer awareness campaign had any effect in dispelling this belief is difficult to say.
40. Office of Fair Trading, *The control of entry regulations and retail pharmacy services in the UK*, OFT 609, January 2003.
41. In the event the OFT's report was incorporated within a wider examination of regulatory change undertaken by the government. As a result, the DTI announced (in August 2004) changes which make it simpler and faster to set up new pharmacies but at the same time allow some restrictions on entry to protect local pharmacies, especially in rural and poor areas. The measures include the right to set up new pharmacies in out-of-town shopping centres but not in large shopping centres within towns; primary care centres are given the right to set up pharmacies but only if they provide comprehensive health care services to at least 18 000-20 000 people; internet pharmacies are allowed to operate as long as they provide a full professional service; and there are no restrictions on pharmacies committing to operate for more than 100 hours a week (DTI press release, 18 August 2004).
42. See Office of Fair Trading, Super-complaints – guidance for designated consumer bodies, OFT 514, July 2003. A number of consumer bodies have been recognized for this purpose including the Consumers' Association (now Which?), the National Consumer Council and the National Association of Citizens' Advice Bureaux.
43. See *United Brands v. EC Commission*, ECR 207, 1978.
44. See European Commission, Notice on the definition of the relevant market for the purposes of Community competition law, OJ C372, 9 December 1997.
45. See, for example, Geroski and Griffith (2004).
46. See *United States v. EI du Pont de Nemour and Co.*, 1956.
47. See *United Brands v. EC Commission*, op cit.
48. See Chapter 5 below.
49. DG Competition, 'The application of Article 82 of the Treaty to exclusionary abuses', Discussion paper, December 2005, p. 17.
50. For further discussion see DG Competition, ibid., pp. 15-17.
51. Council Regulation (EC) No 1/2003 on the implementation of the rules laid down in Articles 81 and 82 of the Treaty, OJ L1, 4 January 2003.
52. See Chapter 1.
53. Council Regulation (EEC) No 17/62 of 6 February 1962, first regulation implementing Articles 85 and 86 (now 81 and 82) of the Treaty, OJ 13, 12 February 1962.
54. See Philip Lowe, 'Current issues of EU competition law – the new competition enforcement regime', speech given 31 December 2003, p. 6; available at http://ec.europa.eu/comm/competition/speeches/index_theme_26.html
55. Philip Lowe, 'Current issues of EU competition law', ibid., p. 6.
56. Again this policy is in line with UK policy, in this case under the Competition Act as amended and introduced in May 2004.

57. *TACA*, COMP/35.134, Decision of 16 September 1998.
58. *Wanadoo Interactive*, COMP/38.233, Decision of 16 July 2003.
59. *Clearstream*, COMP/38.096, Decision of 2 June 2004.
60. *Microsoft*, COMP/C-3/37.792, Decision of 24 March 2004.
61. *Coca Cola*, COMP/39.116, Decision of 19 October 2004.
62. These commitments were only the second that had been accepted (and the first in a dominant firm case) under the new powers in the Modernization Regulation discussed above.
63. DG Competition, 'The application of Article 82 of the Treaty to exclusionary abuses,' Discussion paper, December 2005; hereafter referred to as 'Discussion Paper'.
64. The Competition Commissioner, Neelie Kroes, has indicated that exploitative abuses will be considered at a later stage; see Neelie Kroes, 'Preliminary thoughts on policy review of Article 82', Speech at the Fordham Corporate Law Institute, New York, September 2005.
65. See also Vickers (2005).
66. Note, however, that this 'logic' doesn't address the question whether the test would be necessary and/or sufficient for or against an abuse. As argued below, it cannot be concluded that it is a sufficient condition for there *not* being an abuse (that is, a 'safe harbour' decision).
67. It might be tempting to suggest that setting price below the average costs of an 'as-efficient competitor' would be sufficient for the finding of an abuse. Note, however, that this would be inconsistent with the usual test employed for predatory pricing, that price below average cost but above average variable cost may, but need not, imply an abuse.
68. There are a number of different measures of average cost, depending on how common costs are allocated, and whether only avoidable costs are considered. For a brief discussion of this see further below.
69. See Discussion Paper, para. 65, p. 20.
70. The test might apply in markets that are competitive since it would then not be desirable to see prices below the costs of less efficient firms as exclusionary. This will not apply if markets are imperfectly competitive as discussed below.
71. It perhaps should be noted that in some cases greater competition can force a dominant firm to raise its price (for example, where its demand curve shifts back but becomes less elastic as a result of greater competition). This would complicate the analysis in that at least some consumers will be worse off than without the extra competition.
72. It has been shown by Lahiri and Ono (1988) that if firms compete in outputs there will be some level of costs at which it would be not be desirable for a high cost firm to operate. It would also be true that below this cost level there is an overall welfare gain from allowing a less efficient firm to compete. If firms compete in prices, competition is generally stronger, and it may be that *any* high cost firm that can survive in the market will add to economic welfare by lowering prices to consumers. This would be the case, for example, in duopoly with linear demand curves and constant (but different) marginal costs.
73. Under Article 82, decisions of the courts have determined that firms can have a defence if there are 'objective justifications' for the behaviour observed. This could arise because of 'objective necessity' where the firm is responding to an external factor (for example, a health or safety issue) or as a loss-minimising defence against the competition of others. In the latter case, evidence that the dominant firm had invested in new resources to support its behaviour would indicate that such a defence would not be available: see Discussion Paper, op cit., pp. 24-6.
74. On balance, the Discussion Paper appears to support the former view rather than the latter as elsewhere (as, for example, under Article 81). It also requires that there are direct gains in the short run rather than in the medium to long run.
75. As noted in note 28, the *Store cards* report was published at a late stage in the preparation of this book.

3. UK Merger Policy

Peter Maunder

INTRODUCTION[1]

Measures to reform the framework for UK mergers policy were contained in Part 3 of the 2002 Enterprise Act. These new measures came into force on 20 June 2003. The new framework was a significant development in the policy for merger control that was originally introduced in 1965, nearly 40 years previously, and had not been formally modified since the 1973 Fair Trading Act. The new regime formally incorporated a new legal test – a substantial lessening of competition (SLC) – which followed that adopted in the US in 1914. In this respect, as in others, one can readily see the changes in the UK being influenced by the long-established precedent of merger policy in the US.

There are three key aspects of the 2002 Enterprise Act (the 'Act') as it relates to mergers. The first of these is the change in the role of the agents involved in UK mergers policy. These institutional changes include the establishment of the Office of Fair Trading (OFT) on a statutory basis as a corporate body on 1 April 2003. Under the 1973 Fair Trading Act (FTA), the OFT did not exist as a legal entity but was the administrative support for the Director-General of Fair Trading (DGFT). The statutory position of the DGFT was abolished under the new Act and these functions were transferred to the OFT. The OFT consists of a chairman and chief executive and other members appointed by the Secretary of State for Trade and Industry (hereafter 'Secretary of State').[2] The OFT and the Competition Commission (CC) are each explicitly recognised as specialist and independent competition authorities under the Act which transfers responsibility for mergers policy to these two bodies from government ministers in all but very exceptional cases.

The second significant aspect of the new Act relates to the greater transparency and increased accountability in decision making of the OFT and CC. The OFT is required to publish a statement of reasons for each of its merger decisions. The Act introduces a new provision for reviewing decisions taken by the OFT, CC and government ministers. Parties to a merger, or others who are sufficiently affected by a decision, may apply to a new independent body, the Competition Appeal Tribunal (CAT) for a review. The OFT and CC were required by the 2002 Act to publish detailed guidance as to how they would discharge their new roles and responsibilities. Their new guidelines have considerable similarities to the merger guidelines operating in the US.

The third key provision of the Act requires the OFT and CC assess mergers against a pure competition test – the SLC – rather than the public interest test which was the formal test under the FTA. This, again, brings convergence with the US system as noted earlier.

Together, these changes amount to a reform of the framework for UK mergers policy. This chapter now examines these three key aspects of the new regime. It begins with the changed framework of mergers policy involving the diminished role of the Secretary of State. Second, the developments in the appraisal of mergers are considered and the criteria for referral to the CC by the OFT are explained. Third, developments in procedures affecting the CC, which essentially relate to changes in its timetable of reporting, are examined. A case which prompted a clarification of the OFT's referral procedures as a result of a judicial review by the CAT in late 2003 and the subsequent appeal is also examined in this section. Finally, some conclusions are drawn at the end of the chapter.

DEVELOPMENTS IN THE INSTITUTIONAL FRAMEWORK

The 2002 Act made the OFT, CC and CAT the determinative competition authorities, as outlined in the introduction. Hitherto, under the FTA, the OFT advised the Secretary of State on possible references to the CC, although the latter could make a referral independently of any such advice. On receiving a reference, the CC would report to the Secretary of State whether the relevant merger operated, or might be expected to operate, against the public interest. If the CC reported that a merger failed the public interest test, the Secretary of State had discretion on policy remedies to address the situation.

Under the 2002 Act, merger decisions were taken almost entirely out of the political area. There are three exceptions, however, where ministerial involvement remains. First, the public interest criterion is retained when national security is involved and this provides a potential basis for government intervention, although it has not yet been exercised. Second, the assessment and clearance of mergers in the market for newspapers remains the responsibility of the Secretary of State in the light of advice from both the OFT and the Office of Communications (Ofcom). Thirdly, a similar system to that which applies to newspapers was adopted for mergers of water or sewerage companies where the OFT liaises with the industry regulator, Ofwat.

The virtual disappearance of ministerial involvement in merger decisions as enshrined in the new Act has been welcomed as bringing greater predictability in merger policy. It was, however, not such a significant change in view of the way in which policy was actually operating previously. In the words of the chairman of the CC, 'the change will be rather less novel or dramatic' (Morris, 2002, p. 15) as successive secretaries of state in the late 1990s had become more willing to concur with advice on merger referrals from the OFT. Between December 1998 and June 2001, Stephen Byers reportedly dealt with over 280 merger cases in his role as Secretary of State but referred only one case to the CC against the advice of the OFT, and there were only two cases which he did not refer, contrary to OFT advice.[3] Indeed, it was Byers who proposed in the 1999 Green Paper on mergers that the responsibility for referral decisions should be handed to the OFT and CC.[4]

The formal announcement of the proposed change in the Secretary of State's role as regards merger policy referrals was made in the White Paper of July 2001. Its sub-title, 'A world class competition regime', indicates the government's broad objective which was to make the OFT and CC transparent organisations ranking among the world's best competition authorities.[5] The 2002 Act can be seen as bringing merger policy into line with the recent changes in the other main areas of competition policy under the 1998 Competition Act, further enhancing its status in enforcing UK competition policy.

The virtual abandonment of formal provisions for ministerial involvement in merger cases under the 2002 Act came, ironically, soon after the High Court had for the first time overturned a merger decision made by the Secretary of State in the light of a CC report. The then Secretary of State, Stephen Byers, accepted the Commission's recommendation that Interbrew, based in Belgium, should divest the brewing interests of Bass plc which, in effect, blocked the merger.[6] Interbrew successfully applied for judicial review and, in May 2001, the High Court held that the CC had failed to give Interbrew a reasonable opportunity to discuss alternative remedies. The High Court ordered the Secretary of State to reconsider his acceptance of the CC's recommendation and to seek advice from the OFT. As a result, Interbrew ultimately retained part of the brewing interests of Bass but divested some brewing capacity and brands including Carling, the leading UK brand. *Interbrew/Bass* brought into question the adequacy of the CC's treatment of public interest concerns and possible remedies. Predictably, the then chairman of the CC accepted that the Commission needed to review how it handled the concluding stages of merger cases to avert further legal challenge. The changes made by the Act to the CC's timetable are noted later in this chapter – these aim to allow adequate consultation with relevant parties prior to remedial action being specified in the new regime where there is no ministerial involvement.

As the OFT became fully responsible for deciding which mergers to refer to the CC for detailed investigation under the 2002 Act, it became vital to ensure accountability and transparency in its decision-making. The advice of the DGFT to the Secretary of State on individual merger cases had started to appear on the OFT's website in August 2000, following the consultation on the 1999 Green Paper when interested parties indicated that such publication would be welcome.

The new transparency was extended further when the OFT took full responsibility for merger decisions in June 2003 and was required to publish its reasons for referral or non-referral.[7] At this stage, the Mergers Panel, which had been established in 1965 when merger control policy was first introduced, was abolished. This ad hoc committee of officials drawn from several government departments had acted as a vehicle for the accommodation of political concerns and compromise within an opaque system of determining referrals (Wilks, 1999). Case Review Meetings, which are attended only by OFT officials, were introduced in its place. The decisions, either merger clearances (which may be subject to undertakings) or referrals to the CC are now made available on the OFT website in both summary version and full text.

Both bodies were required by the 2002 Act to publish guidance as to how they would discharge their new roles and responsibilities. The CC issued five draft documents in September 2002 and the OFT issued its draft consultation paper a month later. Following a consultation period, both the OFT and CC published final versions of this guidance advice, including their respective guidelines for merger assessment and guidelines on procedures in both hard copy version and on their websites.[8]

The OFT has a duty to refer a merger to the CC for further investigation if it is likely to result in a substantial lessening of competition with three exceptions.[9] The first is where the merger is insufficiently advanced to warrant a reference. The second is where the relevant markets are not sufficiently important to warrant the costs of investigation by the CC. The third exception – the presence of customer benefits of a merger outweighing its adverse effects – is regarded in the Guidance as a more probable basis for non-referral but, even here, the document states that such benefits (which are discussed later in this chapter) will be a very unlikely basis for not referring the merger to the CC if an SLC is involved.

The 2002 Act also allows the OFT (or the Secretary of State in the exceptional public interest cases outlined earlier) to accept binding undertakings from the merging parties in lieu of a reference to the CC. Such undertakings must address the adverse competition effects identified and be proportionate to them. These remedial settlements may be preferable when there is an SLC which only arises from a small overlap in the product ranges of the merging parties; for example, the divestment of the minor overlapping interests to a third party would avoid more detailed and costly study by the CC of all the activities of the merging parties. The OFT's Guidance makes clear that commitments about the future conduct of the merged concern are unlikely to be regarded as addressing the competition concerns identified and structural change is likely to be required.

The power of the OFT to accept undertakings in its own right under the 2002 Act is a further key element highlighting its new role as an independent competition authority even if this amounted to a formalisation of its recent practice under earlier legislation. In the year ending in March 2004, the OFT considered 56 mergers under the FTA and 211 mergers under the new legislation which came into operation in June 2003.[10] Of the 211 mergers reviewed under the 2002 Act, nine were referred to the CC although only four proceeded to the report stage. Undertakings were given in lieu of a reference in three cases. In the next six months ending September 2004, there were ten referrals, in line with the number of referrals expected in a full year by the OFT (between ten and 20) according to its Annual Report on 2003-04.[11] Thirty-one cases were found not to qualify for examination, 56 were allowed to proceed and undertakings were given in one other case.[12] The role of the CC in determining remedies after full investigation in referred cases is considered later in this chapter.

The reformed mergers framework included the establishment of the CAT where decisions by the OFT and CC can be reviewed on appeal, with Sir Christopher Bellamy as its first President. Hitherto, there had been an Appeal Tribunal as part of the CC but the CAT became entirely separate from the CC as from 1 April 2003. There is now a specific right of appeal against both referral and clearance decisions by the OFT on judicial review grounds. This right of appeal against OFT decisions both by the parties involved and other affected parties, together with the requirement for the OFT to publish a detailed statement of reasons for its decisions, will act as an important check on the OFT in exercising its new role even though the number of cases actually taken to the CAT is likely to be relatively small.[13]

The newly-independent CAT soon made its mark in December 2003 in a review of the OFT's decision[14] not to refer *iSOFT/Torex* to the CC. Its judgement on the appeal brought by IBA Health Ltd threatened to alter the basis on which the OFT had assumed it would decide whether or not to make a referral to the CC.[15] The OFT went to the Court of Appeal on the grounds that the CAT had wrongly interpreted the intention of the Act. In its judgement of February 2004, the Court of Appeal dismissed the case brought against the CAT by the OFT as it found that the OFT had not adequately explained its clearance decision, although it rejected the CAT's interpretation of the 2002 Act. This case is discussed more fully later in the chapter but, first, it is necessary to consider the assessment of mergers under the Act and specifically the SLC test; it was the OFT's interpretation of the proof required under this test which underlay the CAT's ruling on the OFT's decision not to make a referral to the CC in *iSOFT/Torex*.

APPRAISAL AND REMEDIES

The next sections consider the issues involved in merger decisions by the OFT and CC following the adoption of the SLC test in the 2002 Act and their 2003 guidance documents. As the chairman of the OFT put it '... (the) guidelines can be seen as the economics bridge between the law and the facts of cases. They say how the authorities will interpret and apply the law, particularly in respect of economic analysis, to case facts' (Vickers, 2004, p. 462). The following eight aspects are considered in turn with some illustrative examples: the relevant merger situation and market definition; the substantial lessening of competition test; competition with and without the merger (the counterfactual); horizontal mergers; vertical mergers; conglomerate mergers; efficiency gains and customer benefits arising from mergers; and, finally, remedial action.

The Relevant Merger Situation and Market Definition

In general, mergers that meet the size thresholds of the EC Merger Regulation are examined in Brussels and are outside the scope of the UK merger control. There are some exceptions – jurisdiction may be handed back if a merger will have particular effects within a distinct market nationally (as discussed in Chapter 4) and national authorities can also take steps to protect certain legitimate interests such as the plurality of the media, public security and prudential rules.

The UK has a voluntary notification system for mergers falling within the scope of its legislation. There are two jurisdictional tests for determining whether a merger falls under the scope of the UK merger controls. The 'turnover test' is met if the UK turnover associated with the enterprise being acquired exceeds £70m (a figure raised from £45m in the draft documents). The alternative 'share of supply' test is met when, as a result of the merger, the enterprises which cease to be distinct either supply or are supplied with at least one quarter of all the goods and services of a particular description in the UK or a substantial part of it. The OFT will determine whether the share of supply test is met taking into account the narrowest reasonable definition of the appropriate set of goods and services.

Whether the merger is of a horizontal, vertical or conglomerate type, identifying the competitive constraints faced by the merged entity requires a definition of the relevant product and geographic markets affected by the merger. The issues raised by the need to define the market had been addressed earlier in the advice given on the interpretation of the 1998 Competition Act;[16] this considered the extent of possible substitution on the demand and supply side using the 'hypothetical monopolist' test, which is also known as the SSNIP test.

This benchmark for market definition, which is also contained in the current Guidelines, asks (in the case of product market definition) whether it would be profitable for a hypothetical monopolist to make a small but significant (5 to 10 per cent) non-transitory increase in the price ('SSNIP') of a given product (service) or group of products (services). The starting-point in this analysis is the product, or products, immediately affected by the merger; further products are added to the defined market until a price increase of between 5 and 10 per cent would be profitable because consumers would not switch away from the postulated group in sufficient numbers. Applying the hypothetical monopolist test requires the consideration of a range of both quantitative and qualitative evidence from customers, competitors and suppliers. The aim is to determine the smallest group of products for which the hypothetical monopolist could sustain a SSNIP and find this profitable.

As indicated above, the SSNIP test was not a new concept under the 2002 Act. There is little direct evidence, however, that the OFT had given much emphasis to the SSNIP test in merger cases before the 2002 Act came into operation (see Goodman, 2003). For example, in *Kingspan Group/Thermal Ceramics Benelux*, the OFT arguably did not apply a strict SSNIP test in defining the relevant market.[17] The OFT focused on phenolic foam (used for thermal insulation) produced by both companies rather than the wider market of foamed plastic insulation materials. Even though the merging parties had a combined market share of over 80 per cent in the supply of phenolic foam, the OFT advised that the merger should be allowed to proceed in the light of evidence from third parties of the possibility of demand substitution to other foamed plastics. Low barriers to entry and buyer power from distributors reinforced the willingness of the OFT to approve the merger.

In contrast to the OFT approach, there is some evidence of the CC strictly applying the SSNIP test before the 2002 Act came into force. A reference from the Secretary of State in February 2002 concerning the proposed merger of H+H Celcon Limited and Marley Building Materials Limited (MBM) provides a clear illustration of the hypothetical monopolist test in operation.[18] Both parties argued that the relevant market was all concrete blocks, including aggregate blocks, both dense and lightweight, and aerated concrete blocks (known as aircrete). Aircrete accounted for about one-third of concrete block sales in 2001 compared with 40 per cent for dense aggregate blocks and 25 per cent for lightweight aggregate blocks. The evidence offered by house builders indicated almost no willingness to switch between aircrete and aggregate blocks in response to a small but significant (5 per cent) rise in aircrete prices and, having assessed the reasons for this, the CC decided that aerated concrete blocks was the relevant market. It should be noted that the *H+H Celcon/MBM* report was published three months before the draft CC Guidelines indicating a seamless transition into the new regime for the CC in respect of product market definition.

The SSNIP test, including both demand and supply-side substitution, also provides a benchmark in defining the relevant product and geographic markets affected by the merger. In terms of the spatial aspect of market definition, the relevant market may be international, national, regional or limited to certain localities. Product perishability and transport costs are two crucial determinants of the relevant geographical market.

Issues raised by geographic market definition are well illustrated in the OFT's consideration of the completed acquisition by Dadco Alumnia and Chemicals Limited (Dadco) of sole control of Aluminium Oxid Stade GmbH (AOS), an alumina refinery near Hamburg in Germany in October 2004. AOS had been a production joint venture supplying both Dadco and Hydro Aluminium Deutschland GmbH (HAD). Prior to the merger, Dadco and HAD each sourced alumina hydrate from AOS and separately sold it to their own customers. The commodity alumina hydrate, which is used as a raw material in the production of industrial chemicals, is not manufactured in the UK. As almost all UK customers purchase their needs from EEA-based suppliers, the OFT considered the EEA was the appropriate geographic frame of reference even though transportation costs and logistics were not a barrier to supply from locations outside the EEA. Some third parties estimated Dadco's post-merger share of supply in the European Economic Area (EEA) would be as high as 51 per cent. In the light of Dadco's submission that its share of the UK market was 20-30 per cent, however, the OFT took the view that prior to the merger Dadco and HAD were not as strong a constraint on each other in the UK as elsewhere in the EEA. In its decision to clear the Dadco merger, the OFT noted that customers generally had expressed no adverse opinion on the transaction.[19] The majority of UK customers considered that they had a choice of existing suppliers, although some UK customers were unaware that Dadco supplied commodity alumina hydrate prior to the merger. Moreover, they could turn to other potential suppliers, including Glencore in Ireland, which could have supplied customers in the UK with ease.

The Substantial Lessening of Competition Test

In light of their new responsibilities under the 2002 Act, the OFT and CC required a clear test for appraising the likely effects of mergers within the relevant markets. The reforms aimed to ensure that, under the new framework, 'decisions (would) in future be taken by independent, transparent and accountable bodies – the OFT and CC – subject to a clear competition test.'[20] The 'substantial lessening of competition' test was introduced alongside the institutional changes in the new Act (2002 Act, sections 22(1), 23 and 33(1)).

According to the OFT Guidelines, the OFT must refer a relevant merger to the CC if the available evidence indicates there is a 'significant prospect' that the merger may be expected to lessen competition substantially, except in some limited exceptional cases as discussed earlier.[21] This standard for referral has been relatively low, compared, for example, with European standards; and it has not been unusual for the CC to clear cases unconditionally. For example, the CC published ten non-newspaper merger reports between April 2002 and 31 March 2003. In six of these enquiries, the relevant merger was cleared unconditionally.[22] In the following year, however, only one of six merger investigations under the FTA was cleared unconditionally. The second merger case reported under the 2002 Act was cleared unconditionally, unlike the first one. The November 2003 decision not to refer *iSOFT/Torex* under the Act was reviewed by the CAT, as mentioned earlier. Although the OFT's appeal case against the CAT's decision was dismissed, the OFT nevertheless issued a further note of guidance on the criteria for referral decisions, as discussed later in the section on procedure.

The standard of proof required when the test is used after full investigation by the CC is higher than when applied by the OFT, essentially reflecting the more detailed information available at the later stage. Hence the CC Guidelines state:

> . . . for the Commission to reach an adverse decision either the merger must have resulted in an SLC or the Commission must expect such a result. The Commission will usually have such an expectation if it considers that it is more likely than not that the SLC will result.[23]

With the formal adoption of the SLC test for use by both the OFT and CC, the UK merger regime has moved closer to the long established system in the US, as noted in the introduction. In practice, however, merger appraisal in the UK had been based on competition considerations for some considerable time while, for their part, successive Secretaries of State since 1997 had shown very little of the original enthusiasm to seek assessment of mergers based on any wider public interest issue.

Competition with and without the Merger (the Counterfactual)

The key issue in applying the SLC test is to compare the prospects for competition with and without the merger. The competitive situation without the merger is termed 'the counterfactual' in the OFT Guidance document. Generally the prevailing conditions of competition provide the best guide to the appropriate counterfactual. However, in establishing the nature of rivalry without the merger, the authorities may need to take account of possible entry and exit as illustrated in the referral of *Arcelor/Corus* to the CC.

In September 2004, the OFT referred the April 2004 acquisition by Arcelor SA (Arcelor), based in Luxembourg, of Corus UK Limited's UK hot-rolled sheet piling business (Corus).[24] The assets acquired consisted of supplier and customer lists, product specifications and sales information but did not include the Corus production plant at Scunthorpe which Corus had closed down two months earlier as part of its UK restructuring programme. This plant closure was a key aspect in the OFT's deliberations about the counterfactual – that is, what the competitive situation would have been without the merger. The OFT was not persuaded by Arcelor's claim that the steel-piling activities of Corus were loss-making and that Corus would have closed the Scunthorpe mill even in the absence of the Arcelor transaction.

The OFT regarded the Corus decision to close its Scunthorpe mill as presenting alternative suppliers to the UK with an opportunity to compete for the market share it previously supplied from that source. The OFT found evidence that Arcelor obtained business from nine out of the ten top UK customers of Corus so, to that extent, the merger dampened competition and, given the possibility that there might have been a more competitive outcome than the acquisition by Arcelor, the OFT concluded the SLC test was met and made a referral to the CC. The CC, however, concluded (by a majority of four to one) that Arcelor's acquisition might not be expected to lead to a substantial lessening of competition. [25] Some reduction of competition was expected, but this was seen as stemming from Corus's closure of the Scunthorpe mill rather than the deal it made with Arcelor. Thus the CC was satisfied that Corus would have closed its Scunthorpe mill even if the Arcelor deal had not happened whereas the OFT had previously not been so persuaded.

Horizontal Mergers

Both guidance documents deal with two aspects of the assessment of horizontal mergers. The first is the numerical measurement of the degree of competition within the relevant market affected by a horizontal merger. The second aspect, which receives more attention, is how the likelihood of post merger changes in the intensity of competitive pressures will be evaluated.

Turning first to the quantitative measures of intra-market rivalry, two commonly used indicators of the degree of competition within the relevant market – the share of the leading firm and Herfindahl-Hirschman concentration measures – are to be used by both the OFT and the CC, although there are some differences in the specifics within the respective Guidelines. The CC Guidelines state that no particular market share threshold denotes the likelihood of the CC deciding that the merger has resulted in, or is expected to result in an SLC. Nonetheless a combined market share of 25 per cent or above is said normally to be sufficient to raise potential concerns (although this figure should not be confused with the jurisdictional share of supply test). The OFT Guidance makes no reference to any combined market share but, like the CC, introduces benchmarks based on the Herfindahl-Hirschman Index (HHI). Both the OFT and CC are likely to regard any market with a post-merger HHI in excess of 1800 as highly concentrated, and any market with a post-merger HHI in excess of 1000 as concentrated. A merger which increases the HHI by more than 50 in a highly concentrated market may give rise to potential competition concerns. A change in the HHI of 100 would have the same effect in a concentrated market. [26] This guidance is based directly on the US merger guidelines and adopts the same numerical thresholds.

The OFT and CC guidance documents discuss two conceptually distinct means by which a horizontal merger might be expected to result in an SLC. These are termed 'non-coordinated' and 'coordinated' effects. The former may arise from a merged firm being able to exploit its increased market power as a result of the loss of competition between the merged parties. Such non-coordinated effects also include the possible effects on the ability of other firms in the market to benefit independently from the merger. Coordinated anti-competitive effects refer to the greater market power which may arise from the increased scope for tacit collusion among oligopolists. This distinction between 'non-coordinated' and 'coordinated' effects is not new in the UK and was discussed four years earlier in a report on merger appraisal commissioned by the OFT from the independent consultancy firm, National Economic Research Associates (NERA, 1999). It was, however, the first time that it had found formal expression within the legislation. The two types of effects are now considered in more detail.

In the case of non-coordinated effects, both sources of guidance indicate that there is an alternative term – 'unilateral effects' – and each identifies eight characteristics of markets affecting the post-merger likelihood of these effects.[27] For example, what are the options for switching by customers to alternative products? Are competitors to the merged firms under capacity constraints? Is the potential for entry limited or are there significant barriers to exit? Does the merger involve a firm that poses a significant competitive threat to other firms in the market? Unlike the CC guidelines, the OFT guidance uses the term 'maverick' in dealing with the possibility that one of the merging firms is an important rivalrous force in the market representing a competitive constraint greater than its market share indicates. The elimination of this 'maverick' through merger is seen as potentially bringing about an important change in competitive dynamics.[28] The possible influence of mavericks has been recognised in industrial economics for some time (see Scherer and Ross, 1990, for example). The term is also used in the CC report discussed below even though it does not appear in the CC guidelines.

The assessment of the characteristics of markets seen as affecting the likelihood of non-coordinated effects has inevitably featured in CC reports prior to the 2002 Act. Non-coordinated effects among oligopolists could be considered in the UK prior to the recent reform, in contrast to the position in the EU until the recent reforms there (see next chapter). There is, however, little evidence of their importance in UK investigations to date.

Turning to the assessment of 'coordinated' effects among oligopolistic firms, both the OFT and CC Guidance identify three necessary conditions for tacit coordination to be successful. The first is the ability of the participants to align their behaviour in the market. The second is that the firms have an incentive to maintain coordinated behaviour, which means that it must be possible for deviation from tacit coordination to be detected and deviating firms must face a credible 'punishment' in terms of the likelihood of retaliation by others. The final condition is that coordinated behaviour should be sustainable in the face of other competitive conditions in the market. The OFT Guidance notes that this approach is consistent with the approach taken by the Court of First Instance in the EU in its judgement on the Airtours appeal.[29]

The CC Guidelines spell out 15 characteristics of a market which may impinge on coordinated effects. These include high concentration, entry barriers, stability of market shares, switching costs and the extent of capacity in the market. These Guidelines note that the CC, in making an evaluation, needs to consider whether the coordinated effects exist prior to the merger and, if so, whether the merger would exacerbate the coordinated effects to the detriment of consumers. It is recognised that identifying past coordination is difficult in practice, but the Guidelines point to the level of profitability as a possible indicator to help to distinguish whether similar prices in the past are the result of intense competition or the outcome of coordinated effects.[30]

The guidance documents note that a merger might potentially result in an SLC but that competitive constraints could offset this outcome. This may be because a post merger price rise would either encourage rivals to expand capacity or attract new entry. Prospective new entry has to be timely, of sufficient scope and sustainable to be regarded as providing lasting and effective post-merger competition. The OFT Guidance discusses entry barriers with reference to absolute and strategic incumbency advantages and sunk costs,[31] terms which have appeared in earlier OFT publications and reflect earlier guidance.

The ability of a merged entity to raise prices may also be constrained by the countervailing power of buyers but both guidance documents emphasize that even if buyers are large relative to the size of suppliers, this will not necessarily be taken to indicate that buyer power is strong as it also depends on how easy it is for buyers to switch suppliers or set up their own supply arrangements.

Evidence provided by previous cases shows that the guidance on coordinated effects reflects previous policy towards horizontal mergers – as can be shown by reference to two reports by the CC in 2002-3. In the *Cargill Incorporated/Cerestor SA* acquisition, the CC noted that the reference products – glucose syrups and blends – were purchased on the basis of individual negotiation between producer and consumer and thus prices were not transparent. This was seen as making it more difficult for coordinated action to succeed in bringing about price rises. The CC thought coordinated action would be unlikely to succeed in view of the growing demand for the products together with the presence of large and powerful buyers; these would be capable of switching to a new entrant or even of sponsoring new entry if they felt at risk of being too dependent on their existing suppliers. Hence it concluded the merger might be expected not to operate against the public interest.[32] In *Arla Foods amba/Express Dairies plc*, the CC recognised that although the proposed merger would reduce the number of competitors, coordinated behaviour, either tacit or explicit, would be unlikely to occur as a consequence. This view was taken in the light of detailed consideration of the possibility of both non-coordinated and coordinated effects. In its advice to the Secretary of State, the OFT had suggested that the merger could increase the likelihood of tacit collusion. The parties to the merger argued that the necessary conditions for coordinated behaviour were not met. The existence of over-capacity in the fresh milk processing industry would give the national multiple retailers scope to switch their source of supply and, here again, strong countervailing power was a key strand in the CC's decision not to oppose the merger.[33]

The approach taken in these earlier cases can be compared with the CC's approach under the 2002 Act, as illustrated by its report on *DS Smith plc/Linpac Containers Ltd*, an acquisition which affected the market for corrugated cardboard sheet. The CC found that there were some characteristics of the cardboard sheet market which could allow coordinated behaviour amongst the major suppliers. It believed, however, that the smaller suppliers would have the incentive to respond to any cardboard sheet price rises by expanding output through existing and new capacity. Of particular interest in this report is the CC's reiteration of the three necessary conditions for coordinated behaviour and its close scrutiny of the evidence to establish whether these three conditions had been met. The CC concluded that the first two conditions for coordinated effects were broadly met but not the third one, as the competitive constraints on the exercise of monopoly power were weak. Although the CC did not expect the merger to give rise to an SLC, it believed that the customers' concerns about price increase announcements justified further investigation of competitive behaviour in the market for the supply of corrugated cardboard sheet by the OFT. The CC considered the possibility that Linpac Containers was a maverick but, in contrast to the OFT, concluded that the firm's market share reflected its strength in the competitive process.[34]

These cases show that the consideration of the coordinated anti-competitive effects of a merger along the lines suggested by the 2003 guidance documents predates the 2002 Act so, once again, it is clear that the guidance documents reflect past best practice rather than marking any new departure.

Vertical Mergers

Both guidance documents give much less attention to vertical mergers than to horizontal mergers. They both recognise that vertical mergers may strengthen market power by the foreclosure of supply. This may occur, for example, if a rival firm is unable to obtain inputs from the merged firm following a merger between the input producer and another downstream customer and there is no reasonable alternative source of supply. The OFT Guidance document makes the vital distinction between the ability of the merged firm to foreclose competition in some way and the incentive to do so in terms of the profitability of pursuing that strategy. The importance of this distinction can be illustrated by an early OFT decision under the 2002 Act relating to bus manufacture.

In September 2004, the OFT concluded that the vertical acquisition of the bus body and chassis business Transbus International Ltd (Transbus) out of administration by Alexander Dennis Ltd (ADL), a company set up as a bid vehicle for this acquisition, would not lead to an SLC. The investment of Brian Souter and his sister, Ann Gloag, in ADL meant that the acquisition would have brought the largest UK manufacturer of buses into common ownership with Stagecoach, which is one of ADL's largest customers and the third largest UK bus operator. The potential competition concern facing the OFT in *ADT/Transbus* was whether Stagecoach could foreclose competition in the downstream bus market by raising its competitors' costs in relation to bus purchases or spare parts for buses. The OFT thought that, given the need for spare parts among bus operators, it would not be profitable for ADL to deny access to its spare parts as any such strategy would ultimately lead bus operators to cease buying new buses from ADL. Moreover, ADL offered no unique products and faced keen competition. The OFT therefore cleared the bid by ADL.[35]

Apart from these foreclosure concerns, the guidance documents recognise the possibility that vertical integration may facilitate collusion by increasing market transparency between firms. This is likely to be rare and can be dealt with by the approach to coordinated effects in horizontal mergers discussed previously.

Conglomerate Mergers

The possible exercise of 'portfolio power' is seen as a key issue in the treatment of conglomerate mergers (mergers between firms operating in different product/service markets) in both guidance documents. 'Portfolio power' refers to a situation where a firm exercises more market power from owning a range of products in separate markets than it could from each of the markets separately. In particular, it suggests that the market power deriving from a portfolio of branded products exceeds the sum of its parts. Where this power exists, anti-competitive concerns may arise from effects on market structure, the feasibility of entry-deterrence strategies and the increased potential for coordinated behaviour. One aspect of this is whether, for example, customers' purchasing decisions will be affected by the tying or bundling of products. The OFT's Guidance notes that buyers may exercise countervailing power and this could avert an SLC. But it also recognises that the creation of the portfolio of products arising from a merger may constitute a strategic entry barrier limiting the ability of competitors to extend their own portfolios.[36] Portfolio power has been considered as a relevant concern by the OFT in a number of very different markets prior to the 2002 Act, including radio broadcasting[37] and continence care.[38] But it is in the pre-2002 case relating to the computing industry that the OFT has given closest consideration of the possibility of competing products being foreclosed through the exercise of portfolio power.

This case concerned the completed acquisition by Synopsys Incorporated (Synopsys) of Avant! Corporation (Avant), two US-based companies which designed software tools for the electronic design automation (EDA) industry.

The two companies had overlapping interests in the supply of EDA software tools, a market which can be divided into four basic functional categories. Two of these categories are so-called 'front-end' tools for circuit chip design and the remaining two are 'back-end' tools that focus on the physical attributes of microchips. There is minimal demand-side or supply-side substitution within each of the four categories. The OFT considered the *Synopsys/Avant* merger, by itself, would be unlikely to alter the competitive significance of the parties in each of the four product categories but that there was the question of whether Synopsys might prevent its own tools operating with tools supplied by other manufacturers.

The OFT recognised the technical possibility of Synopsys seeking to force its customers to use a complete Synopsys-based design system that fulfilled all four categories of functionality rather than buying from other competing tool suppliers. However, it saw several reasons to doubt whether Synopsys had the incentive to engage in foreclosure. It would be commercially risky, given the ability of microchip designers to source their needs elsewhere and, furthermore, the willingness of customers to rely wholly on Synopsys was doubtful as many customers hold simultaneous licences for competing tools. The OFT concluded that Synopsys was likely to lose a large proportion of its sales of front-end logic synthesis tools if it engaged in foreclosure. By closing the interface between its own products and all other types of EDA tools used by its customers, a failed foreclosure strategy could threaten the firm's total product range, especially as several other EDA software suppliers were developing integrated tool sets that offered an alternative to a complete Synopsys design. Thus the DGFT recommended the Secretary of State not to refer the merger to the CC but noted the possibility of recourse to US antitrust law and the competition provisions of the EC Treaty if foreclosure by Synopsys became a reality.[39] As in *ADL/Transbus*, the vertical merger discussed earlier, the distinction between the technical feasibility of foreclosure and its success in practice[40] played a vitally important role in the outcome of this case.

Efficiency Gains and Customer Benefits Arising from Mergers

The preceding discussion of the three types of merger has considered some of the anti-competitive effects that may arise but the potential beneficial effects of mergers also need to be considered. The 2002 Act allows the OFT to consider efficiency gains claimed by the parties to a merger at two separate points in its first stage investigation. First, efficiency gains can be taken into account where their effect will be to increase rivalry between the post-merger companies such that no SLC will result. Second, efficiency gains can be taken into account in the consideration of consumer benefits which might occur after the merger, even though they do not avert the finding of an SLC. The presence of customer benefits is one of three exceptional circumstances in which the OFT may exercise discretion not to refer a merger to the CC and, as mentioned earlier, it is the most likely of these three.

The OFT Guidance is unequivocal in indicating its sceptical stance on efficiency gains. Any efficiencies claimed must be demonstrable and merger-specific and it must be likely that consumers will enjoy a reasonable share of the benefits. Such gains will not be considered unless the evidence is compelling. In addition, the OFT would normally expect competition to deliver lower prices, higher quality and greater customer choice and it will be rare for the OFT to clear a merger which results in an SLC on the basis that customers will still be better off.[41] Given possible competition concerns and the asymmetries in information between the OFT and the merging parties, this cautious stance by the OFT on possible gains from merger is unsurprising.

The OFT's cautious view on efficiency gains and reluctance to balance the competitive detriment of a merger against possible consumer benefits reflects past practice as seen, for example in *Blockbuster Entertainment/Apollo Video Film Hire* where it was stated 'While there are arguments for and against reference, the balancing of potential consumer benefits as against the potential loss of competition is usually considered to be a matter for the CC.'[42] A similar approach under the Act can be illustrated by the October 2004 referral to the CC of the completed acquisition of James Budgett Sugars Ltd (Budgett) by Napier Brown Foods (NBF). The companies are the two largest sugar merchants in the UK. NBF claimed that the merger would allow indirect cost savings from reduced overheads and direct cost savings from buying sugar on better terms but did not provide a breakdown of its estimated indirect cost savings. The OFT found contradictory evidence on direct cost savings throughout its investigation. Whilst recognising that there could be some customer benefits as a result of the economies of scale available to the enlarged merchant in this commodity business, the OFT was less clear whether NBF would pass these cost reductions on to customers. Although the combined company might constitute a 'third force' to compete with the two vertically integrated producers, British Sugar and Tate & Lyle, the OFT decided that it could not put aside its competition concerns and referred the merger to the CC.[43] The CC concluded in March 2005 that *Napier Brown Foods/James Budgett Sugars* would not lead to an SLC but voiced its concerns about a lack of effective competition in this market. The CC looked to a reform of the EU sugar regime to substantially reduce the price paid by sugar customers to a level closer to that which prevailed outside the EU.[44]

Possible efficiency gains can also be considered by the CC at two stages in its more detailed investigations – in terms of whether it averts the finding of an SLC[45] and as part of a consideration of possible customer benefits in deciding remedies on a merger which results in an SLC.[46] Section 30 of the 2002 Act identifies these benefits as including lower prices, higher quality and a greater choice for consumers or greater innovation in the supply of relevant goods or services. The Act provides that a benefit is only a relevant customer benefit if the CC believes that:

1. the benefit has accrued as a result of the creation of the relevant merger situation or may be expected to accrue within a reasonable period as a result of the creation of that situation, and
2. the benefit was, or is, unlikely to accrue without the creation of that situation or a similar lessening of competition.[47]

Thus the parties need to provide compelling evidence to the CC for the latter to be persuaded of the relevance of customer benefits and the necessity to consider they warrant any modification of the remedy that it would otherwise put in place.

Customer benefits had to be considered after the referral of the proposed acquisition by FirstGroup plc (FirstGroup) of the Scottish rail franchise operated by ScotRail Railways Ltd (ScotRail) to the CC in January 2004. The bidder was the leading supplier of bus travel in the UK and is also responsible for five passenger train operating companies. The CC confirmed the OFT's earlier concerns over the possible loss of competition on routes where bus and rail services overlapped. The CC did not regard the existing undertakings relating to FirstGroup's bus operations as sufficient to prevent the adverse effects expected on some routes after the merger. The CC also expected *FirstGroup/ScotRail* to result in an SLC in wider public transport network markets. The CC considered the benefits to consumers could include new services or increased frequencies, improved quality of service and improved integration with other forms of transport. With regard to this latter aspect, the CC reported that a number of third parties claimed that the merger between a main bus operator and the predominant rail operator in Scotland might assist transport integration. Other third parties, however, argued that transport integration did not require common ownership of bus and rail operations and, in this respect, no benefits might be expected as a result of the merger. FirstGroup itself believed that a higher service quality for passengers, materially over and above the minimum standard imposed by the ITT, and better transport integration would result from its acquisition of ScotRail.

The CC concluded that even if such benefits might result from the merger, they would not be put at risk by the remedies it put forward, and noted that FirstGroup was unwilling to challenge this view. The paragraphs within Appendix IV in the report are heavily excised and thus it is difficult to establish the size of the benefits that the CC had in mind in this case. But the CC's proposed undertakings included requirements relating to FirstGroup's participation in public transport multi-modal ticketing schemes with other bus operators in Scotland. FirstGroup was also required to provide factual, accurate and impartial advice about its own and its competitors' multi-modal tickets.[48] This report shows customer benefits being explicitly weighed up in the final stages of a merger decision in a more formal manner than required under earlier legislation. But, as indicated above, there is a difficulty in identifying the precise trade-offs made by various CC inquiry groups from the published reports since the 2002 Act.

Remedial Action

The role of the OFT in accepting remedies on the basis of its first stage investigation of a merger was discussed earlier. Turning now to the role of the CC in remedial settlements, the CC can exercise its order-making powers or accept undertakings from the parties where it has decided that it should take action to mitigate or prevent an SLC. The Act directs the CC 'in particular to have regard to the need to achieve as comprehensive a solution as is reasonable and practicable to the substantial lessening of competition and any adverse effects resulting from it.'[49] According to the CC Guidelines, direct action to preserve the market structure through prohibition or partial prohibition of a proposed merger or divestment in the case of a completed merger is regarded as likely to be preferable to behavioural remedies that may involve costly monitoring and may even distort competition as market conditions alter over time. Although both the costs of taking action and the effectiveness of that action need to be weighed up, the CC is not expected to consider the costs of divestment if the merger has already been completed unless there are exceptional circumstances.

Two types of possible behavioural remedies are distinguished – those which are intended to increase the competition faced by the merged firm (such as requiring access to key inputs, requiring the licensing of know how or intellectual property rights or dismantling exclusive distribution arrangements) and those limiting the possibility that the merged firm will take advantage of its increased market power (including a price cap, a commitment to non-discriminatory behaviour or an obligation to increase the transparency of prices).

An early referral under the 2002 Act provides a useful illustration of the CC's approach to remedies and use of behavioural undertakings. The CC concluded that the proposed acquisition by Dräger Medical AG & Co. KGaA of the Air-Sheilds neonatal warming therapy business from Hillenbrand Industries Inc could be expected to give rise to an SLC in the markets for closed care incubators, open care warming beds and transport incubators.[50] The substantial market share held by the merged entity was seen as enabling it to raise prices selectively to a significant number of hospital customers. The CC decided that undertakings on product range and service support from the merged entity would be the most appropriate remedy. To allay the concern that product lines would be rationalized, reducing choice for hospital customers, it sought undertakings from the merged company to continue to provide a full range of products, spares and after sales service for at least three years. These were made subject to price controls which would be monitored by an independent trustee. The undertakings were agreed with the merged parties in June 2004. As a separate remedy, the CC recommended to UK health departments and their procurement agencies that they take action to encourage market entry and strengthen the buyer power of NHS Trusts in order to act as a further competitive restraint on the merged company in the longer term. This illustrates how the CC took action to avert a post merger SLC in an environment where ministerial involvement in remedial action has now disappeared.

DEVELOPMENTS IN PROCEDURES, INCLUDING THE ROLE OF THE CAT

The third and final main section in this chapter considers the changes under the Act relating to the CC's rules of procedure.[51] Before turning to the procedural changes affecting the CC in the case of a merger referral, however, the role of the CAT will be discussed with particular reference to the *iSOFT/Torex* case. This case, as mentioned earlier, led the OFT in October 2004 to issue a note regarding decisions about referral to the CC to clarify its earlier Guidance.

The CAT and *iSOFT/Torex*

Very few cases arising from merger decisions have been considered by the CAT to date but it can act as an important new check on the OFT's new role regarding mergers as well as providing a new independent forum in which CC decisions can be challenged. Particularly notable was the early CAT judgement which resulted from *iSOFT/Torex*. In July 2003, iSOFT Group plc (iSOFT) offered to acquire the issued share capital of Torex plc (Torex). Both companies were suppliers of software to hospitals and health-care companies. The proposed acquisition was notified to the OFT on 1 August 2003. Two weeks later, IBA Healthcare Ltd (IBA), a company based in Victoria, Australia and also engaged in the same market, complained to the OFT about the effect of the anticipated merger. The OFT cleared the merger in the context of the proposal by the Department of Health to install a new IT system covering the medical record of each patient across all NHS providers in England.[52] The OFT concluded that, while their strong base of installed systems might give the merging parties a large market presence, it was unlikely, in itself, to confer significant market power in view of the new IT regime. The OFT thus decided the merger did not meet the SLC test and did not make a referral to the CC. In taking this decision, it was fully aware that the combined market share for the relevant products of the two companies in England was 44 per cent in respect of Electronic Patient Records (EPSs) and 66 per cent in Laboratory Information Management Systems (LIMS). The LIMS accounted for 100 per cent of the installed base in Wales and

Scotland. The next largest competitor accounted for 14 per cent of the market. Entry was difficult and there was low supply-side substitutability.

IBA was dissatisfied with the OFT's decision not to refer the merger to the CC and applied to the CAT for a review. The CAT quashed the OFT's decision at this judicial review and referred the matter back to the OFT for reconsideration. It stated:

> . . . we are not satisfied that the OFT applied the right test, or that the OFT reached a conclusion that was reasonably open to them. We are not satisfied that the facts are sufficiently found in the decision or that all material considerations have been taken into account. We are unable to verify whether there was material on which the OFT could reasonably base important findings in the decision.[53]

The President of the CAT, Sir Christopher Bellamy, said that 'only exceptionally' should the OFT try to resolve mergers where there was a real question as to whether there was an SLC. The CAT interpreted the 2002 Act to mean that there was a two part test for referring a merger to the CC – firstly, the OFT must refer a merger if it believed that an SLC was involved and secondly, if there was a credible view that the CC would also decide that there would be an SLC due to merger.

The OFT was granted permission by the CAT to appeal to the Court of Appeal against the Tribunal's decision. Whilst awaiting the Court's judgement, the Chairman of the OFT agreed with forecasts that the number of bids referred to the CC would double if the Court of Appeal upheld the CAT's interpretation of the referral provisions. Although the CAT's 'two-part test' has received some support (see Alese, 2004), the Court of Appeal rejected this approach which it viewed as making the new merger legislation unworkable. The Court of Appeal also found, however, that the OFT had not adequately explained and justified its clearance of the proposed iSOFT merger with Torex and dismissed the OFT's case against the CAT. One observer later commented that in its handling of the case 'the CAT may not have been entirely right; it was not wholly wrong either' (Alese, 2004, p. 474).

In April 2004, the OFT accepted undertakings from iSOFT in lieu of reference to the CC. It agreed to divest Torex's LIMS computer systems used in hospitals or trusts to a purchaser approved by the OFT; the anticipated acquisition by Clinisys Solutions Limited of Torex was approved by the OFT in January 2005.[54]

In the light of the Court of Appeal ruling, the OFT issued a new Guidance Note revising its earlier guidance. It now stated that

> The test for reference will be met if the OFT has a reasonable belief, objectively justified by relevant facts, that there is a realistic prospect that the merger will lessen competition substantially. By the term 'realistic prospect', the OFT means not only a prospect that has more than a 50 per cent chance of occurring, but also a prospect that

is not fanciful but has less than a 50 per cent chance of occurring....The OFT's test may be met in other cases where the OFT believes that there is less than a 50 per cent chance of a merger resulting in a substantial lessening of competition. However, in such cases there is no exact mathematical formulation of the degree of likelihood which the OFT acting reasonably must require in order to make a merger reference. Between the fanciful and a degree of likelihood less than 50 per cent there is a wide margin in which the OFT must exercise its judgement as to whether it may be the case that the merger may be expected to result in a substantial lessening of competition.[55]

This case highlighted the need for the OFT to ensure that it presented well reasoned arguments and adequate evidence to support its decisions. It also emphasized its need to make a judgement in a large number of merger situations as to whether it may be the case that the merger gives rise to an SLC. The final outcome, in the light of the Court of Appeal's judgement of February 2004, has prevented a large number of referrals to the CC compared to the relatively small number made during the first months under the new Act.

In December 2004, the CAT received a further challenge to an OFT decision not to make a merger referral to the CC when UniChem Limited challenged the non-referral of the anticipated acquisition of East Anglian Pharmaceuticals Limited by Phoenix Healthcare Distribution Ltd.[56] In its judgement, the CAT stated that the OFT had not adequately consulted with UniChem and thus quashed the decision remitting the matter back to the OFT for reconsideration.[57] This illustrates the important check on the OFT's procedures provided by the newly established CAT.

The CC Rules of Procedure

The increased transparency of decision-making by both the OFT and CC was noted at the beginning of this chapter and the transparency of the CC's operations is considered further here by looking at the CC's rules of procedure which explain how its methods of operation would become more explicit.[58] The rules provide for a faster 'administrative timetable' and new powers under the 2002 Act for the CC to obtain information in a timely fashion help make such a timetable feasible. There is statutory time limit of 24 weeks in which a report must be completed. Whilst work on most merger cases is expected to be completed in a shorter time than the maximum allowed, there is the possibility of an extension of eight weeks where the CC considers special reasons may prevent any earlier publication.

The content of the proposed administrative timetable drew most comment from those offering responses to the draft rules of procedure during the consultation period. These responses included comment on the desirability of public hearings and views about the time needed for parties to reply to provisional findings, two matters which receive further consideration here.

The draft rules of procedure provided for the group of members considering the reference in question to decide which, if any, of its hearings are to be held in public. Public hearings by the CC had begun in 2001 and so pre-date the new legislation. Some respondents to the CC in the consultation period during late 2002 had urged that public hearings should be the general rule except when disclosure issues arose. Other respondents, however, said that public hearings were not beneficial in most cases. The CC argued that its draft rules offered a balanced approach allowing for a mix of both private and public hearings as appropriate in each reference. The rules, as finally published, allow a group to hold joint hearings with two or more parties if it considers this would assist a proper examination of a particular case.

As regards the CC's provisional findings, the rules provide for the main parties to be notified of these and of any remedies and to be consulted on both aspects. Hitherto, the tight timescale requiring the CC to report to the Secretary of State within 24 weeks had made it very difficult for a provisional findings stage to be included under the FTA. However, in the light of the new rules, together with the elimination of the time previously allocated to ministerial scrutiny, the CC was committed to a greater degree of consultation before its investigation came to a close. The rules now provide for a minimum of 21 days for the parties to reply to provisional findings. Although there was pressure for a longer time to be introduced from some respondents in the consultation process, the CC was adamant that it was unrealistic to promise more than 21 days in every case, especially when dealing with the more complex merger cases. But, whatever the time period, it is important to recognise the relationship between the consultation on the provisional findings and the CC's enhanced role in determining remedies. Hence, in theory, the consultation process permits the parties to help devise the most effective remedies to address the concerns of the CC. Thus the new regime aims, within the time available, to ensure appropriate pro-competitive remedies can emerge in the light of adequate consultation with the relevant parties.

The recognition in the 2002 Act of the need of time to allow consultation with relevant parties should not be understated. It offers the best chance that the CC will be fully informed in its determination of appropriate remedies. The likelihood of judicial review similar to that seen in *Interbrew/Bass* in 2001 should thus be much diminished. Some respondents to the CC's draft rules suggested that third parties should have a chance to comment on remedies before decisions were taken. In response, the CC said that it would consider any representations third parties choose to make in the light of the statement of proposed remedies in its provisional findings given on its website. Third parties do not have to wait for the provisional findings to be published on the CC's website to find out the concerns emerging in the course of an inquiry and start to make representations. The earlier publication on the CC's website of an issues statement, following the group's initial process of gathering information, views and evidence, identifies for all interested parties the areas the inquiry will examine with the merging parties. The issues statement identifies issues concerning market definition, the competitive effects of the merger, the counterfactual and relevant customer benefits that may arise as a result of the merger. These key aspects provide the CC inquiry group with the basis for its hearings with the merging parties to help reach a decision on the SLC test. Thus the issues statement provides an opportunity for all interested parties to contact the CC with relevant views and evidence.

The proposed acquisition by Stena of certain assets operated by P&O on the Irish Sea, referred to the CC in August 2003, was the first case under the new Act which proceeded to the report stage. The CC reviewed its revised procedures in the light of experience in this merger case. The then Chairman, Sir Derek Morris, claimed that the publishing of provisional findings had worked well as had preparing a shorter style of report.[59] The decision to put much more material on the website than in pre-Enterprise Act days also resulted in much greater transparency. In particular, the website listed possible remedies which the inquiry group began to discuss with the parties soon after the publication of provisional findings. The report was published within the maximum 24 week period permitted[60] but the Chairman said that further experience under the new regime was likely to result in future inquiries being completed more quickly.

Having discussed the decision-making procedure of the CC under the new Act, it is worth noting that the new legislation required the OFT to be quicker in reaching its first stage decisions than was required under the FTA. Where the OFT is notified of a merger under the voluntary pre-notification procedure, its investigation has be completed within 30 working days (with some exceptions). This compares with 35 days under the FTA. Where the OFT is informed of a merger by the so-called informal written submission, it would expect to make a decision on a referral to the CC within 40 days, although this is not binding.[61] This compares with 45 days under the previous legislation.

CONCLUSION

The measures within Part 3 of the 2002 Enterprise Act have been in force for just 18 months at the time of writing. This is a very short time period on which to judge how well the new regime for merger control in the UK has been operating, but it is possible to make a preliminary assessment of how the OFT, CC and the CAT have accepted their new responsibilities as competition authorities.

Taking first the changed institutional framework brought about by the Act, the detachment of ministerial involvement in mergers policy has unquestionably been a wholly beneficial feature of the present system. The political controversies over both referrals and non-referrals as late as the 1990s are indeed from another age. Critics can no longer assert that the referral process is opaque.

The demise of the Mergers Panel has meant that what Wilks called 'the whole complexity of Whitehall inter-departmental horse-trading' has disappeared (Wilks, 1999, p. 220). Second, the formal adoption of the SLC test in the 2002 Act came at the appropriate time for the newly-independent competition agencies. The OFT and CC were able to draw on the US experience to show, through their new guidance documents, how they would uphold the pure competition test.

As the Chair of the OFT noted in 2002 when the then Enterprise Bill was still awaiting parliamentary approval, a competition test had become paramount in virtually all merger cases. But, as he put it at that time, 'There is great advantage in focusing the legal test clearly and sharply on competition criteria.'[62] At least part of the controversy surrounding mergers policy as late as the 1990s arose as much from the elusive nature of the public interest test as from ministerial involvement in both the referral process and the consideration of remedies proposed by the CC. The formal demise of the public interest test was necessary because the SLC test, which replaced it, is clearly grounded in economic principles and substantially reduces the scope for uncertainties in interpretation that had been apparent under the FTA. The UK, with the adoption of the SLC test, joined not only the US but also Canada, Australia, New Zealand, South Africa and Japan in its formal stance on merger policy. A similar test has subsequently been adopted in the EU, as discussed in the following chapter.

The second, and largest part of this chapter considered how the OFT and CC appraise mergers with reference to their guidance documents. It was shown that some of the economic principles pre-date the 2002 Act. For example, the SSNIP test and the tripartite framework for assessing the coordinated effects of mergers featured in some of CC reports on mergers prior to 2003. Moreover, the OFT's approach to market definition was clearly established with reference to the 1998 Competition Act. Guidance documents often formalise past practice and thus one should not expect to find a wholly distinctive approach to merger appraisal in these guidelines.

The third main section of this chapter focused on the procedural changes since June 2003. This noted the way in which the Act assisted the CC in determining an explicit tight timetable within which the relevant parties must provide their inputs whilst permitting adequate time, where necessary, to discuss remedies with the parties. Here, again, some aspects of current procedures are not new. Thus the use of public hearings and the publication of preliminary findings both pre-date the 2002 Act. But, since 2003, the CC has taken full advantage of the internet to make its procedures as transparent as possible, whilst recognising commercial confidentiality. The CC might seem to compare favourably with the OFT with respect to the transparency of its decision making. This was certainly the view of the CAT when making its judicial review of the *iSOFT/Torex* merger of two hospital software suppliers. One should note, however, that the advice of the then DGFT on referral or non-referral to the CC was not made public as recently as 2000. There has arguably been a dramatic transformation since that date in the public accountability of the OFT in explaining its first scrutiny of mergers. The OFT may have deserved criticism from the CAT for its initial handling of the *iSOFT/Torex* case but it can, in retrospect, be seen 'to have lost the battle but won the war' with the CAT in respect of applying the SLC test. It is clear that the OFT will face further challenges to its decisions on merger referrals paralleling the growing number of other appeals to the CAT about OFT judgements in non-merger cases, such as those relating to fines under the Competition Act. It is thus no surprise to see the OFT strengthen its legal division to meet the growing volume of litigation on both the consumer and competition aspects of its responsibilities. The OFT made the following simple but easily overlooked observation when it issued its revised Guidance Note following *iSOFT/Torex*:

> Merger review involves assessment of uncertain future prospects often on the basis of imperfect information and in a limited time frame. The degree of uncertainty may vary from case to case depending on the subject-matter of the merger and the nature and scope of evidence available to the OFT.[63]

This recognition of the difficulties in making a scrutiny of merger is an honest one. But in making the required critical judgement on mergers, the OFT now at least does so in a transparent and accountable manner that few could have expected at the start of the present millennium. Arguably both the OFT and the CC have met the challenges facing them with their new responsibilities for merger control. As recently as 1999, it was suggested that the UK had 'a poor policy well administered' (Wilks, 1999, p. 236). Merger policy is certainly now not poor. The recent changes to the OFT and CC to become independent but wholly accountable authorities indicate that the administration of mergers policy has been enhanced. Both the OFT and CC will no doubt face legal challenges to test their new status and responsibilities but the former opaque and back-stage character of the work of the OFT and CC in applying 'a poor policy' is now long gone. This constitutes real progress in a crucial area of economic policy.

NOTES

1. The author is indebted to both of the editors for detailed comments and suggestions on earlier drafts.
2. In March 2005, Philip Collins, a partner in a Brussels-based law firm, was announced as the part-time chairman of the OFT to succeed Sir John Vickers in that role at the end of his five year term of office in September 2005. In July 2005, John Fingleton, the head of Ireland's competition authority, was announced as the new chief executive of the OFT.
3. Stephen Byers, 'A new era in competition', speech to the Social Market Foundation, 28 February 2000 at www.dti.gov.uk/ministers/achieved/byers.
4. Department of Trade and Industry, Mergers – a consultation document: proposals for reform, Green Paper, August 1999.

5. Department of Trade and Industry, Productivity and enterprise: a world class competition regime, Cm 5233, July 2001.
6. *Interbrew SA/ Bass plc*, Decision of 9 January 2001, Cm 5014. Recent CC merger decisions are published on the CC website at www.competition-commission.org.uk/rep_pub/reports. A decision index is also maintained on the CC website.
7. Office of Fair Trading merger decisions are published on the OFT website at www.oft.gov.uk. The OFT also maintains a decision index.
8. See Office of Fair Trading, Mergers – substantive assessment guidance, OFT 516, 2003, Office of Fair Trading, Mergers – procedural guidance, OFT 526, 2003, Competition Commission, Merger references, Competition Commission guidelines, CC2, June 2003 and Competition Commission, Rules of procedure, Competition Commission guidelines, CC1, June 2003. In July 2003, the CC issued a further guidance document on the disclosure of information to Commission groups considering both merger and market investigation references under the 2002 Act. In December 2004, the CC published guidelines explaining its approach to merger inquiries in the water industry. It also issued a document explaining its proposed approach to applying divestiture remedies. All these further forms of guidance are published on the CC's website.
9. See Office of Fair Trading, Mergers – substantive assessment guidance, op cit., paras 7.1-7.5.
10. Office of Fair Trading, Annual Report and Resource Accounts 2003-04, HC 739, pp. 62-3.
11. Competition Commission, Annual Review and Accounts, 2003-04, July 2004.
12. Office of Fair Trading, *Fair Trading*, Issue 39, 2004.
13. CAT decisions are published on the CAT's website at www.catribunal.org.uk/archive.
14. *iSOFT/ Torex*, OFT Decision of 7 November 2003.
15. *1BA Health Limited v. Office of Fair Trading*, CAT case 1023/4/1/03, Judgment of 3 December 2003.
16. See Office of Fair Trading, Market definition, OFT 403, 1999, updated in 2005.
17. *Kingspan Group/Thermal Ceramics Benelux*, OFT Advice of 26 September 2002.
18. *H+H Celcon Limited/Marley Building Materials Limited*, CC Decision, Cm 5540, published 26 June 2002.
19. *Dadco Alumina and Chemicals Limited/Aluminium Oxid Stade GmbH*, OFT Decision of 29 October 2004.
20. Vickers, Sir John, 'Competition economics and policy', speech given at Oxford University on 3 October 2002, available at www.oft.gov.uk/news.
21. See Office of Fair Trading, Mergers – procedural guidance, op cit., para. 3.2.
22. Competition Commission, Annual Review and Accounts, 2002-03, July 2003.
23. See Competition Commission, Merger references, op cit., para. 1.19.
24. *Arcelor SA/Corus UK Group plc*, OFT Decision of 10 September 2004.
25. *Arcelor SA/ Corus UK Group plc*, CC Decision of 10 February 2005.
26. See Office of Fair Trading , Mergers - substantive assessment guidance, op cit. and Competition Commission, Merger references, op cit.
27. See Office of Fair Trading, Mergers – substantive assessment guidance, op cit., para. 4.8 and Competition Commission, Merger references, op cit., para. 3.29.
28. See Office of Fair Trading, Mergers – substantive assessment guidance, op cit., para. 4.8.
29. Case T-342/99 *Airtours v. Commission*, Court of First Instance judgment of 6 June 2002.
30. See Competition Commission, Merger references, op cit., para. 3.41.
31. Office of Fair Trading, Mergers – substantive assessment guidance, op cit., para. 5.21.
32. *Cargill Incorporated/Cerestor SA*, CC Decision, Cm 5521, published 30 May 2002.
33. *Arla Foods amba/ Express Dairies plc*, CC Decision, Cm 5983, 24 September 2003.
34. *D.S. Smith plc/Linpac Containers Ltd*, CC Decision of 21 October 2004.
35. Alexander Dennis Ltd/Transbus, OFT Advice of 23 September 2004.
36. See Office of Fair Trading, Mergers – substantive assessment guidance, op cit., para. 6.8.
37. *BBC Worldwide/Chivers Communications*, OFT Advice of 21 June 2001.
38. *Colopast AS/SSL International*, OFT Advice of 21 December 2001.
39. *Synopsis Incorporated/Avant!*, OFT Advice of 22 August 2002.
40. Office of Fair Trading, Mergers – substantive assessment guidance, op cit., para. 5.4.
41. Office of Fair Trading, Mergers – substantive assessment guidance, ibid., para. 7.10.

42. *Blockbuster Entertainment/Apollo Video Film Hire*, OFT Advice of 11 April 2001.
43. *Napier Brown Foods plc/James Budgett Sugars Ltd*, OFT Decision of 12 October 2004.
44. In *Napier Brown Foods plc/James Budgett Sugars Ltd*, the CC accepted undertakings on 22 November 2004 and confirmed its provisional findings report of 4 February 2005 in its final report on 15 March 2005 when it cleared the merger.
45. See Competition Commission, Merger references, op cit., para. 3.26.
46. See Competition Commission, Merger references, ibid., paras 4.34-4.50.
47. See Competition Commission, Merger references, ibid., para. 4.38.
48. *FirstGroup plc/Scotrail*, CC Decision of 28 June 2004.
49. See Competition Commission, Merger references, op cit., paras 35.4 and 36.3.
50. *Dräger Medical AG & Co KGaA/ Hillenbrand Industries, Inc.*, CC Decision of 19 May 2004.
51. See Competition Commission, Rules of procedure, op cit., paras 7.1-7.5.
52. See note 14.
53. CAT judgement, 3 December 2003, para. 266.
54. *Clinisys Solutions Ltd/Torex Laboratory Systems Ltd*, OFT Decision of 26 January 2005.
55. Office of Fair Trading, Revising 'Mergers – substantive assessment guidance', Guidance Note, OFT 516a, October 2004.
56. *Phoenix Healthcare Distribution Ltd /East Anglian Pharmaceuticals Ltd.*, OFT Decision of 17 December 2004.
57. *Unichem v Office of Fair Trading*, CAT case 1049/4/1/2005, Judgment of 1 April 2005, para. 279.
58. See Competition Commission, Rules of procedure, op cit.
59. See Competition Commission, Annual Review and Accounts, 2003-04, p. 5.
60. *Stena AB/P&O*, CC Decision of 5 February 2004.
61. See Office of Fair Trading, Mergers – procedural guidance, op cit.
62. Vickers, Sir John, 'Competition economics and policy', speech given at Oxford University on 3 October 2002.
63. Office of Fair Trading, Revising 'Mergers – substantive assessment guidance', op cit.

4. Merger Policy in the EU

Eleanor J. Morgan

INTRODUCTION[1]

A new EC Merger Control Regulation (ECMR) came into operation on 1 May 2004.[2] It marked the most significant overhaul of the EU merger regime since September 1990, when merger control legislation was first introduced at EU level. The substantive aspects of the original ECMR were revised for the first time and these revisions were accompanied by various procedural and jurisdictional changes. There were also some important non-legislative developments.

The revision process which led to the new Regulation began with the publication of a Green Paper by the European Commission (hereafter the 'Commission') in December 2001.[3] In December 2002, the Commission proposed a wide range of changes to the merger regime. These included a legislative proposal for a revised ECMR[4] together with various internal initiatives, notably draft guidelines on the assessment of horizontal mergers.[5] The proposals were widely debated (see, for example, Verouden, Bengtsson and Albæk, 2004) and, after some important revisions, the new merger Regulation was finally adopted in January 2004. This was accompanied by several guidelines, most notably horizontal merger guidelines and specific best practice guidelines on the day to day management of merger cases, which were introduced for the first time, as well as a notice on the allocation of cases between the Commission and Member States. There was also a range of internal reforms designed to improve the organisation of the merger regime and the economic analysis underlying its merger decisions.

This chapter examines the main new developments in the EU system of merger control. First, it outlines the key features of the merger Regulation as initially enacted. The chapter then provides a very brief overview of the merger control record prior to the recent changes and points to some of the pressures for reform. The reforms are examined against this background, with most attention being devoted to new developments in merger appraisal. The discussion of appraisal focuses on the assessment of horizontal mergers because no guidelines are yet available on the assessment of vertical and conglomerate mergers, although the Commission has stated an intention to publish these in future. As well as looking briefly at the changes to case allocation between the EU and national jurisdictions, the chapter also examines the main procedural changes and internal reforms.

Finally, it reflects on the likely significance of these new developments, although it is still too early to know how the revised system will actually perform in practice.

THE PRE 2004 SYSTEM AND PRESSURES FOR REFORM

The ECMR, adopted in December 1989, plugged a significant gap in European competition policy by providing a specific merger control at European level for the first time.[6] Previously both Article 81 (then 85), which covers restrictive agreements, and Article 82 (then 86), which deals with the abuse of dominant positions, were occasionally applied to merger cases. These were not suitable instruments of centralised merger control, however, as they relate to *ex post* investigation and remedy rather than *ex ante* scrutiny and prevention. The European Commission first proposed a merger regulation in 1973 but it was only with the rising level of cross border mergers in preparation for the 'single European market' that the political compromises necessary to secure agreement on a regulation were finally achieved.

The ECMR was introduced to control large scale mergers and merger-like transactions affecting the EU. Previously, such deals might have needed a number of approvals under the various different national control systems, as well as facing the prospect of possible scrutiny by Brussels under Articles 81 and 82. A key feature of the ECMR is its 'one stop shop' system, under which the Commission has sole responsibility for scrutinising mergers within the scope of the Regulation (subject to limited exceptions) and national competition authorities can control mergers outside its scope. This system of exclusive powers was intended to establish a level playing field and reduce the transactions costs involved in large, Community level mergers as well as preventing the minority of deals which were expected to be anti-competitive.

The overall framework of the Regulation, which has been little changed since its introduction, is usefully detailed elsewhere (see, for example Neven, Nuttall and Seabright, 1993; Hawk and Huser, 1996; Goyder, 2003, and Morgan, 2001). Briefly, the ECMR covers the largest mergers and merger-like transactions (known as 'concentrations') affecting the Community. These have to be pre-notified to the Commission (that is, notified prior to their implementation/completion) and are controlled exclusively at EU level, subject to the limited exceptions discussed later in this chapter. The assessment is divided into two stages. First, there is a screening stage (Phase I) after which a merger can be approved either unconditionally or with conditions. Second, a full investigation can be launched (Phase II) if there are sufficient concerns about the likely effects that have not been dealt with at the initial stage. The Commission then has to decide whether to permit the merger, possibly with conditions, or ban it. These decisions are governed by relatively tight deadlines. The Commission has considerable remedial powers and can impose conditions on the merger, order divestiture and levy fines for breaches of the Regulation. The Commission's decisions can be appealed in the European Courts.

Although the introduction of the ECMR, the first supranational merger control, was an important step forward in the development of EU competition policy, the Regulation was the product of compromise and certain aspects proved problematic from an early stage (see Neven et al., 1993). Nevertheless, the only legislative changes to the original ECMR before the recent revisions were contained in a comparatively limited package of measures agreed in 1997 and introduced in 1998.[7] These dealt mainly with the scope of the Regulation and particularly the division of jurisdiction between the Commission and Member States. The practice of accepting remedial settlements at the end of Phase I, rather than taking proposals that caused concern into full proceedings, was officially recognised and some other 'housekeeping changes' were introduced to tidy up the legislation (Morgan, 1998).

The system had also been kept under revision through the development of 'soft law' – by issuing interpretative notices as well as through developments in the Commission's approach to the cases themselves. In addition, a number of issues, such as the application of the ECMR to collusive oligopolies and its power to deal with mergers between firms based outside the EU which have an impact on the Community, had been clarified through judicial review.

Although more thoroughgoing than previous changes, the recent reforms can, to some extent, be seen as part of a natural process of evolution in merger control. There had been periodic reviews of the allocation of jurisdiction between the Commission and the national competition authorities, where previous legislative reform had concentrated, through the life of the ECMR. The increasing number of multiple filings in three or more Member States, even without EU enlargement, added impetus to the Commission's established drive to increase the scope of the Regulation's one stop shop and this was reflected in the 2001 Green Paper which, like the previous merger reviews, focused primarily on jurisdictional issues. The need to ensure that there were efficient procedures to cope with potential increases in the case load, as well as to make any necessary changes to the merger control system in time to integrate the ten new members, also played a part in the revision process. The publication of horizontal merger guidelines as part of the recent reforms followed other guidelines produced to clarify specific aspects of policy (for example, on market definition[8] and on remedies[9]) on the basis of experience in applying the Regulation. The introduction of the horizontal guidelines also reflected the influence of increased cooperation with the US, where such guidelines are a well established feature of merger control policy.

After its first decade, however, the EU system of merger control was showing increasing signs of strain, prompting more thoroughgoing reforms than had been on the agenda previously. The number of merger cases within the scope of the ECMR had far outstripped original expectations, reaching a peak in 2000. There were just 63 notifications in 1991, the first full year of operation, and this rose to 131 in 1996 and reached 345 in the year 2000, with 335 notifications in 2001 (see Table 4.1 for a statistical overview). A greater number of cases were being taken into Phase II proceedings[10] and the tight time scales of the ECMR together with inadequate staffing, and particularly the shortage of professional economists, made it difficult for the Commission to cope satisfactorily with these unprecedented demands. The inadequacies of the economic analysis underlying some of the decisions in these complex cases and deficiencies in the procedures were increasingly highlighted. The Commission's prohibition of the purchase of Honeywell by General Electric in July 2001, still under appeal at the time of writing, was a particularly high profile decision in which its appraisal and case handling attracted intense criticism.[11] The EU approach in this case was in sharp contrast to that of the US authorities, who had cleared the merger conditionally after investigating the same products and the same (world) markets.

A marked increase in the number of appeal cases being brought to the European Court of First Instance was one sign of growing unease about decision making under the ECMR. The suitability of the yardstick used to assess mergers in the EU was increasingly being questioned and its possible replacement by the standard used in the US was put on the discussion agenda in the December 2001 Green Paper. The following year, the three high profile CFI judgements against the Commission added to the pressure for reform. The first concerned the bid by Airtours (now My Travel) for First Choice. The Commission's decision to prohibit this oligopolistic merger on the basis of coordinated effects was criticised as 'vitiated by a series of errors of assessment' and overturned.[12] Only five months after this judgement the Commission, which had hitherto survived nearly all merger appeal challenges, suffered two further setbacks within a week. Its decision in *Schneider/Legrand* was annulled on procedural grounds as Schneider's rights of defence had been infringed. This decision also contained strong rebukes about the quality of the substantive assessment.[13] The judgement on the appeal following *Tetra Laval/Sidel* criticised the Commission's analysis of the conglomerate effects of the transaction as well as the assessment of remedies and the inadequate standard of proof adopted.[14] The Commission appealed to the European Court of Justice only in the latter case; this was particularly critical because the appeal judgement had raised the standard for the proof necessary to find against a merger and was seen by the Commission as undermining its ability to control anti-competitive mergers.[15] With the review process already underway, these judgements both encouraged and facilitated the introduction of more radical changes to the EU system of merger control than had originally been envisaged.

JURISDICTIONAL CHANGES

The 2001 Green Paper, like the reviews in 1993 and 1996/7 that preceded it, was largely concerned with who should take merger decisions in the European context

Table 4.1 Notifications and decisions under the ECMR: 21 Sept. 1990 - 31 Dec. 2005 (total numbers)

	1990-94	1995-98	1999-2002	2003	2004	2005	Total
Notifications[a]							
Cases notified	288	648	1251	212	249	313	2961
Cases withdrawn	11	28	42	0	5	9	95
Final decisions							
Phase 1							
Outside scope	25	25	4	0	0	0	54
Compatible	222	524	1068	203	220	276	2513
Compatible with commitments	9	17	70	11	12	15	134
Phase 2							
Compatible	5	7	10	2	2	2	28
Compatible with commitments	10	17	35	6	4	3	75
Prohibition	2	8	8	0	1	0	19
Restore effective competition[b]	0	2	2	0	0	0	4
Other decisions[c]							
Partial/ full referral under Article 9	3	14	31	9	3	6	66
Referral under Article 22.3	1	3	2	1	1	3	11

Notes
[a] Every notification did not lead to a decision or withdrawal in the same year.
[b] Concentration concluded prior to decision.
[c] For details of Article 4.4 and 4.5 referrals under new ECMR provisions, see text.

Source: European Commission.

rather than how those decisions should be taken. Although the need to improve the quality of merger decisions and procedures under the ECMR took centre stage in the debate following this latest Green Paper, as discussed above, some further adjustments to the mechanisms for allocating cases between the Commission and the national authorities were included in the 2004 legislation to supplement the 1998 amendments mentioned earlier.[16] The more recent changes were also accompanied by an explanatory notice on case referral.[17]

The ECMR aims to ensure that mergers are dealt with centrally only when centralised control is more advantageous than control by the individual Member States, broadly in keeping with the principle of 'subsidiarity' (although the Commission exercises discretion in referral decisions). It is also designed to provide legal certainty about which system of merger control applies. The allocation of responsibility for merger control between Brussels and the national authorities is based on turnover thresholds (see Appendix 4.1). The worldwide turnover criterion was designed to reflect the 'aggregate economic and financial power' of firms; the Community turnover threshold was to ensure significance at Community level and the two thirds rule was introduced to exclude mergers with mainly national impact.

The Commission originally wanted the thresholds for investigation to be set at lower levels so that more mergers would fall within the scope of the ECMR. Despite the unexpectedly large number of mergers which have actually been dealt with in Brussels, the Commission has argued for an extension of its powers in the regular reviews of these thresholds. It has been unsuccessful in obtaining any general reduction in the thresholds so, instead, has recently focused on how best to bring more mergers which otherwise require multiple national filings under the scope of the legislation.

Supplementary turnover thresholds were introduced in 1998 to try to include mergers within the ECMR which were otherwise likely to involve multiple filings in three or more national jurisdictions as centralised control would be likely to be more efficient than decentralised control in such cases. The levels of these supplementary thresholds were inevitably arbitrary as a variety of criteria are used by national authorities to establish eligibility for merger control, not all of which are based on turnover. The resulting rules are complex and a merger involving a number of firms active in several Member States can require the analysis of many combinations of turnover to assess whether the deal falls within their scope (see Appendix 4.1).

The evidence, although rather patchy, suggests that these complicated additional thresholds did not work satisfactorily (see the annex to the 2001 Green Paper). From March 1998 to December 1999, 45 mergers had been filed under the supplementary thresholds, equivalent to 9 per cent of all filings. In 2000, only 20 cases were filed under the supplementary thresholds (5 per cent of filings) while 75 cases were filed with three or more national authorities. Information from Member States suggests that these multiple filings cases normally had cross border effects.

Nevertheless, these thresholds, like the general thresholds, have not been changed (except indirectly, insofar as they are affected by the larger territory which now has to be taken into account since accession of the new EU members and by inflation). Instead, further changes were introduced to the way that cases otherwise outside the scope of the ECMR can be reallocated to the Commission.

Two main 'referral clauses' were included in the original Regulation which allowed some fine tuning of case allocation between the Commission and Member States to help ensure control at the appropriate level. Article 9 enabled referral of a merger by the Commission to a national authority on request if it posed a threat to competition in a distinct market within that Member State. Article 22 allowed a Member State to request that Brussels investigated a deal below the normal thresholds for EU control if it raised concerns about the effects on competition nationally as well as having a cross border effect in the EU. This clause was originally included at the request of the Dutch as they did not have a national system of merger control (although they have subsequently adopted one, in common with nearly all EU members). The original provisions of Article 22 were not used very often but there were some significant cases – requiring, for example, the radical restructuring of *RTL/Veronica/Endemol* (Dutch TV and radio broadcasting) and divestiture in *Blokker/Toys 'R' Us* (toy retailing in the Netherlands).

Some aspects of these two main referral clauses had been clarified and extended in the 1998 reforms and were again modified in 2004. The original wording of Article 9 did not include the possibility of the Commission referring only part of a case, although this had happened in practice – for example, the repatriation to the UK authorities in *Steetley/Tarmac* had been limited to bricks and tiles. This possibility was explicitly included in the 1998 amendment. Referral under Article 9 was possible if the notified concern posed a threat to competition in a distinct market 'be it a substantial part of the common market or not'. As the Commission's jurisdiction was limited elsewhere in the ECMR to mergers where effective competition is impeded 'within the common market as a whole or a substantial part of it', the Commission would have had no power to ban a merger in an insubstantial part of the common market anyway. The reforms introduced in 1998 (Article 9(2)(b)) tidied up the legislation making it easier to repatriate this type of merger by requiring the Member State to show only that such a deal significantly affected competition rather than to prove the existence of a competitive threat.

The internationalisation of business and the introduction of merger control laws in all the Member States, except Luxembourg, by that stage meant that it was increasingly common for mergers to fall within the scope of several national jurisdictions. As well as introducing the supplementary thresholds, the 1998 reforms recast Article 22 as a partial answer to the problem of multiple filings by allowing Member States to make joint referrals to the Commission of mergers which fell below the usual ECMR thresholds.

As Table 4.1 shows, Article 9 has been relatively well used with 60 cases being referred either in full or partially (that is, with one or more of the markets affected rather than the whole merger being referred for national scrutiny) back to Member States by the end of December 2004. Much less use has been made of Article 22; there were only eight requests under its provisions by December 2004, of which just three had been made jointly by several Member States by the beginning of that year.

There were some modifications to the referral clauses in 2004, including a change to the substantive test under Article 9 to bring it into line with Article 22; this means that instead of having to show the existence of a competitive threat, the test for all Article 9(2) (a) cases is that the deal threatens to affect competition significantly. The main development in the referral provisions, however, is a system of 'streamlined referrals'. This allows firms to take the initiative to request a referral to/from the Commission/Member States and vice versa under Articles 4(4) or 4(5) at the pre notification stage for the first time. This latter move has been generally welcomed as identifying the competent authority at this early stage should reduce the time and administrative expense both for the firms involved and the Commission.

Under the new system of access to the ECMR for mergers falling short of the thresholds (where the changes seem likely to have more significance), firms can make a pre-notification request to the Commission to take over cases that otherwise would require notification in three or more Member States (Article 4.5). The Commission then has exclusive jurisdiction as long as the application is not opposed by any of the Member States within 15 working days (in which case, the merger is not referred to Brussels).[18] As the firms involved usually have most knowledge of the details of the case, it can be argued that this new option should improve case allocation. At the same time, there have been concerns that it may encourage 'forum shopping' with firms trying to ensure that their proposed merger comes within the jurisdiction of at least three Member States so as to be able to request investigation by the Commission instead.[19]

The evidence to date suggests that the new system usefully adds to the previous arrangements for dealing with multiple filings. By the end of 2004, 19 pre notification requests had been lodged by firms for mergers to be allocated to the Commission that would otherwise have required multiple filings. National vetoes were exercised by Member States in only two of these. In 2005, there were 27 such requests by the end of the year with no refusals to refer. In contrast, there had only been two requests by firms for a transaction which they believed 'may significantly affect competition' within a 'distinct' national market to be reallocated from the Commission to the national authority under the new Article 4(4) by the end of 2004, both of which were successful. By December 2005, there had been 14 additional requests of this type with no refusals and 11 references were actually made in the course of the year. Although a successful pre notification request by the parties involved to be investigated nationally means that they will avoid the administrative burden of filing at EU level (previously necessary even if the merger was eventually repatriated under an Article 9 request), it is perhaps unsurprising that the option of requesting referral back to the Member State initially was not as popular as requesting referral to Brussels. Investigation by the Commission may be expected to be quicker and less troublesome than investigation nationally in some cases and, until more experience is built up, firms may fear that the basis on which such requests have to be made ('threatens to significantly affect competition') is somewhat self incriminatory.

REFORMS IN SUBSTANTIVE APPRAISAL

The Appraisal Test

The main substantive change introduced by the new ECMR is to the test for appraising mergers. The original test states that:

> A concentration which creates or strengthens a dominant position as a result of which effective competition would be significantly impeded in the common market or in a substantial part of it shall be declared incompatible with the common market.[20]

This test, which became known as the 'dominance test', is similar to the wording of Article 82 of the Treaty of Rome dealing with monopolies, which prohibits the abuse of a dominant position. Although the Commission has not explicitly treated the merger appraisal test as a cumulative two-part test, the CFI has interpreted it in this way (as, for example, in its 2002 *Schneider* judgement referenced earlier). Under this interpretation, unless a merger was likely to create or strengthen a dominant position, satisfying the first part of the test, the applicability of the second part did not arise. Where a merger was caught by the first part of the test, the CFI regarded the second part as providing a margin of discretion over whether a merger involving dominance would fall foul of the ECMR. But unless there was a finding of dominance, the second part of the test – impediment to competition – could not be used to challenge a merger.[21]

This interpretation of the dominance test contrasts with the appraisal test in the USA, adopted in the 1914 Clayton Act, which prohibits mergers with an effect which 'may be substantially to lessen competition, or to tend to create a monopoly.' This 'SLC' test is currently interpreted in the US merger guidelines as 'whether the merger is likely to create or enhance market power or to facilitate its exercise.'[22] A similar SLC test has been included in the recent UK merger legislation, as discussed in the previous chapter.

The 2001 Green Paper invited comment on the effectiveness of the appraisal test in the ECMR and, in particular, on how this compares with the SLC test. A great variety of views were expressed. Some suggested that there was little difference between the SLC and EU approaches as both dealt with market power but the balance of opinion was that the dominance test needed reforming. Critics argued that the wording of the test, with dominance as the first hurdle, focused attention on structural change and diverted attention away from the overall effects of a merger on competition. This led to two main criticisms of the dominance test and the way it had been interpreted, as outlined below.

The first criticism, based on the view that dominance is a more restrictive concept than market power, was that the original test was not sufficiently inclusive and could result in an anti-competitive merger being allowed. In particular, although the concept of dominance had been extended beyond single firm dominance to include 'collective' dominance involving tacit collusion between oligopolists, some argued that there was still a loophole as regards mergers involving non-leading firms, especially in differentiated product markets, which

coordinated or unilateral), but anti-

test was that a merger which increased lting in it being wrongly prohibited. er put rivals at a disadvantage and so ion involving the merging parties. l appraisal test in these circumstances nned if competition overall was not n that, in practice, dominance *per se* *ATR/de Havilland*, the first case to be y, the treatment of *GE/Honeywell*, in ains could count against the merging rs could be regarded as equivalent to xample, the discussion in Fox, 2003), ne Commission.

to these two main criticisms of the cope of the dominance test and the ins – are discussed later in this section. es:

pede effective competition, in the common articular as a result of the creation or declared incompatible with the common

nt to effective competition (SIEC), a for judging a merger and is designed to competition are covered. While role is reduced to that of the prime

One reason for keeping the concept of dominance in the text may have been to obtain the unanimous agreement in the Council of Ministers which was necessary for such a change; some Member States have adopted a dominance test in their national merger legislation which could have made it difficult to abandon that standard altogether. Having reached a consensus on this rather subtle compromise wording, it has been suggested that the assessment of the second part of this hybrid test might tend to be left open or gradually neglected in the appraisal without any loss in terms of the actual outcome. The Commission's interest in retaining dominance as part of the test was, however, officially explained in terms of the need to preserve the previous dominance related case law and it clearly expected that the learning from past experience in applying the dominance test would remain relevant under the new standard.

The recitals to the Regulation (which are technically not legally binding but have always carried considerable weight in EU law) and the horizontal merger guidelines (hereafter the 'Guidelines')[24] indicate how the new test is to be interpreted. The introduction to the Guidelines (para. 2-4) reaffirms the importance of dominance (interpreted to include tacit collusion among oligopolists) as a 'primary form of competitive harm' and reiterates the previous definition of dominance. The effect of mergers on competition is now paramount, however, and a framework based on 'non-coordinated' or unilateral effects analysis (discussed further below) is set out in the Guidelines for its assessment. The Guidelines make it clear that the SIEC only extends beyond dominance (interpreted to include tacit collusion among oligopolists) to bring unilateral effects in oligopolistic markets within the ECMR's scope. In addition, they help to clarify how efficiency effects are to be treated under the new Regulation. Developments in the treatment of oligopoly are discussed in the next two sub sections; effects on efficiency are considered later in the chapter.

Coordinated Effects

A major question when the ECMR was first introduced was whether it could be used to control oligopolistic market structures where no single firm is dominant. Its wording did not deal with this aspect, leaving considerable room for debate about the Commission's power in oligopoly cases (see Horspool and Korah, 1992).

The first potential oligopoly loophole to be closed related to oligopolistic mergers which increase the likelihood of tacit collusion (known as 'coordinated behaviour' under the new ECMR). The Commission successfully tackled this under the original appraisal test by interpreting 'dominance' to encompass the creation or strengthening of 'collective dominance'. The Court's judgement on the appeal arising from *Kali und Salz* and its later *Gencor* judgement confirmed the Commission's powers over oligopoly and identified the legal concept of joint dominance within the ECMR with the economic concept of tacit collusion.[25] The investigation and control of possible oligopolistic dominance which might be associated with tacit collusion then became a common application of EU merger control under the original form of the ECMR as, for example, in *Air Liquide/Messer* (March 2004).[26] Note, however, that control under the ECMR was and still is limited to tacit collusion – explicit collusion is illegal under Article 81 and the Court judgement in *Tetra Laval* confirmed that the Commission should not assume that a merger will result in explicit collusion.

Although the Commission had gained the legal power to tackle mergers that might create or strengthen oligopolistic dominance, the decisions could be rather unpredictable (Morgan, 1996). Typically a checklist approach was used to identify factors expected to facilitate tacit post merger collusion and those that might hinder it. Many of these are the same as those regarded as affecting the ability of firms to form and maintain explicit cartels (see Scherer and Ross, 1990, p. 235-315). This framework does not give any guidance as to how the factors should be weighed up in the presence of both positive and negative features, leaving a good deal of discretion to the Commission in deciding individual cases.

In its judgement on the *Airtours* appeal, the CFI introduced a different framework for appraising collective dominance based on a textbook model of tacit collusion (a repeated game with a transparent punishment strategy). The necessary conditions for oligopolistic dominance were specified using this approach, conditions which it judged had not been satisfied in *Airtours/First Choice* (as usefully discussed in Bishop and Lofaro, 2004).[27] The Court's approach to the assessment of oligopolistic coordination in this case has since been adopted in the new horizontal guidelines (para. 39-60).

The Guidelines distinguish two types of circumstance in which a merger may increase the risk of tacit collusion. The first is relatively straightforward, at least conceptually, and is designed to deal with mergers that increase the likelihood of tacit collusion on a market that previously operated as a non-collusive oligopoly:

> A merger in a concentrated market may significantly impede effective competition, through the creation or the strengthening of a collective dominant position, because it increases the likelihood that firms are able to coordinate their behaviour in this way and raise prices, even without entering into an agreement or resorting to a concerted practice within the meaning of Article 81 of the Treaty (Guidelines, para. 39).

The Guidelines (para. 41) outline three features that the Commission needs to establish before claiming that sustained coordinated behaviour is likely to be established for the first time. These are: first, the need for transparency allowing firms to monitor whether the terms of coordination are being adhered to; second, the existence of a credible deterrence mechanism that can be used if deviation is detected and, third, the need for the oligopolists to be insulated sufficiently from the actions of outsiders (including future competitors and customers) that the results of their coordination are not threatened. A necessary condition for the emergence of coordination is also mentioned, namely that it must be relatively simple to establish a common understanding on the terms of coordination whether the focus is price setting, customer and territory sharing or output and capacity limitation.[28]

The second situation in which coordinated effects may cause concern post merger is less clear (see Robert and Hudson, 2004). The Guidelines state:

> A merger may also make coordination easier, more stable or more effective for firms, that were already coordinating before the merger, either by making the coordination more robust or by permitting firms to coordinate on even higher prices (para. 39).

This implies that the Commission must show that all the elements necessary for coordinated behaviour were present pre merger, which is likely to be difficult in practice; the problem of identifying pre existing coordinated behaviour is recognised in the UK merger guidelines published by the Competition Commission.[29] The EU Guidelines do not contain a presumption against mergers where past coordination is found but state that such evidence is important if the market characteristics are relatively static (para. 43).[30]

The Guidelines usefully clarify the meaning of collective dominance as a concept and show the avenues of investigation that the Commission will follow in assessing whether a merger is likely to result in coordinated behaviour. The new text does not solve all the problems in assessing oligopolistic coordination, however, even in cases where the post merger introduction of tacit collusion is the issue. This is perhaps inevitable because economic theory does not identify the point at which a change in market structure will 'tip' the market towards coordination. There is also relatively little guidance on how the effects of the likely changes in oligopolistic behaviour on competition will be assessed; this key aspect, which involves comparing the likely outcome with the way in which the market would have operated if the merger did not occur (the 'counterfactual') could have usefully been explored in more depth. Nevertheless, the Guidelines provide a much clearer framework for the first stages of the analysis than offered by the earlier checklist approach and reduce the scope for discretion in such decisions. If coordination cannot be achieved, if compliance cannot be monitored, if deviation cannot be punished or if outside threats can jeopardise the outcome, then a merger cannot be regarded as likely to result in coordinated effects. Although this framework cannot be applied mechanistically, the evaluation of possible coordinated effects should be more predictable in future.

Non-coordinated Effects

With the Commission's powers to tackle oligopolistic coordination under the original dominance test confirmed by the Court, attention turned to the possible existence of another gap in the control of oligopoly. In principle, oligopolistic mergers can also reduce competition though unilateral effects (termed 'non-coordinated' effects in the EU). Unilateral effects can be said to occur when noncompetitive outcomes result from the individual profit maximising responses of firms to market conditions post merger and can, in theory, result from mergers in oligopolistic markets as well as markets where a single firm dominates. Put simply, if former competitors A and B merge, the competition between these two, which may not become the market leader (that is, the oligopoly situation), has been lost. If there is only a limited amount of surrounding competition, this could reduce competition in the market as a whole. With A and B no longer competing, firms C and D, for example, might decrease their competitive efforts in the market. Any such response by C and D is not, however, a precondition for the merging parties to raise prices after the merger in the unilateral effects story as it would be under tacit collusion; the incentive to raise prices comes from the elimination of the competitive constraint due to the merger itself independently of competitors' responses. This scenario is most likely in differentiated product markets when the merging brands are particularly close competitors, unlike the products of oligopolistic rivals.[31]

The Commission arguably did not have the power to apply a theory of unilateral effects below the level of market dominance under the previous merger test. Arguably it was trying to address possible unilateral effects in the differentiated short haul package tour market in *Airtours/First Choice* through a broad interpretation of collective dominance but this was subsequently rejected by the Court (Motta, 2000). The more recent *Oracle/Peoplesoft* case, although carried out when the original dominance test applied, was taken to full proceedings partly on the grounds of unilateral oligopoly effects. It is notable that the parties' market shares on the relevant markets do not feature at all in this decision.[32]

While the Commission was reluctant to admit to any gap in control under the dominance test,[33] unilateral effects in oligopoly are explicitly dealt with for the first time under Recital 25 of the new ECMR which states:

> ... under certain circumstances, concentrations involving the elimination of important competitive constraints that the merging parties had exerted upon each other, as well as a reduction of competitive pressure on the remaining competitors, may, even in the absence of a likelihood of coordination between the members of the oligopoly, result in a significant impediment to effective competition.

and then confirms:

> The notion of 'significant impediment to effective competition' in Article 2(2) and (3) should be interpreted as extending, beyond the concept of dominance, only to the anti-competitive effects of a concentration resulting from the non-coordinated behaviour of undertakings which would not have a dominant position on the market concerned.

This explicit extension to cover unilateral effects is, therefore, the only area in which the new SIEC test is said to enlarge the Commission's powers, although the application has yet to be tested in the Courts. The distinction between unilateral effects and coordinated effects is clear in theory but it will be more difficult to distinguish in practice between the potential for independent anti-competitive behaviour and collusive behaviour among oligopolists (see Phlips, 1995, p. 4-7).

The framework for the analysis of unilateral effects provided in the Guidelines (para. 24-38) is applicable whether or not a merger creates a market leader, as in the US.[34] This goes wider than the traditional analysis of single firm dominance, which tended to focus on the effect on the prices and outputs of the market leader as a result of its increased monopoly power. It is more in keeping with some of the recent decisions under the old Regulation which had begun to place greater emphasis on the wider competitive effects of merger proposals and increasingly focused on the direct substitutability of the merging parties' products, with more reference to likely unilateral effects. The Guidelines state that the concept of dominance will continue to provide 'an important indication as to the standard of competitive harm' (Guidelines, para. 4) so the precise interpretation of the dominance concept and the extent to which a fuller analysis of the competitive effects will be applied in practice and accepted in the Courts remains to be seen.

The guidelines suggest that market shares and the addition to these will be used to provide an initial but important indication in the assessment of non-coordinated effects; new developments regarding the market share indicators to be applied are discussed in the next section. The other factors are the closeness of competition between the merging firms (in terms of their product attributes, quality and reliability or geographic location), the possibilities that customers have for switching suppliers, the likelihood of competitors increasing supply in response to a price rise, the possibility of the merged firm inhibiting expansion by competitors and whether a merger eliminates a recent but potentially important entrant to the market or a firm with significant 'pipeline' products.

The practical assessment of the closeness of competition is a critical aspect of a non-coordinated effects analysis but, in many cases it will not be clear *a priori* which products are close to those of each merging party. Detailed empirical analysis will be required to assess the cross price elasticity of demand between the various products, increasing the need for appropriate expertise within the Commission to ensure that the analyses are robust and the results are correctly interpreted. The *GE/Instrumentarium* decision in the medical equipment sector, while formally still relying on the dominance test, provides a good example of the extensive statistical work which is likely to be conducted in the assessment of non-coordinated effects under the new Regulation; it included an analysis of win/loss data in recent bidding rounds and various econometric analyses to isolate the impact of the presence of one party on the size of the discount offered by the other.[35]

The potential extension in the Commission's powers under the ECMR to include the non-coordinated effects of oligopolistic mergers may be regarded as somewhat problematic as it again implies tighter *ex ante* control on oligopolistic behaviour than is available to the Commission *ex post* under other competition policy provisions. At the same time, it adds to uncertainty as it is difficult to predict when such effects might be found. Some critics have been concerned that the new provisions add significantly to the Commission's discretion in merger cases and will allow a sharp increase in interventionism (for example, Ridyard, 2005; Baxter and Dethmers, 2005) but very few actual examples have been identified to illustrate the potential for non-coordinated effects in practice and even these are not completely convincing.

The *Heinz/Beech-Nut* merger in the US has been widely cited as an example of a unilateral effects oligopoly case (see, for example, Coppi and Walker, 2004). This was a merger between the second and third firms in the baby foods market that together would have not become the brand leader. It is at least debateable whether the harmful effects of the merger could have been analysed using a coordinated effects analysis. The elimination of the pre-merger rivalry between the merging brands was the main concern (a 'unilateral effect') but the final state of post merger competition would have depended on the nature of rivalry between the merged firm and Gerber, the brand leader (more akin to a concern about coordinated effects). Indeed Kolasky and Elliot (2003 p. 64) have argued that a survey of merger challenges brought by the Justice Department and FTC would show very few cases in which the combined market shares of the parties did not exceed 40 per cent (above which a finding of single firm dominance was a realistic possibility in the EU) and where there was not a 'good coordinated effects story of the kind that would meet the requirements for collective dominance under EU law.'

It remains to be seen how much scope there will actually be for bringing this type of oligopoly case in the EU. Intervention in unilateral oligopoly cases may be controversial as potentially significant competitors will remain on the market following the merger and, following US experience, is perhaps most likely in cases where the number of significant competitors is reduced from three to two. Although its powers have been widened, the Commission seems likely to tread cautiously, at least initially, in this new area of merger control.

Market Definition and Share Thresholds

Under the old dominance test, the need to show that a dominant position had been created or strengthened before the effects on competition could be assessed put considerable emphasis on market definition and market share calculations. Market definition has traditionally been regarded as a key element in EU merger control (see, for example, Alonso, 1994) and was usually the focus of such limited empirical economic analysis as was carried out. According to the Notice on market definition, published in 1997,[36] the hypothetical monopolist or SSNIP (small but significant non-transitory increase in price) test is the reference point for determining demand substitutability, as in the US and UK. In the EU, however, other factors typically feature more prominently in the actual decisions, especially in determining geographic market definition (see Coppi and Walker, 2004).

EU cases have increasingly required many different products and/or services to be analysed as well as numerous geographical markets. This, together with a tendency towards more detailed investigation, has led to increasingly lengthy decisions. For example, *Alcatel/Telettra* (April 1991), the first decision after full proceedings, contained only 45 paragraphs.[37] In contrast, there were 862 paragraphs in the *Exxon/Mobil* decision of September 1999 and it extends over 136 pages in the Official Journal.[38] Decisions taken after initial scrutiny have also tended to become longer and more complicated; for instance, *Glaxo Wellcome/SmithKline Beecham* (May 2000) contained 224 paragraphs and, in common with other pharmaceutical mergers, required very many different product markets to be investigated.[39]

The increased emphasis in the US on empirical estimates of the closeness of competition in unilateral effects cases and on simulations of the likely effects of mergers has reduced their reliance on market definition and market share data in merger decisions. In the EU, such developments are still in their infancy, although there is already evidence of increased sophistication in the use of econometric analysis to assess the closeness of competition, as discussed above, and the potential for using merger simulation analysis in a European context as part of the analysis has been illustrated by Ivaldi and Verboven (2002) in the case of *Volvo/Scania*.[40] The new appraisal test is likely to increase the emphasis on measuring the effects on competition more directly, although the calculation of market shares at some stage in the analysis will remain an important part of the assessment.

Once the relevant market has been assessed, the Commission has taken the combined shares of the merged parties as an initial indicator of the likely effect of the merger. As the Guidelines (para. 17) state, market shares of 50 per cent or more 'may in themselves' be evidence of a dominant market position 'according to well established case law' and past decisions suggest that a merger is more likely to raise concerns as market shares increase above 40 per cent, although lesser shares could cause concern in particular circumstances. The recitals to the new ECMR, like its predecessor, state that market shares of less than 25 per cent are unlikely to raise competitive concerns (recital 32). The Guidelines exclude mergers involving a 'collective dominant position' from this safe harbour provision and introduce further 'safe harbour' thresholds based on the Hirschmann-Herfindahl (HHI) measure of market concentration.

These Guidelines set out a single set of HHI thresholds for use in both unilateral and coordinated cases (para. 19 and 20), broadly following the US approach. Markets with a post merger HHI below 1000 'normally do not require extensive analysis.' The Commission is also 'unlikely to identify horizontal concerns' where the post merger HHI is between 1000 and 2000, with an increase of less than 250, or where a post merger HHI is above 2000 and the increment due to merger is below 150. As many as six special circumstances are identified which override these HHI indicators, including one of the merging parties having 50 per cent or more of the market. If such a major player is involved, a post merger increase of less than 150 in the HHI could give rise to competitive concerns.

The US guidelines which introduced the use of HHI indicators suggested that mergers above the thresholds specified were likely to attract scrutiny, in contrast to the ECMR's wording. In practice, however, the US authorities do not act as if there is a presumption of anti-competitive effects above the thresholds; the median levels of HHI for cases that went unchallenged were far higher than those set out in the guidelines and HHIs were greater than 2000 in every challenge since 1985.[41] This may have influenced the Commission to position its HHIs as tentative safe harbours and to specify them slightly more liberally with higher HHI thresholds and increments than those specified in the US (and UK) – the equivalent of the highly concentrated case is an HHI greater than 2000 in the EU, rather than 1800. Even this seems cautious, however; for example, any merger that reduces the number of firms from six to five will result in an HHI greater than 2000 and most mergers in such an industry will increase the index by more than 150. If this is indeed the threshold used to define the 'at risk' category, it would represent a radical increase in the degree of intervention in EU policy.[42]

When HHIs were introduced in the US in the early 1980's, they were generally regarded as the single best indicator of market power as they increase with the shares of the leading firms and with inequality in firm sizes and, under Cournot assumptions, are positively linked to profitability. Recent literature shows that in differentiated product markets, the HHI loses the theoretical relationship to industry profits that it has in the Cournot model. At the same time, developments in oligopoly theory suggest that it is the similarity of firm shares, rather than inequality, which tends to be associated with tacit coordination (see Compte, Jenny and Rey, 2002). In addition, the most robust empirical relationships between market share indicators and profitability seem to be with the share of the leading firms and at very high levels of concentration (Kwoka, 1981). Although HHIs will give useful benchmarks to help in initial screening in some cases, their superiority as a proxy for market power over other concentration measures – for example, a set of concentration ratios – is no longer regarded as clear cut.

To the extent that concentration indicators can give a useful guide to possible effects on competition, the level of HHI likely to result in merger enforcement under the new policy is of more interest than the tentative safe harbours. It is not clear from the Guidelines under what circumstances the Commission will rely on HHIs rather than market share data or how conflicting results using the two different types of indicators would be evaluated. To date, relatively few decisions have referred to HHIs since the guidelines were implemented and in a number of these, no competition concerns were raised even though the thresholds were exceeded.[43] It is to be hoped that appraisals under the new SIEC test will be less reliant on market shares (although they should still play an important role either as a first or later step in the analysis) and will focus more directly on assessing the impact of the merger on competition, following the trend that was being established in the final months of the previous Regulation.

Mitigating Factors – the Role of Efficiency Gains

The Guidelines identify the factors which could mitigate the potential adverse effects of a horizontal merger, whether it involves potential coordinated or non-coordinated effects, and codify previous best practice regarding their assessment. These include the likely impact of new entry, the possibility that buyer power may limit the scope for anti-competitive behaviour and the failing firm defence. The proper role of efficiency effects was a major issue in debates preceding the new ECMR and the Guidelines also detail their treatment.

The treatment of likely efficiency gains from merger had been controversial ever since a specific merger regulation was first proposed. In the event, the assessment of efficiencies was not included as a formal part of the ECMR's appraisal test. Instead, the original Regulation mentioned that the 'development of technical and economic progress' was only to be taken into account 'provided that it is to consumers' advantage and does not form an obstacle to competition.' This suggested some scope for efficiency effects to be considered as a factor in the merger appraisal but only as part of the competitive analysis rather than to reverse a finding of dominance and justify an anti-competitive merger.

Efficiencies had occasionally been mentioned as a positive feature in EU merger assessment, although they have never explicitly played a crucial role in approving a merger. Some critics have argued that far from taking a positive view of gains in efficiency which would benefit consumers (to the extent that the wording of the ECMR allows), the Commission sometimes treated them as a negative feature – an 'efficiency offence' – due to its concern that increased efficiency could disadvantage rivals and strengthen the dominant position of the merged firm (Jenny, 1993). The Commission's concern in *GE/Honeywell* about likely cost savings from the conglomerate merger leading to more aggressive competition and post merger price reductions recently brought the treatment of efficiency gains into the spotlight and has been cited as a further example of the protection of competitors being put before the protection of competition. This alleged approach has been attributed, in part, to the preoccupation with structural aspects under the original dominance test.[44] Such charges had been strongly denied by the Commission – for example, Philip Lowe, as Director General of the Competition Directorate, stated in 2002 'I nevertheless conclude these remarks on efficiencies by confirming quite categorically that there is no "efficiencies offence" in our merger policy'[45] and Mario Monti in his role as Competition Commissioner confirmed 'I have said this before, but let me clarify it once and for all: there is no such thing as a so-called "efficiency offence" in EU merger control law and practice.'[46] In the same speech, however, Monti admitted that there was a lack of clarity in the Commission about precisely what consideration should be given to efficiency arguments and how these should be defined and measured.

The new Regulation retains the original wording dealing with efficiencies but the emphasis on competition effects under the SIEC test should encourage a more positive approach to possible efficiency savings and help to ensure that they are explicitly treated. The recitals to the ECMR and the Guidelines provide further guidance to the treatment of efficiencies as a potential part of the overall competitive assessment. Recital 29 states:

> In order to determine the impact of a concentration on competition in the common market, it is appropriate to take account of any substantiated and likely efficiencies put forward by the undertakings concerned. It is possible that the efficiencies brought about by the concentration counteract the effects on competition, and in particular the potential harm to consumers, that it might otherwise have and that, as a consequence, the concentration would not significantly impede effective competition, in the common market or in a substantial part of it, in particular as a result of the creation or strengthening of a dominant position.

The Guidelines devote considerable attention to the treatment of possible efficiency gains. These may take various forms, including cost savings leading to lower prices and synergies leading to new or improved products. They emphasise (para. 79) that the 'relevant benchmark in assessing efficiency claims is that consumers will not be worse off as a result of the merger.' These will be considered as part of the overall competitive assessment and will provide grounds for allowing a merger to proceed only:

> ... when the Commission is in a position to conclude on the basis of sufficient evidence that the efficiencies generated by the merger are likely to enhance the ability and incentive of the merged entity to act pro-competitively for the benefit of consumers, thereby counteracting the adverse effects on competition which the merger might otherwise have (Guidelines, para. 77).

The Guidelines make it clear that there is still no 'efficiency defence' based on a welfare trade-off, as advocated by Williamson (1968), despite some calls for its introduction during the review process. This type of efficiency defence implies the adoption of a total welfare standard, including both producer and consumer surplus. Although some economists have advocated the adoption of this standard in antitrust policy, arguing that gains by producers should be balanced against losses by consumers, there is a developing literature which supports the focus on consumer welfare. This literature highlights the inherent bias in favour of the producers due to their information advantages compared with the regulator, their lobbying power and their ability to select mergers in their own interests (see Lyons, 2004) and concludes that merger policy should ultimately be concerned with the effects on consumers to help redress the balance.

The approach to the assessment of efficiency effects within this framework, detailed in the Guidelines, is justifiably cautious. Many studies have shown the lack of efficiency gains typically achieved after mergers have taken place despite the frequency of pre merger justifications to shareholders based on synergies (Tichy, 2001). The Guidelines emphasise that the benefits have to be merger specific and verifiable and stress the importance of an audit trail in verifying efficiency effects, listing the types of documents that can be produced as evidence. Among other features of the Guidelines designed to minimise the chance of anti-competitive mergers slipping through the net on the basis of efficiency arguments, there is an explicit preference for reductions in marginal or variable cost, rather than decreases in fixed cost, as the former are more likely to be reflected in lower prices. Less emphasis will be placed on efficiency gains the further into the future that they are likely to materialise. In addition, the larger the possible negative effects of the merger on market power, the higher standard of proof that will be required; efficiency considerations are ruled out for mergers approaching the level of market power associated with monopoly.

Although the Commission has addressed efficiency claims in the past, the fact that it now actively encourages merging parties to bring these forward is a new development. The Best Practice Guidelines (para. 18)[47] recommend merging firms draw attention at the pre notification stage to any likely efficiency gains that they wish to be taken into account so that there is sufficient time for these to be appropriately considered. A reduction in the perceived risks of committing an 'efficiency offence' should make firms more willing to draw attention to likely efficiencies. The policy guidance should also help to ensure that efficiency is explicitly considered as a potentially positive effect and that any proposals that would increase overall consumer welfare through significant efficiency gains are allowed. It is still too early to know how often explicit efficiency arguments will tip the balance and allow an otherwise anti-competitive merger to be approved but so far there is no evidence to suggest that there will, in practice, be many cases of this type.

CHANGES IN INTERNAL ORGANISATION AND PROCESS

The merger review process in the EU is largely administrative. When the system of merger control was first introduced, a Merger Task Force (MTF) was established within the Competition Directorate (now styled DG Competition) to take responsibility for merger control. It decided which cases to analyse in detail, provided the analysis as part of the investigation and was involved in all aspects of the decision. Its recommendations had to be ratified by the Commission but this was almost invariably a formality. Moreover, in contrast to its American counterparts who have to obtain an order from an independent judicial authority before banning a merger, the Commission's decisions are only subject to judicial review on appeal. Although detailed decisions on each EU merger case are published, in contrast to earlier practice in the US,[48] the way in which the roles of prosecutor, chief investigator and judge are combined in the EU system has led to continuing criticism that the Commission's processes lack transparency and accountability (McGowan and Cini, 1999, p. 190).

The Commission has made much of the fact that it is open to stringent third party review through the appeals procedure but Court judgements often take a considerable time. For example, it took three years to decide the *Airtours* case and the recent critical judgement of the European Commission's procedures leading to the ban on the merger of US telecoms group Worldcom with rival Sprint in June 2000 was only taken in September 2004.[49] A 'fast track' procedure was introduced in February 2001 in recognition of this general problem, but this is not granted automatically and is inappropriate for complex cases.[50] The evidence suggests that even the accelerated procedure is probably too lengthy for a successful appeal to allow the merger to be kept alive as a commercial proposition; for example, the CFI's critical judgements on *Sneider/Legrand* and *Tetra Laval/Sidel* took ten months after the initial Commission decisions.

The Commission has indicated its support for further moves to speed up and strengthen the judicial review process.[51] This seems a key area of reform which would help meet the criticism that the Commission acts as both judge and jury. The creation of specialised judicial panels to deal with certain types of cases or a specialised merger chamber within the CFI are possibilities which have been under discussion, as well as the provision of additional resources to the CFI. The requirement for all documents to be translated into French, the official court language, however, is a major cause of delay.

Despite the delays in obtaining judgement, there has been an increased tendency for decisions to be appealed in the Courts. In addition, the judgements arising from *Airtours/First Choice*, *Sneider/Legrand* and *Tetra Laval/Sidel* marked the beginning of more detailed legal and factual review by the CFI. Previously the CFI had been reluctant to become involved in the economic arguments but its landmark judgements on *Airtours* and *Tetra Laval* have provided frameworks, respectively, for the economic analysis of coordinated effects (reflected in the treatment of oligopoly as part of the new Horizontal Guidelines) and of conglomerate issues (where guidelines are still outstanding).

The harsh criticisms of both the economic assessment and the procedures in these cases highlighted the inadequacies of a system that had allowed such flaws to occur. The 2001 Green Paper had briefly discussed the system of checks and balances in merger control but these adverse Court decisions gave a new urgency to introducing changes to internal organisation and procedural reforms.

DG Competition has been reorganised in the most radical change to its structure since the MTF was introduced in 1990. Previously there were three broad areas of operation, each with their own dedicated hierarchy of staff and investigation teams – the MTF, four sectoral directorates responsible for other antitrust investigations and the state aid directorates. The MTF has been disbanded and replaced by a coordinating unit that is to oversee the consistency of procedure and policy. Responsibility for merger cases has been reorganised on industry lines by integrating this into the sectoral directorates so they now deal with mergers as well as other antitrust cases.

The stated aim of this restructuring was to strengthen in-house knowledge of key sectors within DG Competition and make better use of resources, in view of the fluctuations in merger activity, as well as spreading the benefits of the MTF's working practices to other areas of DG Competition. The changes mean that those handling merger cases should already have extensive knowledge of the industrial sectors. There are, however, two concerns. The first is whether the sectoral units will have the staff to deal with the increased workload when merger activity peaks.[52] The second is whether merger reviews will be more open to influence by the sectoral directorates' own policy agendas. Previously other directorates with sectoral expertise were consulted and the Commission was sometimes accused of reflecting their concerns in its treatment of mergers – for example, by attaching de facto conditions to merger clearance or extracting remedies to speed up liberalisation of an industry rather than focusing exclusively on remedying a merger related concern (as has occurred in electricity and telecoms).[53] The dividing lines between merger investigations and the other interests of sectoral teams have now been blurred so there is a danger that this problem may become more acute.

Preliminary screening, full investigations and recommendations about whether to prohibit or require remedies are carried out by the same case team leading to a danger, in the absence of institutional control, that the team may become too convinced by its own arguments. Peer review panels have been set up to provide case teams with an independent internal review to assess the Commission's conclusions at key stages in the investigation. Members are drawn from both DG Competition and from other DGs. Although using separate teams for Phase I and Phase II investigations would be a more certain safeguard, especially against the initial misgivings which led to full proceedings biasing the eventual outcome, the first cases provide some evidence that scrutiny by the new peer review panels can play a useful role. For example, the peer review panel reportedly altered the course of the investigation in *GE/Instrumentarium* substantially and helped to secure conditional clearance.

Cases such as *GE/Honeywell* showed the need for more in-house economic expertise to increase the rigour of Commission's analysis and to prevent excessive reliance on submissions from the merging parties and their competitors. The assessment of potential unilateral effects calls for more sophisticated econometric work than has characterised EU merger decisions in the past. A new post of Chief Economist has been created in DG Competition and Lars-Hendrik Röller, a prominent industrial economist with an applied orientation, took up the post in September 2003. He is assisted by a new team of professional economists who are seconded to work on case teams throughout DG Competition. They will provide a much needed, though relatively small, injection of specialist expertise that can be deployed to assist merger case teams in the most major, complex and sensitive investigations. The contribution of this team to date has been encouraging (see, for example, *Sony/BMG*).[54]

The role of Hearing Officer was introduced in 1986 to try to ensure that investigations are properly conducted and the parties' right of defence was respected but this was generally regarded as ineffective. Their position and profile was increased in 2001, when two new Hearing Officers were appointed, reporting directly to the Commission and with new terms of reference. Additional resources have allocated since the Commission's recent defeats by the CFI to strengthen their role further.

These developments in internal organisation and resourcing have been accompanied by a number of procedural changes. These strengthen the fact finding and enforcement powers of the Commission, and provide more flexibility in the timetable as well as giving more protection to the parties involved.

The Commission has gained the formal right to interview witnesses and record the results adding to its fact finding powers. The stronger deterrents include an increase in possible fines for supplying incorrect or misleading information from 50,000 Euros to 1 per cent of turnover and the extension of the existing provision for fines of up to 10 per cent of turnover for failing to suspend a transaction to cases where the parties fail to notify before implementing the merger.

The original requirements concerning the timing of notifications have been relaxed. Notification is no longer required within one week of concluding a binding agreement, a requirement which had not been strictly enforced previously, and instead must be made before the merger is implemented. In addition, mergers can now be notified to the EU authorities before a binding agreement has been concluded and public bids can be notified before public launch as long as there is a clear intention to proceed. These changes are in line with the recommendations of the International Competition Network, a recently established informal forum of competition agencies from all over the world that works to improve world wide cooperation and convergence among the competition authorities (Todino, 2003). The changes will facilitate international cooperation on merger cases as regards the timing of investigations as well as allowing companies more flexibility in their merger planning. In addition, requests for referrals under the ECMR's exemption clauses can now be made prior to notification, as discussed earlier.

One of the acknowledged strengths of the EU system of merger investigation is the tight timetable involved but this has also proved problematic. The 1998 revisions allowed the Commission to accept remedies to settle cases in Phase I and at the same time introduced an extension to the time allowed if undertakings were offered or if request to refer the merger for examination was received from a Member State so that these could be properly considered. Remedies have been increasingly used to settle merger cases (see Table 4.1). By December 2005, 134 mergers had been cleared conditionally after Phase 1 scrutiny and 75 after full investigation. Changes to the original timescales have now also been made in Phase II. A further 15 day automatic extension has been introduced where remedies are offered in the later part of a Phase II investigation to allow greater consultation of third parties and Member States (see Table 4.2). There is also provision for a 20 working day extension of the Phase II deadline in complex cases with the parties' agreement (and all deadlines have been converted to working days resulting in slight de facto extensions). The new provisions for 'stopping the clock' are being called upon and proving useful in practice.

Table 4.2 Timetable for merger investigations

Pre May 2004	Current system
Phase I	
One month starting the day after the receipt of notification	*25 working days* starting the day after the receipt of notification
Extended to *six weeks* if undertakings are offered or a referral request is received	Extended to *35 working days* if undertakings are offered or a referral request is received
Phase II	
Four months from the day after the decision to carry out an in-depth inquiry	*90 working days* from the day after the decision to carry out an in-depth inquiry
	plus
	Up to *20 working days* if requested by the notifying parties or by the Commission with the agreement of the notifying parties
	15 working days if companies offered remedies after the 54th working day that followed the initiation of the in-depth inquiry

These changes have been supplemented by the introduction of a number of procedural improvements in the Best Practices Guidelines to address criticisms of the review process, including the lack of transparency and concerns that competitors of the merging parties have been allowed too much influence in the proceedings (see Kekelekis, 2004 for a detailed discussion of these changes). The existing practice of 'state of play' meetings between the Commission and the notifying parties has been codified and systematised and the novel possibility of 'triangular' meetings among the Commission, the notifying parties and third parties prior to, or instead of, the formal Oral Hearing has been introduced.

According to the Best Practices Guidelines (and the updated Notice on access to file[55]) the Commission's file can only be accessed by the parties after they have received the Statement of Objections. This means that the parties are made aware of the full extent of comments or complaints from customers and competitors at a late stage in the proceedings. Although the rights of access to the Commission's file have not been extended under these guidelines, the Commission's commitment to provide earlier access to key documents and to discuss the nature and scope of its concerns prior to the sending of the Statement of Objections may increase transparency and give merging parties more opportunity to defend their point of view. GE's economic experts in *GE/Instrumentarium*, for example, were given direct access to the data and analysis submitted by the third party as well as the analysis undertaken on the Commission's behalf. This allowed the type of scrutiny of the Commission's conclusions that has often been absent in past cases and resulted in substantial criticisms of the third party's econometric analysis.[56] However, the Best Practice guidelines do not confer any legal rights so the Commission has discretion on a case by case basis as to how far they are implemented. It remains to be seen whether the use of these non-binding mechanisms will be sufficient to meet past criticisms and ensure that a sufficient level of communication and transparency is maintained to protect the rights of defence of both the notifying parties and third parties through the merger review process.

CONCLUSIONS

The recent reforms in the EU system of merger control built on the experience gained over more than thirteen years under the original ECMR. The 2001 Green Paper focused on possible ways of dealing with the increasing number of multiple filings and the need to improve the effectiveness of the regime prior to EU enlargement, as well as putting possible revisions to the appraisal test on the discussion agenda. The breadth of the eventual reform package, which encompassed significant substantive, organisational and procedural changes as well as modifications to the jurisdictional divide, was prompted by serious deficiencies in merger assessment and procedures. These were highlighted in the series of high profile CFI judgments against the Commission in 2002. After this, it was essential for the Commission to address the inadequacies in the existing merger regime on a broad front in order to restore credibility, and it became more feasible to gain the unanimous agreement in the Council of Ministers required before the substantive aspects of the Regulation could be altered.

Jurisdictionally, the existing system of case allocation has been fine tuned by retaining the two tiered turnover thresholds and combining them with a streamlined mechanism for referrals. Although the resulting arrangements appear complex and patchwork in nature, there is already considerable evidence of successful pre notification requests by the merging parties to the Commission in potential multiple filings cases. This appears to be the most significant jurisdictional improvement made in the recent reforms and seems to be a useful step towards more appropriate case allocation.

Turning to the substantive reforms, the revised wording of the appraisal test is intended to clarify that it is an effects based competition test in what appears to have been an ingenious compromise in a hard fought debate over the appropriate standard. The new test includes the creation and strengthening of a dominant position but relegates it to a particular case within the SIEC test. It would have been much neater if all reference to dominance could have been deleted and this would also have removed an important source of uncertainty arising from the apparent coexistence of two theories of competitive harm under the new regime – dominance and unilateral effects. Nevertheless, the revised wording of the appraisal test should reduce the emphasis on structure *per se*, in line with more recent practice, and also allows intervention by the Commission in mergers which cannot be interpreted as affecting dominance but which are still expected to be anti-competitive.

The adoption of the new substantive test was apparently intended to preserve the precedents and learning established under the earlier dominance rule but to allow the inclusion of unilateral effects in oligopoly cases. This is the only area in which the scope of EU merger control has apparently been enlarged. Although the wording regarding the treatment of efficiency effects remains unchanged in the ECMR itself, there is some clarification of their role in the new recitals and the Guidelines usefully detail both the circumstances in which efficiency could be a mitigating factor and the type of evidence required.

Questions still remain about the role that efficiencies will actually play in tipping the balance in an otherwise anti-competitive merger and the impact of the new appraisal test, especially in view of the retention of 'dominance' in the wording. There are significant uncertainties about the likelihood of non-coordinated but anti-competitive effects in oligopolistic mergers being found below the normal thresholds for dominance and, indeed, the role that unilateral effects analysis will play where there is a single dominant firm. There are, however, early indications of a continuing gradual shift in the analysis of differentiated products mergers involving a single dominant firm; while the analysis may still be based on the traditional concept of single firm dominance and conventional market definition, the issue of the closeness of substitution of the merging parties' products is moving centre stage (see, for example, *Piaggio/Aprilia*).[57] The full implications will only become apparent once the Commission actually applies the new test in a significant number of cases and the power to use unilateral effects analysis in oligopoly cases is tested in the Courts.

The substantive reform of the ECMR and the accompanying Guidelines bring the rules for treating horizontal mergers, which have accounted for the majority of transactions challenged under the ECMR, more closely into line with the approach of the US authorities. However, this may not be true of conglomerate mergers, where the EU authorities have recently taken a more interventionist stance than their US counterparts that has been particularly controversial.[58] The judgements of the ECJ and CFI in the *Tetra Laval* and *GE/Honeywell* cases, together with the recent *BaByliss* judgement,[59] should help in clarifying the treatment of conglomerate effects prior to releasing guidelines on conglomerate cases. Although guidelines are not always precisely followed (for example, in the case of market share thresholds in the US discussed earlier), the publication of guidelines for the different types of mergers can be expected to help to shape future European merger policy in the same way as the US guidelines have influenced policy in the US.

There has been a notable fall in prohibitions decisions since the recent successes of litigants in the CFI and it is to be hoped that the Commission's decisions will be sounder rather than becoming overly cautious as a result of the earlier Court reverses. Only one merger has been banned since 2001 – the joint acquisition by EDP, the established Portuguese electricity company, and ENI of GDP, the incumbent Portuguese natural gas company (December 2004).[60] In her press briefing on the case, Neelie Kroes, the current Competition Commissioner, stressed that the decision had been 'very carefully considered', was 'based on a very thorough investigation and in-depth economic analysis' and was shared almost unanimously by the Member States.[61] The Court subsequently upheld this prohibition decision.[62]

The changes to the Commission's internal working methods and organisation are significant new developments and the increased emphasis on economic expertise, slight relaxation of time limits and enhanced provision for checks and balances should help to improve the quality of decision taking under the ECMR. The injection of economic expertise was much needed, but there are doubts over whether the small team of economists now in place will be able to make an impact beyond the largest cases. Much depends on how these changes, including the provisions of the Best Practices Guidelines, are actually handled within the Commission.

The reforms do not address the fundamental question of the Commission's combined roles of prosecutor, judge and jury and the relatively slow judicial review process to which it is still subject. This institutional framework has been criticised since the ECMR was first adopted and became much more controversial following the series of high profile setbacks in the Courts. The EU merger regime still does not operate under the shadow of the Courts in the same way as the US regime. Investigations of problematic cases at Phase I and II are still handled by the same team, unlike the UK system. Despite all the other changes and the additional checks and balances which are in place, these institutional features are still a source of concern. It will take time to see whether the results of the recent reforms will be enough to restore the Commission's credibility or whether more far reaching changes to the EU's administrative system of merger control will be necessary in future.

APPENDIX 4.1

The original thresholds of the ECMR covered transactions where:

1. the combined aggregate turnover of all the undertakings exceeds EUR 5 billion and
2. the aggregate Community-wide turnover of each of at least two of the undertakings concerned exceeds EUR 250 million,

unless each of the undertakings has more than two thirds of its aggregated Community-wide turnover in one and the same Member State (the 'two thirds rule').

The scope of the ECMR was extended under the supplementary thresholds introduced in 1998 to include transactions where:

1. the combined aggregate turnover of all the undertakings exceeds EUR 2 500 million;
2. the combined turnover of all the undertakings exceeds EUR 100 million in each of at least three Member States;
3. at least two of the undertakings each have turnover exceeding EUR 25 million in each of the three Member States in (2) above, and
4. Community-wide turnover of each of at least two undertakings exceeds EUR 100 million,

unless the 'two thirds rule' applies.

NOTES

1. I am grateful to Roger Clarke, Teresa Krajewska, Bruce Lyons and Michael Utton for comments on an earlier draft. Any errors and omissions are the author's responsibility.
2. Council Regulation (EC) No 139/2004 of 20 January 2004 on the control of concentrations between undertakings, OJ L24, 29 January 2004. See also the Implementing Regulation, Commission Regulation (EC) No 802/2004 of 7 April 2004 implementing Council Regulation (EC) No 139/2004 on the control of concentrations between undertakings, OJ L133, 30 April 2004.
3. Green Paper on the review of Council Regulation, EEC No 4064/89, COM(2001) 745/6 final, issued on 11 December 2001.
4. Proposal for a Council Regulation on the control of concentrations between undertakings, OJ C20, 28 January 2003.
5. Draft Commission Notice on the appraisal of horizontal mergers under the Council Regulation on the control of concentrations between undertakings, OJ C331, 31 December 2002.
6. Council Regulation (EC) No 4064/89 of 21 December 1989 on the control of concentrations between undertakings, OJ L395, 30 December 1989.
7. Council Regulation (EC) No 1310/97 of 30 June 1997, OJ L180, 9 July 1997.
8. Commission Notice on the definition of relevant market for the purposes of Community competition law, OJ C372, 9 December1997.

9. Commission Notice on remedies acceptable under Council Regulation (EEC) No 4064/89 and under Commission Regulation (EC) No 447/89, OJ C68, 2 March 2001.
10. This may partly reflect the existence of more problematic mergers and partly a more aggressive stance, with the EU trying to follow the US lead in taking a more economics based approach although it had relatively limited economics expertise internally.
11. *General Electric-Honeywell*, Case COMP/M.2220, Decision of 3 July 2001, OJ L48, 18 February 2004. The subsequent Court Judgments on the appeals following this case (Cases T-209/01 and T-210/01) were issued on 14 December 2005.
12. Case T-342/99 *Airtours v Commission* 2002, Judgment of 6 June 2002, ECR 2002 II-02585.
13. Case T-310/01 *Schneider Electric SA v Commission*, Judgment of 22 October 2002, ECR 2002 II-04201.
14. Case T-5/02 *Tetra Laval BV v Commission*, Judgment of 25 October 2002, ECR 2002 II-04519.
15. The opinion of Advocate General Tissano, which is not binding on the Court of Justice, was delivered on the Commission's appeals against the CFI judgments on 25 May 2004. He considered that although the CFI committed various legal errors, in particular with regard to the scope of judicial review, the judgments under appeal should not be set aside. The subsequent judgments in Cases C-12/03 P and C-13/03 P were delivered on 15 February 2005.
16. The types of transaction defined as 'concentrations' under the regulation were not changed significantly. The regulation clarified that the change of control must be 'on a lasting basis' and that it was sufficient for 'parts of undertakings' to be involved. There is no reference to closely connected or conditionally linked transactions being treated as a single concentration, in contrast to the original proposal, although this is mentioned in a recital to the ECMR (which is not legally binding).
17. Commission Notice on case referral in respect of concentrations, OJ C56, 5 March 2005 (available at www.europa.eu.int/comm/competition).
18. In the opposite direction, an extension to Article 9 provisions (Article 4.4) allows the merging parties to make a prenotification request for the case to be examined by a national competition authority rather than the Commission. The Commission's case allocation Notice contains legal requirements for referrals and additional factors to be taken into account when a request for referral is envisaged under Articles 4.4 and 4.5.
19. This approach still seems preferable to the mandatory '3+ system' suggested in the Green Paper (para. 29-33) under which all concentrations liable to notification in at least three Member States would automatically have been subject to Commission jurisdiction.
20. Under the EEA agreement of 5 February 1992, the Commission takes the position in EFTA States into account, as well as the EU, in assessing compatibility.
21. The Commission, however, did not make any procedural distinction between parts of the dominance test in merger appraisal and seemed to treat it as a unified test.
22. US Department of Justice and Federal Trade Commission, Horizontal merger guidelines issued April 1992 and revised April 1997. See www.usdoj.gov/atr/public/guidelines/horizontal_book/hmg1.html
23. *Aerospatiale-Alenia/de Havilland*, Case IV/M.53, Decision of 2 October 1991, OJ L334, 5 December 1991.
24. Guidelines on the assessment of horizontal mergers under the Council Regulation on the control of concentrations between undertakings, OJ C31, 5 February 2004.
25. Joined Cases C-68/94, *France v. Commission* and C-30/95, *SCPA and EMC v. Commission*, Judgment of 31 March 1998, ECR 1998 I-01375 and Case T-102/96, *Gencor Ltd v. Commission*, Judgment of 25 March 1999, ECR 1999 II-00753.
26. *Air Liquide/Messer Targets*, Case IV/M.3314, Decision of 15 March 2004, OJ C91, 15 April 2004.
27. *Airtours/First Choice*, Case IV/M.1524, Decision of 22 September 1999, OJ L93, 13 April 2000.
28. The attitude to collusion has differed under Article 81 and the ECMR. In view of the final outcome of *Wood Pulp* in 1993, firm evidence of concerted practices has been required to find a violation of Article 81 whereas collective dominance has been identified with tacit collusion under the ECMR and established with looser evidence. This arguably reflects a different presumption about the likelihood of collusion under the ECMR rather than just the difficulties of providing clear evidence in *ex ante* control. See D.J. Neven, 'Collusion under Article 81 and the

merger regulation', paper presented to the 3rd Nordic Competition Policy Conference on 'Fighting cartels – why and how?', Stockholm, 11-12 September, 2000.

29. See Competition Commission, Merger references, Competition Commission Guidelines, CC2, June 2003, para. 3.42-3.43.

30. The draft guidelines did contain a presumption against past coordination but this has wisely been dropped.

31. For a useful exposition of the economics of unilateral effects, see Ivaldi, M., B. Jullien, P. Rey, P. Seabright and J. Tirole (2003) available at http://ideas.repec.org/p/ide/wpaper/582.html. This report points to the importance of assessing the full equilibrium effects of a merger, as suggested by a unilateral effects analysis, even in cases where single firm dominance is involved, since it may be misleading to focus on the prices and production of the merged entity alone.

32. There were concerns that *Oracle/Peoplesoft* would reduce the number of competitors from three to two in particular specialized management software applications. In March 2004, the Commission issued a Statement of Objections to the proposed merger under the original ECMR's dominance test. This was partly on the basis of unilateral effects; Peoplesoft was Oracle's next closest competitor and there was a concern that the merged entity would have greater freedom to set prices (as well as the merger giving potential for tacit collusion between the merged firm and the market leader, SAP). The non-coordinated effects issue was abandoned, however, during the course of the bilateral cooperation with the US authorities as the market was found to be wider than originally envisaged. See *Oracle/Peoplesoft*, Case COMP/M.3216, Decision of 26 October 2004, OJ L218, 23 August 2005.

33. According to Mario Monti, the 'dominance test, if properly interpreted, is capable of dealing with the full range of anti-competitive scenarios which mergers may engender', 'Merger control in the European Union: a radical reform', paper presented at the European Commission/IBA Conference on EU Merger Control, Brussels, 7 November. RAPID press release, SPEECH/02.545. It is also notable that in the draft horizontal merger guidelines on non-collusive oligopoly, the Commission referred to previous decisions in which the analytical framework had been used – *Volvo/Scania*, Case IV/M.1672, Decision of 15 March 2000, OJ L143, 29 May 2001, para. 148, and *Barilla/BPS/Kamps*, Case COMP/M.2817, Decision of 14 June 2002, OJ C198, 21 August 2002, para. 34.

34. Non-coordinated effects were divided into two areas in the draft guidelines. The first (the creation of a 'paramount' market position) corresponded to the traditional concept of single firm dominance and the other ('non-collusive oligopoly') was associated with a set of unilateral effects concerns that could be present at smaller post merger market shares. This distinction was considered unnecessary under the SIEC test and both categories are treated together in the current guidelines despite the continuing stress on the concept of dominance.

35. *GE/Instrumentarium*, Case COMP/M.3083, Decision of 2 September 2003, OJ L109, 16 April 2004.

36. Commission Notice on the definition of relevant market for the purposes of Community competition law, OJ C372, 9 December 1997.

37. *Alcatel/Telettra*, Case IV/M.42, Decision of 12 April 1991, OJ L122, 17 May 1991.

38. *Exxon/Mobil*, Case IV/M.1383, Decision of 29 September 1999, OJ L103, 7 April 2004.

39. *Glaxo Wellcome/ SmithKline Beecham*, Case IV/M.1846, Decision of 8 May 2000, OJ C170, 20 June 2000.

40. *Volvo/Scania*, Case IV/M.1672 (see note 33 above).

41. D. Scheffman, M. Coate and L. Silvia (2002), '20 years of merger guidelines enforcement at the FTC: an economic perspective', available at http://atrdocs.GRP@USDOJ.gov

42. An HHI of 1000 is the equivalent of 10 equally sized firms; a market containing 8 firms will always have an HHI above 1000. A merger between two firms each accounting for 11.19 per cent of the market would exceed the 250 HHI threshold while the HHI would change by more than 150 as the result of a merger between two firms each with 8.67 per cent of the market.

43. See, for example, *Kesko/ICA*, Case COMP/M.3464, Decision of 13 November 2004, para. 47.

44. See W.J. Kolasky, 'Conglomerate mergers and range effects: it's a long way from Chicago to Brussels', address before the George Mason University Symposium, Washington DC, 9 November 2001. Available at www.usdoj.gov/atr/public/speeches.

45. P. Lowe, 'Competition Policy in the European Union', remarks at the American Antitrust Institute, 1 July 2002. See www.antitrustinstitute.org/recent2/192.cfm.
46. See Mario Monti, 'Review of the EC Merger Control Regulation: roadmap for reform', remarks to the British Chamber of Commerce. RAPID press release, SPEECH/02/252 of 4 June 2002.
47. DG Competition, 'Best practices on the conduct of EC merger control proceedings', available at www.europa.eu.int/comm/competition.
48. The US has started to publish summaries of its decisions in cases which are not litigated.
49. Case COMP/M.1741 *MCI Worldcom/Sprint*, Decision of 28 June 2000, OJ L300, 18 November 2003; Case T-310/00 *MCI v. Commission*, Judgment of 28 September 2004. This prohibition was overturned mainly for technical reasons as the Commission had banned the transaction a day after the proposed merger had been abandoned.
50. Amendments to the rules of procedure of the Court of Justice of 28 November 2000, OJ L322, 19 December 2000; amendments to the rules of procedure of the Court of First Instance of the European Communities, OJ L322, 19 December 2000.
51. See Mario Monti, 'Review of the EC Merger Control Regulation', op cit.
52. In 2005, there were 313 notifications which was an increase of more than 25 per cent on activity in the previous year.
53. *Telecom Eireann* (Case IV/M.802, Decision of 18 December 1996, OJ C35, 4 February 1997) is an interesting example. The Irish government had previously applied for Commission confirmation that it could delay liberalisation of voice telephony and other telecom services for limited periods beyond the 1 January 1998 liberalisation date applicable to most Member States. The Commission made it clear, however, that the approval of this transaction depended on the Irish assenting to a faster liberalisation schedule.
54. *Sony/BMG*, Case COMP/M.3333, Decision of 19 July 2004, OJ L62, 9 March 2005. The Chief Economist's team carried out an assessment of the large amount of data supplied by each of the largest record companies to see whether the average prices at which transactions were concluded had shown parallel behaviour in the main EU countries. The team reportedly met several times with the companies' economists and attended the oral hearing. This merger, which was investigated to see if it would lead to or strengthen a collectively dominant position, was allowed as the Commission, applying the criteria given in the *Airtours* judgment, found that the market was not sufficiently transparent and there was no effective mechanism for retaliation.
55. Commission Notice on the rules for access to the Commission file in cases pursuant to Articles 81 and 82 of the EC Treaty, Articles 53, 54 and 57 of the EEA Agreement and Council Regulation (EC) No 139/2004.
56. 'Assessing unilateral effects in practice: lessons from *GE/Instrumentarium*', RBB Economics Briefing Note, 14 May 2004. See www.rbbecon.com/publications/downloads/rbb_brief14.pdf
57. *Piaggio/Aprilia*, Case COMP/M.3570, Decision of 22 November 2004.
58. See W.J. Kolasky, 'Conglomerate mergers and range effects: it's a long way from Chicago to Brussels', address before the George Mason University Symposium, Washington DC, 9 November 2001. Available at www.usdoj.gov/atr/public/speeches.
59. Case T-114/02, *BaByliss SA v. Commission*, Judgment of 3 April 2003, ECR II-01279.
60. *ENI/EDP/GDP*, Case COMP/M.3340, Decision of 9 December 2004 (not yet published in the OJ).
61. Neelie Kroes, 'Introductory remarks at a press conference on *Choline Chloride* cartel and *EDP/ENI/GDP* merger decision', Brussels, 9 December RAPID press release SPEECH/04/526, 9 December 2004.
62. Case T-87/05, *EDP v Commission*, Judgment of 21 September 2005.

5. Horizontal Agreements and Restrictive Practices Policy in the UK and EU

Roger Clarke and Eleanor J. Morgan

INTRODUCTION[1]

Horizontal agreements and restrictive practices have long been recognised as a source of public policy concern and policies to deal with them go back at least to the 1890 Sherman Act in the US. A restrictive practices policy was adopted in Article 85 (now 81) of the founding EC Treaty and specific policies towards restrictive practices have been in operation in the UK for some fifty years. This chapter discusses developments in UK and EU policy towards horizontal restraints which are restrictive practices between firms operating in the same market. Vertical agreements between firms at different stages in production are treated in Chapter 6.

Both the EU and UK operate policies which prohibit arrangements between firms that have the aim or effect of preventing, restricting or distorting competition – EU policy is concerned with practices which may affect trade between Member States and UK policy deals with those affecting the UK market.[2] However, exemptions are permitted (under Article 81(3) in the EC Treaty and section 9(1) of the UK Competition Act respectively) even when competition is restricted if the practice can be shown to provide benefits such as improving production or distribution, or supporting technical or economic progress, as long as consumers receive a fair share of the benefits.

Agreements that have the restriction of competition as their principal goal (cartels) are generally regarded as the most harmful to competition of all anti-competitive practices and this has led to the adoption of strong policies against them. This is particularly the case for 'hard core' cartels, usually defined as agreements that fix prices, limit supply or production, share markets or rig bids (see OECD, 2003, p. 7). These agreements have a direct adverse effect on consumers and offer no (or few) off-setting benefits. Also by restricting competition, such cartels may reduce incentives for firms to lower their costs and may stifle new research and innovation. As a result, competition authorities have increasingly sought to take a hard line against such activities both in the UK and EU and also more generally (OECD, 2002, 2003).

A key issue in the control of horizontal agreements is finding evidence to show that such practices exist. Prior to the 1998 Competition Act in the UK, firms were required to register agreements with the Director General of Fair Trading (DGFT) for consideration by the Restrictive Practices Court. Since the sanctions imposed for operating an agreement which was not registered with the DGFT were slight, firms could operate an agreement secretly either by de-registering or not registering in the first place. In addition, firms can operate informal agreements ('gentlemen's agreements') or concerted practices through which they adopt parallel behaviour and do not compete in the market.[3] All of these measures create problems for competition authorities in finding evidence to show that restrictive practices exist. While parallel behaviour might be an indicator, as we will see, the courts in the EU (as well as the US) have ruled that parallel behaviour is not, in itself, sufficient evidence to show the existence of a restrictive agreement or concerted practice.

Against this background, this chapter considers changes in UK and EU policy that have taken place in recent years. In the UK, the older restrictive practices policy based on the 'form' of an agreement has been replaced by a policy focusing on the effects of restrictive agreements and concerted practices, and harsher penalties have been introduced for firms found to have engaged in practices which prevent, restrict or distort competition. In addition, the UK, but not the EU, has introduced criminal penalties in hard core cartel cases which hold individuals personally responsible for engaging in such restrictive agreements. Also, both the UK and EU have adopted leniency policies designed to give firms incentives to come forward in cartel cases, similar to those in the US.[4] By allowing firms that come forward ('whistle-blowers') reductions in fines or full immunity, they strengthen the ability of competition authorities to tackle the central problem of providing evidence in cartel cases. As we discuss later in the chapter, these policies have been very successful in the EU, in particular, as in the US, in uncovering and successfully prosecuting cartels, and hence have been a significant development in policy in this area in their own right.

The rest of the chapter is organised as follows. The next two sections discuss recent developments in policy, first in the UK and then in the EU. The following section examines the important role leniency has played in strengthening policy in this area and compares the provisions in the EU and UK with US policy. Possible future developments in policy are then discussed and a final section concludes.

UK POLICY: THE CHAPTER I PROHIBITION AND THE CARTEL OFFENCE

Prior to March 2000, UK policy on cartels and restrictive agreements was based on the 1976 Restrictive Trade Practices Act (supplemented by the Resale Prices Act 1976).[5] Under the Restrictive Trade Practices Act, the UK adopted an approach to the control of cartels and restrictive agreements which was based on the 'form' rather than the 'effects' of an agreement. This policy had a number of important weaknesses in both its scope and the penalties that could be imposed and a much stronger policy has been adopted in the 1998 Competition Act and the 2002 Enterprise Act.

Under the 1976 Restrictive Trade Practices Act[6] firms were required to register restrictive agreements with the Office of Fair Trading (OFT) which then had the duty to bring cases before the Restrictive Practices Court (RPC). Under the policy, it was assumed that restrictive agreements were *against* the public interest, but the Act allowed firms to defend those agreements in terms of certain specified benefits or 'gateways' (Clarke, 1985, pp. 240-1). These included factors such as 'protecting the public from injury', 'protecting employment in a region' and offering 'specific and substantial benefits to the public'. In addition, firms were required not only to show that their agreement produced one or more of these benefits but also that, on balance, it was in the public interest. Failure to do so meant that the agreement was struck down, and hence could not be enforced in UK law.

Despite its apparent early success,[7] important problems existed with this policy. First, as noted above, the Act focused on the form of an agreement and whether it was registrable under the Act. As such, it primarily related to written agreements between firms and this implied that it did not cover verbal and contractually non-binding ('gentlemen's') agreements where competing firms otherwise coordinate their conduct on the market. This was obviously a major disadvantage in that it allowed firms to de-register their agreements if necessary and continue to operate them in a less explicit form.[8] Second, the policy also allowed firms to defend their agreements in terms of the benefits or 'gateways' laid down in the Act, and these were regarded as quite wide. In practice, however, relatively few cases were upheld in the Court so this did not appear to be a major problem in the law.[9] Finally, the 1976 Act lacked any real sanctions for firms found to operate a restrictive agreement. Under the Act, agreements that were struck down by the Court were declared void but no further penalty was imposed.[10] Similarly, failure to register an agreement meant it was void in law but, again, no further penalties were imposed. At the very least, therefore, the policy offered a poor signal to firms engaged in restrictive agreements or concerted practices and there was clearly need for reform.

Current policy on horizontal agreements is based on the Chapter I prohibition of the Competition Act 1998 together with the 'cartel offence' introduced in the 2002 Enterprise Act. In the Competition Act, the Chapter I prohibition closely follows Article 81 of the EC Treaty, and brings UK policy more into line with policy in the EU. Under this policy,

> agreements between undertakings, decisions by associations of undertakings or concerted practices which (a) may affect trade within the United Kingdom, and (b) have as their object or effect the prevention, restriction or distortion of competition within the United Kingdom, are prohibited unless they are exempt (Competition Act, Chapter I, section 2(1); the so-called 'Chapter I prohibition').

Subsection 2(2) of the Act then provides a non-exhaustive list of agreements to which the prohibition applies; namely, agreements, decisions or practices which

(a) directly or indirectly fix purchase or selling prices or any other trading conditions;
(b) limit or control production, markets, technical development or investment;
(c) share markets or sources of supply;
(d) apply dissimilar conditions to equivalent transactions with other trading parties, thereby placing them at a competitive disadvantage;
(e) make the conclusion of contracts subject to acceptance by the other parties of supplementary obligations which, by their nature or according to commercial usage, have no connection with the subject of such contracts (Competition Act, Chapter I, section 2(2)).[11]

Section 2(4) of the Act then states that such agreements are void using wording very similar to that in Article 81.

Under section 60 of the Act, the UK authorities are required as far as possible to make decisions in line with decisions under Community law. Hence, explicit provision is made in UK policy to follow EU policy closely, including decisions reached by the European Commission supported in the European courts.[12] This requirement is strengthened in the EU Modernization Regulation which requires national competition authorities not to prohibit agreements under national law that would not be prohibited under Article 81.[13]

Several aspects of UK policy deserve further attention. First, while the Act prohibits agreements that prevent, restrict or distort competition, it also requires that such restrictions have 'an appreciable effect' on competition. In this respect, the OFT takes a similar position to that in the EU in adopting rules under which an agreement will, typically, not be seen as having an appreciable effect.[14] These rules involve a market share test for horizontal agreements. The rules, however, are quite stringent: for example, the rule for a horizontal agreement is that it will not be regarded as having an appreciable effect if the combined market share of the firms involved is less than 10 per cent of a relevant market.[15] Yet agreements which have the effect of fixing prices or market shares, limiting production or setting resale prices are not regarded as inappreciable even if this combined market share test is met. Clearly, therefore, the principle of an inappreciable effect is unlikely to operate in most (or all) hard core cartel cases.

Second, the 1998 Act also allows immunity from financial penalties in the case of 'small agreements'.[16] For these purposes a 'small agreement' is defined as one in which the combined annual turnover of the firms involved is less than £20 million. This provision, which does not apply to price fixing agreements, and is not available in Article 81 cases, has been introduced to protect smaller businesses from financial difficulties if a substantial fine were imposed. It does raise the possibility that small agreements (for example, at local level) could be exempted from the operation of the law. In such cases, however, this immunity can be removed if the OFT believes that a significant restriction of competition is involved. Parties to small agreements are not immune to private actions (for example, to seek damages or stop particular behaviour) taken in the Courts. Such actions, however, have not been a feature (at least in the past) of UK policy in this area.

Section 2(1) of the Act allows for possible exemptions from the Chapter I prohibition under similar conditions to Article 81. The Act provides for three types of exemptions: individual exemptions, block exemptions and parallel exemptions.[17] Individual exemptions can be made by the OFT in individual cases; block exemptions relate to particular types of agreement which are thought not to violate the Chapter I prohibition, and parallel exemptions relate to individual or block exemptions made by the European Commission which also, therefore, apply to the UK. Under section 9 of the Act, an agreement can be exempted if it

(a) contributes to:-
    (i)   improving production or distribution, or
    (ii) promoting technical or economic progress,
          while allowing consumers a fair share of the resulting benefit; but
(b) does not:-
    (i)   impose on the undertakings concerned restrictions which are not indispensable to the attainment of those objectives; or
    (ii) afford the undertakings concerned the possibility of eliminating competition in respect of a substantial part of the products in question (Competition Act, 1998, section 9(1)).

These exemptions are almost identical to the ones given in Article 81(3) of the EC Treaty.[18] They imply that agreements which have a minimal adverse effect on competition but also provide benefits, such as improving production or distribution, can be excluded from the prohibition. This is likely to exclude many vertical agreements and also some horizontal agreements. Agreements that restrict competition appreciably, however, are less likely to be exempted unless they provide strong countervailing benefits. In particular, in contrast to earlier policy in the UK, hard core cartels which fix prices, limit production, share markets or rig bids are unlikely ever to satisfy these conditions and hence are almost always prohibited in UK law.

The Act gives substantial new powers to the OFT to investigate cases and to fine firms found to have breached the Chapter I prohibition. In particular, the OFT is able to conduct 'dawn raids' on firms suspected of having infringed the Chapter I prohibition, as in the case of the Chapter II prohibition discussed in Chapter 2 in this book. In addition, following the Modernization Regulation, the OFT now has parallel powers with the European Commission under the whole of Article 81 of the EC Treaty and the Commission looks to the national authorities to deal with all but the most serious cases. Previously the power of the national authorities to apply Article 81 was limited as Article 81(3) was the exclusive domain of the Commission. In view of this, the UK authorities advised firms operating agreements with both an effect on trade and an appreciable effect on competition in the UK to notify the European Commission which had exclusive power to grant an exemption under Article 81 (3) rather than notifying under the Chapter 1 prohibition.

Several other significant developments have taken place following the 1998 Act. First, under the Act, UK policy has been extended to cover concerted practices as well as restrictive agreements.[19] This implies that it is not necessary to establish that a written agreement exists to establish an infringement under the Chapter I prohibition. In considering concerted practices, the OFT has identified a number of relevant factors which are broadly in line with EU policy:

- whether the parties knowingly entered into practical cooperation
- whether behaviour in the market is influenced as a result of direct or indirect contact between undertakings
- whether parallel behaviour is a result of contact between undertakings leading to conditions of competition which do not correspond to normal conditions of the market
- the structure of the relevant market and the nature of the product involved
- the number of undertakings in the market and, where there are only a few undertakings, whether they have similar cost structures and outputs (Office of Fair Trading, Agreements and concerted practices, OFT Guidance, 2004, p. 7).

In its discussion, the OFT rules out the possibility that the prohibition will be applied in cases where there is no evidence of (direct or indirect) contact between firms and this is again in line with policy in the EU.

Second, a significant new development in the UK has been the introduction of a leniency policy in line with the EU and US. This policy was introduced following the Competition Act in March 2000[20] and has now been revised to bring it more closely into line with policy in the EU.[21] Under this policy, firms can obtain full immunity from fines if they are the first firm to come forward to provide information on a cartel, and if they cooperate fully with the investigation. Full immunity is automatically given to the first firm to come forward if the OFT has not started an investigation and does not already have sufficient information in its possession to establish the existence of the alleged cartel activity. However, automatic immunity is not available to a firm which has coerced other firms to participate in the alleged cartel activity. Full immunity is available at the discretion of the OFT to the first firm to come forward if an investigation is already underway.

In addition, fines may be reduced by up to 50 per cent if a firm is not the first firm to come forward but nevertheless provides additional information which assists the OFT substantially in finding a breach of the Chapter I prohibition. A firm which has coerced other firms to participate in the alleged cartel activity can be granted a reduction in its fines of up to 50 per cent. Also, the OFT has adopted a 'leniency plus' policy, similar to that in the US, which enables firms that are cooperating with the OFT under leniency in one case to provide evidence under leniency in a separate case, and thereby receive an additional reduction in fine. This is discussed more fully later in the chapter.

A further significant extension of the policy has been the introduction of a new 'cartel offence' in the Enterprise Act 2002. This introduces criminal penalties for individuals found to be involved in hard core cartel cases, in addition to the civil offence under the 1998 Act.[22] This means that individuals will be personally (and criminally) liable in hard core cartel cases. In such cases, the OFT's powers have been enhanced to include powers to undertake covert surveillance, including the use of listening devices, and to use directed surveillance, in addition to making 'dawn raids'.[23] The maximum penalty under the new offence is five years in prison and/or an unlimited fine. The OFT can also apply for a court order to disqualify a director involved in a cartel offence for a period of up to 15 years. Cases will, typically, be prosecuted by the Serious Fraud Office, although the OFT also has powers to prosecute a case.

The introduction of the cartel offence brings UK policy more into line with US policy than EU policy in this area. The possible punishments will clearly focus the minds of individuals, depending on how the policy is applied. The Enterprise Act has only recently come into force and, as yet, there have been no criminal prosecutions.

The 2002 Act has also introduced the need for an additional leniency programme in relation to individuals. Immunity under section 190(4) of the Act from prosecution for this criminal offence can be obtained in the form of a 'no-action letter' if the individual admits the offence and satisfies a number of additional conditions. These include that the individual provide the OFT with all the information he/she has available on the cartel, that he/she cooperates fully with the OFT investigation and that he/she had not taken steps to coerce others to join the cartel.[24] The OFT, however, reserves the right to proceed with a prosecution if it already has sufficient evidence against the individual(s) concerned. As in the US, individuals associated with firms that are first to come forward and which are given full immunity will receive immunity in the form of a no-action letter.

A number of early cases suggest that UK policy is having some effect, although cases have tended to be quite small. The OFT had, in fact, considered 29 cases[25] concerning the Chapter I prohibition between 1 March 2000 when the Act came into force and the end of 2005. In 12 of these cases, an infringement of the prohibition was found, including nine in which a fine was imposed. Of the other cases, four were given individual exemptions, four varied their agreement to satisfy the requirements of the OFT, one involved a block exemption and seven involved no infringement being found. In addition, a binding commitment was given in one case not to infringe the prohibition.[26]

Whilst the policy has been in place for a limited time, several cases can be used to illustrate the working of the Act.

Hasbro, Argos and Littlewoods (2003)[27]
In this case, Hasbro, a leading manufacturer of children's toys and games, was found to have entered into restrictive agreements and/or concerted practices with Argos and Littlewoods, two of the leading retailers of children's toys and games, to fix the retail prices of Hasbro toys and games, and not to allow discounts on list prices.[28] This agreement, which had lasted from 1999[29] to the summer of 2001, was found to have restricted price competition leading to artificially high prices of Hasbro's toys and games. The OFT imposed fines of £17.2 million on Argos and £5.37 million on Littlewoods.

Interestingly, Hasbro, which had clearly been the instigator of these agreements, escaped a fine by being the first firm to come forward before the investigation was underway and by cooperating fully with the investigation. This reflects an aspect of UK leniency policy which allows leaders/instigators of restrictive agreements to claim immunity under the leniency policy, as discussed later in the chapter. Argos and Littlewoods appealed the OFT's decision to the Competition Appeal Tribunal (CAT) which upheld the OFT's decision in December 2004.

Replica Football Kit (2003)[30]
This case involved a network of agreements between Umbro, a leading manufacturer of replica football kit, and nine of its distributors to fix prices of replica football shirts, including the England football shirt worn in the Euro 2000 championship and football shirts for clubs, including Manchester United and Chelsea. The typical price of a replica football shirt was fixed at just under £40 for a short-sleeve adult shirt and just under £30 for a short-sleeve junior shirt. The OFT concluded that these agreements amounted to price-fixing and imposed

fines totalling £18.6 million on the ten firms involved. The largest fines were £8.4 million for JJB Sports and £6.6 million for Umbro, while Manchester United also paid a £1.7 million fine. Interestingly, the Football Association, which should have been supporting the fans, was also involved and was fined £198 000 (reduced to £158 000 by leniency).

The effect of the removal of these restrictions can be seen in a follow-up survey by the OFT which found that, in April 2003, prices ranged between £24 and £40 for the short-sleeve adult shirt and £18 and £30 for the short-sleeve junior shirt.[31]

Flat Roofing in the West Midlands (2004)[32]

In this case, nine firms were found to have participated in a series of distinct agreements and/or concerted practices to bid for contracts to repair, maintain and improve flat roofing in the West Midlands region between 2000 and 2002. The firms were mainly involved in bid-rigging in tenders for schools, libraries and shopping centres, amongst other things. Fines totalling £290 000 were imposed on the firms involved. Subsequently, two of the firms appealed against the decision but the CAT upheld the OFT's decision, although the fine for one of the firms was reduced.

This case has led to a number of others involving roofing contractors in Scotland and in the north east of England,[33] where similar practices have been uncovered. In the Scottish case, for example, ten contractors were fined £830 000 in total in 2005, although this was reduced to about £560 000 by leniency. A further case in 2005 concerned roofing in Western-Central Scotland and, most recently, in various parts of England and Scotland concerning flat roofing and car park surfacing.[34] These decisions bring the total penalties imposed to date in this sector to £4.3 million (reduced to around £2.5 million by the OFT's leniency programme).

Mastercard (2005)[35]

Finally, in a larger case, the OFT investigated an agreement between members of the MasterCard UK Members Forum and other MasterCard licensees to set the price of the fallback multilateral interchange fee in all MasterCard transactions between 1 March 2000 and November 2004. The OFT found that this system amounted to an agreement to fix prices and was used to recover some costs not involved in the operation of the policy. It concluded that the agreement infringed both the Chapter I prohibition and Article 81 of the EC Treaty. However, no fines were imposed, partly because the agreement was notified to the OFT on 1 March 2000 and partly because it had been terminated.[36]

EU POLICY: ARTICLE 81 OF THE EC TREATY

As is well known, EU policy on agreements between firms is based on Article 81 of the EC Treaty and operated under the procedures laid down under Regulation 17/62[37] until these were replaced by the Modernization Regulation introduced in May 2004. Under Article 81(1) of the Treaty 'all agreements between undertakings, decisions by associations of undertakings and concerted practices which may affect trade between Member States and which have as their object or effect the prevention, restriction or distortion of competition' are held to be incompatible with the common market. Article 81(2) then declares that all such agreements are void. Article 81(3) provides grounds under which an agreement (or other restrictive practice) may be legal even where there is a restriction on competition under Article 81(1). This exemption may apply, as noted in the previous section, if the agreement has the effect of improving production or distribution of goods, or promoting technical or economic progress. In these cases, the firms must be able to show: first, that consumers receive a fair share of the benefits; second, that the restriction is indispensable to obtain these benefits and third, that the agreement does not allow the parties the possibility of eliminating competition in a substantial part of the market. Article 81(3) is applied either to individual agreements or types of agreement through a block exemption and, in the latter case, the agreement will satisfy the exemption criteria as long it as can be shown to benefit from a block exemption.

As noted in the previous section, horizontal agreements do not always appreciably restrict competition and sometimes may on balance even be pro-competitive. Examples include cooperation to develop a new product or new technology, sharing information on technical matters, standardising product specifications and improving information for consumers. These kinds of agreement are usually exempt under Article 81(3).

The adoption of a Notice[38] and two block exemption regulations[39] by the European Commission (the 'Commission') in November 2000 marked a new approach to the application of Article 81(3) exemptions affecting horizontal cooperation.[40] According to the Commission Notice (which covers R&D, production, marketing, purchasing, standardization and environmental agreements):

> Changing markets have generated an increasing variety and use of horizontal cooperation. More complete and updated guidance is needed to improve clarity and transparency regarding the applicability of Article 81 in this area. Within this assessment greater emphasis has to be put on economic criteria to reflect better recent developments in enforcement practice and the case law of the Court of Justice and the Court of First Instance . . . (Commission Notice on guidelines on the applicability of Article 81, para. 6).

These Guidelines placed more emphasis on an economics and market-based approach to the application of Article 81 which had in the past been construed more legalistically. In line with this, the new block exemption regulations (on R&D and specialization respectively) put more emphasis on the effects on competition and on the market shares of the parties involved (although these, of course, are a relatively crude way of identifying cases where market power is most likely to arise) rather than the form of the agreement. Further guidelines published in 2004 built on the approach adopted in the Notice to develop a framework for the application of Article 81(3) in areas of horizontal cooperation and offer further guidance on the requirements (mentioned above) under which agreements can be exempted.[41]

Some horizontal measures and, in particular, hard core activities such as price-fixing and market sharing are unlikely ever to show benefits under Article 81(3) and so, typically, cannot be defended in this way. Such horizontal agreements (cartels) have been attracting considerably more attention from competition authorities around the world and the Commission has devoted more of its energies and resources to countering this type of activity in recent years. In light of this, the Commission set up a specialised cartel unit in 1998 within the Competition DG to deal with most of the cases in this area and, with a gradual increase in resources, a second cartel unit was set up in 2002. The recent reorganisation of the Commission, however, has meant that, since July 2003, all antitrust units within Competition DG have had the task of detecting and prosecuting cartels in their area of responsibility. This appears not to have been as effective as having a dedicated unit to support this key activity and it was announced in 2005 that a new Directorate devoted exclusively to cartel enforcement had been established.[42] Previous success in uncovering and dealing with cartels has brought significant benefits (as we discuss further below) and has also provided convincing evidence of the incidence and harmfulness of hard core cartels and revealed the long periods over which some cartels have been sustained.

The Commission has wide powers to investigate suspected infringements of Article 81 and to impose fines on firms involved. The 1998 guidelines on financial penalties relate the levels of fines to both the gravity of the offence and its duration. Fines of up to one million euros can be imposed for a relatively minor offence; fines of up to 20 million euros can be imposed for more serious offences and more than 20 million euros can be charged for very serious offences (such as hard core cartels).[43] The fines remain at these levels if the cartel has been in operation for up to one year; they can be increased by up to 50 per cent if the cartel has operated for up to five years and by 10 per cent for each year of operation for a cartel which has been established for more than five years. The fines can also be increased further if there are aggravating circumstances (for example, if the firm has previously been found to have been involved in earlier infringements) and can be reduced if there are mitigating circumstances. The maximum fine under current EU policy is 10 per cent of a firm's global turnover which is typically calculated in the previous financial year.

Recent cases in the European courts have clarified a number of issues regarding the Commission's fining policy in cartel cases – including the Court of First Instance (CFI) July 2003 ruling on four appeals against the Commission's decision in 2000 on the *Lysine* cartel (where it reduced the total fine to 74.3 million euro from 81.6 million euro).[44] In particular, it confirmed that the Commission did not need to reduce the fines because the participants in the cartel had already been fined by the Canadian and US authorities. In contrast with earlier cartel cases where it had rejected the companies' defence that the cartel had no effect on the market, the CFI suggested that in determining the gravity of the infringement, the Commission should assess the actual impact of the cartel 'at least where it appears that this can be measured' and, in particular, with respect to its effect on price. In this case, the CFI felt that the impact of the cartel had been satisfactorily assessed. The judgement confirms the degree of discretion the CFI is willing to allow the Commission to exercise as regards setting the fine and that it can do so without regard to the actual size of the market affected by the infringement. The CFI found the fines were not disproportionate, based on deterrence considerations, even though they had been set without taking into consideration the participants' turnover in the relatively small European Economic Area *Lysine* market. This, like the *Pre-insulated Pipes* judgement,[45] marks a clear change from the Court's concern with the turnover of the affected goods seen in its earlier *Parker Pen* judgement.[46]

While the Commission has shown itself ready to adopt a strict approach regarding fines, a surprisingly lenient approach was adopted in the decision on *Electrical and Mechanical Carbon and Graphite Products* in December 2003,[47] the third cartel decision relating to graphite products within three years. The Commission reduced the fine that it would have otherwise imposed on SGL by one third because it was simultaneously involved in the three cartels and was under serious financial constraints. The Commission had already imposed significant fines in the previous two cases and the firm was suffering financial difficulties as a result. Although SGL could have paid the fine, the Commission judged that a higher fine would not be needed to ensure effective deterrence. The Commission is generally not willing to accept financial difficulties as a reason for a reduction in the level of penalties and its decision here is rather surprising. As the Commission acknowledges in its decision, a reduced fine for companies engaged in a number of cartels at the same time might give rise to moral hazard problems, as it reduces the cost of participating in additional infringements. Higher fines have been given in other cases where a firm has been involved in multiple past infringements (see, for example, the discussion of the *Plasterboard* case below).

Several differences between EU and US policy can be noted in relation to penalties. First, in contrast to established US policy, there are no criminal penalties for individuals participating in cartels under EU law which can be seen as an important weakness of current EU policy. As noted in the previous section, criminal penalties have recently been introduced in the UK (under the 2002 Enterprise Act) in hard core cartel cases reflecting the view that individuals engaging in cartel activities are effectively seeking to exploit their position at the expense of consumers. Such measures have not been considered so far at EU level.[48] Second, while EU law is now thought to allow for private civil action to be taken against firms found to be in violation of Article 81, no such cases have yet been successfully brought.[49] The position was clarified in *Courage Ltd. v Crehan* (2001) where the European Court of Justice (ECJ) ruled that a private party should have the right to sue for damages for violation of Articles 81 and 82. In this case, however, it was decided in the UK court that no violation of Article 81 had, in fact, taken place. It remains to be seen whether this ECJ decision will give rise to successful litigation under EU law. There is also no provision for treble damages in cartel cases as in the US. In the US, 90 per cent of all antitrust cases are brought by private rather than public action and this contrasts strongly with policy in the EU (and the UK).[50]

Important changes in EU policy were introduced in the Modernization Regulation which came into force on 1 May 2004.[51] Under this regulation, a 'legal exception' regime was introduced which replaced the earlier notification system. Under the previous policy, firms were able to obtain legal certainty in Article 81 cases by notifying the Commission of an agreement in order to obtain clearance under Article 81(3). Given that the Commission might later find an agreement violated Article 81(1), and hence was void under Article 81(2), there was a strong incentive for firms to notify agreements to the Commission and a very large number of agreements were notified. In fact, this policy operated in a perverse way in that agreements which were likely to be exempted were more likely to be notified than hard core cartel cases. This placed a heavy burden on the Commission which had to deal with a large number of often quite minor agreements under the earlier EC Regulation. Despite efforts to reduce the Commission's workload by the introduction of block exemptions and thresholds to exclude insignificant agreements, as well as issuing 'comfort letters'[52] rather than formal decisions, there was a backlog of cases which tended to divert resources from the investigation of the more serious breaches of Article 81. Under Modernization, firms themselves have now been given the responsibility to ensure that any agreements do not run contrary to Article 81, or if they do, that they satisfy the requirements for exemption under Article 81(3). The aim of this move from an *ex ante* notification procedure to an *ex post* control regime is to reduce the workload of the Commission and allow it more time to deal with the most important cases (including hard core cartel cases but also vertical price fixing cases) which have the largest, and potentially most damaging, effects on consumers and the common market as a whole.

At the same time, the national competition authorities (NCAs) across the EU have received new powers to pursue Article 81 cases . As well as this change, a new policy on case allocation between authorities with jurisdiction in this area has been adopted. Under this policy, NCAs which have a more direct interest in a case (which may often arise because of a parallel investigation under domestic competition legislation) will undertake investigations under Article 81 rather than the Commission. In more serious cases where there is clearly a Community-wide dimension, the Commission will undertake its own investigation as before. This move to decentralise the operation of policy requires coordination between the Commission and the Member States which is now provided through the new European Competition Network (ECN).[53]

In the rest of this section, the main thrust of EU policy in horizontal Article 81 cases is considered and some key cases are discussed. The most notable points to emerge are that, first, EU policy generally finds against agreements between firms in cases of hard core cartels and, second, that parallel pricing is not treated as an infringement of Article 81 *in isolation* from other factors.

Taking the first point first, the Commission, the CFI and the ECJ have taken a relatively hard line against hard core cartels over a considerable period of time (Neven et al., 1998, Chapter 3; Whish, 2003, Chapter 13). While, in the past, many of these cases were 'small', attention has more recently focused on a number of major investigations which have involved very large and often long established cartels. The *Vitamins*, *Plasterboard* and *Organic Peroxide* cases are all good examples and are discussed briefly below. As is now common in cartel cases, a whistle-blower company played an important part in bringing each of these cartels to the Commission's attention. The final hard core case discussed, the *Cement* case, illustrates the length of time it can take to finalise proceedings.

Vitamins (2001)[54]

The *Vitamins* case is particularly interesting because of its geographical scope. In this case, eight leading producers of vitamins operated a world-wide network of cartels between September 1989 and February 1999. While the identities of the firms varied between different vitamins, two firms (Hoffman-La Roche of Switzerland and BASF of Germany) were involved in practically all of these cartels which were highly organized with regular meetings to fix prices, set output quotas and share markets.

The Commission imposed total fines of 855 million euros, the largest fine imposed by the Commission in an Article 81 case up to now, of which Hoffman-La Roche was fined 482 million euros and BASF 296 million euros. In a similar case in the US in 1999, Hoffman-La Roche was fined $500 million and BASF $225 million. Evidence available in the US case was clearly helpful in bringing the case in the EU and this has been a factor in a number of other investigations.

Plasterboard (2002)[55]

In *Plasterboard*, four firms were found to have operated a cartel in the supply of plasterboard in the EU between 1992 and 1998.[56] The cartel covered the UK, France, Germany and Belgium and accounted for 80 per cent of EU trade in plasterboard. The aim of the cartel was to limit price competition and control production and meetings were held usually on the edge of trade association meetings.

In this case, total fines of 478 million euros were imposed in November 2002, the second largest fine imposed by the Commission in an Article 81 case. The leading firm, Lafarge (France), was fined 249 million euros. Lafarge and BPB (UK) had previously been involved in cartels (in cement and cartonboard respectively) and this was an important factor leading to increases in their fines, in particular those of Lafarge.

Organic Peroxides (2003)[57]

A number of producers of peroxides, a chemical used in making plastic and rubber products, were found to have operated a cartel between 1971 and 1999, the longest lasting cartel ever uncovered by the Commission.[58] One of the firms, Atofina, had been involved in four earlier cartels and Laporte (UK) and Peroxide Chemie had each been involved in one previously.[59] The firms held regular meetings to fix prices, share markets and so on and, after 1993, a Swiss consultancy firm, AC Treuhand, took over the responsibility for organising these meetings. The latter produced papers showing the agreed market shares and even went as far as reimbursing the travel expenses of cartel members so that there would not be any trace of the illegal meetings in their expense records. The Commission found that the firms were involved in hard core cartel activities and fines totalling 70 million euros were imposed. An interesting aspect of this case was that a fine, although only a token one (1000 euro), was levied against Treuhand. According to the Commission, the sanction was limited because of the novelty of the case but it suggested that in future it would prosecute facilitators of cartels, not just the actual members, and impose heavier sanctions in such cases.

Cement (1994)[60]

The length of time it can take to conclude Article 81 cases is illustrated by the *Cement* case. This was eventually brought to a close in 2004, almost 15 years after the start of the investigation by the Commission. Initially, the Commission imposed fines of about 248 million euros on 42 undertakings in 1994. On appeal, the total fines were reduced by 140 million euros. The CFI also found that the Commission had failed to prove participation of some of the firms in the cartel and two firms had their fines annulled because they were judged to have had insufficient access to evidence to prepare their defence.[61] Six companies also appealed to the ECJ which, finally, largely upheld the CFI judgement in January 2004.[62] Such long cases are clearly not desirable and the Commission has been trying to reduce the time taken between initiating cartel cases and reaching its decision but the time taken in appeals is a continuing issue.

Turning to policy towards concerted practices, EU policy (like the US)[63] considers a number of different factors in assessing the significance of parallel behaviour. This is because firms (typically oligopolists) may adopt similar pricing behaviour through independent action rather than through a concerted effort (express coordination). The important point is that while no formal agreement is necessary for a finding of an infringement under Article 81, parallel but unilateral behaviour stemming from independent action should not be held to account in identifying concerted practices. The Commission usually considers a number of separate factors in dealing with concerted practices including whether there is evidence of direct or indirect contact between firms, whether they notify each other of price changes and the overall nature of competition in the market.

Several early cases have been important in this area which we deal with briefly.

Dyestuffs (1972)[64]

An example of this approach was provided early on in the *Dyestuffs* case. Evidence of parallel behaviour was observed in three uniform price increases among the ten manufacturers responsible for 80 per cent of EU production in the period 1964-7. In the first, the leading European producers increased prices by 15 per cent on some dyes in January 1964 and by 10 per cent on other dyes in January 1965.[65] Then, in October 1967, they increased prices by 8 per cent in Germany, Holland, Belgium and Luxemburg and 12 per cent in France. The market was effectively segmented into five national markets where there were different cost structures making it very unlikely that such parallel behaviour would be consistent with genuine competition. In addition, the fact that firms pre-announced their price increases in 1965 and 1967 showed that they were 'testing the water' before implementing increases to ensure that price competition would not break out. The Commission had evidence that the companies had met and discussed prices although no formal agreement appeared to exist. In this case, the Court ruled that while uniform price reductions might be seen as normal competitive behaviour, it was much less likely that uniform price increases would be interpreted in this way. In addition, it also accepted that pre-announcing price increases was a means of coordinating behaviour and that this was the main aim of the firms involved.[66]

Wood Pulp (1985)[67]

In the *Wood Pulp* case, the Commission argued that the leading producers of wood pulp were involved in concerted practices to fix prices between 1975 and 1981. Although there was no evidence of an explicit agreement, the firms adopted a policy of setting prices quarterly (in dollars) in advance and there was relatively free exchange of information on prices set by firms. In addition, the Commission alleged that there was limited evidence of any price competition in this market. However, the European Court ruled that the ready availability of price information was not, in itself, evidence of coordinated behaviour, while the method of setting prices on a quarterly basis in advance was the result of pressure from buyers to have a stable price, thereby reducing uncertainty and short run swings in prices. In addition, the Court found that there was some price competition through discounts to the quarterly prices set. It, therefore, overturned the Commission's decision indicating that 'parallel conduct cannot be regarded as furnishing proof of concertation unless concertation constitutes the only plausible explanation for that conduct' and established that a higher standard of proof was required.

Polypropylene (1999)[68]

In the *Polypropylene* case, there was some evidence that concerted practices appeared to exist. In this case, along with others involving large chemical producers at about the same time,[69] the Commission found that firms were meeting on a regular basis and that uniform price increases were taking place. The Commission decided that the Article 81 prohibition had been breached and fines were imposed. The ECJ accepted the Commission's findings and indicated that the onus needed to be put on the parties involved to rebut the evidence of a concerted practice; if they were unable to do this, then a concerted practice might be inferred.[70]

These and other cases show that the ECJ requires a number of factors to be considered in reaching decisions in this area and, in particular, it is not the case that parallel behaviour is evidence that a concerted practice exists. Broadly speaking, it is necessary to establish that there are reasons for believing that competition is not working properly in a market and, linked to this, that there are uniform price increases or other systematic effects; that there is contact between firms leading to these changes and/or that price information is being used to support such concerted action. Since *Polypropylene*, however, a greater onus is placed on the firms involved to explain why such parallel behaviour appears to exist.

Freed of the need to deal with notifications, the Commission is now focusing attention on different sectors where restrictive practices are thought likely to pose a threat to competition. As part of this more proactive policy, it has recently turned attention to restrictive practices within the professions. In February 2004, it issued a Report on Competition in Professional Services in the light of a significant body of empirical work showing that some of the traditional restrictions on price setting, advertising and other elements of competition among the professions have a negative effect on consumers which cannot be justified.[71] The Commission has suggested that professionals, such as accountants, architects, lawyers and pharmacists, review their restrictive practices and the implication is that once this opportunity has passed, either the Commission itself or the national authorities may intervene against practices which appear to be anti-competitive. It has already taken some action in cases relating to professional services.[72] Its first decision condemning fixed tariffs for professional services related to Italian customs agents was taken in 1993;[73] despite this, minimum price levels apparently still persisted in 2004. In June 2004, the Commission concluded that the recommended fee scale of the Belgian Architects' Association, which had been in operation for 35 years, violated Article 81 and imposed a fine of 100 000 euros. The Association decided not to appeal and has withdrawn the fee scale.[74] A subsequent Commission working document shows that there has been some progress in refining and eliminating disproportionate restrictions relating to professional bodies especially in Denmark, the Netherlands and the UK.[75]

THE ROLE OF LENIENCY POLICIES

An important problem in cartel policy is to provide evidence of the existence and operation of a cartel, as mentioned earlier. Since cartels are illegal in most countries, they usually operate in secret and this makes it difficult for competition authorities to detect them and collect enough evidence to prosecute a case. In response to this, following the US example, a number of countries have introduced a leniency policy which offers incentives for a firm or firms to 'blow the whistle' and provide evidence in cartel cases (see OECD, 2002, 2003). The destabilising effects these policies have on cartels have led to significant improvements in the detection rate in these countries, including the US, EU and the UK.

The US introduced a leniency policy as early as 1978 but the policy was largely ineffective in its initial form.[76] In 1993, however, it introduced a more robust policy which provided important safeguards for firms and individuals involved in cartel cases. Under this policy, the first firm to come forward in cases where the Department of Justice (DoJ) has no prior knowledge of a cartel, and has not initiated an investigation, is granted full immunity from prosecution automatically. This replaced the earlier policy in which immunity was at the discretion of the DoJ. Second, in cases where the DoJ has started an investigation, but has not obtained enough information to initiate a prosecution, the first firm to come forward to provide information can also obtain full immunity (although, in this case, at the discretion of the DoJ).[77] Whether leniency is, in fact, given depends on how early in the investigation the firm comes forward, whether the firm is a leader or instigator of the cartel, and whether it coerced other firms to take part in the cartel; in these two latter categories, firms cannot come forward for leniency in US cartel cases. Third, individuals in the first firm to come forward who cooperate fully with an inquiry are also automatically immune from criminal prosecution.

The key features of this revised policy were the legal certainty of the benefits offered (that is, guaranteed complete immunity for the firm from fines and from criminal prosecution for individuals) to the first firm to come forward in cases where the DoJ has not started an investigation and the possibilities also of coming forward also at a later stage.[78] Given that penalties under US law had increased (and include prison terms for individuals), there is a strong incentive for firms and individuals to be the first to come forward. In effect, if the penalties are seen as sufficiently strong, firms are in a situation similar to a prisoners' dilemma game in which each firm has the incentive to be the first firm to come forward.[79] In addition, the DoJ also allows second and later firms to come forward for leniency (but not full immunity) after an investigation has begun, thereby making it easier to get sufficient information to bring the case to a successful conclusion and speeding the process.

The US has since further strengthened its policy in 2004[80] by reducing damages in private lawsuits to single damages for the first firms to come forward. This compares with the treble damages usually awarded in private lawsuits in the US, which continue to apply to other firms.

The EU introduced its own leniency policy in 1996.[81] This allowed leniency to the first firm to come forward provided it supplied 'decisive evidence' of the existence of a cartel before the European Commission had begun an investigation and cooperated fully with the investigation. There was less certainty about treatment compared to US policy as only a 75 to 100 per cent reduction in fine could be expected rather than a guarantee of full immunity. The first firm to come forward after the Commission had initiated an investigation could receive a reduction in fine of 50 to 75 per cent but again only if it cooperated fully. A firm which either came forward later or provided less substantial evidence could receive a reduction in fine between 10 and 50 per cent. Other conditions, apart from full cooperation, which applied for leniency to be granted were that firms should not have instigated the cartel or encouraged others to join it.[82]

Despite the substantial success of this policy in the EU (see below), it was revised in 2002 to increase the incentives for firms to come forward and to make the system more transparent.[83] In its current form, the first firm to come forward before the Commission has started an investigation is now automatically granted full immunity. This policy, moreover, applies even if a firm has instigated a cartel although not if it has coerced other firms to join. The requirement for the firm's evidence to be 'decisive' under the original leniency notice was reduced to providing evidence 'sufficient' to initiate an investigation of the firms involved. In addition, a firm which comes forward once an investigation has begun can also obtain full immunity if it provides evidence sufficient to establish an infringement where this would otherwise not have been possible. In lesser cases, where the Commission has already started an investigation, fines can be partially reduced if the evidence provides significant 'added value' to the investigation. Specific reductions are laid out: the first firm to come forward can expect a reduction in fine of between 30 and 50 per cent, the next firm between 20 and 30 per cent, and subsequent firms up to 20 per cent. In such cases, firms that might have been involved in coercing other firms to join the cartel might also receive leniency.

The EU policy differs from US policy in several significant ways. First, leniency in the EU relates only to corporate fines since individuals are not held liable in EU cartel cases. In this respect, of course, EU policy also differs from current UK policy. Second, EU policy as it currently stands has increased the incentive for firms to come forward in cartel cases, in particular, by allowing possible full immunity to firms that might have been the leaders or instigators of a cartel (as long as they have not been coercers). In doing this, the EU has been concerned to avoid difficult decisions over who might have led or instigated a cartel, but at the cost of possibly allowing firms that had been leaders/instigators to receive no penalty at all. This approach, which is the same in the UK, contrasts with US policy where immunity is only open to firms who did not lead or instigate the cartel and who had not coerced other firms to join.[84] This is compounded in both the EU and UK as reductions in fines of up to 50 per cent are available to firms who may have coerced other firms to join the cartel. These provisions might appear too lenient on such firms but the Commission (and to some extent the OFT) has taken the view that it is better to remove the cartels than to place too much emphasis on apportioning blame. Finally, the EU has a more transparent approach to policy than the US, setting out the levels of leniency when full immunity is not applicable, and this may give stronger incentives for firms to come forward. In the US (and UK), no specific reductions in fines are laid out for second and further firms who provide information.

The development of leniency policies has had a major impact on the effectiveness of cartel policies. In the US, the introduction of the revised leniency policy in 1993 led to a substantial increase in the number of applications for leniency from about one per year prior to 1993 to about one per month in more recent years. In the period 1998-2002, for example, total fines imposed in cartel cases came to more than $1.5 billion, which is considerably higher than accumulated fines in earlier periods (OECD, 2003).

Leniency policy has also had a major impact in the EU. For example, in the period 1986-2000, there were nine decisions in cartel and concerted practice cases under Article 81 involving total fines of 999 million euros.[85] In 2001 (the first year in which the new policy fully took effect), there were ten decisions involving 56 companies who were fined a total of 1.8 billion euros; in 2002, a further nine decisions were reached involving total fines of 950 million euros; in 2003, five cases with total fines of 404 million euros and in 2004, another six decisions involving 30 companies were taken with total fines of 390 million euros. These figures indicate the importance of the leniency programme in obtaining information, even though in some cases firms escape penalties which they might otherwise have paid (assuming that prosecution was possible at all). The Commission has been willing to waive these fines in the broader interest of removing significant cartels involved in trade between Member States.

As noted earlier, the UK introduced its own leniency programme in 2000 and has modified it more recently.[86] Evidence of the operation of this policy is, therefore, more limited in the UK. In the period to the end of 2005, however, there were nine decisions in which penalties were imposed and leniency played a role in all but one of these.[87] These cases include *Hasbro, Argos and Littlewoods* (2003), *Replica Football Kit* (2003) and *Flat Roofing in the West Midlands* (2004) mentioned earlier in this chapter. Since many of the cases were quite small, however, total fines involved were a relatively modest £40.9 million.

Leniency programmes have been adopted by a substantial number of other EU Member States, besides the UK. By September 2005, 18 Member States had adopted a leniency programme and their terms, although similar, are not identical.[88] This means that there is no common leniency programme for all ECN members and firms seeking leniency under different regimes have to apply to different authorities in different countries. This lack of harmonization of the sanctions and leniency rules applied by NCAs under the Modernization Regulation has been criticised, although it essentially leaves the previous position unchanged in this respect.

Although NCAs would not necessarily have applied Article 81 rules before May 2004, cartel members then, as now, ran the risk of sanctions in Member States affected under national law if not then under the European competition rules. However the provisions for the exchange of information by ECN members were a new potential source of concern for firms when the Modernization Regulation was being introduced; they feared that self-incriminating evidence about cartel activity offered in a leniency application to one authority might trigger an investigation by another authority or be used elsewhere as evidence to impose sanctions.

The Commission Notice on Cooperation within the ECN addresses these concerns about the exchange of information between competition authorities resulting from a leniency application[89] and the Commission Notice on

Cooperation between the Commission and the national courts deals with further concerns about information supplied to the Commission being used in national courts.[90] Satisfactory arrangements in these respects are important in ensuring that whistle blowers are not put off coming forward so preventing the leniency programme being undermined. It remains to be seen whether these safeguards will prove sufficient. Firms still have a potentially tricky decision about where to make their leniency application/s taking into account, among other things, which of the authorities that have jurisdiction over the case is most likely to deal with it under the new case allocation policy.

FUTURE DEVELOPMENTS

It is clear that there have been important steps forward in this area in recent years with the abolition of the notification system at EU level to allow the competition authorities to focus on enforcement, some decentralisation of EU power and sharing of the responsibility for enforcement with Member States to bring consistency in the application of the rules (although the Commission still retains widespread discretion, notably in case allocation), and the enhanced powers gained especially by UK authorities, as well as the development of the leniency programmes in both regimes.

The question remains as to whether the policy is having a significant effect when looked at against the total amount of cartel activity in existence or whether it is still dealing with a minority of cases. This question is difficult to answer although recent cases have given some indication of how extensive and sustained cartel activity can be. It is also clear from the experience of the US, UK and EU regimes that more cartels are caught when tougher penalties (in conjunction with clear and transparent leniency programmes) are introduced. This suggests that there may be a need to strengthen policy still further in the EU and UK. This and other possible developments are considered next.

In deciding whether to engage in cartel activity, a rational firm will weigh up the likely gains from that policy and the probability of being caught against the penalties that may be imposed.[91] This is clearly recognised in current policy in the EU and UK. However, while the maximum penalty available in cartel cases is 10 per cent of the world-wide turnover of the firms involved and there has been a trend towards increasing fines in the EU recently (with very substantial fines in some high profile cases such as *Vitamins* and *Plasterboard* as noted earlier), actual penalties are often lower, especially under the leniency programme, which weakens the disincentive effect.[92]

Should sanctions be stronger? In the US, stronger sanctions exist in addition to fines: first, in that cartel activities are a criminal offence and individuals can be fined and/or imprisoned in cartel cases, and, second, because private parties can sue for damages. The rationale for criminalising the offence is that individuals knowingly engage in cartel activities; while shareholders may bear the brunt of fines imposed on firms, nothing can indemnify individuals against the possibility of time in prison. This is clearly the rationale for the adoption of this policy in the UK (and some other EU states).[93] The EU currently does not have the power to introduce criminal procedures and so will have to continue to rely for the time being on civil enforcement by way of financial penalties on firms (McGowan, 2005). However, it seems likely that over time the 'constitutional' difficulties will be removed allowing criminal sanctions to be introduced at EU level and this should significantly increase the deterrent effect of EU cartel policy.

In addition to criminal liability, US policy also provides for private parties to sue for damages in cartel cases. Whilst actions for damages have become a real possibility following the *Courage v. Crehan* (2001) case in the EU, no damages have so far been awarded at EU level. This is actively being considered by the European Commission which has recently published a Green Paper on the issue.[94] In addition, measures have been taken in the UK under both the Competition and Enterprise Acts to make it simpler to take private civil action in cartel cases.[95] At present, however, there are no provisions for punitive damages in either jurisdiction compared to the treble damages available in the US.

Turning to the question of leniency, slightly different approaches have been introduced in the EU and the UK as discussed above. The main differences are that EU policy provides more detail on the reduction in fines for second and later firms who come forward, while in the UK a 'leniency plus' policy has been introduced as in the US. Clearly, these differences are relatively minor although it would seem reasonable also to include 'leniency plus' in EU policy. Equally, there are probably positive gains to being more specific about leniency provisions for second and later firms. The UK and EU policy of allowing firms who had been leaders or instigators in a cartel to claim immunity, so avoiding problems of apportioning blame, is clearly more contentious. US policy, which does not allow leniency for such firms, may be thought to provide a better balance.

If claims for damages become an important feature in cartel cases in the EU and UK, incentives for firms to come forward will be reduced. In this case, it will be necessary for firms also to consider the effects of private actions in deciding whether to provide evidence. It may, therefore, be appropriate to increase the fines that are levied in cartel cases to offset this effect. This issue has been dealt with in the US by allowing firms who come forward first the benefit of only being sued for single damages by private parties but this option is not available in the EU or UK.

Recent changes in the law have given important additional powers to the Commission and the OFT in cartel cases. The new Modernization Regulation which came into force on 1 May 2004 increases the Commission's powers of investigation to include interviewing individuals during inspections of premises, sealing premises to protect information during an inspection, and increased powers to enter and search private homes (this latter on the authority of a judge).[96] Given the possibility that information might disappear overnight or that documents could be kept at home, these changes provide useful extra powers to conduct cartel investigations. As discussed earlier, the UK also has strong powers to investigate cases under the Competition and Enterprise Acts which have significantly strengthened its hand in dealing with hard core cartels.

It is also important to consider the effect of policy developments from the perspective of the firms involved. One significant issue is the question of due process – whether firms' rights are protected given the disproportion between government agencies and the firms involved.[97] While this is primarily a legal question, it seems reasonable to conclude that firms are, in fact, protected by the checks and balances available in current policy.[98] One example is the explicit codes of conduct used in gathering evidence in cartel cases in the UK and EU. More broadly, however, both the Commission and the OFT have developed procedures for dealing with cartel cases designed to ensure that decisions reached are not overturned on appeal. These policies mean that the Commission and OFT will be fairly scrupulous in their treatment of firms under the rules, and this provides a useful safeguard in cartel investigations although appeal cases take a long time to be heard.

On a separate point, the introduction and strengthening of cartel policy in many countries has led to an increase in the compliance costs of firms,[99] especially for firms engaged in cross-border activities. In addition, within the EU, firms which have engaged in cartel conduct face additional costs in the need to make separate leniency filings in cartel cases at EU level and in individual Member States. While the ECN allocates cases to Member States (or the Commission itself) which are seen as most appropriate in dealing with a particular case under Article 81, there is still a need to deal with investigations and apply for leniency within individual Member States. Since conditions for leniency and procedures for obtaining leniency differ between Member States (at least to some degree), this creates a further burden on the firms involved. The problem is recognised by the Commission which believes that greater harmonization would be desirable[100] and this is now under active consideration.[101]

International cartels have been attracting increased attention and the evidence in EU cases, such as the *Vitamins* case, shows that it is possible to deal successfully with international or global cartels within the framework of EU competition policy. A key reason for this has undoubtedly been the leniency programme which has been a major factor in encouraging firms to provide evidence in cartel cases. In addition, however, a number of high profile cases [102] have shown the benefits of international cooperation to fight cartels, in particular with the US. As international cartels may often be the most harmful, it is clearly desirable to target such cases and to use evidence brought to light in foreign prosecutions to deal with EU and UK cases. This is likely to be an important part of future EU and UK strategy, as it has been in the EU in the recent past.

Whilst publicly available evidence in the US and elsewhere is useful in dealing with international cartels, a wider question concerns evidence which is available in the files of foreign authorities but is not in the public domain. In respect of this, it is clearly desirable to have greater cooperation between national competition authorities to exchange information in cartel cases. This has been recognised in a number of bilateral agreements between the EU and the US, Canada and Japan to exchange information, although there are nevertheless significant limitations imposed by confidentiality. On a multilateral basis, information is currently exchanged in the International Competition Network, of which the EC Commission and the OFT are founder members.[103] Also the OECD Competition Committee Working Party 3 recently adopted a paper on 'recommended practices for the formal exchange of information between competition authorities in hard core cartel investigations.'[104] It seems likely that these developments will continue to be pursued and be an important part of future policy in this area.

The economic literature suggests that cartels are more likely to form when certain market conditions prevail.[105] These include, but are not limited to, factors such as firm numbers, market concentration and the homogeneity of products, which appear to be correlated with cartel activity (Grout and Sonderegger, 2005). In addition, certain sectors of the economy seem to be more prone to cartel activity than others and this may be because the factors recognised as conducive to such behaviour are more prevalent in those sectors. This has led the OFT and the Commission to develop strategies to identify sectors in the economy in which cartel activity may be a particular problem as part of their increasingly more proactive role. In the EU, Article 17 of the Modernization Regulation reinforces the Commission's powers to investigate sectors of the economy (or types of agreement) where problems appear to exist and the Commission has announced that it intends to use these powers widely.[106] It proposes, in particular, to examine markets where there are 'only a few players, where cartel activity is recurrent or where abuses of market power are generic'.[107] In the UK, the OFT has also identified a number of sectors which may give rise to competition concerns.[108]

CONCLUSIONS

This chapter has shown there has been significant progress in recent years in dealing with cartel activity and concerted practices in both the UK and EU. This has been particularly marked in the UK where a relatively weak policy with no real penalties under the 1976 Restrictive Trade Practices Act has been replaced by a stronger policy closely based on Article 81 of the EC Treaty. In addition, the UK has introduced criminal penalties in hard core cartel cases (in the Enterprise Act 2002), unlike the EU but in line with policy in the US. At least equally important has been the introduction of leniency policies at both the UK and EU levels which have led to significant increases in the number of cases dealt with by the OFT and particularly by the European Commission.

The Commission reached 66 cartel decisions between 1969 and February 2003, with relatively few decisions in the 1970s and only about three per year between 1980 and the mid-1990s.[109] Nearly a half of all decisions (29) were taken between 1999 and February 2003 (roughly seven a year), with 19 cases in 2001-02. In these 19 cases, fines totalling three billion euro have been imposed on the firms involved. In addition, in 2004, the Commission received 49 applications for leniency in 25 different cases while in the ten months following the introduction of the Modernization Regulation, 11 decisions were reached, of which seven were made by the Commission and five by NCAs.[110] These figures show there has been a major increase in the number of cases in which formal decisions were reached under the new EU provisions compared to the record under earlier policy.

Although these developments are welcome, it is difficult to assess how effective the new policies have been in detecting hard core cartels and concerted practices. Given that the introduction of leniency policies in the UK and EU have led to the discovery of significant numbers of restrictive agreements, the question arises whether additional restrictive agreements or concerted practices may continue to exist undetected. Although it is unrealistic to expect such behaviour ever to be completely eradicated, we have argued that there is a case for strengthening policy further by increasing penalties for firms and individuals involved in restrictive agreements or concerted practices and/or in developing pro-active strategies to uncover such behaviour. In particular, there may be a case for introducing criminal penalties for individuals engaged in hard core cartel activities at EU level when possible, in line with policy in the US and UK, as well as in some other European countries. Further incentives for firms to come forward in such cases are continuing to be considered.[111]

The competition authorities in the UK and EU have powers to investigate specific industries or sectors of the economy where problems seem likely to exist. Recent attention on agreements in the professions, for example, which may exist for non-economic reasons but have the effect of significantly restricting competition, is a move in this direction. More extensive use of these powers should be helpful in highlighting and dealing with agreements which harm competition.

Policy towards restrictive practices in other Member States, besides the UK, has also moved closer to the EU model. In particular, the EU rules have been adopted by the ten newest Member States as part of accession negotiations as well as voluntarily by Italy and the Netherlands, which previously had no history of competition policy. This has allowed greater decentralisation of policy under Modernization and greater consistency of approach within the EU is to be expected in future, although the relationship between the national authorities and Commission under the new arrangements is still evolving. Finally, further effort to increase international cooperation between competition authorities is an additional way in which policy towards horizontal agreements and restrictive practices might be usefully developed.

NOTES

1. We are grateful to Philipp Girardet for his comments on this chapter.
2. Under Article 81(1) of the EC Treaty and section 2(1) of the Competition Act 1998 respectively.
3. Concerted practices may involve no agreement at all but simply imply contact between firms and/or exchange of information designed to support parallel behaviour to prevent competition in the market.
4. These policies offer leniency (or full immunity) to firms that come forward first in a cartel case and operate in a similar way to a prisoners' dilemma game. Thus each firm knows that it will get a reduced fine or may escape a fine altogether if it comes forward first; if they all hold out they get no fine; if they all cooperate they get a reduced fine (which is higher than if they come forward first), and they pay the full fine if one of the other firms comes forward first. Under appropriate assumptions about the penalties, the dominant strategy is to come forward first, to escape or reduce the fine, and this forms the basis of the policy. In practice, leniency (or full immunity) may be granted to the firm that comes forward first in a case recently started, or not yet started, and fines may be reduced for firms that cooperate with an investigation once it is underway, giving incentives for them to provide further useful information. In some cases, additional incentives may be given for firms involved in one cartel to 'blow the whistle' on other cartels it belongs to and other measures, such as immunity from criminal prosecution for individuals, may be used.
5. The Resale Prices Act is of interest here only in that it prohibited collective resale price maintenance.
6. This Act, in turn, was based primarily on the 1956 Restrictive Trade Practices Act.
7. In the earlier legislation of the 1956 Act (see previous note) 2550 agreements were registered under the Act in its first ten years of operation but 83 per cent of these had been terminated or varied to take them outside the scope of the Act. The main reason for this was the relatively hard line taken by the RPC in its early cases (see Clarke, 1985, p. 243).
8. While, in some cases, there is evidence that the Act led to greater competition, there is also evidence that firms continued to operate similar policies following de-registration (see Swann et al., 1974 and O'Brien et al., 1979).
9. The Court had upheld only 12 agreements by 1978.
10. Under the policy, firms could be fined for contempt of court for continuing to operate an agreement once it had been struck down by the Court. In principle, private parties could also

sue for damages arising from the illegal operation of a cartel or restrictive agreement although this appears never to have happened, probably due to the high cost involved and the risk that such action might fail.

11. Note that these examples are identical to those given in Article 81(1) of the EC Treaty.
12. The OFT's view has been that this would only apply as far as relevant principles are concerned and would, therefore, exclude decisions at EU level which aim, in particular, to promote the single European market (Office of Fair Trading, The Competition Act 1998: the major provisions, OFT Guidance, 1999, p. 9). It appears, in practice, however, that this distinction has not played a significant role in decisions by the OFT in cartel cases.
13. Council Regulation (EC) No 1/2003 of 16 December 2002 on the implementation of the rules laid down in Articles 81 and 82 of the Treaty, OJ L1, 4 January 2003. The regulation replaced Council Regulation (EEC) No. 17/1962 of 6 February 1962, first regulation implementing Articles 85 and 86 (now 81 and 82) of the Treaty, OJ 13, 12 February 1962.
14. See Commission Notice on agreements of minor importance, OJ C368, 22 December 2001 and Office of Fair Trading, The Competition Act 1998: the major provisions, op cit., pp. 5-7.
15. For non-horizontal (primarily vertical) agreements the test is that a firm has less than a 15 per cent market share in a relevant market. In both cases, the figure is reduced to 5 per cent if a network of agreements is found to operate in a market.
16. See Office of Fair Trading, Agreements and concerted practices, OFT Guidance, 2004, pp. 32-3.
17. Office of Fair Trading, The Chapter I prohibition, OFT 401, March 1999, p. 11.
18. The only difference is that two words ('of goods') have been deleted in the second line following the word 'distribution'. This allowed the exemption to apply also to services (see OFT, Agreements and concerted practices, op cit., pp. 24-5).
19. See Office of Fair Trading, Agreements and concerted practices, op cit., passim. As noted earlier, UK restrictive trade practices policy prior to the 1998 Act related primarily to written agreements. Concerted practices in so far as they were covered by the law were, however, dealt with under the complex monopoly provisions of the 1973 Fair Trading Act.
20. See Office of Fair Trading, Leniency in cartel cases, OFT guideline, 2001.
21. See Office of Fair Trading, Leniency in cartel cases, OFT guideline, 2005.
22. See Office of Fair Trading, The cartel offence, OFT guidance, 2003, p. 3.
23. These powers were introduced under the Regulation of Investigatory Powers Act of 2000 in orders laid before Parliament in 2003. See Office of Fair Trading, Covert surveillance in cartel investigations, OFT 738, August 2004 and Office of Fair Trading, Covert human intelligence sources in cartel investigations, OFT 739, August 2004.
24. See Office of Fair Trading, The cartel offence, op cit., pp. 5-8.
25. This includes vertical investigations. However, for most of this period non-price vertical restraints were subject to a block exemption and so most of these cases concerned horizontal issues.
26. The Competition Act was amended as of 1 May 2004 to allow the OFT to accept binding commitments in Chapter I cases. The case, *TV Eye* (2005), was the first in which the OFT accepted commitments under the Chapter I prohibition.
27. *Agreements between Hasbro, Argos and Littlewoods fixing the price of Hasbro toys and games*, CA98/8/2003, Decision of 21 November 2003 replacing an earlier decision CA98/2/2003 of 19 February 2003. This case should be distinguished from the earlier *Hasbro* case CA98/18/2002 of 28 November 2002 involving Hasbro and ten independent distributors which however came to similar conclusions to the present case.
28. The agreements in this case were vertical agreements between Hasbro and each of its distributors, as in the replica football kit case noted below. However, taken as a whole, they represented overall restrictive agreements and/or concerted practices to fix prices in the market, as clearly recognised by the OFT. Hence their effect was horizontal and amounted to price-fixing in this market.
29. The infringement itself, however, only covered the period after 1 March 2001 when the Competition Act came into force.
30. *Price fixing of replica football kit*, CA98/06/2003, Decision of 1 August 2003.

31. As in the *Hasbro, Argos and Littlewoods* case, these agreements were vertical but, in total, represented restrictive agreements and/or concerted practices to fix prices. In this case, on appeal, it was also found that the Chairman of JJB and the chief executive of Allsports (two of the leading retailers) had personally agreed to fix the price of the Manchester United football shirt launched in the summer of 2000.

32. *Collusive tendering for flat roofing in the West Midlands*, CA98/1/2004, Decision of 17 March 2004.

33. *Collusive tendering for mastic asphalt flat roofing contracts in Scotland*, CA98/01/2005, Decision of 15 March 2005 and *Collusive tendering for felt and single ply flat roofing contracts in the north east of England*, CA98/02/2005, Decision of 16 March 2005.

34. See OFT press release, 23 February 2006.

35. *Investigation of the multilateral exchange fees provided for in the UK domestic rules of Mastercard UK Members Forum Ltd*, CA98/05/05, Decision of 6 September 2005.

36. A similar investigation involving Visa is currently underway: see OFT press release, 19 October 2005.

37. Council Regulation (EEC) No 17/62 of 6 February 1962, op cit.

38. Commission Notice on guidelines on the applicability of Article 81 to horizontal cooperation agreements covering R&D, production, marketing, purchasing, standardization, and environmental agreements (replacing two previous Commission Notices), OJ C3, 6 January 2001.

39. Commission Regulation (EC) No 2659/2000 of 29 November 2000 on the application of Article 81(3) EU to categories of R&D agreements, OJ L304, 5 December 2000 (replacing Regulation (EEC) No 417/85); and Commission Regulation (EC) No 2658/2000 of 29 November 2000 on the application of Article 81(3) to categories of specialization agreements, OJ L304, 5 December 2000 (replacing Regulation (EEC) No 417/85).

40. RAPID press release, 'Commission reforms competition rules for cooperation between companies', IP/00/1376, 29 November 2000 provides a good summary of these changes.

41. Commission Communication, Guidelines on the application of Article 81(3) of the Treaty, OJ C101, 27 April 2004.

42. See A. Saarela, and P. Malric-Smith, 'Reorganisation of cartel work in DG Competition', *Competition Policy Newsletter*, Summer 2005, p. 43.

43. Commission Guidelines on the methods of setting fines imposed, OJ C9, 14 January 1998.

44. Case T-220/00, *Cheil Jedang Corp. v. Commission*; Case T-223/00, *Kyowa Hakko Kogyo Co. Ltd. and GmbH v. Commission*; Case T-224/00 *Acher Daniels Midland Co. and Ltd. v Commission*, and Case T-230/00 *Daesang Cor. and Sewon Europe GmbH v. Commission*, Judgements of 9 July 2003.

45. See, for example, Case T-31/99, *ABB Asea Brown Boveri v. Commission* (2002) ECR II-1881.

46. Case T-77/92, *Parker Pen v. Commission* (1994) ECR II-549.

47. *PO/Electrical and mechanical carbon and graphite products*, COMP/38.359, Decision of 3 December 2003.

48. At present what is held to be the first European criminal trial carrying the possibility of a jail sentence for price-fixing is taking place in Ireland (under Irish law) in the home heating oil industry (see Irish Examiner, 28 February 2006).

49. Two recent cases were brought in the UK but these were settled out of court (see note 50).

50. There have recently been two follow-on civil damages cases arising from the Commission's *Vitamins* decision (see below) before the UK CAT although unfortunately for precedent setting these were settled out of court. See *(1)BCL Old Co Ltd, (2)DFL Old Co Ltd, (3)PFF Old Co Ltd v (1)Aventis SA, (2)Rhodia Ltd, (3)Hoffman-La Roche AG, (4)Roche Products*, CAT Case 1028/5/7/04, registered on 26 February 2004.

51. Council Regulation (EC) No. 1/2003 (the 'Modernization Regulation'), op cit.

52. Comfort letters are informal letters sent out by the Commission indicating that it does not propose to take any action under Article 81(1).

53. See Commission Notice on cooperation within the Network of Competition Authorities', OJ C101, 27 April 2004. The ECN has set up several working groups to coordinate enforcement activities across the EU, one of which is looking at bringing about further harmonization in the area of leniency programmes.

54. *Vitamins*, COMP/37.512, Decision of 21 November 2002. See OJ L6, 10 November 2003.
55. *PO/Plasterboard*, COMP/37.152, Decision of 27 November 2002. See OJ L162, 10 January 2003.
56. One of the firms, Gyproc Benelux (Belgium), only joined the cartel in 1996. See RAPID Press Release, 'Commission imposes heavy fines on four companies involved in plasterboard cartel', Brussels, 27 November 2002.
57. *PO/Organic Peroxides*, COMP/37.857, Decision of 10 December 2003. This case is of interest not for its size (the market involved was fairly small) but for the length of time the cartel operated without being discovered..
58. Not all the firms were members for the entire period. For example, Peroxidos Organicos (Spain) joined in 1975 and Laporte (UK) (later Degussa) joined in 1992. See RAPID Press Release, 'Commission fines members of organic peroxides cartel', Brussels, 10 December 2003.
59. Atofina was involved in the *Peroxygen* (1984) case, the *Polypropylene* (1986) case, the *LdPE* (1988) case and the *PVC* (1994) case. Laporte and Peroxid Chemie were involved in the *Peroxygen* (1984) case.
60. *Cement*, COMP 138.401, Decision of 30 November 1994.
61. *Cimenteries CBR v. Commission* (2000) ECR II-491, 5 CMLR 2004.
62. *Aalborg Portland A/S v. Commission*, Judgement of 7 January 2004.
63. See Scherer and Ross (1990, Chapter 9).
64. Case 48-68, *ICI and Others v. Commission*, Judgement of 14 July 1972, ECR, 619.
65. In fact several Italian companies refused to implement the price increases in January 1965 so that prices in Italy did not rise in line with other prices in the EU (see Goyder, 2003, p. 72).
66. Note, in this case, that the ECJ ruled that pre-publishing (when aimed at increasing prices) was sufficient to show contact between firms. This, it argued, was in line with the intention of the Treaty to capture coordinated behaviour which falls short of an actual agreement between firms.
67. *Wood Pulp*, Case IV/29.725, Decision of 19 December 1984, OJ L85, 26 March 1985. See also joined cases C-89/85, C-104/85, C 114/85, C-116/85, C-117/85 and C-125/85 – C-129/85, *Åhlström and Others v. Commission* (1993) 1-ECR, 1307, 188, 211-7.
68. *Polypropylene*, 38 CMLR 739-765.
69. Further cases involved *PVC* and *LDPE*: see the discussion in Goyder (2003, p. 146).
70. The ECJ, like the CFI, also accepted the Commission's finding that agreements and concerted practices constituted a single infringement as both seek to catch the same types of collusion.
71. Communication of the Commission of 9 February 2004, Report on competition in professional services, COM(2004) 83 final .
72. See F. Amato, B. Collins, S. De Waele and R. Paserman, 'Professional services: more competition, more competitiveness, more consumer orientation', *Competition Policy Newsletter*, Summer 2004, pp. 71-4.
73. *CNSD*, Case IV/33.407, Decision of 30 June 1993, OJ L203, 13 August 1993.
74. *Orde van Architecten*, COMP 38.549, Decision of 24 June 2004.
75. 'Progress by Member States in reviewing and eliminating restrictions to competition in the area of professional services', Commission Staff Working Document, Com(2005) 405 final, Brussels, 5 September 2005.
76. For details of US policy see OECD (2002, 2003) and Motta (2004). The main weaknesses of earlier policy arose because full immunity was discretionary, creating uncertainty for the firms involved, and because leniency was given to firms but not to individuals. In addition, penalties in cartel cases were relatively light in the 1970s and 1980s, although they had become much stronger by 1993 (see OECD, 2003, pp. 20-1).
77. Under the 1978 policy, leniency was only available where the DoJ had no prior knowledge of the existence of a cartel and had not initiated an investigation.
78. US policy also imposes certain requirements on firms who come forward in cartel cases (see the Department of Justice Guideline, Corporate leniency policy, available at http://www.usdoj .gov/atr/). For example, firms must cooperate fully with an investigation and must desist from taking active part in the cartel from the time they come forward. Immunity is not available to

firms who have coerced other firms to join the cartel or who are/were the leaders or instigators of the cartel.

79. See note 4.
80. In the Antitrust Criminal Penalty Enhancement and Reform Act 2004, see Scott Hammond, 'An overview of recent developments in the Antitrust Division's criminal enforcement program', paper presented to the American Bar Association Midwinter Leadership Meeting, 10th January 2005, available at http://www.usdoj.gov/atr/public/speeches/207226.htm. Other reforms in 2004 include increasing the maximum fine on corporations to $100 million, the maximum individual fine to $1 million and the maximum term of imprisonment to 10 years.
81. Commission Notice on the non-imposition of fines in cartel cases, OJ C207, 18 July 1996.
82. In the case of a 10 to 50 per cent reduction in fine, only cooperation was required and not the other conditions.
83. Commission Notice on immunity from fines and reduction of fines in cartel cases, OJ C45, 19 February 2002.
84. The US DoJ has, however, taken the view that when firms are regarded as equal co-conspirators or there is more than one leader, any firm can apply for leniency – see Gary R. Sprattling, 'Making companies an offer they shouldn't refuse', speech given at the 35th Annual Symposium on Associations and Antitrust, Washington DC, 16 February 1999. It does this to increase as far as possible the number of firms eligible to become whistleblowers.
85. Source: http://europa.eu.int/comm/competition/citizen/cartel_stats.html and press releases.
86. See Office of Fair Trading, Leniency in cartel cases, op cit., 2005. See also Office of Fair Trading, Guidance as to the appropriate amount of a penalty, December 2004 and Office of Fair Trading, Leniency and no-action: OFT's interim note on the handling of applications, OFT 803, July 2005.
87. The cases were: *Arriva/First Group* (2002), *John Bruce* (2002), *Hasbro* (2002), *Hasbro, Argos and Littlewoods* (2003), *Replica football kit* (2003), *Flat roofing in the W. Midlands* (2004), *UOP* (2004), *Flat roofing in the N.E. England* (2005) and *Flat roofing in Scotland* (2005). There was no leniency given in the *John Bruce* case. In addition, evidence of an infringement was found in two further cases (*N. Ireland livestock* (2003) and *Lladro Commercial* (2003)) but due to special factors, no fines were imposed.
88. A list of NCAs with leniency programmes is published on the Commission's competition website, see http://europa.eu.int/comm/competition/antitrust/legislation/authorities_with _leniency_programme.pdf.
89. Commission Notice on cooperation within the Network of Competition Authorities, op cit.
90. Commission Notice on cooperation between the Commission and the Courts of the EU Member States in the application of Articles 81 and 82 EC, OJ C101, 27 April 2004.
91. Standard papers on cartels are Green and Porter (1984) and Abreu, Pearce and Stachetti (1986). A useful survey of the literature is given in Jacquemin and Slade (1989).
92. See Philip Lowe, 'What's the future of cartel enforcement', speech delivered at the Understanding Global Cartel Enforcement Conference, Brussels, 11 February 2003.
93. There has been a move towards the introduction of criminal liability and fines and imprisonment in a number of EU countries in recent years. Cases where imprisonment is an option include France, Germany, Luxembourg and Ireland, in addition to the UK (see Shearman and Sterling, 'Cartel policy – Europe catches up', at htpp://www.shearman.com.
94. European Commission, Green Paper on damages actions for breach of the EC antitrust rules, COM(2005) 672 final, 19 December 2005. See also Neelie Kroes, 'Taking competition seriously – antitrust reform in Europe', speech given at the Antitrust Reform in Europe: a Year in Practice Conference, Brussels, 10 March 2005.
95. Under these changes it is now possible for private parties to bring class actions against cartels ('a group litigation order') on a no win, no fee basis. These cases will be heard by the Competition Appeal Tribunal or in the ordinary courts.
96. The power to conduct interviews is designed to counter the tendency for employees to be evasive when asked questions during inspections. The ability to seal premises was often used on the authority of national agencies rather than the Commission's own powers: see Philip Lowe, 'What's the future of cartel enforcement', speech given to the Understanding Global Cartel Enforcement Conference, Brussels, 11 February 2003.

97. See the comments of Philip Lowe, 'Chairman's closing remarks', speech given at the Antitrust Reform in Europe: a Year in Practice Conference, Brussels, 10 March 2005.
98. Firms involved in cartel investigations may, however, have a different view on this.
99. Compliance costs have also increased with the adoption of the legal exception regime at the EU level.
100. See the comments of Neelie Kroes, 'Taking competition seriously – antitrust reform in Europe' and Philip Lowe, 'Chairman's closing remarks', speeches given at the Antitrust Reform in Europe: a Year in Practice Conference, Brussels, 10 March 2005.
101. As noted in note 53, an ECN leniency working group (currently co-chaired by the UK and France) is actively considering harmonization proposals to create greater convergence in this field.
102. Including the *Lysine* (2003), *Sodium Gluconate* (2002), *Graphite Electrodes* (2002) and *Vitamins* (2001) cases.
103. See Philip Lowe, 'What's the future of cartel enforcement', speech given to the Understanding Global Cartel Enforcement Conference, Brussels, 11 February 2003.
104. OECD Competition Committee, Working Party 3 (2005), 'Best practices for the formal exchange of information between competition authorities in hard core cartel investigations.'
105. See, for example, Werden (2004) and Ivaldi, Jullien, Seabright and Tirole (2003).
106. European Commission, A pro-active competition policy for a competitive Europe, COM(2004) 293 final, 20 April 2004. Note that the power to conduct inquiries into a particular sector was provided for in Regulation 17 but was rarely used.
107. European Commission, A pro-active competition policy for a competitive Europe, ibid., p. 16. It also provides a longer list of relevant factors which include the degree of concentration, price trends not connected to cost or demand changes, irregular price differences, lack of innovation and lack of entry.
108. OFT, Annual Plan: 2005-6, available at www.oft.gov.uk. Not all of these sectors involve infringements of Chapter I and/or Article 81 although in some cases (such as the construction industry and public procurement) specific cartel concerns may arise.
109. See Philip Lowe, 'What's the future of cartel enforcement', speech given to the Understanding Global Cartel Enforcement Conference, Brussels, 11 February 2003, pp. 2-3.
110. Neelie Kroes, 'Taking competition seriously – antitrust reform in Europe', speech given at the Antitrust Reform in Europe: a Year in Practice Conference, Brussels, 10 March 2005.
111. At time of going to press, the Commission has put forward an amendment of the 2002 leniency notice to provide more certainty in relation to private remedies for firms confessing to their participation in a cartel.

6. EU and UK Vertical Restraints Policy Reform

Paul W. Dobson

INTRODUCTION[1]

The appropriate policy treatment for vertical restraints has long been a contentious subject. Vertical restraints are essentially restrictions on the freedom of behaviour for one or more undertakings resulting from a vertical agreement between trading parties. The central problem is that while vertical restraints may serve to prevent, restrict and/or distort competition, they may equally offer efficiency improvements (for example, through reduced costs or improved quality), and thus the net economic effect is *a priori* ambiguous in most cases where market power is or might be an issue.[2]

Purely as an illustration, consider so-called 'exclusive dealing', whereby a distributor agrees to take its supplies from a single supplier and in the process prevents other suppliers from using this distributor. On the one hand, this arrangement may restrict or even prevent competition if access to the market (including final consumers) is difficult to achieve for these other suppliers. On the other hand, having an exclusive relationship may encourage the supplier to make (relationship-specific) investments in the arrangement (for example, to improve distributor service quality), secure in the knowledge that other suppliers will not be able to free ride on this investment. The former aspect may be viewed as anti-competitive while the latter may be seen as pro-competitive, and if both effects are present the net outcome is not immediately obvious. The same problem arises with most other examples of vertical restraints.

Clearly, where the anti-competitive effects of a restraint outweigh any efficiency benefits, then social welfare[3] would be improved by the restraint being prohibited. Unfortunately, pinning down precisely the conditions where this is the case is far from straightforward and it is not possible to rely solely on the form of restraint as effectively every type can in principle exhibit both anti-competitive and efficiency-enhancing effects, indicating the need for case-by-case analysis.[4] However, economics has contributed some important insights into the effects of these practices and EU and UK policymakers have sought to draw on these insights in developing a new, essentially common, policy approach towards vertical restraints.

Indeed, the last few years have witnessed a fundamental reform of competition policy towards vertical restraints in both the EU and the UK. In 2000, the European Commission adopted a new general block exemption regulation, replacing the existing industry-specific (for example, covering beer and petrol) or context-specific (for example, covering franchising) exemption regulations.[5] At the same time, the European Commission issued very detailed guidelines on the proposed enforcement of policy, explaining the 'effects-based' approach underlying the new regime, with its emphasis on (economic effects-based) self-assessment rather than (form-based) notification (as was previously the case).

Meanwhile, in the UK, the passing of the Competition Act 1998 has moved the UK closer to the EU position on competition policy. Yet, for an interim period, following full implementation of the Competition Act, the UK adopted a 'Vertical Agreement Exclusion Order'. This excluded non-price vertical restraints from the Chapter I provisions of the Act. However, from 1 May 2005, this has been rescinded and instead the UK has fallen directly in line with the EU approach on vertical restraints.

As this chapter highlights, the reform in EU policy in particular, and in UK policy to a lesser extent, marks a fundamental shift in approach with a much greater emphasis on the economic effects of restraints rather than their contractual form. The change in policy has important implications for trading relations, particularly for firms with large market shares and perhaps industries that have previously received special treatment. This chapter reviews the changes in policy, appraises the economic arguments put forward by the EU and UK authorities in their vertical restraints guidelines, and discusses the likely effects on business of these changes.

EXAMPLES OF VERTICAL RESTRAINTS

It is not an exaggeration to suggest that most ongoing trading relationships involve one or more vertical restraints. For simple, one-off, arms-length transactions, it is quite possible that the terms and conditions of trade may be no more than a simple contract specifying the price, quantity, and timing/nature of exchange/provision of the traded goods/services. However, with ongoing or repeated exchanges, it is usual for contracts to have additional terms and conditions, in part to encourage compliance with the terms of the contract, as well as to counter potential opportunistic behaviour (that is, to ensure parties keep within the intention or spirit of the contract). For example, there might be incentive and/or penalty clauses or detailed specification of behavioural requirements in order to avoid potential moral hazard problems, where one party's behaviour is not fully observable by the other party (that is, where monitoring becomes problematic).

In many instances, contracts may make extensive use of terms and conditions that collectively amount to several vertical restraints simultaneously applying. Moreover, not all the terms and conditions will necessarily be about ensuring compliance and overcoming potential problems in the supply or use of the traded goods or services. Some, whether intentionally or inadvertently, may affect the behaviour of one or both trading parties in a manner that adversely affects the economic outcomes of the markets they respectively operate in. However, this is only likely to arise where market power is an issue and where vertical restraints serve to magnify or exacerbate competition problems. It is with regard to tackling these instances, and distinguishing them from the vast bulk of cases where restraints do not harm competition, that competition policy towards vertical restraints policy has now been directed.

To provide an idea of the range of possible restraints, as well as indicate the scope of this topic, it might be useful to begin by highlighting some of the possible types of vertical restraints that might be employed by trading parties. The following list is far from exhaustive but provides ten commonly cited types:

- *non-linear pricing*: such as a volume-related discount or a two-part tariff (with a lump-sum fee plus a constant per-unit charge as paid by a franchisee to the franchiser)
- *rebate schemes*: where a retailer is offered discounts depending on quantity sold or purchased (for example, a progressive rebate) or on the number/range of products stocked (that is, an aggregated rebate)
- *service requirements*: where the retailer is required to provide a specified level of pre- or post-sales service or promotional effort in support of the manufacturer's product
- *resale price maintenance*: where the supplier specifies the resale price of the product at a fixed or minimum level, thereby preventing the retailer undercutting this level (in contrast to the setting of maximum prices or recommended resale prices)
- *selective distribution*: where a manufacturer supplies only a limited number of dealers that are then restricted in their ability to re-sell products (for example, they may not be allowed to sell on to unauthorised distributors)
- *exclusive distribution*: a particular form of selective distribution where the manufacturer supplies only one distributor or retailer in a particular territory or allows only one distributor/retailer to supply a particular class of customer (for example, businesses or consumers)
- *exclusive purchasing or dealing*: where the retailer agrees to purchase, or deal in, goods from only one manufacturer

- *tie-in sales and bundling*: where the manufacturer makes the purchase of one product (the tying product) conditional on the purchase of a second product (the tied product) (where a set of tied products is commonly referred to as a bundle of products)
- *full-line forcing*: an extreme form of tie-in sale where, in order to obtain one product in the retailer's range, the retailer must stock all the products in that range
- *quantity forcing/fixing*: where the retailer is required to purchase a minimum or an exact quantity of a certain product or a substantial percentage of its annual requirements.

Note that in all ten of these examples, the restraint is applied to the receiving (so-called 'downstream') party – that is, the distributor, retailer or franchisee – as determined by the providing or supplying (so-called 'upstream') party – that is, the supplier, manufacturer or franchiser.[6] In many of the above examples, the restraints are likely to arise by mutual agreement – for example, the retailer agrees to the manufacturer's restraint as long as there is some reward, such as financial compensation for exclusive dealing or conferred monopoly privileges coming with exclusive distribution. However, in other cases, the restraint may be effectively imposed when one party has sufficient market power over another trading party – for example, an imposition of full-line forcing as a take-it-or-leave-it trading offer.

Yet, beyond the examples given above there may be other restraints that arise from neither contractual agreement nor contractual imposition on another trading party as they affect trade in other ways. A good example is 'selective distribution' which may well arise through agreement between a manufacturer and selected retailers but affects those retailers outside the selective distribution system who are deliberately refused supplies. In other words, there is a dual combination of restraints – selective distribution for 'inside' retailers and refusal to supply to 'outside' retailers. Nevertheless, for the sake of clarity, this chapter will take vertical restraints simply as contractual-based restrictions, unless otherwise stated.[7]

The above examples are also in keeping with the emphasis by policymakers and competition authorities on restraints placed on downstream parties by upstream parties. This does not necessarily have to involve a producer supplying a distributor – as the above examples all indicated. It could instead involve a producer (of, say, components or raw materials) supplying another producer (for example, an assembler of components or user of raw materials). Equally, it could involve a distributor, like a wholesaler, supplying another distributor, like a retailer. More generally, vertical restraints can, in principle, occur at any stage of the supply/distribution process for a product or service. Moreover, vertical restraints can work in both directions. Just as a producer might seek to impose restrictions on a retailer's behaviour, a retailer might seek to impose restrictions on its suppliers. For example, the retailer might impose on the supplier an obligation for exclusive supply or a requirement to use a third-party supplier nominated by the retailer (for example, for packaging or transport), or deliberately shift risk (for example, through enforced sale-or-return or by delaying payments).[8]

With these examples and background in mind, we move on next to examine the respective changes to EU and UK vertical restraints policy, prior to considering the guidelines for assessing the economic impact of vertical restraints.

EU POLICY REFORM

The European Commission's 'Green Paper on Vertical Restraints in EU Competition Policy' (published in January 1997), effectively began the vertical restraints reform process in Europe. The Green Paper highlighted the shortfalls in existing EU policy and offered suggested options for change.[9]

The Green Paper came at a time when there had been growing disquiet over policy and a widespread view that implementing some changes in policy direction and/or form might be desirable. At the time, the old Article 85, now Article 81, of the EC Treaty provided the basic policy framework. Article 85(1) prohibited agreements in fairly broad terms, but many, or even most, vertical agreements benefited from either block exemption or individual exemption under Article 85(3). Specific block exemptions existed for exclusive distribution, exclusive purchasing (including special provisions for beer and petrol), motor vehicle distribution arrangements, franchise arrangements, and intellectual property licensing. These exemptions did not permit blanket approval, but rather allowed the practices subject to certain provisions. In addition, the old Article 86, now Article 82, could also be relevant where one firm clearly operated in a dominant position in the industry and imposed restraints (for example, tie-ins or full-line forcing on those it supplied). But, in general, the legislation in the area was, and still is, largely framed in terms of agreements. Thus (service) franchising agreements, for example, were treated for the purposes of the block exemption as a generally benign method of business operation, even though distributors agreed to substantial restrictions in their activities. Even if the restrictions included elements such as tying or full-line forcing, which would in other contexts have attracted opprobrium, these could be treated as acceptable if they were viewed as having been (freely) agreed to.

The Green Paper identified three major shortcomings in this policy approach. Firstly, the then existing Block Exemption Regulations comprised rather strict 'form-based' requirements and as a result were generally considered too legalistic and tended to work as a straitjacket. Secondly, for those agreements that fell within the old block exemptions there was a real risk that the

Commission could have exempted agreements that distorted competition (due to them being *form*-based rather than *effects*-based). Thirdly, as the old block exemptions only covered vertical agreements concerning the resale of final goods and not intermediate goods or services, a significant proportion of all vertical agreements were not covered by the then existing block exemptions, even when the parties involved had no market power.

Following a consultation period, the European Commission issued a Communication setting out the EU's preferred course of action to remedy these three shortcomings and protect competition better.[10] The approach advocated was to consider vertical agreements in their market context. A central tenet was that restraints do not pose problems unless inter-brand competition (that is, rivalry between producers) is weak and market power exists. In the absence of market power, the advocated approach was to facilitate a relaxation of the form-based requirements, ensuring that fewer agreements were covered by the old Article 85(1) (now Article 81(1)). For those companies with substantial market power, however, the approach would ensure closer scrutiny, that is, concentrate attention and resources on cases where anti-competitive effects were most likely to arise.

Subsequent to the Communication and the setting out of the Commission's economic thinking, two key regulations were amended in April 1999 that paved the way for the implementation of new policy rules as formalised by Commission Regulation (EC) No. 2790/1999 of 22 December 1999 on the application of Article 81(3) of the Treaty to categories of vertical agreements and concerted practices, the so-called EU Block Exemption Regulation.[11]

This new regulation dispensed with the old form-based block exemptions and instead gave rise to a single broad-umbrella block-exemption approach, covering all vertical restraints for the distribution of all goods and services. This uses a market share threshold test to distinguish between agreements that are or are not block exempted, taking essentially a blacklisting approach, that is, defining what is not block exempted as opposed to defining what is exempted. In this way, it is argued, it avoids the straitjacket effect and facilitates the simplification of the applicable rules.

The core element of the new EU policy approach is thus for one, very wide, Block Exemption Regulation ('BER') that covers all vertical restraints concerning intermediate and final goods and services except for a limited number of hard core restraints. As a base premise, the Commission's line is that in the absence of market power, a presumption of legality for vertical restraints can be made with the exception of what it terms 'hard core restrictions', but that when market power exists no such favourable presumption can be made. The level of market power (as measured by market share) required for vertical restraints to produce negative effects is below the level normally required to meet the dominance test under Article 82 which, following case law, is usually taken to be a market share exceeding 40 per cent (although the ability to act independently of competitors, customers and suppliers is the more refined test). Rather the critical threshold the Commission has settled on is a 30 per cent market share. Below this level (other than for the hard core restrictions) it is assumed that the practices have no significant net negative effects (at least, when operating in isolation and not part of parallel networks). Above the threshold there is no presumption of illegality. Instead, the threshold is intended to serve as a means of distinguishing the agreements that are presumed to be legal from those which may require individual examination. The latter must be assessed to determine whether they are caught by Article 81 and, if so, whether each of four exemption criteria are met.[12] In principle, this is a question of 'self-assessment' although the Commission may provide assistance and, in appropriate cases, it may issue a 'guidance letter'.[13]

With the critical firm-level market share threshold set relatively high at 30 per cent, the intention was that the vast majority of vertical agreements where no net negative effect could be expected would no longer require individual scrutiny, thereby leaving competition authorities to concentrate on perceived important cases.

In the case of hard core restraints, however, the view taken is that, irrespective of the market shares held by the trading parties, these should not be exempted.[14] Here, the prohibited hard core ('blacklisted') restraints identified by the Commission are:

1. resale price maintenance (except maximum or recommended resale prices provided that these do not amount to fixed or minimum resale prices)
2. restrictions concerning the territory into which, or the customers to whom, the buyer may sell (other than for certain trade used in exclusive or selective distribution)
3. restrictions on active or passive selling[15] to end-users by authorised retail distributors in a selective distribution system (as long as the distributor sells only from a given location)
4. restrictions on authorised distributors in a selective distribution system selling or purchasing from other members of the network (that is, relating to cross-supplies amongst distributors)
5. restrictions on the sale of components as spare parts by the manufacturer of the component to end-users, independent repairers and service providers (that is, relating to after-market sales).

For each of these cases it is argued that the anti-competitive effects are likely to be high and the efficiency benefits relatively weak (or at least not significantly greater than could be attained from using other arrangements).

In respect of the five hard core restrictions, we can note that the first of these relates to vertical price fixing, something that is *per se* prohibited in most developed countries on the basis that it completely bars intra-brand price competition (that is, competition between distributors/retailers selling supplier brands) and can facilitate supplier collusion (that is, weaken inter-brand competition by making it more straightforward to identify and move towards 'focal prices' and assist in monitoring collusion through increased price transparency). Thus resale price maintenance has the effect of potentially preventing both intra-brand and inter-brand competition.

The other four restrictions, though, relate to various aspects of selective and exclusive distribution, but again where there are restrictions on intra-brand competition. However, rather than a concern about diminished inter-brand competition (which could only be expected to arise indirectly, say from the deliberate separation of downstream markets), the prime concern with these four restraints appears to be that they can lead to segmented markets (particularly for consumers) and increased scope for price discrimination – something very much at odds with the EU's policy desire for integrated markets (preferably Community-wide) and an absence of barriers to trade across territories within the EU. In other words, while there may be competition concerns, there appears also to be a strong political motive behind the special treatment afforded these four restrictions – certainly compared to the much more benign view taken towards other non-price vertical restraints.

In addition to the prohibited hard core restrictions, there are some rules governing the use of other restraints. For example, exemption does not apply to any non-compete obligation, like exclusive dealing or tying, if its duration is indefinite or exceeds five years. Furthermore, the Commission may withdraw the benefit of the Block Exemption when cumulative effects are observed as applying widely to a sector (that is, where there is a network of similar agreements or concerted practices).

A central element to this new effects-based approach was also to view different forms of vertical agreements having similar effects in a similar way – as reviewed later in this chapter. Specifically, the new policy is intended to prevent unjustified differentiation between forms or sectors and avoid a policy bias in the choice companies make concerning their formats of distribution (that is, similar policy treatment for similar effects so avoiding the problem of 'form shopping', that is, choosing the form of agreement that creates the least competition concerns).

To go with the new Block Exemption regulation, the European Commission issued Guidelines on Vertical Restraints (hereafter the Guidelines) detailing the Commission's enforcement policy.[16] The Guidelines set out the general rules to be adopted when evaluating the effects of vertical restraints, the relevant factors for the assessment of Article 81(1) and Article 81(3), and analysis of specific vertical restraints with examples. The Guidelines also provide insights on policy towards individual exemption above the market share threshold and possible withdrawal of the Block Exemption below the threshold (for example, where blacklisted practices are used or where cumulative effects from parallel networks are a concern).[17]

UK POLICY REFORM

The UK has taken its lead from the EU in this area of competition policy.[18] Where previously the legal position was complicated by different elements of vertical restraints falling under different Acts and associated procedures, the Competition Act 1998 paved the way for simplification and alignment with the EU approach.

In the old regime, the need to register vertical agreements was governed by the Restrictive Trade Practices Act 1976. Here, registration was dependent on the form of the agreement. Some forms were exempted while others were not, thus opening up the prospect of firms adopting 'form shopping' to avoid the need to register agreements. For example, Schedule 3 to the Act exempted some exclusive dealing arrangements. Moreover, whereas multipartite agreements regarding exclusivity might typically have required registration, an equivalent set of bipartite agreements (for example, covering exclusive territories) might not have, even though the economic effect may have been the same.[19]

In contrast to the case-by-case treatment generally afforded to most vertical restraints, resale price maintenance has for a long time been treated more harshly in the UK. The Resale Prices Act 1976 made the imposition of vertical resale price maintenance illegal in most cases. Subsequent to the passing of the Act, all outstanding instances of fixed or minimum RPM were made illegal through successful challenges by the authorities in the Restrictive Practices Court. The Office of Fair Trading was finally able to remove the last two vestiges of RPM, for books and non-prescription medicaments, respectively in 1998 and 2001.[20]

For all other vertical restraints, including exclusive purchasing, selective and exclusive distribution, franchise arrangements, tie-in sales, and full-line forcing, the legal framework used to be driven primarily by the Fair Trading Act 1973 and the Competition Act 1980. However, these Acts did not proscribe activities. Rather, they simply provided for investigation in appropriate cases. Thus, for example, the anti-competitive provisions of the Competition Act 1980 enabled the Office of Fair Trading to investigate particular practices and produce a report which may have then led to a Monopolies and Mergers Commission (subsequently, Competition Commission) reference. However, of greater significance were the monopoly investigations that could be initiated under the Fair Trading Act. In the 1990s, in particular, a number of highly significant industries, often involving particular exclusivity arrangements, were subjected to such investigations. In several notable cases, no action was taken.[21] However, in some cases, structural remedies (for example, the enforced divestitures in the beer industry) or behavioural remedies (for example, applying to carbonated drinks, new motor cars, national newspapers, and films) were applied.[22]

These industry investigations effectively reflected the policy approach towards (non-price) vertical restraints, but such a piecemeal approach naturally raised concerns about consistency in treatment both across industries and over time. Indeed, a good example relates to the successive inquiries into the ice cream market by the Monopolies and Mergers Commission in 1979, 1994, 1998 and 2000 concerning freezer exclusivity, that is, manufacturers that supplied freezers requiring shops to stock them exclusively with their own ice creams.[23] In 1979 and 1994, it was concluded that freezer exclusivity did not restrict competition. Yet, in 1998 and 2000, and with little change in the market circumstances, it was concluded that the practice did restrict competition.[24]

The key reform towards a more integrated policy approach in the UK emanated from the Competition Act 1998, with the intention of bringing the UK into line with EU competition policy. Specifically, the prohibitions contained in Article 81 of the EC Treaty and section 2 of the Competition Act 1998 (the so-called Chapter I prohibition) prohibit agreements between undertakings which have as their object or effect the prevention, restriction or distortion of competition, while Article 82 of the EC Treaty and section 18 of the Act (the Chapter II prohibition) prohibit conduct by one or more undertakings that amounts to an abuse of a dominant position.

In regard to vertical restraints, the Competition Act 1998 signalled the intention to shift the UK policy position away from a reliance on *ex post* redress (to block any abuse of market power arising or exacerbated by vertical restraints) to the EU's *ex ante* approach where vertical agreements should not be exempted from the general prohibition of anti-competitive agreements when one or more parties has significant market power.[25]

However, the move to the *ex ante* approach was not immediate. At the time, the changes to EU vertical restraints policy were still to be resolved and the prevailing view in the UK was that vertical agreements which did not include a restraint on prices would not usually have an appreciable adverse effect on competition. Instead of adopting the *ex ante* approach applicable to other agreements (notably horizontal ones), the *ex post* redress approach towards vertical restraints was essentially retained under the Competition Act 1998 (Land and Vertical Agreements) Order 2000, the so-called 'UK Exclusion Order'.[26] The UK Exclusion Order, made under section 50 of the Act, excluded non-price fixing vertical agreements from the application of the Chapter I prohibition.

The Exclusion Order did not mean that all non-price fixing vertical agreements could operate without restriction. First, the UK Exclusion Order offered protection from the Chapter I provision but did not preclude the application of EU Article 81 where there was an effect on trade between Member States.[27] Second, agreements giving rise to an abuse of a dominant position could be challenged under Chapter II of the Competition Act 1998.

To an extent, the UK Exclusion Order covered similar agreements to the EU Block Exemption, given its intention to follow closely the treatment of vertical agreements in the European Community. Nevertheless, there were two fundamental differences:

- The UK Exclusion Order was not subject to a market share threshold test – although, like the Block Exemption, the OFT could withdraw the benefit of the exclusion in certain cases and where one party is dominant it did not preclude the application of Article 82 and/or the Chapter II prohibition.
- The UK Exclusion Order had only one 'hard core' restriction, which related to vertical price fixing (that is, fixed or minimum resale price maintenance). An agreement that included a price fixing restriction could not benefit from the exclusion.

From EU case law, however, challenge under Article 82 or the Chapter II prohibition would seem unlikely if each party had less than (about) a 40 per cent market share of its respective economic market, though, in the past, the UK authorities have seen a 25 per cent market share as a critical level (viewing this level as a 'scale monopoly' threshold). Accordingly, if EU case law were followed on market share thresholds for 'economic dominance', this would suggest that about a 40 per cent level has been the relevant UK threshold while the Exclusion Order had been in operation, compared to the 30 per cent market share level adopted by the EU.

In contrast to the one 'hard core' restriction, the EU approach, as explained earlier in this chapter, has four other 'hard core' restrictions relating to restrictions on re-sales, after-market sales, cross-territory sales and cross-supplies in a selective distribution system. These hard core restrictions distinguish the EU from other systems of competition policy as they reflect the fact that one of the historical goals of EU competition policy was and still is the creation of the single European market, with no national barriers to trade.

Thus there are significant differences between these two approaches, giving rise to the prospect that particular agreements could be (or, at least, could have been) treated very differently under these two regimes.

This has now changed, however, in that the UK has aligned itself fully with the EU position. This change in stance follows the EU's adoption of the 'Modernization Regulation' (Regulation 1/2003) in December 2002 'decentralising' the enforcement of Article 81 to national competition authorities and courts as from 1 May 2004. This regulation prompted the UK government to reconsider the way that vertical agreements are dealt with in UK law. After a period of consultation, the government announced the decision in January 2004 to repeal the Exclusion Order and apply the EU Block Exemption Regulation for all vertical agreements whether they affect interstate trade or only trade within the UK.[28] Formally, the Exclusion Order has been repealed with effect from 1 May 2005.[29]

This change will potentially have a considerable impact on those parties either caught by the difference in implied market share thresholds (down from a dominance threshold usually taken at around 40 per cent to the Block Exemption threshold of 30 per cent) or where one or more of the EU's other four hard core restrictions are used.[30] An example of just such an industry caught in this manner is the supply and distribution of national newspapers and consumer magazines. Here, there are parties with slightly over 30 per cent (but less than 40 per cent) market share.[31] The products are also distributed through an exclusive territory system that operates with a prohibition on cross-territory passive sales – amounting to a hard core restriction under the EU interpretation, but a practice that has been approved (due to its considerable efficiency benefits) by UK competition authorities in the past (notably by the Monopolies and Mergers Commission (1993)[32]). It remains to be seen what, if any, support the UK authorities will be willing and able to offer this industry in order for this distribution system to be maintained.

On a more general level, the repealing of the Exclusion Order opens up the question of whether it is always appropriate for practices operating at the national level to be treated the same as Community-wide practices. Certainly, not all members of the European Union share this view – for example, the French and German authorities have allowed instances of RPM to continue. Yet, by falling completely in line with EU policy, it would appear that UK policymakers do not see the need to distinguish between national and community objectives, where the latter embrace not only the desire for effective competition but also for pan-European market integration or at least prevention of market segmentation. However, from a competition perspective, it is far from clear that the latter aspect is always supportive of the former. For example, it is conceivable that instances of deliberate market segmentation serve to enhance effective competition – exclusive territories for wholesaling newspapers and magazines being a prime example – while at the EU level, separation of national markets on this basis would be seen as anathema, regardless of the economic merits or otherwise. In particular, a concern must be that the move by the UK to repeal the Exclusion Order and blacklist additional restraints, that is, beyond RPM, may mean that the UK is embracing an EU perspective which is not solely about economic effects, but in part politically motivated by the desire for integrating markets within the European Union.[33]

ECONOMIC ASSESSMENT OF VERTICAL RESTRAINTS

In order to consider more fully the merits or otherwise of the policy reforms outlined above, particularly the EU effects-based approach and the guidelines offered, it appears appropriate to start by considering in more detail the economic role played by vertical restraints and their effects on the economic performance of markets.[34]

As observed earlier in this chapter, vertical restraints can, in principle, occur at any stage of the supply/distribution process for a product or service. They are essentially agreements between trading parties that restrict the actions or place an obligation on the behaviour of one or both of them in some way. For example, this could be the seller obliging the buyer not to trade with any rival supplier (that is, exclusive dealing), the seller agreeing to exclude sales to some or all other buyers (that is, respectively, selective or exclusive distribution), or the supplier dictating the buyer's resale price (resale price maintenance – RPM). The purpose of such restraints is to tackle distribution and/or supply problems that in some way damage the joint profits of the parties (even though they may favour one party over another) – for example, problems arising from sub-optimal investment, effort or sales, excessive transaction costs, or excessive competition. Moreover, given the multiplicity of distribution/supply problems that can arise, vertical restraints can occur on their own or in combination with others, apply to one trading relationship, several relationships, or be generally applicable in a market (that is, where they are operated in parallel by different parties).

The view traditionally held in the economic analysis of vertical restraints is that they are motivated by the desire for vertical control within a principal-agent relationship, where the principal (for example, a manufacturer) imposes contractual obligations on its agent (for example, a retailer) when delegating responsibility for selling its good.[35] In this framework, vertical restraints are viewed as responses to supply and distribution problems facing the principal. The problems stem from a divergence of the parties' interests, typically over the level and type of retail service. The notion is then that the principal uses vertical restraints in order to bring the agent's interests into line with its own interests.

The key problems for which a manufacturer as a 'principal' may wish to control are summarised in Table 6.1. These fall into two groups. Firstly, problems may arise for a manufacturer, independently of concerns about competition with other manufacturers, from retailers taking actions designed to maximise their own profits, but which act against the manufacturer's interest, that is, concerns about intra-brand competition. These are represented by the first four problems in the table. Secondly, problems may stem from the actions of rival manufacturers that have an adverse impact on the firm's profits, that is, concerns about inter-brand competition. In this case, a firm may wish to use particular vertical arrangements to deal with the other two problems listed in the table; that is, concerning competition at the same level as the firm.

As shown by Table 6.1, it is apparent that different restraints may serve the same basic purpose though, in practice, they may vary in their effectiveness,

Table 6.1 Vertical restraints as responses to supply and distribution problems

	Problems in supply and distribution	Contractual solutions
1.	Successive (manufacturer then retailer) mark ups which result in prices being set higher than the optimal level (attained by setting a single mark up)	Two-part tariffs Quantity requirements Retail price ceilings
2.	Damaging price competition between retailers which may dissuade retailers from stocking the firm's products	Resale price maintenance Exclusive distribution
3.	Free riding by retail price discounters on the pre-sales services and/or reputation of full price dealers leading to under-investment by retailers	Service requirements Resale price maintenance Exclusive distribution Selective distribution
4.	Providing the optimal number and density of dealers and capturing economies of scale in distribution	Resale price maintenance Selective distribution
5.	Free riding by rival manufacturers on a product's image, advertising, and customer drawing power or on investment in dealers leading to under-investment by manufacturers	Exclusive dealing Fidelity rebates/discounts
6.	Profit damaging price competition between rival manufacturers offering similar (that is, substitutable) products	Exclusive dealing Tie-in sales Exclusive distribution

Source: Adapted from Dobson and Waterson (1996).

which along with legal and practical considerations is likely to determine the firm's choice. For instance, with a form-based policy, where a particular restraint is prohibited, for example, minimum resale price maintenance (RPM), then a problem, say dealer free-riding, could be tackled by implementing an alternative restraint. Accordingly, with this policy framework firms may be tempted to adopt 'form shopping', that is, use permissible restraints which have the same economic effects as prohibited restraints. On the other hand, it might be argued that such a policy approach may be preferable where the prohibited restraint has potentially multiple anti-competitive effects.

From the perspective of tackling distribution and supply problems, vertical restraints are imposed in order to increase the firm's profits. However, the problem for the policy maker is that the net economic effect of a restraint on society (that is, taking account of the interests of the consumers and the firms operating in the market or sector) is not immediately obvious. For while vertical restraints may benefit society when they increase efficiency, say by allowing for improved investment decisions, reduced costs, and improved product/service quality, they may equally have a detrimental effect by restricting and distorting competition.

More specifically, an anti-competitive effect can arise through a restraint serving one or more of the following:

1. raising barriers to entry or expansion (that is, a so-called 'foreclosure effect'),
2. reducing the intensity of competition between existing firms (either for one particular brand with reduced intra-brand competition or between different brands with reduced inter-brand competition), or
3. facilitating collusion (including tacit collusion through conscious parallel behaviour).

Accordingly, each case needs to be examined on its merits and the market circumstances and other features will be particularly important in determining which effect (pro- or anti-competitive) is likely to dominate. Here, economics has contributed some important insights into the effects of these practices, on which the EU and UK competition authorities have sought to draw in developing new guidelines.

The Guidelines on Vertical Restraints, issued by the European Commission in 2000, for instance, consider the negative and positive welfare effects of vertical restraints in turn. In regard to possible negative effects,[36] vertical agreements are divided into four groups: a single branding group, a limited distribution group, a retail price maintenance group and a market partitioning group. It is argued that the division is appropriate since the 'vertical restraints within each group have largely similar negative effects on competition' (Guidelines, point 104).

The *single branding group* comprises non-compete obligations and quantity forcing on the buyer as well as tying. The common element is that the buyer is induced to concentrate his orders for a particular type of good with one supplier. The chief competition effect is through reduced *inter-brand* competition as a consequence of foreclosure of certain suppliers and no in-store competition when retailers sell only one brand.

The *limited distribution group* covers exclusive distribution, exclusive customer allocation, exclusive supply, quantity forcing on the supplier, qualitative and quantitative selective distribution, and after-market sales restrictions. The common element is that the producer is selling only to one or a limited number of buyers.[37] The chief effect on competition is that it leads to foreclosure of certain buyers, which consequently may directly reduce *intra-brand* competition, which in turn may have the effect of reducing in-store *inter-brand* competition, particularly if the restraint is widely practised.

The *resale price maintenance group* covers minimum, fixed, maximum and recommended resale prices. Concern about maximum and recommended resale prices is that they may work as fixed RPM. The competition effects of (fixed) RPM are that *intra-brand* price competition is totally eliminated and the increased transparency on price and responsibility for price changes make horizontal collusion between manufacturers easier, at least in concentrated markets. The absence of intra-brand competition may also have the indirect effect of reducing inter-brand competition.

The *market partitioning group* is made up of exclusive purchasing, territorial resale restrictions, customer resale restrictions, and prohibitions of resale. The common element is that the buyer is restricted in where it either sources or resells a particular good, leading to a reduction in intra-brand competition that may aid the supplier or buyer to partition the market and thus hinder market integration and facilitate price discrimination.

In regard to the positive effects of vertical restraints, the Guidelines note these as arising from a number of sources that can solve a variety of distribution/supply problems giving rise to sub-optimal investment and sales. For example, vertical restraints may (in the absence of strong anti-competitive effects) be justified on the grounds of (1) solving a free-rider problem (causing under-investment), (2) encouraging new investment, (3) facilitating new entry into markets, (4) allowing for a different promotional strategy in different markets, (5) achieving economies of scale in distribution, (6) alleviating capital market imperfections, or (7) allowing for uniformity and quality standardisation.

In evaluating the overall effects of restraints, that is, weighing the negative and positive effects, the Guidelines propose some general rules. Firstly, competition effects can only arise if market power is present, that is, where there is insufficient inter-brand competition. Secondly, it suggests that vertical restraints that reduce inter-brand competition are generally more harmful than restraints that only reduce intra-brand competition.[38] For example, non-compete obligations, by foreclosing other brands, may prevent these brands from reaching the market, but exclusive distribution, which instead forecloses certain buyers, does not in general prevent the good from reaching the final consumer. A further general rule claimed is that exclusive agreements are generally worse for competition than non-exclusive agreements as the degree of foreclosure is likely to be higher. Also, negative effects are likely to be compounded when the practice is common within a sector. Moreover, vertical restraints at the intermediate level are likely to be less harmful than restraints affecting the distribution of final, especially branded, goods and services.

Concerning differentiation of vertical restraints between groups, the view taken in the Guidelines is that RPM and market partitioning are likely to be more restrictive and offer fewer efficiency benefits than the other two groups. In addition, single branding (non-compete obligations) is generally considered to be more restrictive than limited distribution, reflecting the European Commission's view that inter-brand competition is more critical than intra-brand competition.

In terms of assessing the impact of a vertical restraint, the Guidelines propose the following four-step procedure:

1. Define the relevant markets for the supplier and buyer and calculate their respective market shares.
2. Check to see that neither market share exceeds 30 per cent, in which case the vertical agreement is covered by the Block Exemption Regulation, subject to the hard core restrictions and conditions set out in the regulation.
3. When a relevant market share exceeds 30 per cent, assess whether the vertical agreement falls within Article 81(1).
4. If the vertical agreement falls within Article 81(1), examine whether it fulfils the conditions for exemption under Article 81(3).

For a restraint where the 30 per cent market share threshold is met, the procedure effectively calls for a full competition analysis for assessing whether the vertical restraint fulfils the conditions for exemption. For restraints involving a Community dimension (that is, potentially affecting trade between Member States), this analysis is with respect to Article 81(3) of the EC Treaty. For restraints that have no possible impact on trade between Member States, then the UK authorities (specifically, the Office of Fair Trading) would make an assessment with respect to Section 9 of the UK Competition Act.[39] In both cases, given the full alignment of UK policy with that of the EU, the assessment would be with regard to the same four economic tests:[40]

1. *Economic efficiencies*: Does the vertical agreement contribute to improving production or distribution or promoting technical or economic progress (that is, offer efficiency benefits)?
2. *Consumer benefits*: Does it allow consumers a fair share of these benefits (for example, by increasing choice, quality or accessibility and/or lowering prices)?
3. *Absence of any unnecessary restrictions*: Does the arrangement constitute the minimum necessary restriction to yield these benefits?

4. *Continuing effective competition*: Does it operate in a manner that does not eliminate competition in respect of a substantial part of the market?

Only with all four tests satisfied would the restraint meet the conditions for exemption.[41]

The EC's Guidelines offer a range of hypothetical examples covering each group of restraints to illustrate the relevant factors that would be considered in such an analysis.

SOME REMARKS ABOUT THE POLICY REFORMS

In principle, Article 81 provides an appropriate legal framework for a balanced assessment of vertical restraints, recognising the distinction between welfare-reducing and welfare-enhancing effects. Specifically, Article 81(1) restricts the scope of Article 81 to agreements that appreciably restrict or distort competition, while Article 81(3) allows agreements caught by Article 81(1) to be exempted (from the consequences of Article 81(2)) if they provide sufficient efficiency benefits.

While it may be ideal to assess the balance of effects on a case-by-case basis, in practice it may be argued that the sheer number of cases involved means that some simple, formal rules are required for the application of Article 81 to limit what would otherwise be a very resource-intensive activity. The new approach using a market share test is clearly designed to allow for resources to be devoted to those cases where social welfare losses may be most apparent (that is, where anti-competitive effects are likely to significantly outweigh efficiency benefits of restraints).

Unlike the previous policy with its sector-specific rules (for example, exclusive purchasing arrangements for petrol and beer) and special cases (for example, franchising), the new policy is a blanket one, intended not to favour or discriminate against particular sectors and/or particular distribution systems (other than by the thresholds).

The new approach indicates a marked change with the past in terms of moving from a central focus on market behaviour to a more formalistic, mechanistic approach, at least for screening, with rules based on market structure.

Nevertheless, this move can be seen as placing a serious regulatory burden on firms, given that the new approach relies primarily on self-assessment rather than notification.[42] This means that firms (large or small) will need to define markets and assess market shares, which will add considerable legal uncertainty. Given the difficulties inherent in market definition, the potential for divergences of opinion over what constitutes the 'relevant market' (especially in the context of differentiated goods and the interpretation of close or not close substitutes) is considerable. This may lead to a firm having a very low market share under one plausible market definition, but a high market share under an alternative, equally plausible, market definition. Added uncertainty is created by the risk of block exemption removal hinging on the actions of other firms and by the uncertainty over exactly how the European Commission (or OFT for UK cases) will assess the competitive nature of the market (for example, covering market structure, barriers to entry, the degree of integration of the single market and the cumulative impact of parallel networks).

However, it is not just the regulatory burden on firms and the general legal uncertainty that may be entailed in a system reliant on self-assessment that may be costly. There are also economic issues that suggest possible weaknesses and limitations of the new approach and the guidelines offered.

First, an important message from economic theory is that the effects of vertical restraints are entirely dependent upon market conditions and market behaviour. The new policy approach adopts a structural rule, based on market share alone – as a proxy for market power. This may be regarded as a crude way of capturing or releasing vertical agreements from regulation and, notwithstanding the comments in the European Commission's (1997) Communication and subsequent Guidelines (2000), economics has yet to provide clear guidance on what might be appropriate levels of market share for thresholds, or even whether a sufficiently strong relationship exists between market share and the likelihood of anti-competitive effects outweighing efficiency effects to allow for thresholds to be used with any degree of confidence. Thus the 30 per cent market share rule appears to be somewhat of an arbitrary level. Even with high market shares in evidence, it is of course entirely possible that the market may be acting in a competitive manner, particularly if market shares are highly unstable (that is, volatility of market shares needs to be taken into account as well as the absolute levels). Equally, it is conceivable that firms with low market shares may be able to exert market power, where perhaps the vertical restraints may be market-wide and act to strengthen market segmentation and allow firms to avoid intense (for example, head-to-head) competition (that is, the extent of coverage of the restraint in the market may be crucial). Nevertheless, a market-share threshold test does at least offer an important degree of simplification (if not quite certainty) in undertaking self-assessment, and in principle allows competition authorities to direct their resources to focusing on cases where market power is most likely to arise.[43]

Second, while the Guidelines offer perspectives on a good number of vertical restraints, the coverage is far from comprehensive. Specifically, certain restraints are not mentioned in the Guidelines, and it might not be immediately obvious where they fit into the EU's scheme. Perhaps the principal class that is largely ignored concerns non-linear pricing and incentive arrangements, such as two-part tariffs and discount schemes. For example, a manufacturer-induced restraint might be in the form of a distributor paying an up-front lump sum fee (for example, a franchise fee) and a per unit charge. More complicated pricing procedures might be in the form of aggregated rebate schemes, for example, with end-of-year lump sum payments to distributors based on sales' levels and/or for taking the producer's full product range. This topic raises important issues about the difference between vertical restraints that provide formal obligations and those that provide financial inducements. In practice, the economic effects may be the same, even though competition authorities may take a more favourable view of the latter, given that these, in theory, allow for discretion on the subjected party.[44]

Third, a more fundamental issue is that most of the concerns expressed in the Guidelines, and indeed going back to the Green Paper, are, at least by inference, to do with producers placing restraints on distributors. Indeed, this is reflected in the analysis and discussion set out in the Guidelines. This begs some important questions. Are restraints symmetric in effect when buyers rather than sellers induce them? Is buyer power seen as a problem equivalent to seller power in the context of vertical restraints? Unfortunately, the Green Paper was silent on these questions since issues of buying power were explicitly excluded from discussion, and the Guidelines offer little insight here into the Commission's new thinking except for the discussion on exclusive supply obligations, but this relates to a manufacturer (as a buyer) imposing restraints on its component suppliers (Guidelines, point 213). Yet, it is apparent that in practice retailers often employ a variety of restraints on manufacturers, other than the mentioned case of exclusive supply arrangements, for example, the UK Competition Commission's (2000) inquiry into supermarkets[45] identifying 52 different buyer-led practices. In this regard, the European Commission's views on suitable treatment for slotting allowances ('shelf-space fees'), listing fees, retroactive discounts, buyer forced application of most favoured nation (MFN) clauses, and reciprocal dealing, amongst other retailer-induced restraints, would have been a welcome inclusion in the Guidelines.[46]

Fourth, and partly related to the previous point, the emphasis in the Guidelines on the primary importance of protecting inter-brand competition (for example, Guidelines, point 119) is somewhat at variance with the categorisation of hard core practices that are directly concerned with intra-brand competition. In particular, vertical restraints that directly affect inter-brand competition (for example, from the non-compete group) are given a relatively more lenient treatment than the hard core restraints that directly affect intra-brand competition (that is, those from within the resale price maintenance and market partitioning group). Indeed, this perspective is markedly different from the policy approach in the US where tying (as from the non-compete group) has traditionally received harsher treatment than most other restraints, with the notable exception of RPM. Yet, the apparent contradiction within the EU approach is evident in the Guidelines where it is stated that: 'Vertical restraints which reduce inter-brand competition are generally more harmful than vertical restraints that reduce intra-brand competition. For instance, non-compete obligations are likely to have more negative effects than exclusive distribution' (Guidelines, point 119 (2)).

In fact, economic theory does not lend support to either of the Commission's stances. Specifically, protecting intra-brand competition can be just as important as protecting inter-brand competition and the negative effects of restraints that impede inter-brand competition can be just as damaging as those that impede intra-brand competition, and vice versa – for example, Steiner (1991) and Dobson and Waterson (1996). This observation serves to reinforce the view that the hard core treatment of aspects of exclusive and selective distribution, in particular, is really more about the political motivation to see markets integrated within the European Union rather than about the competition and economic welfare effects of these restraints. Indeed, this view is further reinforced by the somewhat arbitrary pigeon-holing of vertical restraints into four different groups when most economists would probably just think of there being two groups: those restraints that directly affect intra-brand competition and those that directly affect inter-brand competition – for example, Motta (2004).[47]

Finally, apart from the form of restraint, whether induced by sellers or buyers and whether affecting inter- or intra-brand competition, another issue that may prove contentious concerns contract duration. Specifically, how long is it appropriate for a restraint to last, both in the sense of present commitments (and their possible renewal) and also their absolute duration? In the case of non-compete obligations on a buyer, a five-year duration limit is applicable (Guidelines, point 58). However, like market share thresholds, this level seems somewhat arbitrary. In practice, each case may be expected to differ as different trade-offs and market conditions may be involved. Specifically, firms should be able to recoup investments made in developing highly specific trading relationships that offer efficiency benefits, but equally they should not be allowed to foreclose a significant part of a market for a considerable amount of time and thereby protect themselves from the rigours of competition. Similarly, there may be less need on efficiency grounds for lengthy contracts when markets are well established. More general guidance on this matter, applicable to each restraint (but notably ones involving exclusivity), in the form of official guidelines, appears warranted as this may be a critical point if firms with high market shares are required to self-assess.

CONCLUSION

Change of any sort in the regulatory environment throws up opportunities and threats for firms. The new policy approach on vertical restraints certainly offers some benefits but it also offers some costs for firms. The same applies for the authorities left to apply and enforce the new approach.

In its fact-finding exercise for the Green Paper, the European Commission found many industry associations calling for wider block exemptions, allowing their members greater freedom in developing vertical arrangements, tailored to their specific needs. This, indeed, is what the new approach delivers – that is, a less restrictive policy compared to the previous form-driven system. This allows firms greater flexibility in how they conduct business and agree terms and conditions with trading parties without necessarily losing the protection of a market-wide block exemption.

However, the cost to firms of the new broad block exemption approach is the regulatory burden associated with self-assessment and the lack of legal certainty (given that there is no guarantee that authorities will not challenge self-assessed agreements). The difficulties associated with self-assessment start with the need to determine market shares, which in turn begs the question of how the market should be appropriately defined. Defining the relevant market requires both an understanding and a broad agreement on the extent of the market in both geographic and product terms. The latter aspect requires determining the appropriate set of (substitute) products constituting a singly defined market, which can prove notoriously difficult and contentious when goods are differentiated in a variety of ways. Also, even if there were full agreement on the market definition and all the relevant individual market shares were below 30 per cent, there would remain the possibility that vertical agreements could be challenged. This could arise when vertical agreements involve elements that were interpreted (perhaps mistakenly) as amounting to 'blacklisted' practices (for example, price ceilings as *de facto* RPM). It could also arise where there are perceived (again, possibly mistakenly) to be network effects, giving rise to concerns about the cumulative impact of restraints commonly practised in a market.

The new approach is not more restrictive than the old regime in every sense. Economics tells us that *all* vertical restraints can have negative and positive competition effects. This applies to the prohibited practices under the new EU regime, just as it does to all the other types of vertical restraints. In practice, firms employ vertical restraints for a variety of motives, generally as responses to supply and distribution problems. To some extent, the control of a particular problem may be facilitated by more than one restraint – leaving firms with a choice between alternatives when policy treats restraints equally. Of course, in practice, there may be particular reasons why one form of restraint is favoured over another; for example, if one offers greater efficiency benefits such as reduced transaction costs. However, the new policy prohibits the use of certain restraints, some of which may not have suitable replacements. For example, it is not immediately evident how the efficiency benefits will be preserved in the distribution of UK newspapers and magazines if the UK authorities do not continue to support adequately the current exclusive territory wholesaling system following the repeal of the UK Exclusion Order.

For some industries, though, releasing firms from the straitjacket of the previous block exemptions may encourage experimentation and yield efficiency benefits, while also possibly stimulating competition. Alternatively, it could, of course, exacerbate any anti-competitive effects, when combinations of restraints are employed, further adversely affecting social welfare. In this regard, it will be interesting to see the developments in the years to come for the petrol, beer and motor vehicle markets.

The major impact of the policy changes, though, can be expected to fall on firms with large market shares. They are now faced with the prospect of a detailed case examination to determine whether they should receive the same benefits of exemption as their smaller rivals. If exemption is seen as crucial to financial success, then they will be under pressure to justify the efficiency benefits of their existing restraints and perhaps make concessions to the authorities on business practices (for example, on closing price differences across different Member States) or alternatively undertake voluntary divestments to ensure that they fall below the critical upper market share threshold (although this seems less likely). Either way, large firms' positions may be compromised, and their business performance may suffer. This may be good for consumers if it is the result of large firms having to end anti-competitive practices. Equally, it may be bad for consumers if it reduces the ability of large firms to take advantage of potential economic efficiencies.

While there remain some shortcomings and unresolved issues in the new policy approach, these need to be put into the context of the considerable benefits offered by the recent changes. In particular, from an EU perspective, the new approach should broadly be seen as a considerable step forward in developing a sensible and reasonable means of treating vertical restraints for public policy purposes. The change for the EU is particularly marked as the emphasis is now firmly on consideration of vertical restraints on grounds of their economic effects on markets, rather than merely their legal form. In this respect, the approach should be seen as a very welcome change that will serve to protect competition and enhance economic efficiency.

Nevertheless, this assessment is qualified in view of the EU approach conflating justifiable competition policy objectives with the political objective of increasing market integration. Even if one accepts the worthiness of the EU's market integration objective, it is questionable whether it should still feature as strongly today in influencing vertical restraints policy, and perhaps other aspects of competition policy, as it has done previously. Despite the recent accessions (and presumably more to come), it might not seem unreasonable to ask whether the market integration aim is or should be a permanent aspect of vertical restraints policy. In particular, will there ever come a time when we can consider the EU market sufficiently integrated so that parties do not have to be constrained in their commercial dealing because of this policy?

For the UK, the last few years has seen a near blanket exclusion of vertical arrangements from UK competition law, essentially with an unused 'claw-back' provision and only prohibition of resale price maintenance. However, the decision to repeal the Exclusion Order brings UK policy fully into line with that of the EU. This move gives greater recognition to the both positive and negative effects of vertical restraints. Noticeably, it corrects a widely held perception that having a largely unqualified exclusion order meant that policy was too skewed towards the view that vertical restraints are benign. Nevertheless, it also means that the UK has implicitly taken on board the EU's market integration objectives and its tough stance against exclusive and selective distribution arrangements even though this might not be so relevant or appropriate at the national level.

NOTES

1. I am very grateful for the comments and suggestions received on this chapter from Roger Clarke, Thomas Heide, Simon Holmes, Michael Hutchings, Mike Walker, and Mike Waterson.
2. Where market power is absent it can usually be assumed that vertical restraints will have no significant detrimental effects on competition. However, competition authorities may still make exceptions and, as discussed in this chapter, they may adopt a tough stance to all vertical price fixing arrangements as well as other arrangements when they are industry-wide, or at least very common, regardless of the industry's structural features (for example, all firms having low market shares).
3. The term 'social welfare' is treated here as synonymous with economic welfare, which is generally taken as a weighted sum of consumer surplus (that is, the amount above the actual price that a consumer would willingly pay, if necessary, to consume the units purchased) and producer surplus (that is, the level of economic profit in the sense of the largest amount that could be subtracted from the supplier's revenue that would still induce the provider to offer the product). In practice, competition authorities may be expected to give greatest if not all weight to consumers' interests (for example, adopt a 'consumer welfare standard' as opposed to a 'total welfare standard' when consumers' and firms' interests might be expected to be in conflict).
4. Specifically, a potential welfare trade-off is typical with most vertical restraints, if to differing degrees and usually depending on the circumstances.
5. The notable exception has been in relation to the block exemption covering the supply and distribution of motor vehicles, which has subsequently been revised (Regulation No. 1400/2002). The motor vehicle Block Exemption Regulation (BER) covers the distribution of motor vehicles and spare parts, as well as servicing agreements. In this context a wide range of vertical restraints are evident, including exclusive dealing, exclusive purchasing, exclusive supply, franchising, and selective distribution. The motor vehicle BER closely follows the approach taken by the general vertical restraints Block Exemption Regulation (Regulation No. 2790/1999); for example, the 30 per cent market share test to benefit from the exemption and prohibition of hard core restrictions. In addition, there is a list of provisions that must be included in the vertical agreements in order to benefit from the exemption. The mandatory stipulations include the right to transfer rights and obligations to another distributor or repairer within the distribution system, the supplier's obligation to provide detailed reasons for terminating an agreement, a minimum termination period of two years on behalf of the supplier, and a provision that the parties may refer contract disputes to an independent third party or arbitrator.
6. Here it is useful to think of the vertical relationship as goods flowing down a river, for example, with an 'upstream' producer supplying goods to a 'downstream' distributor, who in turn re-sells the goods into a 'sea' of consumers.
7. Furthermore, the emphasis in this chapter will mainly be on formal/explicit contractual restrictions, as opposed to informal or implicit restrictions that arise through an 'understanding'

rather than being a contractual obligation. Nevertheless, it needs to be appreciated that the effect on competition may be the same whether it is an explicit or implicit arrangement. An example is (fixed) resale price maintenance (RPM) that might arise in the form of an explicit contract provision or, as an alternative, by a supplier recommending a retail price that the retailer is then obliged to follow in setting its retail price under the threat of being refused supply if it does not do so. In the effects-based approach that the EU and UK have now adopted, it is the resulting impact (on the market) that is critical, not the legal form of the restraint. Thus, for example, where RPM is strictly prohibited (that is, *per se* illegal), the prohibition applies to both explicit fixed-RPM contracts as well as practices that give rise to the same outcome (that is, where the retailer is induced – for example, through a reward or fear of a penalty – to set prices as prescribed by the supplier).

8. See, for example, Competition Commission, 'Supermarkets: A Report on the Supply of Groceries from Multiple Stores in the United Kingdom', Cmnd. 4842, London: TSO, 2000 for details of 52 practices employed by supermarket retailers in the UK in regard to trading with suppliers.

9. See European Commission, Green Paper on Vertical Restraints in EC Competition Policy, 1997, available at www.europa.eu.int/comm/competition/antitrust/96721en_en.pdf. For details on the evolution of the EC's thinking on the subject of vertical restraints and the policy reform process see Peeperkorn (1999), Subiotto and Amato (2001), and Verouden (2003).

10. European Commission, Follow-up to the Green Paper on Vertical Restraints: Communication on the Application of the Community Competition Rules to Vertical Restraints, 1997, available at www.europa.eu.int/comm/competition/antitrust/com1998544_en.pdf.

11. Commission Regulation (EC) No 2790/1999 of 22 December 1999 on the application of Article 81(3) of the Treaty to categories of vertical agreements and concerted practices (the EU Block Exemption Regulation), OJ L336, 29 December 1999.

12. See section below on the economic assessment of vertical restraints.

13. This is provided for in the Commission's Notice on informal guidance relating to novel questions concerning Articles 81 and 82 of the Treaty that arise in individual cases (guidance letter), OJ C101, 27 April 2004.

14. It should be noted that, for the other (that is, non-hard core) vertical restraints, where the parties have a small market share, say less than 15 per cent, the 'de minimis' notice usually applies (see Commission Notice on agreements of minor importance, OJ C368, 22 December 2001).

15. The distinction between 'active' and 'passive' selling is that with active selling a distributor for a producer directly approaches or makes itself directly amenable to customers in another distributor's territory or market segment, whereas with passive selling the distributor merely responds to unsolicited requests for supply.

16. European Commission, Commission Notice – Guidelines on Vertical Restraints, OJ C291, 13.10. 2000, available at europa.eu.int/eur-lex/pri/en/oj/dat/2000/c_291/c_29120001013en 000 10044 .pdf.

17. The Modernization Regulation (EC Regulation 1/2003 of 16 December 2002), on the implementation of the rules on competition laid down in Articles 81 and 82 of the Treaty, OJ L1, 4 January 2003, also has an important bearing since this regulation allows national competition authorities and the courts of Member States to apply and enforce Articles 81 and 82.

18. For more on the antecedents of the recent UK and EU policy shifts, and relations with the US approach, see Kunzlik (2003).

19. See Waterson (1993, p. 42).

20. See Utton (2000a) on the formal ending of RPM on books. Interestingly, while the UK has now managed to prohibit all overt RPM, some Member States still allow certain exceptions – for example, RPM on books in Germany.

21. These included reviews of the Supply of Petrol (1990), New Car Parts (1992), Fine Fragrances (1993), Ice Cream (1994), and Recorded Music (1994). However, with the exception of fine fragrances, these industries have been subject to further OFT reviews and MMC/CC inquiries. For example, the supply of ice cream featured in two further MMC inquiries (1998 and 2000), leading ultimately to behavioural remedies being imposed. See Monopolies and Mergers Commission, 'Birds Eye Walls Ltd – A Report on Courses of Conduct Pursued by Birds Eye Walls Ltd in Connection with the Supply of Wrapped Ice Cream', Cmnd. 3871, London: TSO,

1998 and Monopolies and Mergers Commission, 'The Supply of Impulse Ice Cream', Cmnd. 4510, London: TSO, 2000.
22. See Dobson and Waterson (1996) for some details.
23. See Monopolies and Mergers Commission, 'Ice Cream and Water Ices', Cmnd. 7632, London: HMSO, 1979; Monopolies and Mergers Commission, 'Ice Cream', Cmnd. 2524, London: HMSO, 1994; Monopolies and Mergers Commission, 'Birds Eye Walls Ltd', op cit., 1998 and Monopolies and Mergers Commission, 'The Supply of Impulse Ice Cream', op cit., 2000.
24. See the comments and suggestions by Hutchings (2004).
25. See Glynn and Howe (2003).
26. Competition Act 1998 (Land and Vertical Agreements) Order 2000 (SI 2000 No. 310).
27. The issue whether agreements might affect trade between Member States has an important bearing in regard to exemptions, since agreements exempt under EU law can obtain a parallel Competition Act exemption.
28. The DTI issued a press release on 21 January 2004 announcing the Government's proposal to remove the UK Exclusion Order but with the removal not taking effect until 1 May 2005. For more details on the arguments for the change, see the consultation paper by Department of Trade and Industry (2003).
29. Upon entry into force of the Competition Act 1998 (Land Agreements Exclusion and Revocation Order) (SI 2004 No. 1260).
30. See Office of Fair Trading, 'Vertical agreements: understanding Competition Law', 2004 for further details of the changes and guidelines offered to businesses.
31. Specifically, there is one newspaper publisher, one magazine distributor and one wholesaler with a share of their respective economic markets greater than 30 per cent but less than 40 per cent.
32. See Monopolies and Mergers Commission, 'The Supply of National Newspapers', Cmnd. 2422, London: HMSO, 1993.
33. On this matter, Motta (2004, pp. 32-3) is extremely forthright in his view that the list of hard core practices 'are justified more by the desire to promote identical prices and sales conditions in the EU than by an economic rationale', adding (pp. 377-8) that 'there is no economic justification for a policy that treats restraints in a different way' and that 'an efficient policy towards vertical restraints would grant exemption to all the vertical restraints and mergers of firms which do not have large market power'. In a similar vein, see Bishop and Walker (2002, point 5.50).
34. For more detailed technical accounts on the economics of vertical restraints, see Dobson and Waterson (1996), Irmen (1998), Motta (2004, Chapter 6), Rey (2003), Rey and Tirole (forthcoming) and Secrieru (2004). For a good non-technical introduction to the subject relating theory to policy, see Bishop and Walker (2002, points 5.32-5.44).
35. As examples of this vertical control principal-agent perspective see Mathewson and Winter (1984), Rey and Tirole (1986a,b) and the survey by Katz (1989).
36. In addition to these three anti-competitive effects, the European Commission also explicitly includes in its consideration of 'negative effects on the market' the EU competition law aim of preventing 'the creation of obstacles to market integration, including, above all, limitations on the freedom of consumers to purchase goods or services in any Member State they may choose' (Guidelines, point 103).
37. Note, the term buyer here relates to an 'intermediate' buyer such as a producer who uses the product or a wholesaler, distributor or retailer who sells on the product – that is, not a 'final' buyer like a consumer.
38. However, there is little basis for this distinction from economic theory (for example, Steiner, 1991). The EU's position really relies on the view that the variety and range of goods offered are significantly more economically important than the variety and range of distribution services offered to consumers, when in fact both are likely to take on importance to consumers.
39. Of course, under the Modernization Regulation, the OFT can now also undertake Article 81 and 82 investigations.
40. These four tests are derived directly from Article 81(3).
41. It should be emphasised that a competition authority is not obliged to grant a formal exemption even if these tests are passed. While an exemption might offer the parties a high degree of legal certainty, and thus be much desired by them, the authority may decide to offer only informal

guidance or at most a written opinion, which might at least be expected to carry some weight if the restraint is legally challenged, for example by potential competitors or customers.

42. As of 1 May 2004, the system of clearance for individual agreements under Article 81(3) has been abolished. Instead, agreements, decisions and concerted practices caught by Article 81(1) which satisfy the conditions for exemption under Article 81(3) will not be prohibited, with no prior decision to that effect being required (Article 1(2), Council Regulation 1/2003). Rather, the undertakings, themselves, have to assess whether a vertical agreement within the scope of Article 81(1) may be nonetheless admissible pursuant to Article 81(3).

43. There is clearly a trade-off involved here between making the system as simple, transparent and as least burdensome as possible while trying to make sure that arrangements that allow for or exacerbate market power abuse are prohibited. If the threshold level is set 'too high' then cases where market power is a problem may slip through the net, while if the threshold is 'too low' then too many harmless arrangements will needlessly be caught and not automatically exempted. In statistical parlance, the choice of threshold is about trying to balance Type I errors (false positives) and Type II errors (false negatives), whilst recognising any choice inevitably entails a trade-off between the likelihood of each error type occurring.

44. An example of how the matter has been controversial when it concerns firms with high market shares has been the supply of impulse ice cream in the context of 'freezer exclusivity' as a surrogate for 'outlet exclusivity'. Here, as investigations in the UK, Ireland and Germany have shown, the potential for incentive-based restraints to affect competition detrimentally can be particularly pronounced when operated alongside other restraints (see Hutchings, 2004). However, in isolation, a practice that offers financial inducements, say to retailers to provide a supplier with additional in-store selling space or even to exclude rivals, may be just a manifestation of natural competition, especially when it allows for retailers to pass on lower prices and so long as it does not amount to predatory behaviour and the exclusion of rival suppliers from the market (as opposed to individual outlets). Indeed, in this specific context, the view generally taken is that 'refusal to buy' is not as potentially detrimental as 'refusal to supply'. Yet this view rests on the perception that it is the supplier rather than the buyer (for example, retailer) that is most likely to have market power – which may not in fact be the case; for example, the distortion to supplier markets when powerful supermarket retailers delist suppliers (see Competition Commission, 'Supermarkets', op cit., Clarke et al. (2002), and Dobson (2005)).

45. Competition Commission, 'Supermarkets', op cit.

46. Of course, the same point applies to other situations where buyer power arises in the supply chain, such as a powerful manufacturer imposing restraints on an input supplier.

47. Moreover, the EU's classification of restraints is not always clear-cut. For example, a series of resale restrictions that amount to territorial exclusivity (in the market portioning group) is really just an example of exclusive distribution (in the limited distribution group). Similarly, exclusive purchasing (in the market portioning group) is really just a non-compete obligation (in the single branding group).

7. Competition and Regulated Industries

John Cubbin

INTRODUCTION[1]

Anyone attempting to write about competition policy and the utilities 25 years ago would have been confronted with an 'empty box'[2] but competition policy and the development of the utilities nowadays are very much intertwined within the EU and within the UK, in particular. Indeed, it can plausibly be argued that it was primarily the success of the UK experiment that created a convergence between competition policy and utility regulation in Europe. Another factor in this recent convergence is the reduced dominance of the Franco-German nexus as the EU has grown.

Some elements in Germany, and rather more in France, might be seen as the champions of the 'continental model' in which utilities are core to the performance of the whole economy, and therefore too important to be left to the 'whims' of market forces. Other countries have different traditions. For example, the Scandinavian countries have been in the forefront of market orientation, particularly in the energy sector, and former Warsaw pact countries have shown a strong enthusiasm for the use of markets.

The Anglo-Saxon alternative to the continental model involves the introduction of competition into the utilities, wherever feasible, with regulation being relied on elsewhere. This basic framework implies policies such as privatisation, the vertical unbundling of assets and activities and deregulation of the competitive activities. Furthermore, direct competition in the market may be supplemented or substituted by competition for corporate control (for instance in mergers and acquisitions), competition for the market (franchising), and competition in the input market (contracting out). In principle, competition can be further encouraged by setting non-discriminatory terms of access to the naturally monopolistic network element. Finally, where competition is not feasible, the form of regulation is designed to mimic the market with the continuing downward pressure created by price cap regulation sometimes being regarded as a competition surrogate.

The experience to date suggests that, of all these measures, direct competition in the market facilitated by vertical ownership separation is the most effective. The European framework relies heavily on open access and only limited vertical separation. However, open access may need to be supplemented by structural changes in order to create effectively competitive markets in energy and fixed line telecommunications. As will be seen, the process of liberalisation has been helped along by invoking the competition policy provisions of national and European law, including those relating to the abuse of dominance, anticompetitive practices, merger control and EU policy on state aids. However, such controls have proved insufficient in themselves to guarantee effective competition on a European scale.

While the UK model has been very influential, not least in the development of EU policy, it is, of course, far from the only source of innovation in the regulation and liberalisation of the utilities. Cross border market integration was an important feature in the Scandinavian electricity reforms of the 1990s. Similarly, experiments with different models have been going on in Latin America, Asia, New Zealand and Australia and elsewhere around the world and, of these, only Australia can be said to be following the UK model in broad outline. Nevertheless, the UK is a clear exemplar, at least in energy and to some extent telecommunications, and some interesting lessons can be learned by studying developments in these sectors as well as in less successful areas of UK policy, particularly the railways. UK policies towards the utilities are examined in the next section. A consideration of the EU framework follows this and, finally, some concluding comments are presented in the last section of the chapter.

THE UK MODEL

The UK model, as it has emerged since the 1980s, attempts to introduce competition in the market; for the market; for corporate control; for inputs, and, where competition in the market is not feasible, it introduces a form of regulation which is seen by some as mimicking the behaviour of the markets. This section looks at each of these forms of competition in turn. It starts with corporate control since historically this was the key to unlocking the other forms of competition. It shows the considerable amount of new learning and adaptation that has taken place in the light of experience.

The full version of the 'UK model', in which competition is promoted through all the mechanisms identified above, has really only been successfully applied in the electricity and gas markets; its application to the gas market required British Gas to be broken up. The model has worked quite well in telecommunications, although problems remain because of the continued vertical integration of

British Telecom (BT). Water also remains vertically integrated, with the cost structure being regarded as a hindrance to the effective introduction of competition in water services on a scale similar to that in energy and telecommunications.

Competition for Corporate Control: the Regulated Industries, Privatisation and Mergers Policy

Privatisation in Britain originated with a desire to tackle the stagflation of the 1970s that, in terms of the economic views of the government of the day, led to a preoccupation with reducing the Public Sector Borrowing Requirement (PSBR). This was seen as politically easier to achieve through asset sales[3] than through additional public expenditure cuts (Brittan, 1984). However, supporters of the 1980s privatisation policy regarded it as having useful spin offs in other respects (Jackson and Price, 1994, Chapter 1). One of these was the reduction in the power of the public sector trade unions; another was the possibility that the political preferences of the country could be changed by a move towards wider share ownership. But the fact that the soft budget constraints faced by nationalised industry managers would be replaced by hard budget constraints was also appealing. If public limited companies (plcs) were not efficient they would be taken over, which would sharpen the incentives on senior management.

Table 7.1 shows when the major regulated industries in the UK were privatised. Only postal services (and water in Scotland) remain in the public sector and subject to regulation by the Postal Services Commission (Postcomm) and the Water Industry Commission for Scotland, respectively, in much the same way as the privatised utilities.

Although takeover by another plc in the UK or an entity from overseas is one sanction for perceived inefficiency, this has not been the only fate of financially distressed privatised utilities. Two companies – Network Rail and Glas Cymru (water service in Wales) – have been transformed into 'companies limited by guarantee'. Such a company does not have share capital and cannot distribute its profits to its members, who are guarantors instead of shareholders. The conversion to this corporate form in the case of Network Rail was partly out of recognition that continuing subsidy, which is required for significant parts of the rail network, sits uneasily with the plc model; in the case of Glas, a political element related to the concern for Welsh national feeling was possibly involved.

Questions about the effects of takeovers and mergers in the utilities go beyond the usual concerns of the competition authorities about competition in the market. Some mergers in the electricity supply industry have tended to reverse the vertical separation imposed at privatisation and there has been a good deal of sale and resale of assets – some of it resulting from the Ofgem policy of de-concentrating generation capacity over the period 1996-8. Six integrated companies emerged from this process: Innogy; Powergen; TXU Europe; Scottish Power; Scottish and Southern, and EDF. The generating capacity of most of these six companies is broadly comparable with their level of retail demand and vertical integration through mergers and takeovers might therefore be seen as a risk reduction strategy equivalent to long term contracts.

Table 7.1 Dates of privatisation in the UK

Sector	Date sold	Economic regulator
British Airports Authority	1987	CAA + CC
British Telecom	1984	Oftel=> Ofcom
British Gas	1986	Ofgas=> Ofgem
Water companies	1989	Ofwat
Electricity companies	1990	Offer => Ofgem
Railways	1994	Office of the Rail Regulator Strategic Rail Authority
Postal services	n.a.	Postcomm
Water in Scotland	n.a.	WICS

In the case of the water industry, there has been a concern that mergers will reduce the benefits from Ofwat's use of comparative efficiency assessments in its periodic price setting. The policy of price capping is discussed later on in the chapter, but for now it is important to note that a special regime for mergers between water and sewerage companies was put in place in the 1991 Water Industry Act and was updated by the 2002 Enterprise Act because of this concern. Mergers in the water industry have to be referred to the CC and it must have regard to the principle that the regulator's 'ability to make comparisons between different water companies' should not be prejudiced. This has slowed down the rate of consolidation of the industry, although there are now only 23 companies that can be used for comparative purposes against 32 immediately after privatisation.

Competition in the Market: Vertical Separation and Competition

The UK's experience suggests very strongly that effective competition relies heavily on complete separation of the ownership of the monopolistic network facility from the provision of the retail services rather than simply on making provision for open access. The problem frequently raised by open access is that of finding an objectively justifiable access price sufficiently low to generate significant competition. This may be because of information asymmetry, which benefits the vertically integrated incumbent and disadvantages both potential competitors and the regulator.

The first utilities to be privatised, BT and British Gas, were privatised in 1984 and 1986 respectively with minimal provision for either competition or vertical separation. In BT's case, this amounted to licensing Mercury (a subsidiary of Cable and Wireless) as a second telephone operator. Mercury supplied some core network and final retail services (such as billing and alternative tariff structures), but depended on BT for 'access' – in this case, call origination via BT's local copper wire loop, which connects customers to the local exchange. This decision has taken rather a long time to undo; competition in electronic communications has developed the most in market segments such as mobile telephony or internet service provision which did not exist at the time of privatisation, so the incumbent possessed little in the way of first-mover advantages.

Later decisions to build in competition at the privatisation stage were due to a growing confidence in the government's ability to sell former nationalised industries as well as a response to the behaviour of BT and British Gas in the early years. Both British Gas and BT initially took a rather assertive approach to their independence from direct ministerial control and new commercial freedoms. For example, the early Ofgas price control reviews seemed to be referred to the Monopolies and Mergers Commission (MMC), the predecessor of the CC, almost as a matter of routine.

On privatisation under the 1989 Electricity Act, the CEGB was therefore divided into generation on the one hand and transmission, control and despatch on the other. Generation was split into three. Nuclear Electric remained in the public sector after soundings from the City suggested that issues such as its decommissioning costs would make it unsaleable, and the non-nuclear capacity was divided between PowerGen and National Power. National Grid Co. (NGC) was launched as a private company owned jointly by the Area Authorities. These became the Regional Electricity Companies (RECs), subsequently known as public electricity supply companies (PESs), and currently District Network Operators (DNOs). The latter, as their current name suggests, have at their core the distribution of electricity to final consumers. Some of their activities, namely 'supply' (the buying of electricity from generators and selling it to customers), metering, and provision of connections (for example, to new housing developments) gradually became subject to competition over the following decade. As competition was introduced, the need for price regulation dwindled so there has been regulatory withdrawal in electricity. This has been true of gas as well.

The 1993 Monopolies and Mergers Commission (MMC) report on gas, one of a number of MMC reports on the regulated utilities, is of more than historical interest for both water and electronic communications. This stated that British Gas was

. . . both a seller of gas and owner of the transportation system which its competitors have no alternative but to use. In our view, this dual role gives rise to an inherent conflict of interest which makes it impossible to provide the necessary conditions for self-sustaining competition.[4]

British Gas was eventually induced to lighten its regulatory load by a process of vertical separation, which led to competition in many of the activities parallel to electricity. As a result, only those parts of the value chain that are natural monopolies through the existence of networks – essentially distribution and transmission of energy – are now subject to regulation. The prices for generation and supply are no longer regulated, but are subject to monitoring in terms of the extent of competition and possible market abuse.

Many initially viewed the electricity experiment as an unqualified success. As a result the privatisation of British Rail (which had previously been unthinkable even to the then Prime Minister, Margaret Thatcher, a leading proponent of privatisation), was put on the agenda. There was to be competition everywhere in the privatised rail system: *for* the market (operating franchises); *in* the market ('on-rail competition'); *upstream* (track maintenance and rolling stock leasing), and everywhere else possible. The plans for privatisation of the railways, however, had little regard to the underlying economic issues and it took place without the degree of care in design that went into electricity privatisation and without ensuring that key technical and managerial expertise was retained. The role of competition through franchising in the railways and the evidence about actual performance are taken up in a later section.

Competition in water has been more limited and more difficult in practice, in part because the network elements (control and distribution) form such a large part of the value added compared with resources, treatment and supply. This is arguably even more the case in sewerage and sewage treatment. Nevertheless the Water Act 2003 extends the opportunities for competition within the water supply industry in England and Wales so that customers with an annual consumption of at least 50 mega litres become eligible to switch supplier.[5] The new regime will commence in Autumn 2005.

Telecommunications is the most contentious area as regards the possibility of introducing competition, with BT still holding around 84 per cent of fixed line call revenue.[6] The indirect result is that the introduction of competition in telecommunications leads to a need for more regulation largely because BT remains a competitor to its own customers in a whole series of 'competitive' markets to which it provides supplies, and is in some ways in a similar position to British Gas at the time of the MMC report referred to above. This was a major consideration in the strategic review of the telecoms market undertaken by Ofcom in 2004-5 (see below), which resulted in a significant change in the way in which BT is organised.

The agenda for the introduction of competition is by no means complete and further moves find support among Members of Parliament as well as customers of the liberalised services. For example, the Parliamentary Transport Select Committee study on airports in the South East of England[7] has proposed splitting the ownership of the separate airports presently owned and operated by BAA.

In some UK sectors, the EU has initiated the opening of services to competition. For example, on 1 January 2003 under the European Postal Services Directives (97/67 EC[8] and 2002/39[9]), Postcomm opened to competition large or 'bulk' mailings over 4000 items (which would expose 30 per cent of inland letter revenues to competition), consolidation and some other 'defined activities', and committed Postcomm to opening a further 30 per cent by 1 April 2005, with full liberalisation of the market promised by 1 April 2007. The relationship between EU and national policy is discussed in more detail later in the chapter.

In summary, competition has been introduced into a wide range of activities which were previously organised as state owned monopolies, including electricity generation, electricity and gas supply, metering, electricity and gas connections, some aspects of the postal services, retail telephone services, telecommunications networks and services, train service operation (to a limited extent), water retailing (also limited), and airline operation. In addition, new services – which in previous eras would have perhaps been assumed to be best controlled by the state – have been developed as competitive from the start. These include mobile telephony, internet service provision and broadband network operation.

Competition Policy Issues in 'Competitive' Markets

The 1998 Competition Act grants sector regulators concurrent powers with the Office of Fair Trading (OFT) with respect to abuse of dominance and anticompetitive agreements (cartels). Chapter I of the Act prohibits those agreements that have the effect of preventing, restricting, or distorting competition. So far there have been just two cases under the Act. In the first, the Federation of Wholesale Distributors complained that the terms of distributor agreements for the sale of mobile telephone pre-purchase vouchers ('pay-as-you-go') amounted to the imposition of resale price maintenance (RPM).

The case is an interesting application of the interplay between licence conditions and the rules of competition.[10] Condition 58.3 of Vodafone's licence (issued under the Telecommunications Act 1984) required Vodafone to 'provide services… at the charges, terms and conditions…published, and … not depart there from.' This meant that the Competition Act was 'disapplied', under an 'exclusion for compliance with a legal requirement.' Subsequently the requirement to comply with Condition 58.3 was itself disapplied when Oftel removed the determination that Vodafone had market influence, and Vodafone promised not to enforce the RPM clause and to provide new agreements without any RPM condition.

The *Swan Solutions* case concerned an alleged breach of both the Chapter I and Chapter II prohibitions.[11] Swan provided software for computer-telephone integration. Oftel found that the agreement did not have an appreciable effect on competition and that Swan did not hold a dominant position in any relevant market, so the complaint was not upheld.

Several abuse of dominance cases have been completed for the network industry sector over the period 2001-2004. BT heads the list with 14 investigations. The water, electricity, and rail industries each had three inquiries, and two concerned mobile telephone operators. The sector regulators also have powers to make market investigation references under the 2002 Enterprise Act, but these powers have not so far been deployed.

In order to give a flavour of the UK approach to policy in this area, four aspects of continuing work to achieve competitive outcomes in energy and telecoms are examined in the following subsections. It appears from these that, while separation in ownership of the monopolistic network elements is important, it is not a final solution in itself, and continued monitoring and willingness to act is required.

The market abuse license condition

With the benefit of hindsight, it has been persuasively argued that the initial break up of the Central Electricity Generating Board into three generators plus a grid company was not sufficiently radical to guarantee a competitive outcome at all times. In the mid 1990s, Powergen and National Power (now part of Innogy) were suspected of manipulating the wholesale Pool price at certain times. They were able to do this because the price for the whole market was effectively set by the bid into the Pool for the plant that was marginal at the current level of demand which, most of the time, was likely to be owned by one of the two owners of the large coal-powered generating stations (see, for example, Green and Newbery, 1992). One of the symptoms was the existence of 'spikes' in the Pool price at certain times, but there was also a suspicion that prices in general were higher than they would have been if the market had been more competitive.

The regulator (Offer and later Ofgem) addressed this problem in four ways. The first was to impose a price cap on Pool prices for a limited period. The second was to encourage divestiture of plant by Powergen and National Power. The 6 GW of plant purchased by Eastern Electricity was subsequently run at a higher level (Littlechild, 2000). The third was to jettison the Pool mechanism for New Electricity Trading Arrangements (NETA). The fourth was to attempt to change the generators' licences to add a market abuse licence condition.

This attempt to change the generators' licences was rejected by one company so the matter was referred to the CC. Ofgem argued that it could not apply general competition law in relation to the electricity wholesale market because of the special characteristics of electricity – it cannot be stored and supply and demand need to balance at each point in time for system stability. The CC rejected Ofgem's case for a variety of reasons including insufficient evidence of market abuse and concern that it would create regulatory uncertainty.[12] The companies are, of course, still subject to general competition law and could have sanctions applied should they decide to abuse any position of dominance they might have, however temporary.

Meanwhile, wholesale electricity prices fell. It is debateable whether this was primarily due to the deconcentration measures or, as Ofgem believe, the introduction of NETA (Evans and Green, 2003).

Complaints notified to Ofgem in relation to 1998 Competition Act
Ofgem exercises functions on behalf of the Gas and Electricity Market Authority, which has concurrent powers (with the OFT) under the 1998 Competition Act to apply and enforce the Act in relation to the gas and electricity sector in Great Britain.[13] It has received complaints in a number of areas with issues concerning supply attracting the most complaints. Between March 2000 and February 2004, 44 cases were received, of which 13 related to non-price discrimination; eight to price discrimination; four to predation; two each to excessive pricing and anti-competitive agreements, and the basis was unclear in a further 15.[14]

It appears, however, that the evidence provided by the complainants was generally lacking in cogency. In none of the 41 cases that were closed was an infringement found (see Table 7.2). In reporting the outcome of these complaints, Ofgem urged complainants to be more specific. Although the poor quality of the submissions by complainants is, in one sense, disappointing, it is encouraging in another sense, as the evidence suggests that the gas and electricity sector now raises relatively few real competition issues.

Call termination on mobile networks
Before the EU process of market reviews in the telecoms sector started as a result of the '2003' package (see below), Oftel had already developed a track record in market analysis and *ex ante* regulation of markets originally under the Telecommunications Act 1984 and Telecommunications (Interconnection) Regulations (SI 1997/2931), which were an implementation of EU Directive 97/33/EC.[15] Companies had been offering discounted or free mobile telephone handsets and recouping some of the losses by charging more for voice termination. Oftelcom found that there was no effective substitute for voice termination on individual mobile networks (hence it was a relevant antitrust

market) and suggested a regulatory solution in its Review of the Charge Control on Calls to Mobiles.[16] This involved a price control defined as the retail price index (RPI) minus 12 per cent during a four year period ending in March 2006. The companies rejected this, so the issue went to the CC, which reported in February 2003.[17]

Table 7.2 Complaints to Ofgem under the Competition Act 1998

Reason given by Ofgem for closure of cases	Total March 2000 – February 2004
Infringement decision	0
Non-infringement decision	2
Company agreed to change behaviour	1
Referred to OFT or other regulator	5
'Lack of evidence'/insufficient grounds for investigation	23
Investigation under sectoral powers	3
Other	7
Total	41

Source: Ofgem.

The CC agreed with Oftel's market definition and considered the issue of cross subsidisation (including a rejected claim by some firms that they were 'Ramsey pricing').[18] The CC took the view that the price structure was inefficient, leading to excessive turnover of customers in the market for handsets. The CC then imposed a price regulation which was tougher than Oftel's original proposal, including a price reduction of 15 per cent by July 2003.

This investigation was interesting from many standpoints, not least because of the intervention in the structure rather than in the overall level of prices offered by companies with identified market power. Moreover, the market definition proposed by Oftel and the CC in the UK has affected telecoms policy elsewhere in Europe.

Possible vertical separation or organisational change for BT
Ofcom was set up under the Communications Act 2003 to provide an integrated regulator for the converging electronic communications sectors. It decided that one of its first major tasks would be to review the UK telecommunications sector with 'a particular focus on assessing the prospects for maintaining and developing effective competition in UK telecommunications markets, while

having regard for investment and innovation'.[19] The consultation was to be in three phases: phase one was to be a review of current position and prospects for the telecommunications sector; options for Ofcom's strategic approach to telecommunications regulation would be examined in phase two, and phase three would develop specific proposals for Ofcom's approach to telecommunications regulation.

Ofcom concluded after its phase one investigations that the present structure was generally delivering relatively good value, competition was developing and call prices were amongst the lowest in the world. The problems which still remained in ensuring effective competition in the fixed line market were highlighted, however, and were regarded by Ofcom as both undesirable and unacceptable.

Three options were considered, namely deregulation (reliance on competition law), a market investigation reference under the Enterprise Act, or 'real equality of access'.[20] Ofcom proposed that the best way of ensuring competition in the fixed line market would be to 'address head-on the barriers preventing competitive wholesale access to BT's network'.[21] Respondents to the consultation were also overwhelmingly in favour of ensuring equality of access, though there was no unanimity about how best to achieve it.

The Phase 2 consultations reflected this preference for equality of access and resulted in a demand from Ofcom that BT make commitments to 'substantive behavioural and organisational changes' resulting in 'real equality of access' for competitors. After extensive discussions with Ofcom, the Board of BT agreed on 21 June 2005 to offer legally binding undertakings to Ofcom in lieu of a reference under the Enterprise Act, an offer that was accepted the following day by the Ofcom Board.

This involves the creation of a new 'access services division' (ASD) as a separate business unit with its own management and considerable operational independence. The remit of its management board will be to deliver equality of access between BT and its competitors. ASD will publish 'an annual plan including a remit, mission statement and performance targets.' The undertakings will be legally binding. In the event that the undertakings are breached, Ofcom can seek enforcement against BT in court. BT's Board will be responsible for ensuring that BT complies with the court's decision. Furthermore, third parties can also seek damages via the court to recover losses incurred if BT breaches any of the undertakings.[22]

Competition for the Market: Franchising

The main locus of franchise competition has been in the rail industry. Rail privatisation in Britain involved separation of the infrastructure (track and signalling) from train operation and the contracting out of the infrastructure maintenance operations. The rolling stock was put under separate ownership and leased to train operating companies with the aim of making the letting of train operating franchises more competitive. In addition, there were hopes for a significant expansion of on-rail competition.

The separation of infrastructure was always going to be difficult, however, since the interface between trains and its infrastructure is more complex and difficult to monitor than in electricity, gas or telecommunications. A section on a locomotive wheel that has worn flat can do enormous damage to track, for example, and one operator's faulty train can hold up other operators.

Furthermore, franchise design raised difficult issues. On the one hand, if a franchise is too short, the incentives to invest in service improvements will be reduced below a desirable level; on the other, the government was nervous of having very long franchises for fear of hold-up problems. In the event, the franchise lengths did vary somewhat to reflect investment requirements, although it has been suggested that the lengths chosen were far from optimal from a transactions cost perspective (see Yvrande-Billon, 2003).

The regulatory design matched the complexity of the industry structure. There was an infrastructure regulator separate from the franchise director. This design created further problems of planning co-ordination.

A series of major rail accidents after privatisation led to a loss of confidence in the safety of rail travel, with a knock-on effect on the whole privatisation scheme. After a serious crash at Hatfield in October 2000, caused by a broken rail that should have been replaced, speed limits were severely reduced throughout Britain. Train travel was disrupted for months and Railtrack became financially embarrassed. In a controversial move, the ownership of the railway system was transferred to Network Rail, a newly-created 'not for profit' company limited by guarantee, in October 2002.

The Railtrack experiment has not, on the whole, proved successful. Annual spending on national rail projects has roughly tripled from £1 billion to £3 billion, unregulated fares have risen in real terms, and there is a common feeling that the old British Rail, despite shortcomings, delivered better value for money. The general perception is that quality of service has declined overall, despite some route-specific improvements. Measures show that punctuality has declined; there has been a reduction in inter-operability owing to limited incentives to co-operate, and the common experience of rail information and booking systems, as well as the cleanliness of trains, is generally disappointing.

This experience has been particularly unfortunate since the recent high growth rate in the demand for rail travel owing to the healthy performance of the national economy, combined with growing road congestion, would have boosted rail finance and investment significantly if the problems caused by rail privatisation had not intervened. Passenger kilometres rose by one third in the eight years to 2003-4, after decades of stagnation in demand. A substantial increase in demand has also been felt in rail freight[23] despite the shift from coal to gas in electricity generation, and is usually reckoned as one of the qualified and unsung successes of rail privatisation.

The political price for this failure has been borne by the franchising organisation, the Strategic Rail Authority (SRA), whose functions have now been largely absorbed into the Department for Transport. The experience of railway privatisation is supportive of the view that vertical separation alone is not enough to achieve a good outcome. Poor market design, poor monitoring and control of market operation, and an *ad hoc* approach to retail regulation (see below) are likely to lead to poor sector performance.

Competition in the Input Market

The final form of competition considered here is competition in the input market. Many UK utilities, especially water and energy companies, have used competitive tendering processes to contract out the provision of certain inputs. Glas Cymru (Welsh Water) was under severe pressure to cut its costs as a result of Ofwat decisions on the price cap and contracted out much of its operational activities to United Utilities. The four-year, £450 million contract, which ran from 2001, involved operating and maintaining 15 reservoirs, many more water treatment works, the water distribution network and sewage treatment works. Billing and income services have been contracted out to Thames Water.

Many other water and electricity companies have also contracted out key operations like operation and maintenance, generally with few problems. Of course, there are always issues of contract compliance – the need to ensure that specified standards are maintained. There is a potential for catastrophe where this is not done adequately. For example, the Hatfield rail disaster has been attributed to a failure of the contracted-out maintenance regime, and the poor compliance regime in hospital cleaning in the nationalised health service has been blamed by some for the growth in hospital-acquired infections, which kill in even larger numbers.[24]

Surrogate for Competition: Price Cap Regulation

Where competition cannot be introduced, a price cap – based on a price control review every four or, more normally, five years – is imposed. This therefore applies to almost all of the activities in the water industry, transmission and distribution in electricity, transmission and distribution (but not storage) in gas, infrastructure provision and most commuter fares in railways, landing charges for airports, and air traffic control services. In telecommunications, BT is regulated in respect of its fixed network services at both the retail and wholesale level, as are call termination charges for mobiles. The Office of Rail Regulation sets revenue for Network Rail but rail fares, except for some peak and season and long distance 'saver' tickets, are unregulated.

The different sector regulators have developed their own approaches to regulation as they have seen fit for the particular circumstances of the sector. However, a common set of know-how and good practice has gradually developed and cooperation between them has grown. For instance, they jointly commissioned a report recently on the cost of capital (Wright, Mason, and Miles, 2003).

Other aspects have also seen some convergence. For example, a key decision relates to the transparency of reasoning in decisions and extent of consultations. Legal requirements on transparency have tended to increase the range of topics on which opinions are sought before a decision is taken, and it is now routine to spend time getting agreement about the key areas of work and a timetable for the review before a price review actually gets underway.

Price cap regulation is, of necessity, a forward-looking exercise. Nevertheless, it is essential to get a good understanding of costs in the most recently available year from the regulatory accounts, and to ensure that these are an accurate assessment of the real requirements in that year. The regulatory body has to take a view on the reasonableness or otherwise of the plans submitted by the companies. The data within the set of business plans may be used to estimate relative efficiencies if there are enough comparators (as in water and electricity distribution), even though this can be rather problematic in econometric terms mainly due to the paucity of observations. Internal and/or international benchmarking may be used for efficiency estimation in other cases.

A spreadsheet-based financial model incorporating all the assumptions helps to arrive at particular recommendations. The use of an explicit model allows sensitivities to be tested and implications for financial ratios or other outcomes of interest to be analysed. Draft conclusions are published and, after consultation with the public and interested parties, final decisions are published. The companies can then either accept these in the form of licence modifications or reject the proposed licence changes, in which case the CC examines the evidence and comes to its own conclusions. Although this is often referred to as an appeal, this is not the correct term since the CC is not restricted in the kind of evidence it may consider in arriving at its conclusions, as it would be in an appeal case.

Since prices are typically set for five years, companies have an incentive to outperform the financial model and have succeeded in doing so more often than not. As just described, the price regulation process is tailored to the particular company's circumstances. This does not appear to be the case for regulated rail fares; these were set initially at a blanket level of the Retail Price Index (RPI)-1 per cent for all situations and subsequently changed to RPI+1 per cent for the three years 2004-7.

EU POLICY

The European system of law, as defined by the Treaty of Rome and updated with the Single European Act of 1986 and Maastricht Treaty, involves the principle of subsidiarity. This means that actions are taken at Community rather than Member State level only if there is a Community dimension to the issue. As a consequence of this, national regulatory and competition authorities play their part in policies that are agreed at the Community level. Directives are the key link between the Community level and the Member State. These allow for some compromise between centrally-determined objectives and local conditions.

Directives, which are agreed in the EU by the Council of Ministers, set out the 'required result' that is to be achieved by the legislation within each Member State. A Member State can be prosecuted through the European Court of Justice and subject to fines if it fails to meet the requirements. Furthermore, if a Member State fails to transcribe the directive into national law, individuals may be able to rely on a 'direct effect' of the directive rather than the defective or absent local legislation. Once a directive has been transcribed into national law, the European Commission (the 'Commission') still retains control and can challenge and amend decisions of those National Regulatory Authorities it deems not to be in accordance with Community Law (see below for examples).

One of the key issues is the extent to which EU directives have been adopted by Member States in letter or spirit. Implementation may require a radical change in traditional ways of thinking in some Member States which members of the national government, parts of the electorate, or pressure groups such as trade unions may find difficult to accept.

The EU system works within the framework of the EU's competition policy. In addition, there are a number of directives relating to electronic communications, energy (principally gas and electricity), to transport, and to postal services, amongst others.[25] There are extensive sets of directives, recommendations, and guidelines, as well as cases in each industry from most Member States. This section concentrates on providing an overview of telecommunications and energy (particularly electricity) with some illustrative examples. It is worth noting that regulation of the water industry at EU level is largely concerned with environmental rather than competition matters since the environment is the aspect with the largest Community dimension, and regulation in rail is concerned as much with developing long distance routes crossing national boundaries and with interoperability as it is with competition.[26]

Telecommunications (Electronic Communications)

The new EU regulatory framework

The liberalisation of these markets has been developing since 1988, when the special rights of the national incumbent over terminal equipment, such as handsets, were removed. The 1990 Services Directive (Directive 90/388 EEC)[27] required the abolition of special and exclusive rights over public telecoms services (but not networks), except for the provision of voice telephony services. This was extended to satellite services and equipment in 1994 (Directive 94/46/EC)[28] and cable TV networks in 1995 (Directive 95/51/EC).[29] 'Full liberalisation' of services and infrastructures across the EU Member States took place on 1 January 1998 (with the exception of some small countries which were granted a transition period) under Directive 96/19/EC.[30]

A review of the regulatory framework in the EU and how it should change in the light of market developments, new technology and changes in consumer demand was published in 1999.[31] This resulted in draft directives in November 2000. The European Council of Ministers gave its approval in February 2002, the European Parliament in March 2002 and the new measures came in to force in July 2003. The 2003 regulatory package consists of four directives, two measures, and various sets of guidelines, plus the setting up of some consultative groups. These are set out in Table 7.3.

The term 'electronic communications' rather than telecommunications has been used to describe this sector since July 2003, reflecting the convergence between different applications such as data, voice, information and entertainment, on the one hand, and physical media such as telephone lines, cable, terrestrial and satellite broadcasting on the other. Broadcasting content, however, remains outside this legislation.

The 2003 package aims to reduce and codify the existing complex set of regulations and directives. In recognition of convergence between different electronic information activities, regulation is extended to cover broadcasting networks (but not content) as well as telecoms and cable TV networks and services. It adopts the principle of technological neutrality – that the same regulatory approach should apply to all telecoms networks, whether fixed or mobile, and all broadcasting networks, whether cable, satellite or terrestrial. Markets should be defined according to services offered, rather than the technology used to provide them. The package attempts to increase harmonisation by giving a greater role to the Commission. Greater consistency across Member States is sought by requiring greater consultation between regulators and the EU.

The Commission envisages steadily increasing competition for electronic communications services, with commensurately less need for sector-specific

Table 7.3 The 2003 regulatory package in electronic communications

Directives	Reference
Framework Directive	(2002/21/EC) OJ L108/33, 24 April 2002
Access and Interconnection Directive	(2002/19/EC) OJ L108/7, 24 April 2002
Authorisation Directive	(2002/20/EC) OJ L108/21, 24 April 2002
Universal Service Directive	(2002/22/EC) OJ L108/51, 24 April 2002
Radio Spectrum Decision	(676/2002/EC) OJ C9/7, 11 January 2002
Regulation on Local Loop Unbundling	(2887/2000 EC) OJ L336/4, 30 December 2000

Other measures

Recommendation on relevant product and service markets 2003/311/EC, OJ L114/45, 8 May 2003

Guidelines on market analysis and the assessment of significant market power 2002/EC, OJ C165/6, 11 July 2002

European Regulators Group (for encouraging consistency of approach to regulation) 2002/627 OJ L200/38, 30 July 2002

Radio Spectrum Policy Group (for harmonising use of radio spectrum) 2002/622 IP/03/418

Source: http://europa.eu.int/information_society/topics/telecoms/regulatory/new_rf/index_en.htm. Up-to-date details on the package can be found on this site.

regulation. Consequently, the new regulatory package is more in line with the principles used in general competition law rather than sector regulation. For example, the definition of significant market power ('SMP') was changed to bring it more into line with the concept of 'dominance' as used in EU competition law:

> if, either individually or jointly with others, it enjoys … a position of economic strength affording it the power to behave to an appreciable extent independently of competitors, customers and ultimately consumers (Article 14(2), Framework Directive).

An operator will be presumed to be dominant in a relevant market when its market share exceeds 50 per cent,[32] rather than 25 per cent which was the old standard under the Open Network Provision Directive. The intention is to apply the same criteria *ex ante* as competition authorities apply *ex post* to the analysis of effective competition in any given market. For example, the framework directive reflects the concern found elsewhere in EU competition policy about the effects of leveraging – that a dominant position in one market can be abused in another related market – stating that where an undertaking has SMP in a specific market, it may also be deemed to have SMP in a closely related market where the links between these markets are strong enough. This approach must be applied in the series of market analyses that every Member State's regulatory authority (NRA) is required to undertake in a set of 18 specified national markets (such as wholesale broadband access, access and call origination on public mobile telephone networks and wholesale unbundled access to metallic loops and sub-loops for the purpose of providing broadband and voice services) in order to identify the operators with SMP that must be regulated *ex ante*.[33] The process consists of three main steps, namely market definition; the assessment of SMP, and the definition of ex ante obligations to be imposed on SMP operator(s) depending on the NRA's assessment of the competitive situation in the national market. The new rules grant regulators more flexibility than under the previous regulatory framework in that the finding of dominance does not automatically trigger a series of obligations that are the same in all cases. Instead, the regulator may choose from the 'menu' of available obligations according to the specific market conditions.

Experience under the new framework

By December 2004, 20 Member States had notified the Commission that they had completed the adoption of primary legislation. However, Belgium, the Czech Republic, Estonia, Greece, and Luxembourg had not yet adopted primary legislation to transpose the framework into national law, and the Commission launched infringement proceedings for non-notification. Proceedings are pending before the European Court of Justice against Belgium, Greece and Luxembourg.[34]

Although they had completed the primary legislation, another eight Member States (Spain, France, Cyprus, Latvia, Lithuania, Poland, Slovenia and Slovakia) had failed to enact the necessary secondary legislation to give effect to the package, so at the time of writing the Commission was considering its options with regard to pursuing this matter with these states. In contrast, some Member States (notably Austria, Finland, Portugal and the UK) have been active. As of 1 October 2004, the Commission had received 101 notifications of draft measures from nine Member States, mostly from the four listed above.

Even where Member States have notified the Commission that national primary and secondary legislation has been adopted, however, the details of what is enacted do not always correspond to the 'required result.' For example, the Commission has expressed its concerns that the principles of impartiality and independence are not always adhered to in the national approaches. The separation between the State's shareholding and regulatory decisions is not always ensured. Sometimes ministries intervene by giving instructions or 'guidance' affecting the NRAs' regulatory decisions. In other cases, the problem is a lack of enforcement or lengthy appeals procedures during which all remedies are suspended rather than adopting interim measures. Lack of suitably trained staff relative to the workload is also a problem in some Member States.[35]

Notifications to the Commission of draft measures are required to ensure that market definition and market analyses are carried out in accordance with EU competition rules and to allow for harmonization within the Single European Market. The Commission can require the withdrawal of draft measures if it considers them incompatible with Community law. In the period to 1 November 2004, the Commission had used its veto powers on only three occasions.[36]

In October 2004, for example, the Commission made a decision requiring the Austrian telecommunications regulator to withdraw a draft regulatory decision that no company had SMP in transit services for the fixed public network telephone network in Austria. This would have had the effect of lifting *ex ante* regulation. The Commission formed the view that the NRA had overestimated the potential for demand-side substitutability:

> . . . the draft measures lacked the evidence to include those operators in the relevant market which have rolled out their networks and no longer demand transit services. Further, insufficient consideration was given to the possibilities that would be open to operators currently dependent on regulated transit services in the event regulation were lifted, and which have insufficient traffic volumes to justify further roll-out of their networks.[37]

As regards the requirement for market reviews, the more active NRAs are reviewing the specified telecommunications markets identified by the Commission and the UK (specifically Ofcom) has adopted the July 2003 package with enthusiasm. As NRAs are expected to review the markets identified as susceptible to *ex ante* regulation periodically to take into account changes in the competitive conditions, this task will keep each of the NRAs (and the companies for which they are responsible) busy for years to come.

As seen above, competition policy principles and methodologies underpin the ongoing review of *ex ante* regulation in the telecommunications sector. In addition, it is worth noting that there has been a growing number of instances where the Commission has investigated the abuse of dominant position under Article 82. The Commission has been involved in margin squeeze cases in the telecoms industry, notably *Wanadoo* (discussed in Chapter 2) and *Deutsche Telekom* (DT). The Commission adopted a decision under Article 82 against DT in May 2003 on the basis that there was a margin squeeze between its wholesale and the retail tariffs for full local loop unbundling and imposed a fine of 12.6 million Euro.[38] DT made commitments to the Commission to end the margin squeeze as from 1 April 2004. It also undertook to make a substantial reduction in local loop unbundling line sharing tariffs as from January 2005, and to increase some of its downstream (ADSL) tariffs. This decision required the endorsement of the German NRA, RegTP.

As the market reviews take place, a good deal of information will emerge about the state of competition in each of the 450 or so markets in the EU. A sizeable fraction of these will involve SMP which, in the absence of major structural changes, means that there will be a great deal of *ex ante* regulation to undertake, implying significant growth in regulatory activity. Paradoxically competition does not mean regulatory withdrawal in this case, but rather an increase in regulation.

Electricity and Gas

Gas and electricity markets are highly interdependent. Not only are they substitutes in some applications, but the building of new, highly efficient, low carbon emission combined cycle gas turbines has been at the core of new capacity building and therefore of new entry into national markets. Competition in the one tends to increase competition in the other.

David Newbery (2002) has provided a neat summary of what needs to be done to achieve effective competition in electricity markets (see also Bergman et al., 1999). This involves securing effective competition in generation; regulated third party access to networks, regulated by specialized agency, and enough generators with sufficient capacity operating in a well designed market with adequate provision for ancillary and balancing services. Good international links and/or divestment of plant may be necessary to keep market concentration low enough.

As this section will show, there have been a variety of EU level initiatives towards the reform of energy markets through directives and competition law enforcement. There is still some way to go, however, before the single European electricity market becomes a competitive reality. As with electronic communications, implementation varies in both quantity and quality across Member States.

The first attempt to integrate European electricity markets was represented by a working paper in 1988 and a Transit Directive of 1990,[39] which attempted to open access to electricity markets. Progress during the early 1990s was slowed down by opposition both from vested interests and those who had a genuine mistrust of liberalisation. There were also structural problems – for example, state ownership of single integrated companies, as in France, or more generally high concentration (in most parts of Europe except the Nordic countries). Subsidies, and implicitly the policies behind them, create distortions, which would tend to be unwound by a successful competitive process. Finally, transmission constraints which physically limit the amount of electricity that can be transported from one region to another – an inheritance of separate national markets – created barriers to the effective functioning of a single European market. Many of these problems remain, and the process of liberalisation is further complicated by considerations of universal service and other obligations, indigenous fuel preferences, and environmental policy.

The 1997 Directive

The first electricity directive came into force on 19 February 1997 and set a target date of 19 February 1999 for transcription into national legislation.[40] At the time, it was seen as extending the 1985 single European market concept to the electricity industry.

The 1997 directive created requirements in the areas of generating capacity, transmission systems and other operations and distribution. As regards generation, Member States had to build new capacity using either authorisation or tendering. With authorisation, the initiative comes from companies wishing to build power plants. Under tendering, the initiative comes from a designated authority, which decides what capacity is needed and then invites competitive tenders. Whichever mechanism applies, the process must be impartial.

In the case of transmission, the designated transmission system operator (TSO) must despatch plant according to transparent and fair rules – for example, if the TSO also has plant, the rules must not favour the TSO company's own plant. There is, however, some ability to discriminate in favour of renewable fuels or fuels indigenous to the Member State. As far as distribution is concerned, system operation had to be non-discriminatory as between entrants and incumbents.

At the heart of the 1997 directive was the access system. Although regulated access would arguably provide the strongest form of liberalisation, the directive also allowed a single buyer arrangement (favoured by France) and a negotiated access arrangement (favoured, at the time, by Germany). Additional barriers to competition were kept in place by allowing the imposition of public service obligations in distribution, and by the failure to require separation of supply from distribution.

Bergman et al. (1999) have provided a useful evaluation of the policy by the late 1990s and made a considerable number of recommendations for future policy. Among the most important of their findings was that concentration in generation is too high in many countries and should be reduced, although they recognised that this is more difficult in small countries such as Hungary. They emphasised that both low concentration in generation and transparency are required for an effective trading mechanism. Although vertical unbundling, including ownership separation, imposes losses in technical efficiency, it is desirable in order to improve the workings of the market. In their view, it is more important to separate distribution from retail (supply) than from transmission. Overall, they felt that the case for continued state ownership is weak, given the need for clear and transparent regulation. Ownership at the municipal level, as in

Norway or Germany, was seen as less problematic, as it results in a greater number of companies that can compete with each other in generation and supply.

Bergman et al. (1999) supported the case for an independent sector-specific regulator, as well as a joint electricity-gas regulator. They pointed out that merger policy should take account of the need to preserve vertical separation and sufficient numbers of comparable companies for yardstick operation to be effective. In addition, they argue that regulated third party access (TPA) is preferred to negotiated TPA; the single buyer model has proved unattractive, and even France has adopted regulated TPA. They acknowledged that it is difficult to get transmission pricing right and, overall, felt that large customers had benefited much more than small customers from liberalisation.

The 2003 Directives

The Electricity Directive 2003/54[41] (alongside Regulation 1228/2003[42] and the Gas Directive 2003/55[43]) reflects a number of these points, but also takes concerns about fuel diversity, public service obligations and security of supply into consideration. These energy directives gave deadlines for the 'full opening' of the market, namely 1 July 2004 for all business customers and 1 July 2007 for households. They also required the separation of transport system operators (transmission and distribution) from other activities (production and supply) through legal and operational unbundling of these activities, and the designation of an NRA. By the deadline in July 2004, only two Member States (Slovenia and the Netherlands) had notified the Commission of their transcription into national law, and three other countries (Denmark, Hungary and Lithuania) had adopted most of the measures.

The Commission expressed some concern about the rate of progress in its annual benchmarking report.[44] Although evidence of improvements in total factor productivity was good news, serious concerns were expressed relating to the lack of switching by customers (even large ones); the lack of penetration across national boundaries; continued high concentration; insufficient investment in infrastructure (transmission capacity, for example); the failure of transparent wholesale markets to develop, and the continued regulation of end user prices or long term power purchase agreements (PPAs) which would present severe obstacles to new entry. The distribution of some of these problems across Member States is shown in Table 7.4

The latest Commission reports suggest that on average around 15 to 20 per cent of large users have changed suppliers since market opening within the EU. The figures range from none in Greece and five to 10 per cent in Belgium towards more than 50 per cent in the Nordic countries and the UK. The data are summarised in Table 7.5; this shows, for instance, that Greece has no competition in either electricity or gas, and the UK is the only Member State where the process of introducing competition in both electricity and gas is complete.

Table 7.4 Summary of main obstacles to competition in energy

Obstacles	Member States involved	Customer switching: large users
No major obstacles	Sweden, Finland, Denmark, Norway, UK	>50%
Unbundling/regulation	Luxembourg, Austria, Germany	Range 10% (Luxembourg) - 35% (Germany)
Market structure or lack of integration	France, Belgium, Greece, Ireland, Spain, Netherlands, Lithuania, Italy, Slovenia, Czech Republic, Slovakia, Latvia	Range 0% (Greece) - 35% (Netherlands)
Long term PPAs/ regulated end-user prices	Portugal, Estonia, Poland, Hungary,	Range 0% (Estonia) - 25% (Hungary)

Source: European Commission, Annual report on the implementation of the gas and electricity internal market, COM(2004) 863, 5 January 2005, Table 2.

The exact formula for classification in Table 7.5 is not specified but appears to be based on a number of factors such as the percentage of the market open to competition, concentration in generation and the type of unbundling of transmission and distribution operators. For example, in the 'not functioning' category, the threshold consumption to be eligible for market opening is the relatively high 40GWh in Estonia and Latvia yet this accounts for only 10-11 per cent of the market. In Greece, the 1kV threshold in theory accounts for 34 per cent of the market but the leading company holds 85 per cent of the generating capacity and there was no switching by consumers in 2002.[45] At the other end of the spectrum, Austria has a 'well developed' market, with all customers eligible for a competitive supply. Table 7.4 indicates that the 'obstacle' for Austria is in the nature of unbundling – in Austria's case the unbundling of the distribution operator is only accounting, not legal separation and only 5 per cent of domestic and small business customers had switched.

Table 7.5 Extent of competition in energy, March 2004

Level of competition	Electricity	Gas
Not functioning	Greece, Estonia, Latvia	All new Member States, Finland, Portugal, Greece
Initial steps only	Belgium (francophone), Luxembourg, Portugal, Poland, Czech Rep., Slovenia, Slovakia, Lithuania	Germany, Luxembourg, Sweden, Belgium (francophone)
Some progress	Germany, Spain, Belgium (Flanders), Ireland, Italy, France, Hungary	Austria, Belgium (Flanders), France, Italy, Denmark
Well developed	Austria, Netherlands	Netherlands, Ireland, Spain
Complete	UK, Sweden, Finland, Norway, Denmark	UK

Source: European Commission, Towards a competitive and regulated European electricity and gas market, Memorandum from DG for Transport and Energy, 2004 available at http://ec.europa.eu/ energy/gas/publications/doc/2004_07_09_memo_en.pdf.

According to the Commission, and as the above examples suggest, the introduction of competition in electricity and gas in some Member States has been made more difficult by the existence of companies with a large degree of market power at national or regional level. It is noticeable that there is no small overlap in the countries which have a poor record of implementing the electronic communications package and those where little progress has been made in electricity reform (for example, Greece, Belgium and several of the newest members).

Based on its policies (rather than the benchmarking reports themselves), the Commission sees the lack of sufficient cross-border transmission capacity as the principal problem in achieving a single European market in electricity. At the Barcelona European Council in March 2002, Member States agreed a list of projects to improve electricity inter-connection in a trans-European network framework. However, progress on most of these projects seems to be slow. As a consequence, the Directorate responsible for energy and transport, DG TREN, has proposed a new Directive on infrastructure and security of supply. In addition to measures relating to energy efficiency, security of supply, and 'ensuring an adequate level of interconnection between Member States, through general, transparent and non-discriminatory policies', it contains proposals for the further development of Trans-European networks in electricity and gas.[46] In a recent paper, John Bower (2004) has challenged the premise on which the proposed infrastructure directive is based. He claims that regulatory failures have been the principal cause of the apparent capacity shortfall. These have caused artificial price differentials between countries that would not exist in a competitive equilibrium, which artificially boosts the demand for transmission capacity, coupled with barriers to the efficient use of what transmission capacity there is. One problem is excessive generator market power; another is the shortage of transmission capacity resulting from vertical integration between generators and transmission, and the third arises because transmission pricing fails to allocate scarce capacity efficiently. As he points out:

> any country where a single firm controls 40 per cent or more of the generation output share has a highly concentrated wholesale electricity market. In 17 of the 23 countries represented the largest generator has a market share of 40 per cent or more. Of the remaining 6, Luxembourg is effectively subsumed into the French and Belgian market because of its small size, both of which are near generation monopolies. Norway, Germany and Denmark are effectively dominated by two or three competitors each with shares in the 30 per cent range so also fall into the definition of highly concentrated markets (Bower, 2004, p. 6).

Bower suggests that the problem of the generators' excessive market power could best be dealt with by divesting mid-merit and peaking generation capacity. In his view, the shortage of transmission capacity could be dealt with by the divestment of vertically integrated transmission capacity; the implementation of a market to allocate transmission capacity when there is congestion would ensure scarce capacity was used efficiently.

The failure of ten Member States to enact the Directives has resulted in action being taken against them at the time of writing:

> Today [16 March 2005] the European Commission sent reasoned opinions to Germany, Belgium, Estonia, Ireland, Lithuania, Latvia, Sweden, Greece, Spain and Luxembourg for failure to transpose into national law either one or both of the two EU Directives on the internal gas and electricity markets. In October 2004 the Commission sent letters of formal notice to 18 countries and this is now the second stage in the infringement proceedings. The situation has improved, but the Commission regrets that ten Member States have still not transposed the Directives nearly two years after they were adopted in June 2003. It's not enough to legislate: the Member States must apply the rules that they have made for themselves. The Commission will use all the means at its disposal to insist on this.[47]

Figure 7.1 shows the breakdown of electricity prices for a 50 MWh customer as collected by the Commission. Prices and retail margins are lowest in the UK and Scandinavian countries, which is consistent with liberalisation having consumer benefits.

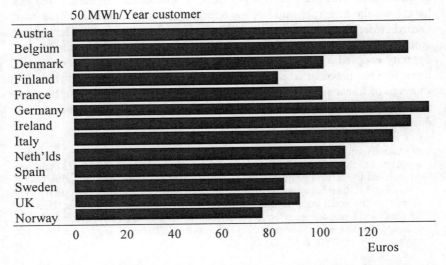

Source: European Commission, 'Third benchmarking report on the implementation of the internal electricity and gas market', DG Transport and Energy Draft working paper, March 2004.

Figure 7.1 Tariffs for small industrial customers

Competition law enforcement in energy markets

Two cases are now discussed to illustrate competition law enforcement in energy markets. These are actions taken to deal with high prices in Germany and the facilitation of liberalization in the Spanish gas market.

As Figure 7.1 shows, Germany has suffered relatively high electricity prices. This has been due, in part, to protection of its coal industry and, more recently, its strong commitment to renewable sources such as wind power. Conflicting approaches to energy liberalisation on matters such as mergers in the energy sector may have not helped.

In 2002, for example, electricity company E.ON merged with Ruhrgas, a dominant gas importer and transporter in the German market which controlled nearly all gas deliveries to companies within its area, and accounted for 58 per cent of sales nationally, as well as controlling almost all imports, high pressure transmission, and storage facilities in Germany. The *E.ON/Ruhrgas* merger would have combined Ruhrgas's strength in the gas sector with E.ON's strong position in the electricity sector, resulting in Europe's biggest energy company. The Cartel Office prohibited the merger, since it would substantially lessen competition in gas and there were concerns about foreclosure of entry into electricity generation (since gas is now the major fuel needed for entry into electricity generation). The Minister of Economic Affairs approved the merger, however, overruling the Cartel Office and his own advisors in the Monopolies Commission.[48] This is an interesting contrast with the *Endesa/Gas Natural* case in Spain (see below) where even a long term supply contract was overturned.

The German electricity market was liberalised in 1998, with the announcement that all customers could choose their retail supplier. This did benefit large industrial customers, but not smaller retail and commercial customers. There were no published non-discriminatory terms of access to transmission and distribution networks so access terms had to be negotiated, and many believe the resulting terms amounted to a margin squeeze for entrants. After an initial fall in prices of some 20 per cent, prices have risen again. This has been attributed to mergers and takeovers in the energy industry, and the system of self-regulation, using negotiated third party access, combined with ex-post investigation (at least in theory) of abuse by the federal and state cartel offices. There have been numerous complaints of high charges for the use of the grid and local distribution systems as a result (Glachant, Dubois and Perez, 2004). From the beginning of 2005, however, the German market had its own regulator linked to the regulatory body for the telecommunication and postal services (RegTP) and this provides for a move towards regulated access to networks and possibly more effective competition. In other countries, the initiatives from DG TREN have been supplemented by activity from DG Competition and NRAs operating under EU law and national legislation.

The Commission has also intervened to facilitate liberalisation in the gas market in Spain. In 2000, it forced Spanish Gas Natural SA to rewrite its contract with Endesa SA, the market leader in Spanish electricity generation.[49] The contract which was initially supposed to last 20 years stipulated that Endesa could use the gas bought from Gas Natural only for the purpose of generating electricity. The Commission was concerned about the potential anti-competitive effects of such long-term restrictive contracts, since they believed it would have raised barriers to entry into the liberalized Spanish gas market. Entrants would be losing an attractive client in terms of volumes, as electricity generators are among the larger customers of gas. The Commission's investigation indicated that the agreement could consitute an infringement of Article 82 as it had the effect of strengthening an already dominant position. Gas Natural (GN) and Endesa responded to the Commission's probe by reducing the contract length to 12 years and removing the restrictive clause regarding resale. The EU, in turn, dropped its investigation.[50] Although the primary concern was the state of the gas market, the Commission also noted the potential impact on the electricity market.

Since then, the Spanish authorities have pursued liberalisation of the gas market and Table 7.5 shows that the Commission now considers competition 'well developed'. In 2002, CNE (the gas regulator) forced GN to spin off 65 per cent of the shares of Enagas, the private company owned by GN that controls Spain's gas transportation system. The government plans to force GN to reduce its ownership to less than 5 per cent by 2007. In 2001, the Spanish regulator awarded 25 per cent of the natural gas contracted to Gas Natural from Algeria's Sonatrach to six private companies. It is largely the electricity utilities such as Endesa, Union Fenosa, and Iberdrola who have had the most success in gaining market share in the liberalized gas market.[51]

Signs of progress in the development of the single European energy market
The focus of European policy has been primarily towards the development of competition in the market, through the opening up of access to networks, rather than for the market (by awarding franchises) or in the market for inputs. However, the partial opening that has occurred has had some knock-on effects, suggesting that the process is gaining some momentum of its own.[52] For example, there is continued growth in the number of power exchanges (where spot electricity is traded) operating in Europe.[53] There have been several sales of electricity capacity, mainly as a result of undertakings made by dominant incumbents wishing to purchase capacity abroad. For example, the purchase of South-west Germany's EnBW by France's EDF[54] led to the release of 6,000 MW 'virtual capacity'.[55] Similarly, there have been a number of gas release schemes as the result of attempted mergers.

Privatisation as such (and hence competition in the market for corporate control) is not a requirement of the directives. However, many countries such as Italy and Spain have chosen to follow this as a matter of policy, and some like the Netherlands do not have such a big legacy of public ownership. In other Member States, pressure for privatisation can be an indirect consequence of the directives when combined with other developments, such as rulings on state aid which restrict the availability of government-guaranteed debt finance, and the effects of merger activity.

For example, France has from time to time announced intentions to privatise EDF and GDF (gas) in order to raise finance, since these companies have been eager purchasers of privatised entities overseas, with predictable effects on the companies' balance sheets.[56] So far, however, organised opposition from trade unions has persuaded the government not to go ahead. The purchase by French nationalised industries of overseas companies, combined with lack of opening of the French market has, at times, been a source of some friction in other Member States.

At the time of writing, the latest move involves the promise by the Italian Prime Minister, Silvio Berlusconi, to reverse a 2001 decision by the Italian parliament limiting EDF's voting rights in Edison (Italy's second largest energy producer) to 2 per cent in retaliation against France's failure to open its own market to competition. This will enable France to gain a foothold in the Italian electricity market, but the need to finance the deal may be the final trigger for EDF's privatisation.[57]

CONCLUDING REMARKS

The cases above indicate that a good deal is going on to increase the degree of competition in the electronic communications and energy markets. We now turn to an assessment of the policy and the state of play. The largest successes of the UK model have been where effective competition has been successfully introduced, and vertical separation has been more effective than access pricing in achieving this (as in gas and electricity). Regulation, whether of the price cap variety or otherwise, seems distinctly second best. To pursue this within a European-wide market context is going to be extremely challenging.

In electronic communications, there is some competition in the newer markets where the advantages of incumbency are less (an extreme case would be mobile telephony). Nevertheless, the current situation amounts to a massive regulatory exercise requiring the periodic examination of up to 450 markets. Where SMP is found, it will be due to a combination of two factors: lack of competition at the local loop and vertical integration of the local loop operator with other retail services.

Nothing can be done about the first factor except regulate local loop provision until competitors, such as wireless local loop and cable, become more effective substitutes. The UK may be leading the way in dealing with the second factor (vertical integration), but the detailed implementation of the separation is absolutely crucial, otherwise it could lead to another Railtrack-type situation with poor quality of service[58] and problematic incentives for investment. It is interesting to note in this context that the US route to competition in telecoms via separation of local exchange carriers has not been a particularly resounding success. However, a truly effective separation could lead to a massive winding down of the regulation of electronic communications. In the best case, instead of 450 markets, only 25 local loop operators would need to be regulated.

In the case of electricity and gas, some Member States seem to have been slow in implementing the directive either in terms of transcription into national law, or completion of secondary legislation. The long period over which reforms were introduced has, in some cases, been used to allow market concentration to increase or otherwise frustrate the intentions of the policy. It was discovered that some divestment of plant in the UK energy markets was necessary in order to arrive at an effectively competitive outcome. Whilst there have been some sales of virtual capacity and releases of gas capacity – 3 per cent of demand in Italy and France[59] – these are still not on the scale of deconcentration which came to be regarded as necessary in the UK.

Although markets in electricity and gas have emerged, the predominance of long term contracts in gas, whilst helping to secure supplies, reduces the liquidity on the spot market, which leads to price spikes and an increased perception of riskiness. On the evidence of the UK electricity market, the EU will need to grasp the nettle and force more divestment of generating plant if it is serious about creating competitive markets. Simply building more transmission capacity seems unlikely to be enough.

However, the lessons of botched liberalisation measures in the UK (railways) and elsewhere (Californian electricity) is a salutary reminder that picking items *à la carte* from a deregulation menu without understanding the likely consequences for incentives, investment, and capacity formation is unlikely to be successful. Good market and regulatory design is crucial. Nevertheless, the goal of competitive markets in European utilities has some strong supporters, and the examples given in this chapter demonstrate that the competition rules of the Community are playing a key role in facilitating this process.

NOTES

1. I am extremely grateful to Eleanor Morgan and Roger Clarke for their comments on earlier drafts.
2. In the phrase of the eminent economic historian, J.H. Clapham (1922).
3. BT was targeted for privatisation in part because it was projected to require a massive investment programme to undertake digitisation, which would add to the PSBR and in part because there was potential for competition in the coming years.
4. Monopolies and Mergers Commission, Gas and British Gas plc, 1993, Cmnd. 2314 – 16, Vol.1, paragraph 1.6.
5. Environment Agency, The Water Act 2003: an explanatory leaflet, 2004.
6. For Q4 2003; see Ofcom, Fixed telecoms market information update, May 2004. Ofcom publications are readily accessible through its website http://www.ofcom.org.uk.
7. House of Commons Select Committee on Transport, Sixth Report, 10 July 2003, HC 454-1.
8. Directive 97/67/EC of the European Parliament and of the Council of 15 December 1997 on common rules for the development of the internal market of Community postal services and the improvement of quality of service, OJ L15, 21 January 1998.
9. Directive 2002/39/EC of the European Parliament and of the Council of 10 June 2002 amending Directive 97/67/EC with regard to the further opening to competition of Community postal services, OJ L176, 5 July 2002.
10. Vodafone's distribution agreements for pre-pay mobile phone vouchers, Decision of 5 April 2002. The details can be found in the OFT website (www.oft.gov.uk) in the 1998 Competition Act Public Register.
11. *Swan Solutions Ltd/Avaya ECS Ltd*, Decision of 6 April 2001. OFT merger decisions are published on its website in the Business section under mergers.
12. AES and British Energy: A report on references made under section 12 of the Electricity Act 1989, CC 453, January 2001.
13. Northern Ireland has its own regulator, Ofreg.
14. Ofgem, Complaints considered by Ofgem under the Competition Act 1998, 1 March 2000 to 29 February 2004, 1 March 2004, reference 46/04 on Ofgem website (http://www.ofgem.gov.uk).

15. Directive 97/33/EC of the European Parliament and of the Council of 30 June 1997 on interconnection in telecommunications with regard to ensuring universal service and interoperability through application of the principles of Open Network Provision (ONP).
16. Oftel, Review of the charge control on calls to mobiles, 26 September 2001.
17. Vodafone, O2, Orange and T-Mobile: Reports on references under section 13 of the Telecommunications Act 1984 on the charges made by Vodafone, O2, Orange and T-Mobile for terminating calls from fixed and mobile networks, CC, February 2003.
18. Ramsey pricing results in a set of prices that maximise consumer welfare subject to the requirements of the fixed and joint costs associated with the provision of multiple products. It is named after an English economist, Frank Ramsey (1903-1960). Ramsey (1927) considered the problem of raising a certain amount of tax revenue but the problem has many parallels in economics. Taxation creates distortions leading to a loss of economic welfare and Ramsey worked out the conditions for this loss to be minimized. In its application to regulated firms which need to raise a certain amount of revenue to cover joint costs, the price-cost margins tend to be higher for those products or services for which demand is least elastic (such as call termination). Calculating such prices can require more information than is typically available.
19. Strategic Review of Telecommunications Phase 1 Consultation Document, April 2004, p. 10, Ofcom website.
20. Strategic Review of Telecommunications Phase 2 Consultation Document, November 2004, Ofcom website.
21. Strategic Review of Telecommunications Phase 2 Proposals, news release, 18 November 2004, Ofcom website.
22. Ofcom 'A new regulatory approach for fixed telecommunications', news release and statement, 23 June 2005, Ofcom website.
23. Annual Abstract of Statistics, various issues.
24. 'The number of death certificates mentioning MRSA rose from 487 in 1999 to 955 in 2003. But this figure is much lower than the 5,000 annual deaths from hospital-acquired infections estimated by the National Audit Office, based on calculations rather than death certificates. The chances are that the actual figure lies somewhere between the two,' TimesOnLine, 25 February 2005.
25. Directive 2003/54/EC of the European Parliament and the Council of 26 June 2003 concerning common rules for the internal electricity market, OJ L176, 15 July 2003; Directive 2003/55/EC of the European Parliament and the Council of 26 June 2003 concerning common rules for the internal gas market, OJ L176, 15 July 2003; Regulation (EC) 1228/2003 of the European Parliament and the Council of 26 June 2003 on conditions for access to the network for cross-border exchanges in electricity, OJ L176, 15 July 2003; and Proposal for a regulation of the European Parliament and the Council on conditions for access to the network for cross-border exchanges in gas, COM(2003) 0741.
26. A third railway package was announced in March 2004, see COM(2004) 40. The objectives of this package are: to revitalise the international rail passenger market through extending competition in that market and establishing a harmonized system of minimum passenger rights, addressing also the particular needs of 'persons with reduced mobility' (PRM); to contribute to the interoperability of the European rail system by facilitating the movement of train drivers between undertakings and across national borders through training provisions, and to enhance the performance and size of the EU rail freight market, in advance of the development of effective competition in the entire market, through mandatory requirements for performance elements in contracts with freight customers.
27. Directive 90/388 EEC of 28 June 1990 on competition in the markets for telecommunications services, OJ L192, 24 July 1990.
28. Directive 94/46/EC of 13 October 1994 amending Directive 88/301/EEC and Directive 90/388/EEC in particular with regard to satellite services, OJ L268, 19 October 1994.
29. Directive 95/51/EC of 18 October 1995 amending Directive 90/388/EEC with regard to the abolition of the restrictions on the use of cable television networks for the provision of already liberalized telecommunications services, OJ L256, 26 October 1995.
30. Directive 96/19/EC of 13 March 1996 amending Directive 90/388/EEC with regard to the implementation of full competition in telecommunications markets, OJ L74, 22 March 1996.

31. The Communication [COM(2000)239] of 26 April 2000 to the European Parliament and the Council gives the results of the public consultation on the 1999 Communications Review and orientations for the new regulatory framework.
32. Commission Guidelines on market analysis, Recommendation of 11 February 2003 on relevant product and service markets within the electronic communications sector susceptible to *ex ante* regulation 2003/311/EC, OJ L114, 8 May 2003, para. 75.
33. Ibid.
34. European Commission, European electronic communications regulation and markets, SEC(2004) 1535.
35. Ibid.
36. These cases concerned the market for international calls (Case FI/2003/0024 and FI/2003/0027) and the market for access and call origination on public mobile telephone networks (Case FI/2004/0082) in Finland, and the market for transit services in the fixed public telephone network (Case AT/2004/0090) in Austria (see below).
37. Commission Decision of 20 October 2004 pursuant to Article 7(4) of Directive 2002/21/EC ('Withdrawal of a notified draft measure') Case AT/2004/0090: transit services in the fixed public telephone network in Austria.
38. Case COMP/C-1/37.451, 37.578, 37.579 – Deutsche Telekom AG. See OJ L263, 14 October 2003.
39. Transit Directive, 90/547/EEC 29 October 1990, OJ L313, 13 November 1990.
40. 96/926/EC Electricity Directive OJ L27, 30 January 1997.
41. Directive 2003/54/EC of the European Parliament and of the Council of 26 June 2003 concerning common rules for the internal market in electricity and repealing Directive 96/92/EC, OJ L176, 15 July 2003.
42. Regulation (EC) No 1228/2003 of the European Parliament and of the Council of 26 June 2003 on conditions for access to the network for cross-border exchanges in electricity, OJ L176, 15 July 2003.
43. Directive 2003/55/EC of the European Parliament and of the Council of 26 June 2003 concerning common rules for the internal market in natural gas and repealing Directive 98/30/EC, OJ L176, 15 July 2003.
44. European Commission, Annual report on the implementation of the gas and electricity internal market, COM(2004) 863, 5 January 2005.
45. European Commission, 'Third benchmarking report on the implementation of the internal electricity and gas market', DG Transport and Energy Draft Working Paper, March 2004,. Tables 1 and 4.
46. European Commission, Memorandum from DG for Energy and Transport towards a competitive and regulated European electricity and gas market. Opening of the internal energy market: progress so far, July 2004. Available at: http://europa.eu.int/comm/energy/electricity/publications/doc/2004_07_09_memo_en.pdf.
47. RAPID press release (europa.eu.int/rapid/), 'Opening up of energy markets: ten Member States have still not transposed the new EU rules', IP/05/319, 16 March 2005.
48. Lies-Dóxcy, E., NERA Energy Regulation Brief, 14 August 2002.
49. RAPID press release, 'Commission closes investigation on Spanish company GAS NATURAL', IP/00/27, 27 March 2000.
50. *Gas Natural +Endesa*, Case COMP 37.542, Decision of 17 March 2000.
51. US Government Energy Information Administration, Country Brief: Spain, March 2005.
52. Capgemini, European Energy Markets Deregulation Observatory, 6th edition, November 2004.
53. These include Amsterdam (Netherlands), Slovenia, Austria, Germany, UK, France, Spain and Nordpool (Norway/Sweden/Finland).
54. For a discussion of the EDF purchase of EnBW, see *EDF/EnBW*, Case M.1853, Decision of 7 February 2001, OJ L59, 28 February 2002.
55. This 'virtual capacity' is a mechanism whereby the dominant operator in an area, for a defined period of time, turns over control of the energy generated at its power stations to other competitors. The ownership of the plant does not change, but some portion of its production becomes managed by a third party. France agreed to this mechanism in early 2001 as the result of pressure from the Commission.

56. France Telecom was partially privatised in 1997, though the government retained a controlling interest. Threats of redundancies in the debt-ridden company may have added to trade union opposition to the privatisation of EDF and GDF.
57. Italian breakthrough for EdF, at http://business.timesonline.co.uk/article/0,,13130-1605767, 00.html.
58. When a service consisting of linked activities (such as end-to-end provision of a voice circuit) is broken into constituent parts, there are negative externalities when one link in the chain is of poor quality as the revenue for other link providers suffers. There will be market failure in the form of poor service quality if this externality is not fully internalised.
59. Capgemini, op cit.

8. Competition and Intellectual Property Rights in the European Union

Claude Crampes, David Encaoua and Abraham Hollander

INTRODUCTION[1]

It is generally recognized that, notwithstanding their distinct histories and individual enforcement agencies, competition law and intellectual property law are not just compatible instruments of economic policy; they are complementary instruments. The two bodies of law pursue the common goal of economic efficiency. This does not preclude a certain tension between them. To understand why, it is useful to briefly recall the more specific objectives of each body of law.

The contemporary economist views competition policy as 'the set of policies and laws which ensure that competition in the marketplace is not restricted in a way as to reduce economic welfare' (Motta, 2004, p. 30). This perception of the role of competition policy has not always been paramount in Europe. Integration towards a single market used to be a central objective of competition policy. Although the aforementioned present day view of the role of competition policy has been in ascendancy at the Community level and in Member States after creation of the single market, European competition authorities still hold the view that national intellectual property rights (IPRs) hinder economic integration.

According to Landes and Posner (2003, p. 1) intellectual property consists of 'ideas, inventions, discoveries, symbols, images, expressive works, ... or in short any potentially valuable human product (broadly, 'information') that has an existence separable from a unique physical embodiment, whether or not the product has actually been 'propertized', that is brought under a legal regime of property rights'. Therefore, intellectual property laws represent the set of statutes, institutions and policies that grant exclusive rights to authors and inventors, for a limited time, over the expression of their writings and intellectual creations (copyrights) or over the ideas themselves embodied in their technical inventions (patents).

To what extent is the existence of such exclusive rights compatible with competition? In this regard it is important to note a key difference between the European Union and the United States (Korah, 2001). Unlike the US, the EU grants no intellectual property rights other than trademarks. Patents and copyrights are granted under the law of Member States, complemented by the so-called European patent, created by the European Patent Convention (1973)[2] currently signed by 28 contracting states. According to Articles 2 and 3, a European patent granted by virtue of this Convention and covering one or more of the contracting states shall have the effect of and be subject to the same conditions as a national patent granted by a contracting state. Therefore, a European patent is just a bundle of national patents granted by the European Patent Office (EPO). The EPO provides a one-stop shop that makes it possible to get around the transaction costs associated with having examinations carried out in individual states. A patent granted by the EPO is recognized in a Member State if translated into the national language. A proposal for a Council Regulation on the Community Patent relying on the EPO,[3] that would have established a single patent for the whole European Union, has not been adopted. Although cases are litigated before national courts, the European Court of Justice (ECJ) has given Community authorities a powerful instrument when it 'drew a distinction between the grant or existence of a national intellectual property right, which was not subject to the Treaty, and its exercise, which was ... The Court took power to override Member States with respect to intellectual property rights that threatened to divide the common market along national boundaries' (Korah, 2001, p. 805).

Initially, the European Community had an inimical perception of property rights. They were considered as impediments for the achievement of the common market. 'The ECJ used the distinction between the existence and exercise of property rights in the early 1970s to develop a judicial doctrine of the Community exhaustion of intellectual property rights: once a protected product has been put on the market by the holder ... or with its consent in one Member State, the right was exhausted and a parallel intellectual property right could not be used to restrain the commercial importation of the product to another Member State' (Korah, 2001, p. 805).

Things began to change in the 1980s (Encaoua et al. 2003).[4] The major role of intellectual property rights in stimulating innovation and growth gained greater recognition. New governing bodies have emerged, for example the World Trade Organization (WTO), the World Intellectual Property Organization (WIPO), and the Court of Appeals for the Federal Circuit (CAFC) in the US.[5] Moreover patent legislation has entered a harmonization process across countries via bilateral and multilateral treaties.[6]

From a competition policy perspective it also matters that over the same period there have been important changes in the motives that drive firms to obtain patents. A number of studies point to the fact that firms increasingly file applications covering technologies that are neither developed nor licensed. In some high-tech industries, firms seek patents for strategic purposes, specifically to exclude potential rivals (Carlton and Gertner, 2002, Cohen, Nelson and Walsh, 2000, Hall and Ziedonis, 2001). For example, the US semiconductor industry builds patent fences around core inventions. One observes a proliferation of mutually blocking patents that coalesce into patent thickets that exclude potential rivals. This comes in addition to implicit threats of infringement suits that serve as bargaining chips to obtain access to other firms' technologies or to force others to accept cross-licensing arrangements (Shapiro, 2001, Encaoua and Hollander, 2002).

These practices raise a host of issues at the interface of intellectual property and competition policy.[7] More specifically they may require a fresh exploration of areas where the grant of exclusive rights may shackle competitive market processes. Two forms of competition should be considered: product competition and research competition. Product competition yields allocative efficiency and gives consumers the opportunity to obtain products at prices that are close to costs. Research competition produces new products and new technologies. It allows firms to escape the constraints of product competition, especially in closely competitive industries where firms have access to the same technologies and produce under the same costs (Aghion, Harris and Vickers, 1997, Aghion, Harris, Howitt and Vickers, 2001, Aghion *et al.*, 2005, Encaoua and Ulph, 2004).

However, market incentives may be insufficient to produce the optimal amount of innovation. Not only is the outcome of R&D uncertain, as everyone recognizes, but, more importantly, its output is an information good, that is, it is non-rivalrous and non-excludable, except by legal means. Granting the original inventor an exclusive right appears as an *ex ante* incentive to innovate inasmuch as it encourages investment in research by prevention of free riding. Note that it is the *ex ante* incentive that matters for the purpose of investment rather than the *ex post* reward to an inventor. The *ex post* reward approach that is prevalent among lawyers, would lead to the conclusion that since the investment cost is already sunk, the exercise of the exclusive right has to be strictly scrutinized under competition law. The *ex ante* approach leads to the opposite conclusion that the successful investor shall not be deprived of the exclusive right to commercialise or sell an invention in order to keep the *ex ante* incentive to invest.

Thus the grant of an exclusive right that limits competition in the product market is part and parcel of a trade-off. 'Like ordinary property rights that promote competition in production by preventing competition in consumption, intellectual property rights are a way (but not the only one) to promote innovation, by restricting some kinds of competition in production.'[8] Even so, later competition is encouraged because a patent is granted on condition of disclosure of the knowledge that underpins the invention. The disclosure favours the diffusion of know-how, allowing others to build around or improve on earlier inventions (Encaoua and Ulph, 2004). Protecting an innovation by secrecy does not allow such diffusion. The dissemination of knowledge also benefits from licensing agreements and other arrangements such as the pooling of patents.[9] Licensing also improves static efficiency because innovators are not always the best equipped to exploit existing know-how.

Most economists and legal scholars 'acknowledge that analysis and evaluation of intellectual property law are appropriately conducted within a framework that seeks to align that law with the dictates of economic efficiency. Cases, doctrines and principles have to be examined from the standpoint of whether they are efficient in an economic sense and, if not, how they might be changed to make them efficient' (Landes and Posner 2003, p. 4).

Still, as soon as one pronounces on fundamental objectives in order to understand the consequences of specific rules, it becomes plain that there exist areas of stress between the two bodies of law. The following sections show how European courts have managed these stresses in three areas: (1) parallel imports and market segmentation, (2) refusals to supply essential inputs protected by patents and copyrights and (3) forms of conduct by copyright collectives.

PARALLEL IMPORTS AND COMPETITION

Firms segment markets for efficiency reasons and in support of collusive agreements. They do so to gain a capacity to discriminate in terms of prices or qualities. Because intellectual property rights enhance right holders' ability to segment markets, courts are constantly required to balance a need to protect the holders of patents, copyrights and trademarks with a desire to give consumers access to products at competitive prices. From an economic perspective, the issue is not merely how to balance dynamic and static efficiency; it is also how to assess the effects of market segmentation on static welfare.

With respect to international segmentation, there are specific issues related to exhaustion regimes[10] and the legal treatment of parallel trade. Parallel trade takes place when products put into circulation in one country are exported to another country via distribution systems not set up, or consented to, by the party who put them on the market first. Parallel trade – also called grey trade – is not the same as trade in counterfeited goods[11]. Products that circulate in parallel trade are genuine. They are generally marketed first by a firm that holds the IPRs in these products, or by a licensee of such a firm. What sets parallel trade apart from ordinary commerce is the diversion of products from the markets ostensibly targeted by IPR holders.

Parallel trade responds to cross-country price disparities.[12] It limits the capacity of firms to segment national markets. This means that from an economic perspective, restrictions on parallel trade should be looked at as devices that facilitate territorial segmentation.

In the following, we summon up the incentives firms have to segment markets. Then we consider the stances of European institutions on the barriers to parallel trade. We look first at parallel imports originating from outside the Union, then we look at parallel trade among Member States.

Market Segmentation

A firm with market power can increase profits by segmenting markets and engaging in geographic price discrimination. However, there is no unambiguous answer to the question how this affects overall welfare. Price discrimination brings about a welfare reducing misallocation of output across markets but total output may be larger than under uniform pricing – possibly because additional markets are being served. The latter is welfare increasing.[13] Malueg and Schwartz (1994) have shown that when there is a large disparity in the willingness to pay across national markets, a mixed regime of discrimination across groups of countries differentiated from each other by substantial differences in willingness to pay, but not among countries within individual groups, yields greater world welfare than uniform pricing on a global scale.[14]

A capacity to discriminate may be necessary to insure that profits are positive. This applies mainly to industries where fixed costs are very large compared to variable cost. One thinks of industries that rely heavily on R&D or other creative effort. The argument essentially boils down to the claim that in certain industries, a mere right to exclude conferred by intellectual property law does not insure that returns are sufficient to elicit a socially optimal level of innovation.

In this regard it is important to stress that economic theory does not give an unequivocal answer to the question whether a switch from uniform to discriminatory pricing increases industry profits when firms confront rival producers.[15] While it is true that each firm benefits from acquiring a capacity to discriminate, it loses when rival producers obtain the same capacity. The net effect on profits depends on the intensity of the rivalry. Allowing discrimination intensifies competition in market segments where buyers view the products of different producers as good substitutes, but, at the same time, it allows firms to capture larger profits in market segments that have a strong preference for their particular variety.

It is not always the desire to discriminate that steers firms towards market segmentation. Manufacturers may grant distributors exclusive territories to encourage them to invest in promotional activities such as presale information, product advertising and quality control. In the absence of exclusivity, the investment by one distributor benefits rival distributors. Distributors who do not invest could attract customers who have already sought information from distributors who invested by undercutting them. The very fact that their costs are lower gives them the option. The result is that each distributor has less incentive to invest than is optimal from the manufacturer's perspective. To address this problem the manufacturer can take measures that reduce the likelihood that buyers in a territory allocated to one distributor would be served by distributors in another territory.

While the alignment of distributors' and manufacturers' incentives is likely to be welfare enhancing, it could come at a cost. For example, the elimination of downstream competition can lead to double marginalization.[16] This reduces manufacturers' profits and consumers' welfare. It also reduces inter-brand competition. Rey and Stiglitz (1995) have shown that the latter is due to the fact that distributors with market power do not fully pass on to their buyers increases in the wholesale price. Therefore the demand faced by manufacturers is less elastic than it would be if distributors were in competition. The outcome of the reduction in elasticity can mirror collusion.[17]

Manufacturers adopt a variety of measures to curtail grey trade and enhance their capacity to profit from price discrimination. They sometimes put quotas on the quantities delivered in a national territory.[18] At other times, they limit the coverage of guarantees to the territory where the product was first put into circulation. Every so often, they use technical means that preclude use in one country of an article originally sold in another territory.[19] At times, they try to create in the mind of consumers residing in high price countries, the belief that grey goods are counterfeit, pirated or of lesser quality.[20]

The laws that protect intellectual property provide another avenue for the segmentation of national markets. A central issue concerning intellectual property protection is which rights are relinquished upon the first legal sale of a product in which rights are initially held. Consider for example the case of CDs containing music. Composers, publishers and, possibly, makers and performers hold initial rights in the music as well as in the CD that contains the music. However, upon first sale of the CD they lose the right to prohibit its resale. That right has been exhausted.[21] In the discussion below, exhaustion of a right will always refer to the loss of the right to control reselling.

IPRs are territorial. The right to control a particular use of protected material applies only within the national boundaries of the jurisdiction that grants that right. This applies equally to the exhaustion of rights; that is the national law determines under what circumstances a right holder – resident or foreigner – exhausts the right to control resale in the national territory.

There are several exhaustion regimes. Under a regime of national exhaustion, the person holding an IPR on a product waives the right to prohibit resale of that product in the national territory upon the first legal sale within the boundaries of that territory.[22] In countries that accept international exhaustion, the original right holder forfeits the power to control resale within national boundaries as soon as the product is legally put into circulation anywhere in the world.

The particular regime a country chooses may vary from one type of IPR to another. For example, a country may adopt international exhaustion in the case of trademarks and national exhaustion for patents. Furthermore, exhaustion regimes may be product-specific. The exhaustion regime a country chooses reflects a somewhat uneasy balance between, on one hand, a desire to protect the interest of IPR holders, and on the other hand, the wish to guarantee consumers and businesses the opportunity to make informed purchases in a competitive environment.

In the following, we discuss the approach of the European Union towards parallel imports from a perspective of competition policy. The EU makes a distinction between parallel trade between Member States and trade between the Union and non-members. The most important difference between the EU and other jurisdictions is the adoption of a regime of regional exhaustion under the Trade Marks Harmonization Directive.[23] Article 7 of the Directive prescribes a regime under which the owner of a trademark cannot avail himself of the right conferred by trademark law to prevent the sale anywhere in the EU of a good marketed first by him or with his consent in any territory of the European Economic Area.[24] This, however, ceases to apply when the proprietor of the trademark has legitimate reasons to oppose further commercialization, especially when the condition of the goods is changed or impaired after they have been put on the market. Trademark rights in Member countries are not exhausted by first circulation of the product outside the EEA.[25]

Grey Goods Originating Outside the EEA

The conditions under which exhaustion of right conferred by trademarks occurs have been clarified in several decisions rendered by the European Court of Justice (ECJ). In the *Silhouette* case,[26] the ECJ ruled that a Member State could not adopt a wider exhaustion regime than set out in Article 7 of the Trade Mark Directive. This was founded in part on the wording of the Directive, and on the observation that 'if some members practiced international exhaustion and others did not there would be barriers to trade, and this would affect the functioning of the internal market, and this is precisely the objective pursued by the Directive'.[27]

The notion of consent received elucidation in the *Sebago* judgment in which the ECJ rejected the validity of an importer's claim that the trademark holder exhausted his right to prevent the sale within the EU of all batches of a good once he had consented to the marketing of a single batch of identical goods.[28]

The meaning of consent was also at the heart of the later *Davidoff* and *Levis* cases.[29] The ECJ held that consent cannot be inferred from the absence of contractual provisions or communication to that effect, or from the fact that the goods carry no warning that sale outside a specific area is prohibited. The ECJ held that consent requires an unequivocal demonstration of renunciation of one's right to oppose importation into the EEA.

While the aforementioned decisions bear on the question whether trademark law can be used for blocking parallel imports into the Union, they do not address the question whether contractual provisions between private undertakings that commit one party to sell only in assigned territories outside the EU are prohibited. This question was addressed by the ECJ in response to a question raised by a French court. The case involved proceedings brought by Yves St Laurent Parfums (YSLP) against Javico. The perfume manufacturer had entered into a contract for the distribution of its products in selected territories outside the EEA. The contract provided that the distributor would not sell the product outside these territories or to unauthorized dealers in the territory. When YSLP discovered that products sold to Javico were marketed in several countries of the Community, it broke the contract and started legal proceedings. When a French court upheld both termination of the contract and its claim for compensation, the defendant appealed on the ground that the controversial contractual provision was prohibited by Article 85(1) (now 81(1)) and therefore automatically void.

The ECJ ruled that in order to determine whether agreements such as the one concluded between YSLP and Javico run afoul of Article 85(1), one must consider whether their purpose or effect is to restrict to 'an appreciable extent competition within the common market and whether the ban may affect trade between Member States'.[30] The Court held that agreements could not be struck down unless they were capable of affecting trade between Member States. It ruled that the provisions at issue 'did not constitute agreements which, by their very nature, are prohibited by Article 85(1)' (paragraph 21 of the judgment). It remained for the national court to determine whether they did in fact have such effect.[31]

The significance of the Javico ruling may be rather limited in view of the ECJ's decision in Davidoff and Levis. A possible consequence of the latter is that firms concerned about the importation of their trademarked products into the EU will find such prohibitions as imposed on Javico redundant.[32] This would be true all the more if it was determined that international exhaustion applies in circumstances where contractual measures designed to prevent importation into the EU contravene Article 81 or Article 82.

Partitioning of the EU into National Markets

The stance of competition authorities with respect to territorial restrictions that restrain grey trade within the Community appears less flexible. The courts have held that an agreement whose object it is to prevent grey trade within the Community is by its very nature a violation of Article 81(1).[33] This means that in order to find a breach of Article 81(1) it is sufficient to show first, that the measures taken amount to an agreement and second, that the object of the agreement is to prevent parallel trade within the Community. The following decisions illustrate the point.

Yamaha[34] sold instruments through a network of official dealers located in various EU countries. It signed contracts with its dealers that bound the latter to the following four conditions: to sell solely to final customers; to buy solely from Yamaha's national subsidiary; to supply solely distributors authorized by the national subsidiary, and to contact Yamaha Europe in Germany before exportation via the Internet.[35] In addition, the contract between Yamaha and its Icelandic dealer contained an explicit prohibition of parallel trade.[36]

The European Commission (the 'Commission') concluded that commitments to sell exclusively to final consumers, buy solely from Yamaha's national subsidiary and supply solely distributors authorized by the national subsidiary had the object of preventing cross-supplies within Yamaha's dealer network.[37] It reached this conclusion by examining the possible consequences of the aforementioned provisions. The Commission also argued that 'although the object of the agreement (to contact Yamaha before exporting) may not have been to directly restrict exports, it clearly had the potential effect of discouraging dealers from exporting products to other Member States' (paragraph 109 of the decision). Interestingly, the Commission did not even broach the question of object or effect in regard to the Icelandic contract. It simply invoked the ruling without considering Yamaha's claim that, given Iceland's remote location, it was unlikely that the contractual clause would in fact restrict trade.[38]

The question what type of conduct produces an agreement within the meaning of Article 81 was at the heart of the subsequent *Bayer* case. The local distributors of the pharmaceutical firm had signed contracts containing provisions that were designed to eliminate grey trade among Member States. The Commission held that there existed an agreement between Bayer and its dealers. For that reason it fined Bayer.[39] The Commission's finding was based on the observation that the dealers had continued their business relationship with Bayer, and, in response to the contract, had adapted the way they placed orders. The Commission noted but did not discuss the implications of the fact that, in response to Bayer's measures, the wholesalers placed their orders as if the product they received would serve to meet only the demand of their national market, and that they did their best to inflate the national quotas imposed on them by Bayer. The evidence examined by the Commission also showed that wholesalers tried to get additional quantities by ordering from other, generally smaller, wholesalers who were not monitored by Bayer.

The Court of First Instance (CFI) overturned the Commission's decision.[40] It held that the Commission had erred by considering that it had established the existence of a concurrence of wills between Bayer and the dealers. The mere absence of such concurrence meant that there was no agreement within the meaning of Article 81(1).[41] The CFI argued that the Commission was wrong in concluding that the reduction in orders could only be understood by Bayer as a sign that dealers had accepted its demands. It held that the Commission could not maintain that the reason wholesalers had to order additional quantities from other dealers was because they agreed to Bayer's demands. It opined that these orders were not indicative that wholesalers did acquiesce.[42] The CFI also explained why Bayer's behaviour justified a decision at variance with the earlier Sandoz ruling in which it had determined that an agreement existed.[43] Sandoz had on repeated occasions indicated on the bills sent to its clients that export of the goods was prohibited. The fact that its distributors had continued to order without protest and had *de facto* respected the ban meant that they had tacitly acquiesced to Sandoz's terms. Whereas Sandoz had put a specific anti-competitive clause in the contract, a formal prohibition to export was lacking in Bayer. Furthermore, Bayer had not implemented a systematic monitoring of the final destination of the product and there was no evidence that the manufacturer had threatened or punished a wholesaler who exported, or made the delivery of products conditional on wholesalers' compliance with the alleged export ban.

The ECJ upheld the CFI's judgment.[44] It indicated that while existence of a monitoring system and penalties may amount to an indicator of an agreement, they do not prove its existence. The Court emphasized that the mere fact that Bayer imposed a quota that may have had the same effect as an export ban, did not imply it had imposed a ban, or that an agreement existed. The Court stressed that the concurrent existence of an agreement that is neutral from a competition standpoint and a measure restrictive of competition that is imposed unilaterally does not amount to a violation of Article 81(1). Because there had been no claim that Bayer was dominant, the need to examine whether Article 82 had been violated did not arise.

The decision in Bayer does not fully answer the question whether unilateral behaviour by a dominant actor designed to rein in parallel trade would be treated by competition authorities in the same way as other potentially abusive forms of conduct.[45] The answer to this question ultimately depends on how competition authorities and the courts view discriminatory practices, in particular price discrimination. It appears that exemptions to the prohibition of price-discrimination by competition authorities are rare.[46] This is somewhat surprising[47] in view of the fact that there is no basis in theory for a claim that discrimination is more harmful to the competitive process than the other forms of conduct mentioned in Article 82. As indicated at the beginning of this section, the economic literature points to several circumstances under which price discrimination yields higher welfare than uniform pricing. Even from a consumer welfare point of view one cannot argue that discrimination always lacks redeeming value. Furthermore, the empirical evidence on the price effects of parallel trade within the EU remains sparse. Some analysis suggests that the rents captured by parallel traders exceed the benefits to consumers in countries that import via parallel channels, and consumer gains are small or moderate.[48] This and the fact that parallel trade consumes resources would suggest that grey products may affect welfare adversely or not at all. One must admit, however, that at this stage it is not clear whether the assumptions underlying the conclusion that consumers in the EU draw little benefit from parallel trade, are critical to that finding.[49]

REFUSAL TO SUPPLY: AN ESSENTIAL INTELLECTUAL PROPERTY RIGHT

Rights of exclusion differ according to the category of IPR. A patent owner can prevent others from making, using or selling the patented invention for a period (typically) of 20 years from the issue of the patent. Copyright protection which applies to original works of authorship embodied in a tangible medium of expression normally expires in the European Union 70 years after the death of the author. Unlike a patent, a copyright protects only the form of expression. It does not protect the underlying idea. This means that a right holder in a work 'a' holds no rights in an independently created work 'b' based on a similar idea. Trade secrecy protection applies to information whose commercial value depends on non-disclosure. Of course, trade secrets have no expiry date and they do not provide a legal barrier that stops others from independently producing and using the same invention.

From an intellectual property perspective, one's right to exclude others is key. Competition authorities do recognize the right to exclude since it is granted under patent and copyright laws. Their concern arises when that right protects an input that is indispensable to another party. They may consider that a refusal to licence an essential input is abusive when it prevents competition. This creates a potential for friction between intellectual property law and competition law.

According to the essential facilities doctrine a firm holding a dominant position in the provision of an input that is indispensable for the production of another good that competes with the good in which the firm is dominant, acts abusively when, without objective justification, it refuses to supply the input under fair conditions. The application of this doctrine must obey a number of stringent conditions: (1) the facility must be under the control of a dominant firm, (2) the access to the facility is required to allow a competitor to operate in a downstream market, (3) it is practically impossible to duplicate the facility, (4) access to the facility by competitors is technically feasible under standard safety rules, (5) the plaintiff is willing to accept the standard commercial terms and (6) the refusal to supply access to the facility has no objective reason.[50]

The application of this doctrine is much more difficult when the so-called essential input is an intangible asset. In principle, firms that produce patented or copyrighted information goods and wield substantial monopoly power are not shielded from antitrust liability. However, it is only in exceptional circumstances that courts in the EU and the US have invoked the doctrine. This raises the difficult question of whether licensing should be made compulsory in some circumstances.

The Economics of Compulsory Licensing

Gilbert and Shapiro (1996) argue that conditions such as the ones listed above cannot by themselves justify compulsory licensing on economic grounds: 'These conditions do not characterize the circumstances under which compulsory access to a facility or to intellectual property would be beneficial to economic welfare. A firm may choose to deny access to an actual or potential competitor ... for many different reasons. These include reasons that are likely to enhance economic efficiency' (Gilbert and Shapiro, 1996, p. 12751). Preventing free riding that would diminish incentives for investment and innovation, preserving a desired level of service quality and designing appropriate contracts that compensate the intellectual property owner for the loss of revenue that may result from access may justify the refusal to deal. Still one cannot dismiss a pure strategic motive behind a refusal to license. Therefore, a detailed inquiry on a case by case basis is needed to determine the consequences of a refusal to license an essential intellectual property right. The inquiry must take into account the economic conditions under which welfare would be diminished if access to the facility were denied (Katz and Shapiro, 1985, Gilbert, 2000, 2002, 2004, Scotchmer, 2004, Maurer and Scotchmer, 2004).

On economic grounds, the short run effects of a refusal to license depend on how the price of the license is determined. Under a fixed fee regime, if the competitor had access to the IPR, its decisions would not be affected by the value of the fee. The fixed-fee license does not change the market outcome (assuming it is not prohibitive) and its effect is purely distributive. But even in this case, the effect on welfare of an order to license depends on the licensee's efficiency. If the licensee is not very efficient or at least less efficient than the patent's holder, an order to license can be detrimental to economic welfare.

However, there are also situations where licenses to efficient competitors are welfare enhancing but are not voluntary.

Under a regime where royalties are a linear function of units supplied, the outcome may depend on whether the patent holder also produces. If the patent holder does not produce, linear royalties combined with fixed fees are sufficient to support the maximum profit (Scotchmer, 2004, pp. 187-9). If so licensing is based on private incentives and there is no scope for compulsory licensing. But when the patent holder is also a producer, the situation can be different since a linear royalty can lead to an inefficient outcome, except in cases where the licensee is more efficient than the patent holder (Maurer and Scotchmer, 2004, p. 10).[51] One solution to this allocative problem could be either to impose a royalty rate that is a decreasing function of the licensor's output or to cap the licensor's output by imposing an upper bound (Maurer and Scotchmer, 2004, pp. 12-17).

Since the proponents of compulsory licensing only require that the royalty be reasonable and do not propose a certain payment formula, it is difficult to assess the short run consequences of a compulsory license for economic efficiency.

Compulsory licensing also affects long run incentives to invest in R&D. Consider the case where investment in R&D is represented by a bid for an innovation produced by an upstream laboratory. Gilbert and Shapiro (1996) identify two adverse effects of compulsory licensing

> First, a compulsory license reduces the profits of the winning bidder by forcing the winner to license in situations where it is not privately rational to do so. Second, compulsory licensing is likely to lower the value of the winning bid because it increases the profits of the losing bidder. Under compulsory licensing, the losing bidder is assured to benefit from the innovation, assuming the owner of the technology is compelled to license the technology at a price that the licensee would be willing to pay. The size of the winning bid is determined by a firm's value of owning the technology, less the value to the firm if the technology is in the hands of its rival. Compulsory licensing lowers the first component and raises the second. Thus, compulsory licensing can have two negative effects on economic welfare. It can reduce welfare in the short run by compelling inefficient licensing. It can also reduce welfare in the long run by reducing incentives to innovate (Gilbert and Shapiro, 1996, p. 12753).

Decisions of the European Courts

To illustrate these difficulties, we discuss a number of competition cases that address refusals to license essential inputs protected as intellectual property. Some major decisions clarify under what circumstances European competition authorities consider that a right holder abuses a position of dominance by refusing to sell or license a protected input to a competitor.

Renault[52] and *Volvo*[53]

The facts of the two cases are similar. Renault and Volvo had design rights on their models for car body panels. They denied access to their design rights to independent repairers, preventing them from supplying spare parts. The ECJ did not set out the circumstances in which a refusal to sell is abusive. It did, however, provide examples of abusive conduct, pointing out that the latter can result from the exercise of intellectual property rights. They include the arbitrary refusal to supply, fixing prices at an unfair level, and ending the production of spare parts for models still in circulation. The ECJ ruled that the freedom of an IPR owner is at the core of the exclusive right and that a mere refusal to deal is not be an abuse of a dominant position under Article 82. Refusal to license could be an abuse only if there was additional abusive conduct of a type referred to above. Therefore the ECJ did not condemn the defendants.

Magill[54]

In the Magill decision, the ECJ set out for the first time circumstances in which a refusal to license can be said to constitute an abuse of dominance.[55] They include preventing the emergence of a new product for which there is a potential demand, a non-justified refusal to license, and the monopolization by the right's holder of a secondary market by exploiting market power in a primary market.

The facts of Magill are as follows. Three Irish TV broadcasting stations held copyrights on their individual programme listings. Each station published its own TV guide to inform viewers of its programme for the following week. Each station also granted a license to daily papers to publish its list of programmes one day in advance. The license was granted free of charge. When Magill decided to publish an all-inclusive weekly guide for all three stations, they sued for copyright infringement and got a preliminary injunction. When the stations subsequently refused to grant licenses to Magill, the company filed a complaint with the Commission. The Commission concluded that the refusal was in breach of Article 82. It ordered the stations to put an end to their abusive conduct by supplying 'third parties on request and on a non-discriminatory basis with their individual advance weekly programme listings and permitting reproduction of those listings by such parties'.[56] This decision was upheld on appeal by the CFI and the ECJ. In a famous decision[57] the highest court said that, although the right to exclude is the substance of the exclusive right, the refusal to license in the special circumstances listed above violates the general obligation of dominant firms to supply a downstream competitor. The ECJ held that although 'mere ownership of an intellectual property right cannot confer a dominant position', there was a *de facto* monopoly over the information produced by the TV stations since they were the only source. The refusal to supply a license was preventing the emergence of a new product for which there was apparently a market demand, and finally there was no justified reason for the refusal.

The refusal to license was decided under the heading of the essential facilities doctrine. The Court did not address the question whether one's obligation to license depends on the economic value of the asset protected under intellectual property law. The social benefit of the right to prohibit publication of a TV guide is hardly obvious. Neither the inspiration behind an artistic creation nor the perspiration behind a research effort is present: there was no significant sunk cost to justify an IPR protection. The economic rationale may be that the public wants to be confident that the published programmes are reliable. This, however, does not explain why the holder should be granted exclusivity, except if there is a risk of error in the competitors' publications.

Much of the litigation on the refusal to license would not take place if intellectual property rights were granted on more solid grounds. The proliferation of IPRs, many of dubious background, exacerbates problems at the interface of intellectual property law and competition policy. It would be useful to assign a screening function to the intellectual property system by sorting out inventions that would be undertaken without any intellectual protection from those that would not. Without such selection, frivolous intellectual property rights will most likely proliferate without adding a real social benefit and possibly provoking expensive litigation.

Tiercé Ladbroke[58]

The association that organizes horse races in France holds the copyright on the sounds and pictures of races. It refused to grant Tiercé Ladbroke – a Belgian bookmaker – a license to rebroadcast French horse races live. The Commission rejected a complaint by Ladbroke and the CFI rejected an attempt by Ladbroke to invoke Magill. The CFI limited the obligations of a dominant actor under Magill by holding that there was no duty to license live rebroadcast of French horse races to a firm that was already the leading provider of betting services in Belgium. But, it also made explicit the obligation of a producer to provide access to an indispensable input. The courts held that there might be a duty to supply where access was essential because there were no substitutes.[59]

Oscar Bronner[60]

Although it does not deal directly with intellectual property, the Oscar Bronner case has much in common with the previous cases. Mediaprint, an Austrian newspaper publisher and distributor, refused to distribute the daily newspaper of Oscar Bronner – a small publisher – through its national home-delivery network. Bronner complained to an Austrian court that, as a small publisher, it could not invest in a separate distribution network next to that of Mediaprint's dominant distribution service. Mediaprint argued that it was not required to help a competitor. The Austrian court referred to the ECJ the question of whether the refusal by a group holding a substantial share of the market in daily newspapers to allow the publisher of a competing newspaper access to its home-delivery network constituted an abuse of a dominant position. The Court argued that refusal would not constitute an abuse if there were alternatives to home delivery or if it were possible to develop a competing home delivery system. Considering that the plaintiff had not shown that it would be uneconomical for competitors to set up a second system, the Court ruled that there was no breach.

The ECJ decision has contributed to a better understanding of the essential facilities doctrine. Most importantly, the Advocate General stressed that in assessing the balance between the need to keep incentives for creation of the facility and the need to protect competition 'particular care is required where the goods or services or facilities to which access is demanded represent the fruit of substantial investment. That may be true in particular in relation to refusal to license intellectual property rights. Such exclusive rights are granted for a limited period that in itself involves a balancing of the interests in free competition with that of providing an incentive for research and development and for creativity. It is therefore for good reason that the Court has held that the refusal to license does not of itself, in the absence of other factors, constitute an abuse'.[61]

NDC/IMS[62]

IMS supplies reports on the regional sales of pharmaceutical products in different countries including Germany. In order to respect confidentiality pharmacies are grouped by zones called bricks or modules. IMS had created a database that partitioned German into 1860 modules. The database was used for marketing pharmaceuticals. In 1999, National Data Corporation (NDC) and Azyx entered the German market. They created a database compatible with that of IMS. IMS sued for infringement and won. When IMS refused to issue a license to NDC, the latter complained that this constituted an abuse of a dominant position. The Commission compelled IMS to grant a license to undertakings already present in the market. However, the order was suspended on appeal to the CFI. This suspension was later upheld by the ECJ. The Commission has now withdrawn its decision.

The IMS case puts the views of the Commission and those of CFI and ECJ in stark contrast (Derclaye, 2003). The Commission apparently reasoned that there had been an implicit adoption of the essential facilities doctrine and those earlier decisions, particularly Magill, yielded an unambiguous formula. For that reason it simply checked that the conditions listed by the ECJ in the earlier decision were met. Because it found that IMS had a dominant position in the German market, that its refusal was unjustified, that the refusal eliminated competition and that there was no actual or potential substitute to the IMS structure, it made an order to license.

The CFI emphasized that the circumstances of Magill were exceptional and that the facts in Magill and IMS were different. The judge advocated that 'the applicant has made out a provisional *prima facie* case that the Commission has misconstrued the scope of the principles set out in Magill'.[63] According to Derclaye (2003), the judgment suggests that there are two interpretations of the Magill case: the cumulative and the alternative interpretation. Under the cumulative interpretation the Commission failed to apply the first condition set out in Magill, namely that the refusal to license prevented the appearance of a new product which the IPR holder did not offer and for which there was a potential demand. Since such a condition was not apparent in the IMS case, the CFI overturned the decision of the Commission. Under the alternative interpretation, blocking access in order to weaken competition would have been sufficient to invoke Article 82.

Microsoft[64]

The European case against Microsoft involves two issues, both related to potential abuses of a dominant position. The first deals with the restriction of access to the interface between Windows and non-Microsoft work group servers; the second addresses the tie between the Windows Media player and the Windows operating system. In 2003, the Commission issued a preliminary injunction requiring that Microsoft provide greater technical information to its server competitors and that it cancel the tie between the operating system and Media Player. After the collapse of the settlement talks between the Commission and Microsoft in 2003, the Commission ruled (on 24 March 2004) that both practices constituted an abuse of dominance. As regards interoperability, Microsoft was required to disclose within four months complete and accurate interface information that would allow competing servers to achieve full compatibility with Windows PCs. Microsoft was enjoined to update this information when bringing out new versions of its product. As regards tying, Microsoft was required, with a delay of not more than three months, to offer PC manufacturers a version of its Windows PC operating system without Media Player. The Commission held that this remedy would allow the bundle configuration to reflect what consumers want and not what Microsoft imposes. Finally, Microsoft was also fined 497 million euros for abusing its market power in the EU.

Microsoft applied for interim relief, requesting from the CFI a suspension of the measure on the grounds that it would do irreparable damage. The CFI dismissed the application for interim measures.[65] More recently, Microsoft has accepted it must comply with the measures and at time of writing it appears to be going ahead with this.

We focus here on the disclosure order. The technical documentation allowing interoperability does not concern the Windows source code, which is not necessary for the development of interoperable products. It concerns only the specifications of the interface between the Windows PC operating system and the non-Microsoft work group servers.[66] Whether these specifications are covered or not by IPR is a complex and technical issue. Even if it does not rule out the possibility that these specifications may be covered by copyright, the Commission maintains that their implementation by others does not constitute a breach of copyright since they lead to clearly distinct works (point 168 in the CFI Order). If these specifications had been protected by patents, the issue would probably have been decided differently. What would happen if these specifications were only protected by trade secrecy law? The argument of the Commission is not completely convincing on this: 'the Commission acknowledges that Directive 91/250[67] does not require the inventor to disclose the information on his own initiative. However, from the aspect of any trade secret that Microsoft may have, disclosing interoperability information is not comparable to licensing a competitor to copy a work protected by intellectual property legislation. That assertion is supported by the technical relevance of such disclosure, by the practices in the software industry and by Microsoft's own behaviour when it entered the market' (point 183 in the CFI order).

At this stage, it is difficult to draw a definite conclusion about refusal to license from the Microsoft case except the very general one that the evolution of technology raises new and complex issues at the interface of IPR and competition law. It could be interesting to develop some guidelines clarifying the exceptional circumstances under which access would be mandatory. For instance, it could be helpful to state that non-access is acceptable except when all three of the following conditions hold: first, access is indispensable for providing a product on a secondary market; second, there is an objective potential demand for the would-be product, and third, there are no objective justifications for the refusal. But even if these conditions are met, other questions remain open. For instance what would be the *reasonable price* for the licensing of the disclosed information if access and interoperability were made compulsory?

To conclude this section, we would like to emphasize that the treatment of refusal to license essential intellectual property rights is a very important question in the framework of cumulative innovation, particularly in ICT and biotechnology.[68] The cumulative character of successive innovations, in which improvements and applications derive from previous inventions, raises concerns that intellectual property rights may create difficulties for follow-up inventions. But, rather than compelling intellectual property holders to license their right when it is essential, another suggested way is to develop bilateral or multilateral agreements such as cross-licensing, patent pools and collective management of intellectual property rights. We turn now to this last issue.

COLLECTIVE MANAGEMENT OF INTELLECTUAL PROPERTY RIGHTS

Background

Collective management of rights allows authors to overcome the transaction cost hurdle that impedes the individual exercise of rights granted to them under copyright law. Copyright collectives – also called collection societies – emerged to manage rights in works that have a great number of potential users but where the value of a single work to the individual user is small. In such situations, management of rights by individual holders is not economically justified. Under individual management, the costs of negotiating with users, collecting payments, identifying those who infringe and suing them would exceed the amount the right-holder could expect to collect. Collective administration of copyright addresses the problem by spreading the costs over a great many works.

Under collective management, individual right-holders assign their right(s) to an organization which carries out the following tasks on their behalf: it monitors the use of works in its repertory, it takes legal action against those who infringe copyright in these works, it negotiates fees with users and collects payments, and it distributes payments to its members after deduction of overheads.[69]

The oldest and largest collectives manage public performance rights for music in a repertoire that contains millions of works. They grant licenses to music users such as broadcasters, restaurants, concert halls and sports arenas.[70] The typical license granted by a performing rights society is a blanket license. Such licenses give the licensee the right to unlimited use of all the works in the repertoire managed by the collective. Typically, the licensing fee correlates with the scale of users' operations and the importance of music to their activities.[71] The amounts redistributed by the collective to members depend on the amount of use of their music, and on whether that music played a central or ancillary role for the purposes it was used.

By tradition, collectives are active only in the territory of the country where they are located. However, within that territory they administer a worldwide repertoire made up of works entrusted to them by local authors, and works assigned to them under reciprocal representation agreements with foreign collectives. This arrangement allows local users to obtain via the collective located in their national territory, unlimited access to a (virtual) worldwide repertory of copyrighted music. Such a right is important to music users who need unlimited and unplanned access to a large repertory. The blanket license offers the guarantee that any music performed in public will not infringe copyright.[72]

In almost all countries a single society manages the performing rights. Users who need spur-of-the-moment access to a very large repertoire cannot circumvent the national society when it holds the exclusive license to manage the performing rights in all present and future works of its members, and when a substantial portion of authors who produce the type of work required by the user are members. As a rule, performing right societies are assigned exclusive rights by their members.[73]

The role of collectives in copyright management has been expanding. Collectives are active in areas such as synchronization, reproduction, neighbouring rights and public lending.[74] More often than not, one society is responsible for the collective administration of a specific right for a particular class of works.[75]

This section will deal almost exclusively with performing rights societies in music because they are the oldest societies and they have been the subject of most antitrust scrutiny.

Competition Issues

The forms of conduct that have come under scrutiny on both sides of the Atlantic are usefully grouped under the following headings: actions that strengthen the collectives' capacity to exploit existing market power vis-à-vis users, and actions designed to favour some members at the expense of other members.[76]

1. Blanket licenses versus limited repertory licensing

The question whether collectives abuse their position of dominance when they refuse to grant licenses for a portion of their repertory was addressed by the European Court of Justice in the *Tournier* Judgment. Years before, the claimants – a group of discotheque owners – had initiated a case before the French competition authority, arguing that the SACEM – the French performing rights society – was acting abusively when it refused to grant them licenses for a repertoire that contained only popular dance music of predominantly Anglo-American origin. The claimants argued that they should not have to pay for the rights in other works that they would never use. The foreign collectives had already refused them licenses for such music.

The ECJ (where the case was referred by a French court for a preliminary ruling) held that 'the refusal by a national society for the management of copyright in musical works to grant the users of recorded music access only to the foreign repertoire represented by it does not have the object of restricting competition in the common market unless access to part of the protected repertoire could entirely safeguard the interest of the authors, composers and publishers of music without thereby increasing the costs of managing contracts and monitoring the use of protected musical works'.[77] The apparent implication is that a refusal to issue limited repertory licenses would be illegal if collectives could somehow fully uphold authors' interests without incurring cost increases.

The economic rationale behind a demand for partial repertory licenses is not clear. The royalties paid to collectives do – in principle at least – reflect the value of the music to users. The mere fact that an individual uses a small subset of a repertoire does not imply that the music he uses is less valuable to him. To some users (for example, discotheques) the music is vital. One must assume that the demands for limited repertory licenses derive from a belief that some regulatory authority would enforce a form of price control under which the royalty for a limited repertory license would relate to the royalty charged for a blanket license in a way that reflects the difference in the number of works cleared.

Also, there is little doubt that making limited repertory licensing available is costly. While the costs of dividing the repertoire are not likely to be significant, there is a possibility that litigation costs will be incurred when users and societies disagree on how particular songs should be classified.[78] Also, because a substantial portion of a collective's repertory consists of new songs, users who acquire a limited license would have to verify on an ongoing basis whether the new releases they want to play are in fact covered by their license. In addition, monitoring costs are higher because societies want to insure that users do not perform works for which they have not cleared the rights.

Because of the extra cost associated with fractional licensing, and because the product being licensed is a public good, it is likely that the parties would settle on a blanket license even if the collective was bound to issue a limited repertory license on demand.

2. The assignment of rights to collectives
The questions raised by competition authorities concerning collective societies include:

- Does a society act abusively when it administers a specific right only on condition that the right holder hand over other rights pertaining to the same works?
- Does a society lessen competition unduly when it declines to administer a specific right on behalf of a person who refuses to assign that right in respect to all possible uses or users of a work?
- Does a collective abuse its position of dominance when it demands that rights be assigned in a form that rules out direct and independent licensing by members with respect to the same rights?
- Does a society unduly restrict competition when it accepts members on condition that the rights they assign embrace all the works in which they hold such rights?

The following principles were laid down by the Commission in the important *GEMA*[79] case: members of collectives must have the right to choose which rights, among a number of rights or utilisation categories established by the Commission, they wish to exploit through the collective, and a collective may demand that a member assign a specific right to all works within the categories that it administers.[80]

The Commission considered the issue of partial assignment again when two members of Daft Punk (a French techno-music group) applied for membership in SACEM in respect of all their rights, except two categories identified in the GEMA decision. They were advised by the French society that membership would be denied unless they showed that another society had been appointed in respect of the excluded rights. In response to a finding by the Commission that such a requirement was abusive of SACEM's dominant position, the French society amended the internal regulation that barred membership of authors who reside in the EU and do not assign all rights to it or another society. Under the amended rule, SACEM can remove this restriction and accept the author. This change was accepted by the Commission, which stressed that refusals to do so should be exceptional and based on objective reasons.[81]

Neither the GEMA nor the SACEM decision disputed the legality of a collective's demand that a right assigned to it should be exclusive. It is significant in that regard that some jurisdictions have expanded the list of conditions under which members can withdraw from collective management. In Ireland and the UK, for example, performing right societies are required to allow members to divide the performing right into categories and decide which of the categories they entrust to collective administration. Upon request from a member, the local societies are duty-bound to license back, on a non-exclusive basis, all or part of the performing right in members' works performed in live concerts – the so-called 'live event right' – by the members. This arrangement allows members to negotiate a performance royalty at the time they settle on other contractual terms with promoters of concerts or owners of venues.[82]

3. Rivalry between collectives

As indicated above, the licenses granted by societies allow for the public performance of music within the national boundaries of the territory in which the societies operate. The main justification for such territorial limitation is the need for a local presence to monitor the uses of works entrusted to the collective. Such presence is not necessary for on-line distribution because specialized software allows monitoring at a distance of all the music delivered via a particular server. This makes worldwide management via a single organization possible. For that reason it holds the promise of significant cost savings. It also removes a key justification for societies not to compete in the cross-border provision of services. To enhance the management efficiency of the rights in music delivered via the Internet, a number of societies established in different national territories have entered into agreements that allow some users to clear rights for many national territories via a single organization.

The Commission has recently handed down an important ruling in regard to agreements that cover the rights of performers in music distributed concurrently by broadcast and on the Internet. This form of distribution is called simulcasting.[83] The competition issues raised by simulcasting were brought to the Commission's attention by an application for a negative clearance for an agreement among 29 European and other societies. The agreement allowed music users to clear rights for multiple territories and/or pay equitable remuneration via a single party.[84]

Under the original agreement a collective could grant a multi-territorial license only to simulcasters whose signals originated in its national territory. The licensing fee would have been equal to the sum of the individual tariffs set by each society for simulcasting on its own territory.[85] Because of concerns expressed by the Commission, the agreement was amended to allow any party that had entered the agreement, and was established in the EEA, to grant a multi-territorial simulcasting license to any broadcaster whose signal originated in the EEA. This amendment opened a door to some competition among EEA-based collectives that were party to the agreement. However, price competition remained limited because aggregation of national tariffs meant that all participating societies would grant one and the same product at an identical price. The only price-related competition that could benefit users related to such factors as conditions of payment and rebates.

The Commission argued that such limited price competition was too feeble to benefit small or medium scale users. It reasoned that the amalgamation of the royalty and the administrative fee into a single price, as provided under the original and amended agreements, was not necessary to the existence of the agreement and that it 'prevents prospective users from assessing the efficiency of each one of the participating societies and from benefiting from the licensing services from the society capable of providing them at a lower cost.'[86] The Commission held that competition would be enhanced if the aggregate payments were broken into separate components: a copyright royalty and an administration fee.

The parties responded by submitting a second amendment that provided for a mechanism under which collecting societies in the EEA would specify which part of their tariff corresponds to the administration fee charged to the user. This part would be determined with reference to actual administration cost of the individual grantor society.

With this change, the Commission accepted the agreement arguing that this arrangement was the 'least restrictive of the alternatives in the present circumstances so as to create and distribute a new product'. It also held that in the absence of a 'minimum degree of control over licensing terms' societies could earn revenue lower than by not participating in an agreement necessary to provide a new product to users. If so, their incentive to participate would disappear.[87] The Commission's decision was also motivated by the fact that the form of co-operation between societies required under the agreement did not take the place of existing competition.

4. Opening up alternative options

The potential for increased competition depends on whether it will be possible for new actors to license the rights managed by the collectives. The options that matter from a competition perspective are primarily those that allow right holders and users to bypass the collective.

Consider the option of non-exclusive licenses. Such an option removes the contractual impediment to direct negotiation between music users and right holders or their representatives, in regard to rights managed by collectives. To exert competitive pressure, the option must be credible, that is, it must be attractive to some users and to the owners of the music they wish to perform. Direct licensing of the right may be appealing to a user who has no need for unlimited and unplanned access to a large repertoire of copyrighted works. It may also draw users who require such access for a segment of their activities if they can acquire a mini-blanket license for that segment at a price sufficiently less than the standard blanket licence.[88]

Transaction costs are larger under this option than under blanket licensing. A major component of transaction costs is the cost of monitoring users of music. Another increase in transaction costs may be due to the cost of negotiating terms. However, the latter is likely to be lower when the user commissions new music than when he seeks to acquire the performing right for an existing work.[89] Nevertheless, transactions costs, in many cases, may be high.

The performing right is only one component of the cost of performing music. Blanket licensing rules out price competition for the performance of components of the repertoire. It does not, however, preclude efforts by rights holders to bring price strategies into play in order to stimulate the demand for their music. Some users – film makers, for example – may have to acquire both a performing and a synchronization license. As long as the royalties paid to clear other rights pertaining to the same works are set individually, there remains some competition for the works. A user of music is concerned about the sum of payments for all the rights he must clear. The decomposition of payments into performing royalties and other royalties hardly matters. As long as some important complementary rights are licensed individually, a higher price in the blanket performing license should be accompanied by some decrease in the price of the complementary licenses.

CONCLUSION

This chapter has looked at three areas where the exercise of intellectual property rights appears to conflict with competition policy objectives. It has discussed major judgments handed down by the European courts that clarify how Articles 81 and 82 of the EC Treaty rein in rights to exclude granted under intellectual property laws.

The analysis of parallel trade suggests that courts are more likely to strike down agreements that segment the EU into national markets than arrangements that serve to protect the EU market from imports originating from outside the Union. The Trade Marks Directive illustrates in the clearest possible fashion the paramount goal of creating a single European market. It is now established that unless explicit authorization to sell into the EU is granted, the holder of a European trademark can block such imports. Also, private agreements that pursue this objective are not considered, by their very nature, to be anti-competitive. Further evidence of the weight assigned to creating a single market is provided by the Commission's *per se* treatment of explicit private agreements to stop parallel trade among Member States.

Such harsh treatment of segmentation is difficult to justify on purely economic grounds. An interesting question, therefore, is whether competition authorities will take the same view of unilateral conduct that partitions the EU into national territories. The courts may well face this issue in the near future because the existence of a significant gap in purchasing power between old and new Member States is likely to raise the benefits from geographical segmentation.

The judgements that concern refusals to license know-how, or products protected by patents or copyright, do not provide a coherent picture of the conditions under which a right holder is compelled to issue a license. It is clear that competition objectives do limit the scope of the right to exclude granted by intellectual property laws, but the circumstances when they do seem case-specific. The conditions of the much cited Magill decision have been termed exceptional. The Oscar Bronner judgment, which stresses that the cost of developing the essential input is crucial, appears well founded in economics. However, its impact on future rulings remains uncertain.

Copyright collectives have always raised challenging questions from an antitrust perspective. Blanket licensing and requirements that authors assign all rights or none to the collective certainly appear to have anti-competitive potential. Also, the organization of markets in which collectives operate gives collectives a position of dominance. Yet, because of the specificities of the markets in which these societies operate, they have been allowed to engage in conduct that would otherwise run afoul of competition rules. European courts have rightly been concerned that mandating alternative contractual arrangements between on the one hand, collectives and users, and on the other hand, collective organizations and their members, would undermine the capacity of authors to exercise rights granted to them by law. It appears that national authorities rather than European authorities have gone furthest in experimenting with some alternative arrangements.

The trade-off between the desire to promote the emergence of new products and the desire to promote competition comes across very clearly in the process that led to adoption of the final version of the Simulcast agreement. The Commission finally settled for a formula that rules out price competition for the product itself but gives parties to the agreement an incentive to minimize overall charges.

NOTES

1. We thank Roger Clarke and Eleanor Morgan for their insightful comments on a previous version.
2. Available at www.european-patent-office.org/legal/epc/.
3. Proposal for a Council Regulation on the Community Patent, COM (2000) 412 final, OJ C337 E/278, 28 November 2000.
4. See also C. Martinez and D. Guellec, 'Overview of recent changes in patent regimes in United States, Japan and Europe', IPR, Innovation and Economic Performance conference, OECD, 28 August 2003.
5. The Court of Appeals for the Federal Circuit has nationwide jurisdiction and hears specialized cases like patent and international trade cases. See www.fedcir.gov.
6. The agreement on Trade Related aspects of Intellectual Property Rights (TRIPS), which has over 140 members, goes beyond the requirement that protection applies to foreign inventors as to domestic ones by also specifying a minimum set of rights that each Member State must provide (see Scotchmer, 2004, p. 320).
7. For an overview of the tensions at the interface of IPR and competition policy, see Federal Trade Commission 'To promote innovation: the proper balance of competition and patent law and policy', 2003, available at www.ftc.gov/os/2003/10/innovationrpt.pdf.
8. J. Vickers, 'Competition policy and innovation', speech to the International Competition Policy Conference, Oxford, 27 June 2001 available at www.oft.gov.uk.
9. A patent pool is an agreement under which the owners of different technologies license them as a bundle. See Merges (1999), Carlson (1999), Lerner and Tirole (2002), Lerner, Strojwas and Tirole (2003) and Scotchmer (2004, pp. 175-80).
10. As detailed below, 'exhaustion regimes' refer to how intellectual property rights are weakened by the trade of protected goods and services.
11. 'Grey trade' means that the products are neither black, that is, counterfeited, nor white since they are sold against the will of at least one IPR holder.
12. The price gaps may be due to differences in demand elasticity or to divergent pricing by regulators across countries, as is the case of pharmaceuticals.
13. When additional markets are being served, consumers in these countries will benefit and consumers in countries which would have been served under uniform prices need not lose.
14. Adoption of such policies would, however, run afoul of importers' most favoured nation obligations under WTO rules. WTO membership does not limit a country's freedom to choose its policy with respect to parallel trade. However, it requires the country to abide by the most favoured nation rule regardless of the policy it chooses.
15. The relevant literature is reviewed in Stole (forthcoming). See also Encaoua and Hollander (2004).
16. That is both the manufacturer and the distributor set price above marginal cost.

17. Gallini and Hollis (1999) give a detailed overview of the pros and cons of market segmentation, focussing on the restrictions on parallel imports achieved via trademark protection.
18. See Crampes, Hollander and Macdissi (2004).
19. For example, the international distribution of films on DVD has been technologically and legally segmented into geographical markets. The regional coding system requires that all DVD players be manufactured for distribution and use in one of six geographic regions around the world. It is a global initiative by agents of the film and DVD industries aimed at preventing the free movement of licensed copies of copyright DVDs around the world. Dunt, Gans, and King (2001) have studied whether the restrictions on DVD usage across regions can be justified as a means of generating potentially socially desirable price discrimination for content providers or are simply a means of restricting competition. They conclude that 'the conditions that may theoretically allow such restrictions to be efficient are unlikely to hold in the case of DVDs and that social welfare is likely to be significantly enhanced by eliminating such technical restrictions' (p. 1). Their argument is that among the four potential consequences of such restrictions on regional flows (price discrimination, collusion, free-riding and the prevention of consumer confusion), the latter two – potentially socially desirable – consequences are unlikely to be important.
20. However, in some instances a moderate amount of parallel imports may actually benefit a manufacturer: see Anderson and Ginsburgh (1999).
21. Some of these right-holders can still prohibit certain uses of the CD. For example, they can forbid its performance on radio or in any public place. The reason is that the right to perform the CD in public is not exhausted upon the first sale of the CD.
22. This assumes that the goods have not been altered after they have been put on the market by the owner of the trademark or with his consent. Repackaging is not *per se* forbidden: see 'Commission Communication on parallel imports of proprietary medicinal products – frequently asked questions', MEMO 04/7, Brussels, 19 January 2004.
23. The Directive was adopted in 1989 (Council Directive 89/104/EEC, 21 December 1988) but became effective only in 1996. 'A trademark may consist of any sign capable of being represented graphically, particularly words, including personal names, designs, letters, numerals, the shape of goods or of their packaging, provided that such signs are capable of distinguishing the goods or services of one undertaking from those of other undertakings' (Article 2). The objective of a trademark is to help buyers to identify the source of products. This gives producers the incentive to improve quality.
24. The European Economic Area currently consists of the EU countries together with Norway, Iceland and Lichtenstein.
25. Before the Directive went into effect, most EU countries operated under international exhaustion. A concise review of the history of the Directive appears in Trogh (2002). Although the exhaustion regime is mainly applied to trademarks, it also concerns the topography of semiconductors (Article 5(5) of Council Directive 87/54/EEC, 16 December 1986), patents (Article 28 of Agreement 89/695/EEC, 15 December 1989), biological inventions (Article 10 of Council Directive 98/44/EC, 6 July 1998) and designs (Article 15 of Directive 98/71/EC, 13 October 1998). The European Court of Justice applied the principle to copyrights (*Musik-Vertrieb Membran GmbH* Case 55/80 and *KKK-Tel International v. GEMA* Case 57/80) and to patents (*Centrafarm v. Sterling Drugs* Case 15/74). Our focus here is on the competition issues raised by the protection afforded by trademarks.
26. *Silhouette International v Hartlauer Handelsgesellschaft*, Case C-355/96.
27. Opinion of Advocate-General Jacobs, paragraph 41 cited by Trogh (2002). The case involved the attempt by the Austrian owner of the Silhouette trademark to prohibit the importation into Austria of a type of genuine Silhouette sunglasses legally marketed in Bulgaria but no longer sold in Austria. Prior to accession to the EU, Austria operated under a regime of international exhaustion. Having failed in its action for trademark infringement before the lower courts, Silhouette appealed to the Supreme Court of Austria which submitted a reference to the European Court of Justice. The ECJ, therefore, overturned the decision in the Austrian courts.
28. Case C-173/98. The case involved a suit brought by the owner of the Sebago trademark against a Belgian firm that imported shoes from the Salvadorian manufacturer of the genuine product for resale under the original label. The claimant argued that the importer had infringed his trademarks because he had not received consent to market the shoes in the EU.

29. C- 414/99 and C- 416/99.
30. *Javico International and Javico AG v. Yves Saint Laurent Parfums SA*, Case C-306/96, 28 April 1998.
31. The Court said that a violation may take place 'where the Community market in the products in question is characterized by an oligopolistic structure or by an appreciable difference between the prices charged for the contractual product within the Community and those charged outside the Community and where, in view of the production and sales in the Member States, the prohibition entails a risk that it might have an appreciable effect on the pattern of trade between Member States such as to undermine attainment of the objectives of the common market' (paragraph 28 of the judgement).
32. Unless such provisions allowed the owner of the trademark to claim damages for infringement that would otherwise not be awarded.
33. For example, in *VW*, Case IV/35.733, '(t)he obstruction of parallel exports of vehicles by final consumers and of cross deliveries within the dealer network hampers the objective of the creation of the common market, a principle of the Treaty, and is already for that reason to be classified as a particularly serious infringement.'
34. *PO/Yamaha*, Case COMP/37.975, Decision of 16 July 2003.
35. The details of the contractual provision differed to some extent from one country to another but their essence was very similar. The contracts also contained provisions that restricted the dealers' pricing policies.
36. Iceland is part of the EEA and hence is 'within' Europe in this discussion.
37. It also noted that under settled case law there is no need for the purpose of application of Article 81(1), to show an actual anti-competitive effect of agreed conduct whose object it is to restrict competition within the Common Market.
38. The *Javico* ruling mentioned earlier states that 'an agreement which requires a reseller not to resell products outside the contractual territory has as its object the exclusion of parallel imports within the Community and consequently restriction of competition in the common market ... Such provisions, in contracts for the distribution of products within the Community, therefore constitute by their very nature a restriction of competition.' *Javico International*, Case C-306/96, paragraph 14.
39. Commission decision 96/478/EC. Article 3 of the decision imposed a fine of ECU 3 million and Article 4 fixed a penalty of ECU 1000 for each day's delay in informing the wholesalers that exports are allowed within the Community and are not penalized.
40. Judgement òf 26 October 2000, OJ C95, 24 March 2001.
41. Remember that establishing the existence of a potentially anti-competitive agreement relieves the Commission of the obligation to show an effective or probable lessening of competition as a result of the agreement.
42. This begs the question whether some forms of cheating on a mundane price-fixing cartel could similarly protect a participant from being accused of tacit collusion.
43. *Sandoz v Commission*, Case C-277/87, rec. P.I-45.
44. Joined cases C-2/01 P and C-3/01 P.
45. After all, restrictions of parallel trade go against a fundamental objective of the Treaty of Rome which is integration of national markets.
46. In August 2001, the Commission cleared certain provisions of the Visa international payment card system, in particular the so-called 'no-discrimination rule' which prohibits merchants from charging customers a fee for paying with a Visa card, or offering discounts for cash payments. The Commission had originally objected to this rule arguing that it was a restriction on competition but changed its opinion in the light of the results of market surveys carried out in Sweden and the Netherlands, where the no-discrimination rule had been abolished following the intervention of national competition authorities. See the statistical studies at europa.eu.int/comm/ competition/antitrust/cases/29373/studies/sweden/report.pdf and europa.eu.int/comm/ competition/antitrust/cases/29373/studies/netherlands/report.pdf.
47. It is consistent with the view, as noted above, that a primary aim of EU policy is to create the single European market.

48. See Ganslandt and Maskus (1999) and NERA 'The economic consequences of the choice of a regime of exhaustion in the area of trademarks', Final Report prepared for the European Commission, 1999, available at www.nera.com/Publication.asp?p_ID=808.

49. Nevertheless European Competition authorities seem to take a particularly dim view of restrictions designed to prevent arbitrage. In the words of the Director General of DG Competition at the Commission '... sales restrictions may be used to prevent arbitrage and support price discrimination between different markets. This will in general lead to a loss of consumer welfare. While some consumers will pay a higher price and others will pay a lower price, collectively consumers will have to pay more to finance the extra profits obtained by the supplier and to cover the extra costs of supporting the price discrimination scheme. Therefore consumer welfare will in general decline unless it can be clearly shown that otherwise the lower priced market(s) would not be served at all and that therefore the price discrimination will lead to an undisputable increase of output. It's only in the latter case that consumer welfare may actually increase' (cited by Lowe, 2004).

50. A useful introduction to the essential facility doctrine can be found in Temple Lang (2000). Different illustrations related to the transport sector under EU competition rulings are given in Motta (2004, Chapter 2, note 53).

51. Maurer and Scotchmer assume that marginal costs are increasing and that fixed costs are such that only two firms can operate in the market. Inefficiency can then arise if production is not allocated optimally between the two suppliers.

52. Case C-53/87, ECR 6039, 1988.

53. Case C-238/87, ECR 6211, 1989.

54. Case T-69/89, ECR II-485, 1991.

55. The presentation of this case is inspired from Korah (2001) and Derclaye (2003).

56. Commission decision 89/205/EEC.

57. Cases C-241/91 P and C-242/91 P, 1995, ECR I-743.

58. Case T-504/93, 1997, ECR II-923.

59. 'The refusal to supply the applicant could not fall within the prohibition laid down by Article 86 (now 82) unless it concerned a product or service which was either essential for the exercise of the activity in question, in that there was no real or potential substitute, or was a new product whose introduction might be prevented, despite specific, constant and regular potential demand on the part of consumers' (*Tiercé Ladbroke v. Commission*, CFI, Case T-504/93, paragraph 131).

60. Case C-7/97, 1997, ECR II-923.

61. Advocate General Jacob's opinion in *Oscar Bronner v. Mediaprint*, Case C 7/97, paragraph 61.

62. *NDC Health v IMS Health*, Case COMP D3/38.044, OJ L 59, 28 February 2002, CFI judgement: *IMS Health Inc. v Commission*, Case T-184/01, 2001, ECR II-3193.

63. *IMS Health Inc. v Commission*, Case T-184/01 R, at 24.

64. Case T-201/04R, *Microsoft v Commission*.

65. Order of the President of the CFI, 22 December 2004, available at www.europa.eu.int or curia.eu.int.

66. A group server operating system runs on central network computers that provide services to office workers around the world in their day-to-day work (file sharing, printing, etc.).

67. Council Directive 91/250/EEC of May 1991 on the legal protection of computer programmes.

68. See J. Walsh, A. Arora and W. Cohen, 'The patenting and licensing of research tools and biomedical inventions', prepared for the Science, Technology and Economic Policy Board of the National Academies, USA, 2002.

69. Members repossess their rights when they leave the society.

70. The right to perform a work of music in public is one among several exclusive rights that copyright law grants composers.

71. The tariff base often equals the revenues earned by the user during a representative period; for example, the tariff rate is lower for sports arenas where music plays a lesser role than for concert halls where its role is central.

72. Although public performance often requires that complementary rights be cleared, collectives rarely provide a one-stop-shop. For example, a broadcaster may have to copy songs onto hard disk in order to perform them in public. This means that the right to reproduce the work must also be cleared. For such a user a collective becomes a one-stop-shop only if it administers the public

performing right, the reproduction right, and the remaining copyrights and neighbouring rights that must be cleared to perform the music.

73. The most notable exception to this arrangement is found in the United States where the two main societies – ASCAP (www.ascap.com) and BMI (www.bmi.com) – are bound under the terms of consent agreements to accept only non-exclusive licenses.

74. A review of various types of collective administration can be found in Ficsor (1990) and D. Gervais, 'Gestion collective du droit d'auteur et des droits voisins au Canada: perspective internationale', Rapport prepare pour le Ministère du Patrimoine Canadien, 2001, available at www.pch.gc.ca/progs/ac-ca/progs/pda-cpb/pubs/collective/collective_f.pdf

75. For example, there may be two societies that manage reproduction where one will deal with the reproduction of musical works while the other specializes in the reproduction of literary works.

76. To address the concerns of monopoly power, some countries, including the UK and Canada, have adopted systems of compulsory licenses or regulation of tariffs by specialized administrative tribunals. Other countries rely primarily on the enforcement of competition law.

77. *Ministère Public versus Jean-Louis Tournier*, Case 395/87, 13 July 1989.

78. In this regard see Broadcast Music Moor Law Inc. Civ. A 77-325.

79. GEMA (Geselschaft für Musikalische Auffuerungs und Mechanische Verfielfaetigungsrechte) is the German performing rights society.

80. GEMA, OJ L134, 20 June 1971 and GEMAII, OJ L166, 24 July 1972.

81. D. Wood, 'Collective management and EU competition law', European Commission, 2001, available at europa.eu.int/comm/competition/speeches/text/sp2001_025_en.pdf. and Bulletin EU 7/8-2002 Competition (24/40).

82. The reason given by the UK Monopolies and Mergers Commission for recommending that members be entitled to administer their own live performances rights is that the circumstances in which this would occur would be tightly and clearly defined, and that live performances, such as major tours, were in many respects similar to performances of operas and ballets which are classified as grand rights where the articles of association permit direct agreement between their copyright holder and the organizer of the performance. See Monopolies and Mergers Commission, 'Performing Rights: A Report on the Supply in the UK of the Services of Administering Performing Rights and Film Synchronization Rights', Cmnd. 3147, London: HMSO, 1996.

83. *IFPI Simulcasting*, Case COMP C-2/38.014, Decision of 8 October 2002, OJ L107, 30 April 2003. Another agreement (the Santiago Agreement) deals with performance licensing when no simulcasting is involved; see press release IP/04/586. A third agreement (the Barcelona Agreement) deals with reproduction rights.

84. Clearance was sought by the International Federation of the Phonographic Industry (IFPI).

85. The latter could be based on a percentage of the revenue generated from the simulcast within its territory.

86. *IFPI Simulcasting* Case COMP C-2/38.014, Commission decision of 8 October 2002 relating to a proceeding under Article 81 of the EC Treaty and Article 53 of the EEA Agreement.

87. *IFPI Simulcasting*, paragraphs 111-13.

88. Such a user could be a broadcaster who uses only pre-recorded music.

89. This is because the user and the supplier are already engaged in dialogue.

9. EU State Aid Control

Fiona Wishlade

INTRODUCTION

The control of State aids is a key component of the EU competition rules and has become an important strand of the internal market provisions. The European Commission's role in disciplining subsidies is unique in international law. This is not only because its supranational authority is unparalleled, but also because the context for its decisions extends beyond considering the economic impacts that are familiar to trade economists; the Commission must assess the potential trade and competition effects of State aid against the contribution that intervention could make to wider EU Treaty objectives such as economic and social cohesion, sustainable development and research and development.

Provisions for the control of State aids were included in the Treaty of Rome from the outset; the authors of the Treaty clearly recognised that some means of limiting subsidies and other forms of government intervention were vital in the establishment of a 'common market'; as barriers to trade were being outlawed, the temptation for Member States to resort to other types of protectionism was considered likely to increase.

The key provisions are Articles 87 to 89 of the EC Treaty. However the Treaty does not define what a State aid actually is, probably because a clear definition might simply have encouraged governments to find ingenious ways of circumventing the rules (Schina, 1987, p. 13). In consequence, the definition of a State aid is frequently the subject of Commission decisions or European Court of Justice rulings that fine-tune, or sometimes radically extend, the range and type of measures that are subject to control.

In essence, Article 87 prohibits State aids, subject to certain exceptions; Article 88 sets out the role of the European Commission and of the Member States, and Article 89 enables the Council to adopt Regulations for the implementation of Article 87 and 88. Although State aids are in principle banned under the Treaty, Articles 87(2) and (3) provide for a number of exceptions. Article 87(2), which provides for some mandatory derogations from the ban is relatively restrictive in scope and has generally been uncontroversial. In broad terms, the three categories of aids that are *de jure* exempted from this general ban are: aids of a 'social' nature;[1] aids related to the damage caused by natural disasters; and aids to parts of the Federal Republic of Germany affected by the division of Germany. Those types of aid that may be considered to be compatible with the common market are outlined in Article 87(3) and the interpretation of this provision by the Commission has resulted in a significant body of soft law and, increasingly, secondary legislation. This has led to the authorisation of State aid for a range of policy purposes such as regional development, research and development, supporting small and medium-sized enterprises (SMEs) and environmental protection.

EU State aid control was long regarded as the Cinderella of EU competition policy and the use of the State aid provisions was very tentative in the early years of the Community. The control of State aid moved up the Commission's policy agenda in the early 1990s as trade barriers were further dismantled under the Single Market programme[2] and it is increasingly seen as a policy that has come of age. Procedures have been progressively formalised over the last few years, and a higher priority has been given to the enforcement of Commission State aid decisions (Hansen, van Ysendyck and Zühlke, 2004).

In terms of substance, the scope of Commission scrutiny has broadened beyond the 'classic' instruments of government intervention such as grants, soft loans and capital injections, to include aspects of fiscal and social security systems and the financing of public service obligations. Moreover, the liberalisation of large segments of hitherto State-owned monopoly sectors has increased the range of activities potentially subject to the State aid rules. In parallel, however, the environment in which policy operates has become increasingly complex. Successive Treaty amendments have emphasised the linkages between policy areas, such as the requirement for national and EU policies to contribute to economic and social cohesion. The recent enlargement to embrace ten new Member States presents significant challenges both to the substance of policy and to its application.

At macroeconomic and political levels, attitudes towards State aids have been influenced by the so-called Lisbon agenda,[3] with the Council of Ministers taking a growing interest in the scale and efficiency of government intervention, reflected in the declared objective of 'less aid, but better'. However, while the Council has ostensibly become increasingly supportive of Commission attempts to rein in State aids, this commitment is often noticeably absent when national interests are at stake in individual cases. As former Commissioner Peter Sutherland observed 'in my time in the Commission I have detected a marked tendency in all Member States to regard other people's State aids as bad and their own as fully justified.'[4]

Against the backdrop of this changing economic and geopolitical environment, this chapter provides an overview of the key elements and recent evolution of State aid control policy. The rest of the chapter is structured in four further parts as follows. The second part sets out the broad context of State aid control. The third part identifies the types of instrument regarded as State aid and subject to scrutiny. The definition of State aid is a crucial issue since measures that distort competition, but do not involve State aid, must be dealt with under other Treaty provisions, with notably less powerful means of redress. The fourth part of the chapter reviews the Commission's approach to State aid in different policy areas, exploring how the Commission has interpreted its role in balancing trade and competition considerations against the wider objectives of the EU. The final part of the chapter discusses a number of current themes in the evolution of policy, considers key recent developments against this background and highlights some future issues and challenges in State aid control.

THE CONTEXT OF STATE AID CONTROL

Role of the European Commission

The European Commission arguably has more autonomy and authority over the Member States in the field of State aid than in any other arena of EU policy; it has progressively extended the scope of its discipline over government intervention and increasingly sought to monitor and to reduce overall levels of expenditure. This section begins by discussing the role of the European Commission while the next section provides an indication of the overall scale of State aid spending.

Article 88 of the Treaty gives the European Commission wide-ranging powers in the sphere of State aid control. There are three principal aspects to these powers. First, the Commission has a general duty to review aid and propose 'any appropriate measures required by the progressive development or by the functioning of the Common Market' (Article 88(1)). Second, Member States must notify the Commission of any plans to offer aid in advance of implementation, in order for the Commission to assess their compatibility with the common market. This means that there is a 'stand still' requirement – aid cannot be paid until the Commission has given its approval. Aid that is not notified aid or aid paid prior to approval is illegal and the Commission can require its repayment. Third, after formal investigation, to which other Member States and third parties may contribute, the Commission can require Member States to abolish or amend aid measures if it considers them incompatible with the Common Market.

The basic provisions of Article 88 have been subject to much case law.[5] This was largely codified in a procedural regulation adopted in 1998,[6] which also reinforced the Commission's powers to order the repayment of illegal aid. It is also important to note that aggrieved competitors can complain to the

Commission about aid believed to have been paid out illegally, or can bring a case before the national courts, which can declare aid unlawful and order its repayment. For its part, the European Court of Justice has played an important role in buttressing the Commission's authority, particularly in the early case law on procedural matters, and has employed a relatively light touch in its scrutiny of the Commission's interpretation of substantive matters, thereby reinforcing the discretionary powers of the Commission.

The combination of discretion and exclusive competence might lead to the impression that the Commission is legislator, policeman, prosecutor and judge in matters of State aid. For all this, the Commission's task in disciplining State aids is not unfettered. Commission's decisions are subject to appeal before the European Courts by Member States or by interested parties, such as competitors of aid beneficiaries. Moreover, the very fact that it is the policies of Member State governments that are subject to control means that decisions are often highly sensitive, especially where national interests are stake. Cases of major national importance – such as aid for the restructuring of a firm where many jobs are at risk – are often the subject of face-to-face negotiations between ministers and the Commissioner for Competition Policy. In consequence, outcomes have frequently been regarded as politically motivated. The perception that the Commission simply bows to pressure from Member States is, however, increasingly outmoded; in recent years, the Commission has been more and more willing to reach negative decisions on State aid in sensitive cases and to enforce decisions with recovery orders where aid has already been paid. For example, in July 2004 the Commission ordered the repayment of aid estimated at up to €1.1 billion by France Télécom.[7] Where Member States fail to recover illegal aid, the Commission can, and does, refer the matter to the European Court of Justice. Commissioner Kroes has confirmed her intention to 'take a very strict line with Member States that fail to comply with Commission decisions on state aid. Taking a firm stand is the only way of ensuring the credibility of our state aid policy.'[8]

The Commission typically registers up to 1000 State aid cases annually, around half of which concern manufacturing and services.[9] Recent trends in the origin of these latter cases are set out in Table 9.1.

In practice, the scale of Commission activity in monitoring State aid is difficult to assess meaningfully. In particular, a notified aid may involve an aid scheme or programme for which there may ultimately be thousands of beneficiaries or it may involve ad hoc assistance to one firm; each counts as one notification. Similarly, the table suggests an overall decline in the number of aids notified. However, this partly reflects the adoption of a number of block exemption Regulations that enable national authorities to implement particular types of aid scheme, without prior authorisation from the Commission, on

Table 9.1 State aid cases registered (excluding agriculture, fisheries, transport and coal)

	1994	1995	1996	1997	1998	1999	2000	2001	2002	2003
Notified aid	510	680	550	515	342	469	473	322	349	306
Un-notified aid	68	113	91	140	97	98	86	46	67	53
Existing aid	16	10	3	1	5	2	10	49	5	18
Complaints	-	-	-	-	-	-	94	152	192	175
TOTAL	594	803	644	656	444	569	663	569	613	552

Source: Compiled from European Commission, Report on Competition Policy, annual (various editions).

condition that certain precise criteria are met. The aim of these Regulations, which concern support for SMEs, for training and for employment, is to reduce the administrative burden on the Commission. Perhaps most interesting is the significant rise in the number of cases arising from complaints (although it would appear that data was simply not disaggregated in this way prior to 2000, rather than there being no complaints before this date). In the 1990s, the Commission actively promoted the role of third parties in enforcement. To some extent, though, the implications were double-edged; the Commission was sometimes forced into reactive mode by challenges from third parties, with implications for the coherence of policy and for the Commission's ability to set the policy agenda (Smith, 2001).

Table 9.2 shows that the Commission raises no objections to the majority of State aids it considers. This might lead to the conclusion that the Commission is relatively ineffective in disciplining State aids. However, the opposite conclusion can also be reached: the Commission has become increasingly explicit about the types and forms of aid[10] that can be exempted from the State aid prohibition so that policymakers can, with some confidence, design measures that are likely to be 'rubber-stamped' for approval. The UK government explicitly endorses this approach in its guidance to administrators.[11] For its part, the Commission must open the formal investigation procedure if it has any doubts about the compatibility of the measure concerned with the common market.

It is now well-established that the Commission has the authority to require the repayment, with interest, of aid paid out illegally. Moreover, provisions of national law, involving, for example, the principle of legitimate expectation[12] can provide no shelter. In 1993, for example, British Aerospace repaid £57.6 million (of which £13.2 million was interest) of illegal aid paid by the UK government in connection with British Aerospace's purchase of Rover.[13] In practice, however, enforcement of repayment orders is generally problematic, depending, as it does, mainly on national authorities. Commission Kroes has noted recently that only a small percentage of aids banned by the Commission are ever recovered and has stressed the duty of the Member States to act to improve compliance.[14]

No systematic information appears to be available either on the number and scale of recovery orders or on the amounts actually repaid. However, the Commission's 1998 annual competition report indicates that 24 repayment orders were made in that year, most involving individual awards to firms (principally firms in difficulty), but some involving aid schemes with many hundreds of beneficiaries.[15] The same report listed 19 recovery orders dating back to 1987 that had not yet been repaid. More recently, the Commission took 11 (partly) negative decisions in 2003 involving the recovery of over €1.3 billion. At February 2004, some 88 recovery orders were pending, of which 40 concerned Germany and 20 concerned Spain.[16]

Table 9.2 Trends in Commission decisions

	1994	1995	1996	1997	1998	1999	2000	2001	2002
No objection	440	504	373	385	308	258	330	315	271
Initiation of formal scrutiny	40	57	43	68	66	62	65	67	62
Positive	15	22	14	18	16	28	11	15	29
Negative	3	9	23	9	31	30	5	26	37
Conditional	2	5	3	5	8	3	0	3	5
Appropriate measures/other	27	22	18	17	31	63	34	25	33
TOTAL*	527	619	474	502	460	444	445	451	437

Note: The totals in Table 9.2 differ from those in Table 9.1 because some notifications are withdrawn so no formal decision is taken and there is no relationship between cases registered and those taken in a particular year.

Source: European Commission, Report on Competition Policy, annual (various editions).

Scale of State Aid Spending

In the mid-1980s, the Commission began to focus on the scale of State aid as part of its attempts to target particular categories of support in the run-up to the completion of the internal market. The aim was to produce an inventory of aid schemes and accompanying expenditure data. In practice, owing to pressure from the Member States at the time, only the latter has ever been published. Initially this took the form of so-called State aid Surveys which were published every two years. Latterly, these have been superseded by regular 'Scoreboards',[17] instigated to monitor the Stockholm European Council commitment in 2001 to 'demonstrate a downward trend in State aid in relation to GDP by 2003' and to reduce the types of aid considered most harmful.

European Commission sources suggest that EU15 expenditure in 2002 totalled almost €49 billion for all sectors, except railways and amounted to €34 billion when agriculture, fisheries and transport were excluded (see Table 9.3). In terms of its weight in the economy, there is a fairly clear downward trend over the past decade. Nevertheless, these aggregate figures conceal some significant differences between countries. Aid as a percentage of GDP in 2002 ranges from 0.16 per cent (Sweden) to 0.72 per cent (Denmark); measured in Purchasing Power Standards (PPS) per head, spending in 2000-2 averaged just 36 in the UK, as against 228 in Denmark.

There are also national differences in policy priorities. For example, according to Commission sources, 53 per cent of Danish expenditure (excluding that on agriculture, fisheries and railways) is targeted at environmental protection, but in most other countries (Austria, Finland, Germany, the Netherlands and Sweden being the exceptions), this amounts to less than 5 per cent of the total. Research and development (R&D) aid accounts for 45 per cent of the total in Finland and around a third in Austria, but just 5 per cent of spending in Portugal and Denmark. In the UK, aid targeted at particular sectors accounts for over one quarter of aid paid with non-manufacturing activities receiving almost all of this; R&D (27 per cent) and regional aid (21 per cent) are the other main categories.[18]

There are, however, considerable methodological difficulties involved in gathering and analysing the data, some of which undermine its usefulness. Depending on data availability, the figures mix expenditure committed and that actually paid out. Also, many aid schemes have multiple policy objectives, so that the apparent absence of spending may simply reflect the classification of measures for statistical purposes. Notwithstanding these caveats, the Commission reports remain the only source of comparative information on aid spending.

Table 9.3 Trends in State aid expenditure (EU15)*

	1992	1993	1994	1995	1996	1997	1998	1999	2000	2001	2002
Total aid exc. railways (€ billion)	70.4	75.2	72.4	71.0	71.5	67.1	60.5	52.5	50.9	49.5	48.8
Total aid exc. agriculture, fisheries and transport (€ billion)	54.4	60.2	55.4	52.6	54.2	50.2	46.4	37.6	36.6	35.4	34.0
Total aid exc. railways (% of GDP)	1.09	1.18	1.11	1.00	0.98	0.88	0.77	0.64	0.59	0.57	0.56
Total aid exc. agriculture, fisheries and transport (% of GDP)	0.85	0.95	0.85	0.74	0.75	0.66	0.59	0.46	0.43	0.41	0.39

Note: At constant 2000 prices.

Source: European Commission, State Aid Scoreboard – Spring 2004 Update, COM(2004) 256 final of 20 April 24, Brussels.

WHAT IS A STATE AID?

The absence of a concrete definition of State aid was noted earlier. Article 87(1) states that:

> Save as otherwise provided in this Treaty, any aid granted by a Member State or through State resources in any form whatsoever which distorts or threatens to distort competition by favouring certain undertakings or the production of certain goods shall, insofar as it affects trade between Member States, be incompatible with the common market.

These provisions have been elaborated in a substantial body of case law and Commission decisions spanning a period of over 30 years. The scope of what is currently considered as State aid will be outlined briefly (but see Bacon, 2003 for a more extensive discussion).

There are five main aspects of the definition of a State aid: the notion of 'aid'; that it must be granted 'by a Member State or through State resources'; that it may be 'in any form whatsoever'; that it must 'distort or threaten to distort competition'; and that it must do so by 'favouring certain undertakings or the production of certain goods'.

Concept of Aid

The notion of aid was considered early on by the European Court of Justice in the context of the European Coal and Steel Community Treaty. The Court concluded that an aid was a wider concept than a subsidy and extended to intervention which mitigated charges normally incurred by an undertaking.[19] The Court later also argued that if the effect of a measure was to provide a benefit, then it should be regarded as aid, even if this was not the primary intention of the measure.[20] In other words, aid involves an advantage that would not be conferred in the normal operations of an undertaking.

State and State Resources

Commission decisions supported by Court of Justice rulings have resulted in a wide definition of the terms 'State' and 'State resources'. It is now clear that the Treaty provisions cover measures by all public bodies, or agencies acting on their behalf, at national, regional and local levels.

The extent of this definition has important consequences not just for the range of measures potentially concerned and their complexity, but also for domestic arrangements for ensuring compliance: it is the national government that is held to account for unnotified or illegal aid, irrespective of whether it is responsible for the administering body offering the aid. For example, a Commission

Decision that a land sale by Derbyshire County Council to Toyota involved illegal State aid (because the land was allegedly sold at less than the market price) and had to be repaid was addressed to the UK government and not the Council.[21]

Form of Aid

Article 87 concerns aid 'in any form whatsoever'. Reflecting this, there is no definitive listing of the types of assistance that fall within the ambit of the Treaty provisions. Clearly, grants, tax exemptions, preferential interest rates, the acquisition of land and buildings on favourable terms are all covered. The Commission has issued specific guidelines for some instruments – for example, guarantees,[22] the sale of land and buildings,[23] fiscal aids,[24] and, most recently, venture capital[25] – largely as a consequence of the difficulties involved in determining when certain forms of intervention constitute State aid. Moreover, such guidelines often arise from measures notified to the Commission – in October 2000, the Commission opened the investigative procedure against the proposed Regional Venture Capital Fund for England and closed it in June 2001 (with a decision approving the scheme), two weeks after having adopted guidelines on venture capital, which then formed the basis for its decision.[26]

Complicated issues arise in the case of State shareholdings or capital injections. Consideration of these issues by the Commission and the Court has resulted in the so-called 'market investor' principle.[27] In short, if a transaction is undertaken in circumstances which a private investor would not be prepared to accept, then this would constitute a State aid. Over time, this notion has become more sophisticated. For example, it has been accepted that a private investor might be prepared to endure a loss in the short-term in making an investment if this were likely to secure the long-term survival of the enterprise. Also, the Court developed the concept of 'public creditor' in Tubacex in considering whether a debt repayment and rescheduling agreement constituted State aid. In that instance, it concluded that the public authority was acting in the same way as a private investor would have done and the Commission consequently revised its recovery decision.[28]

The Distortion or Threat of Distorting Competition

The provision of State aid does not, of itself, contravene the Treaty; in order to fall foul of Article 87, it must distort or threaten to distort competition (and, as discussed below, it must do this by favouring certain firms or products). In practice, this is not a serious limitation on the scope of Article 87, given the increasing interdependence of markets within the EU economy. Nevertheless, the European Court rejected the Commission's contention in Philip Morris[29] that aids always distort competition and that it was therefore not necessary to assess their actual effects.

Evans and Martin (1991, p. 85) have argued that the Commission's approach almost amounts to a *per se* rule: 'if aid is granted, the conclusion that the aid distorts competition is almost automatic'. Notwithstanding this rather sweeping approach, the Commission has also asserted that: 'while all financial assistance to enterprises alters competitive conditions to some extent, not all aid has a perceptible impact on trade and competition between Member States.'[30] This was the justification for the introduction of the so-called *de minimis* facility, on which basis the Commission considered that Article 87(1) could be said not to apply for aid below a given threshold. *De minimis* aid was the subject of a block exemption Regulation in 2001,[31] meaning, in essence, that aid of less than €100,000 in a three-year period to the same firm need not be notified for approval. More recently, there is evidence of Commission attempts to limit the scope of Article 87(1) by finding that there are no impacts on trade between the Member States. A recent example concerned support for the renovation of Brighton Pier UK, which a neighbouring competitor had challenged, but which the Commission considered had no effects on competition beyond the domestic market.[32]

Favouring of Certain Undertakings

Article 87 does not apply if all undertakings in the Member State benefit from the measure without distinction between them. Aid is selective if it applies to a particular type of activity, a sector of the economy, a particular geographical area or to firms with the same characteristics. Thus a line is drawn between measures of general economic policy and measures which directly or indirectly assist certain firms or activities.[33] This line is not always clear and measures that are ostensibly general may, in practice, fulfil the selectivity criterion. For example, in a landmark case, an Italian social security concession which provided higher rates of concession in respect of female employees was found to constitute sectoral aid (and banned by the Commission) since it favoured the production of goods in which female labour predominated, such as textiles and clothing.[34]

The interpretation of the 'specificity criterion' is crucial in distinguishing between what constitutes a State aid within the meaning of Article 87 and so-called 'general measures'. Moreover, the need to make the distinction is paramount because Article 88 only empowers the Commission to take action against measures that distort competition to the extent that they constitute State aid; general measures that distort competition must be addressed through other mechanisms, with notably fewer and less powerful means of redress.

The setting of interest rates is typically used as an example of a general measure; the base rate applies throughout the economy and no particular groups are favoured. In practice, however, changes in rates of interest impact very differently – cash-rich firms will benefit from higher interest rates whilst indebted ones will be disadvantaged. Nevertheless, such broad policy decisions are viewed as part of general economic policy-making and few would argue that it should be otherwise.

State Aid as an Evolving Concept

A notable feature of State aid policy is the extent to which the notion of State aid is continually being refined, or even, on occasion, redefined. In the sphere of taxation, for example, the activities of the Council in the context of harmful tax competition[35] led the Commission to embark on a review of the tax arrangements in force in the Member States. An early casualty of this interest was the Irish 10 per cent tax rate for manufacturing. In the 1980s, the Commission had not objected to this, reaching the rather surprising conclusion that it did not constitute State aid.[36] By the late 1990s, the Commission had changed its mind and, following protracted negotiations with the Irish authorities, issued proposals for a standard rate of corporation tax to be phased in.[37] This is now being implemented by the Irish government.

An important recent definitional issue has been the treatment of arrangements for funding services of general economic interest (SGEI).[38] This has mainly come to the fore because liberalisation and deregulation have altered the context for providing public services and raised new issues about public service obligations. This, in turn, has thrown into sharp relief the question of whether monies paid to organisations entrusted with providing SGEIs should be regarded as compensation or State aid (a distinction with important procedural consequences for all tiers of government and a wide range of public services). A series of cases culminated in the Altmark judgment in July 2003[39] that identified a number of criteria which such payments must fulfil in order to escape notification and scrutiny under the State aid rules. For its part, the Commission has adopted a number of draft instruments designed to increase the legal certainty concerning the financing of SGEIs.[40] Notwithstanding this, considerable uncertainty remains and it has been argued that yet more extensive legislative proposals are required to improve the transparency and predictability of the financing of public services in relation to the State aid rules (Rapp-Jung, 2004).

THE GOOD, THE NOT-SO-GOOD AND THE UGLY: COMMISSION TREATMENT OF DIFFERENT AID TYPES

As outlined above, the first stage of analysis for the Commission in considering a given measure is to establish whether or not it involves State aid within the meaning of Article 87(1); the second stage is to determine whether it can anyway be deemed compatible with the Treaty. The prohibition on State aid in Article 87(1) is far from absolute, as noted earlier, but is tempered by a number of mandatory, and, more importantly, discretionary exceptions to the general ban. The discretionary exceptions are set out in Article 87(3) as follows:

(a) aid to promote the economic development of areas where the standard of living is abnormally low or where there is serious underemployment;

(b) aid to promote the execution of an important project of common European interest or to remedy a serious disturbance in the economy of a Member State;

(c) aid to facilitate the development of certain economic activities or of certain economic areas where such aid does not adversely affect trading to an extent contrary to the common interest;

(d) aid to promote culture and heritage conservation where such aid does not affect trading conditions and competition in the Community to an extent that is contrary to the common interest; and

(e) such other categories of aid as may be specified by decision of the Council acting by qualified majority on a proposal from the Commission.

It is for the Commission to decide whether one of these exceptions applies. By far the most important of these exceptions is Article 87(3)(c), although, as will be seen, Article 87(3)(a) has been used since the late 1980s to justify the authorisation of State aid to the worst-off areas of the EU on regional policy grounds. In broad terms, four main categories of State aid can usefully be identified: horizontal aids, where measures are not sectorally or geographically restricted and aim to contribute to objectives that are viewed positively, such as support for SMEs, research and development and training; regional aids, where support is tightly controlled, or prohibited, in the more prosperous areas, but allowed to reach generous levels in the poorest countries and regions; restructuring aid, where the Commission's a priori attitude is essentially negative; and sectoral aid, where frameworks have been developed to reflect the particular needs and characteristics of certain activities.[41] An exhaustive review of the rules developed in the various policy areas is beyond the scope of this chapter but the following discussion highlights some of the key features of the Commission's approach.

Before turning to this, a general point is that the Commission takes a negative attitude to two types of aid: support for exports to other Member States, and operating aid. The former is never authorised by the Commission, for obvious reasons, and its opposition extends to aid schemes which explicitly favour export-oriented activities. So-called operating aid (support which is not tied to an investment or job creation project, but is of an ongoing nature or, for example, simply feeds into working capital) is rarely authorised. Last, it is worth noting that the aid types discussed in the rest of this section (horizontal aid, regional aid and restructuring aid) have no formal status.[42] Although the Commission refers to these categories of aid, their precise content varies between documents.

The 'Good': Horizontal Aid

In a number of policy areas, the Commission's attitude towards State aid is broadly positive, often reflecting the existence of the EU's own proactive policies. The Commission has adopted a block exemption Regulation in several policy areas, removing the need for prior notification and scrutiny of aid measures that meet certain criteria. The Regulations in operation concern aid for SMEs, aid for employment and aid for training.[43] In several other policy areas, the Commission's approach is essentially positive, but prior notification and approval is required and proposed measures are assessed by the Commission against published guidelines. Examples include support for R&D and environmental protection.

Under the block exemption Regulation for SMEs[44] aid schemes must respect the rules on the types of expenditure eligible for aid (essentially general investment, consultancy and R&D) and the aid ceilings. These range from 7.5 per cent to 75 per cent of eligible costs and favour small firms over medium-sized ones and assisted regions over non-assisted ones.

The block exemption for training concerns aid for firms of any size. Training may be specific (for instance, directly related to the current employment) or general (which is perceived to have wider benefits). The standard maximum rate (for instance for large firms in non-regional aid areas) for specific training is 25 per cent of eligible costs while the standard maximum for general training is 50 per cent; in both cases 'top-ups' are available in designated regional aid areas and for SMEs.

The block exemption for employment aid only allows aid to large firms located in a designated regional aid area or where the recruits are disadvantaged. SMEs are eligible everywhere and higher rates apply in the regional aid areas.

The principles governing R&D aid date back to 1986.[45] They concern aid for firms undertaking R&D, other than that commissioned according to market conditions (for example, by open tender); public financing of R&D activities by public not-for-profit or higher education establishments falls outside the State aid rules. The guidelines distinguish different phases of the R&D process, allowing up to 100 per cent of eligible fundamental research costs to be assisted, but only 50 per cent of industrial research and 25 per cent of pre-competitive research expenditure to be subsidised. Higher rates of award apply to SMEs and to firms located in designated problem regions. The R&D guidelines are scheduled for review before the end of 2005. Commissioner Kroes has noted the need to consider support measures that address the market failures which hinder innovation in a wider sense of the term.[46] More generally, the Commission will have to decide how to reconcile the Barcelona Council objective of raising R&D expenditure in the EU to approach 3 per cent of GDP by 2010 with that of continued State aid discipline.

The guidelines on State aid for environmental protection[47] aim to balance the Treaty requirements of sustainable development against the imperative of undistorted competition. The underlying principle is that the 'polluter pays' so that only SMEs may qualify for assistance to meet existing environmental standards; however, larger firms may receive assistance to improve on compulsory standards, for relocation on environmental grounds, investment in combined heat and power, renewable energy and the rehabilitation of polluted sites. As under the R&D framework, higher rates of award apply in the designated problem regions and for SMEs. The current framework is due to expire at the end of 2007 but has been criticised on a number of grounds, including the restrictive interpretation of the guidelines to cover pollution caused by the beneficiary, the impediment to innovative environmental policy that improves on lowest common denominator standards, the interference with national environmental policy options, and the failure to prevent distortions of competition, notably by allowing higher than necessary levels of aid (Holmes, 2004; Ewringmann, Thöne with Fischer, 2002).

The 'Not-So-Good': Regional Aid

Regional policy was the first area in which the Commission developed guidelines to discipline State aids; these date back to the early 1970s. The system of regulating regional aids has become progressively more elaborate with the Commission increasingly involved in determining the extent of the regional aid maps, the types of assistance offered and the value of aid, such that large firms may now only receive general investment aid if they are located in the designated problem regions. At the same time, the emergence of EU cohesion policy (the Community's own regional policy) has raised important issues of policy coordination.

The current approach to regional aid is set out in the 1998 Guidelines which apply until end 2006.[48] Under the guidelines, regional aid control is perceived in terms of the need to restrict assisted area coverage expressed as a percentage of the population (Table 9.4). Within the stipulated ceiling – 42.7 per cent of the EU15 population – regions where GDP (PPS) per head was below 75 per cent of the EU average were deemed eligible for the Article 87(3)(a) derogation[49] (around 21 per cent of the EU population).[50] The remaining population (around 22 per cent) was allocated among the Member States as 'quotas' for the designation of areas on the basis of Article 87(3)(c). For most countries, this resulted in significant cutbacks in assisted area coverage, although all of some Member States (Greece, Ireland and Portugal) remain eligible for national regional aid until December 2006.[51]

Table 9.4 Final coverage figures for 2000-2006 under Article 87(3)(a) and (c)

	Article 87(3)(a)	Article 87(3)(c)	Total assisted area %
Austria	3.5	24.1	27.6
Belgium	0.0	30.9	30.9
Denmark	0.0	17.1	17.1
Finland	13.4	28.9	42.3
France	2.8	33.9	36.7
Germany	17.2	17.7	34.9
Greece	100.0	0.0	100.0
Ireland	26.6	73.4	100.0
Italy	33.6	10.0	43.6
Luxembourg	0.0	32.0	32.0
Netherlands	0.0	15.0	15.0
Portugal	66.6	33.4	100.0
Spain	58.4	20.8	79.2
Sweden	0.0	15.9	15.9
UK	8.6	22.1	30.7
EU15	21.9	21.1	43.0[*]

Note: The 42.7 per cent ceiling was exceeded owing to the special treatment given to Northern Ireland.

Source: Wishlade (2003), Figure 34 at p. 205.

Although Member States were responsible for selecting the assisted areas within their respective quotas, the methodology was constrained by the guidelines and the outcome had to be approved by the Commission. Last, the Commission adjusted aid maxima in line with regional prosperity and lowered the ceilings compared with 1999 levels.[52]

A key feature of regional aid control has been the emphasis on devising frameworks within which aid schemes could be authorised, thereby obviating the need for case-by-case analysis of individual awards. The downside of this approach is that it shelters many thousands of awards from scrutiny, enabling them lawfully to be offered without any assessment of their competition effects. In the 1990s, the Commission, and to some extent the Council, became concerned about this lacuna in regional aid control and began to develop approaches for individual scrutiny and control of aids to exceptionally large projects, culminating in the first so-called 'multisectoral' framework in 1998; this failed to have any real impact (Wishlade, 2003, p. 127) and was replaced by the current (2002) Multisectoral Framework[53] which takes a more straightforward approach than its predecessor.

The new framework applies an arithmetical formula to reduce aid rates to projects involving eligible expenditure exceeding €50 million. This operates in a progressive way so that the larger the project, the lower the rate of award. Moreover, the Commission must individually approve aid for investments of more than €100 million where the aid proposed exceeds a specified amount; the onus in such cases is on the Member State to demonstrate that the aid will not reinforce a high market or increase capacity in a stagnant sector. Significantly, the framework provides for the Commission to adopt a list of sectors in which regional State aid would be banned altogether. In practice, this was postponed due to 'methodological and technical difficulties' and to take account of Member State requests.[54] The Commission will examine the 'technical feasibility and the political and economic opportunity' of adopting a list of sectors with structural difficulties again before the end of 2005.[55]

The impact of EU competition policy on regional aid has been significant (Wishlade, 2003, Chapter 7). Successive policy revisions have constrained the types of regional aid on offer and subjected the extent of the assisted area maps to intense scrutiny. Most recently, award values have been progressively reduced. However, arguably the most striking feature of the Commission's approach to date is that it focuses on whether regional aid is justified, rather than on whether competition is distorted. Moreover, the emphasis has been on competition between Member States rather than between firms. In short, while the Commission has clearly achieved considerable discipline in the availability of investment aid to large firms, it is by no means clear that its approach to regional aid control actually ensures that distortions of competition are prevented since national and sub-national authorities retain wide discretion to assist large firms, albeit within the assisted areas and subject to aid ceilings set by the Commission.

The impact of the regional aid rules has also spilled over into other policy areas. In the UK, the rules have severely hampered urban regeneration policy, which has long since outstripped regional policy in expenditure terms. In the English Partnerships (EP) case, the finding that 'gap' funding to property developers in designated urban areas constituted State aid (as discussed below) led to a major reorientation of the initiative.

In 1995, the Commission had concluded that the Partnership Investment Programme (PIP) fell outside the scope of Article 87(1), but it reviewed its position in 1999 following concerns that the measure had been used by motor vehicle manufacturers.[56] The UK authorities maintained that PIP did not constitute State aid because the grant given was the minimum necessary to bridge the gap between development costs and the market value of the regeneration site; it did not confer an unfair competitive advantage on the developer because any undertaking could apply for assistance under PIP, all costs and values were assessed at open market rates, and there was negligible (if any) intra-Community trade in the development of derelict land and buildings. However, the Commission ruled that PIP involved the use of State aid because gap funding provides a quantifiable financial incentive to a developer to invest in a location where little or no private investment would otherwise have happened; the aid favoured certain undertakings, and PIP had the potential to distort trade between Member States.

An important factor, in the Commission's view, was that some recipients of EP's funding were undertakings active in trade between Member States (for example car manufacturers). This led to a ruling that PIP could only be considered compatible with the common market if it were aligned with existing State aid codes or frameworks.[57] In practical terms, this meant that where the property developer was not an SME, gap funding could only be provided if the project were located in a regional policy assisted area; these do not necessarily coincide with designated urban areas. Against this background, loss of PIP was described a 'disaster' and the perverse effects of EU competition rules have led to calls for the Commission to adopt a framework on regeneration aid.[58]

The 'Ugly': Rescue and Restructuring Aid

Rescue and restructuring operations have given rise to the most controversial State aid cases. Support for rescue and restructuring is perceived as one of the most distortionary types of aid by the Commission which, in principle, views the exit of failing firms from the market as a normal feature of a functioning market economy. Nevertheless, under EU rules, intervention may be justified in such cases by social or regional policy considerations by examining the distortion of competition set against the employment effects of redundancies owing to closure and/or the regional effects resulting from the impact of closure on suppliers. Exceptionally, rescue and restructuring aid may be justified on competition grounds, for example where the disappearance of a given undertaking would result in a monopoly or tight oligopoly.

Guidelines setting out how the Commission intended to handle such cases were first introduced in 1994 and tightened in 1999. In 2003, the Commission began a review of the 1999 guidelines (which expired in October 2004) and identified a number of issues. The notable ones were: the lack of a definition of firms 'in difficulty'; the problem of applying the special criteria applicable to firms that are part of a group; the fact that rescue aid often has to be granted prior to Commission approval in order to prevent the firm collapsing – the UK government notified rescue aid to British Energy the day after it had been awarded (but although the aid was technically unlawful, it was ultimately deemed compatible with the Treaty);[59] the 'one-time-last-time' principle and the instances of firms ineligible for restructuring aid receiving further rescue aid; the need to clarify the various time limits; and the scope of compensatory measures – when can these be said to be sufficient 'to mitigate the potentially distortionary effects of the aid on competition?'[60] Various commentators endorsed and added to this list of shortcomings (see particularly Nicolaides and Kekelekis, 2004; Anestis, Mavroghenis and Drakakakis, 2004).

The current (2004) guidelines on aid for rescue and restructuring[61] require all proposals to support large firms in difficulty to be notified individually.[62] The number of such cases is relatively small – 120 over the period 1990-2002[63] – but the amounts involved may be significant – ranging from under €1 million to over €20 billion. Of these, 35 cases involved Germany, 20 were in France and there were 15 each in Italy and Spain.[64] In broad terms, a firm in difficulty is one that is deemed to be unable to stem its losses and that, without public intervention, will go out of business in the short to medium term. Rescue aid is temporary assistance to keep the company afloat while a viable restructuring plan is worked out. Restructuring aid is based on an approved plan to restore a firm's long-term viability.

According to the 2004 guidelines, rescue aid may take the form of loan guarantees or loans bearing normal commercial interest rates; however, it must be restricted to the amount needed to keep the firm in business and to the time needed (a maximum of 6 months) to devise the recovery plan. In addition, it must be warranted on the grounds of social (labour-related) difficulties and have no adverse effects on the industrial situation in other Member States. Last, it must be a one-off operation.

Similarly, restructuring aid can only be granted if certain criteria are met. These include: the submission of a restructuring plan to return to viability within a 'reasonable' time; the adoption of compensatory measures to avoid undue distortions of competition (such as reductions of capacity or divestment of assets); the limitation of aid to the minimum needed to implement restructuring measures, to which beneficiaries must also make a significant contribution (normally at least 50 percent for large firms), and monitoring and annual reporting. None of the aid must be used to finance new investment that is not essential to restoring the firm's viability. A firm may be required to close its plants completely in markets where there is long-term structural overcapacity, in which case the only aid the Commission will allow is to alleviate the social costs (for example, redundancy payments and early retirement packages) of restructuring and environmental clean up. Restructuring aid can be granted once only (the 'one-time-last-time' principle).

In practice, the 2004 guidelines retain the key principles of the existing rules, but introduce a number of important changes in response to some of their perceived weaknesses. Specifically, the 2004 guidelines apply simplified and accelerated procedures for the approval of rescue aid and a formula for determining the maximum amount of rescue aid. In addition, as noted, the compensatory measures required for restructuring aid may be up to 100 per cent of the beneficiary's capacity if the market concerned has long-term structural problems. Also, minimum contributions towards restructuring costs, varying by firm size, were introduced so that the obligations on shareholders are more explicit than before.

Nicolaides and Kekelekis (2004) suggest that while these provisions represent an improvement on the 1999 guidelines, they are too generous in their treatment of rescue and restructuring aid for SMEs and fail to address a number of the points which the Commission had itself identified, including the definition of firms in difficulty and the timescale over which a return to viability is required. Nevertheless, it can be argued that, while not involving a radical departure from the 1999 guidelines, the new framework tightens up the rules, especially for large firms, so that increasingly only firms that have clear prospects of returning to viability and whose efforts to restructure will not damage competition should benefit from State aid (Valle and Van de Casteele, 2004).

Although frequently controversial, the real impact of Commission decisions in rescue and restructuring aid cases is difficult to assess. A recent study by London Economics points to 'basic data difficulties' that hamper the evaluation of the sectoral impacts of aid but, nevertheless, concludes tentatively that 'perhaps, in a number of cases the recovery of a State aid receiving company appears to occur at the expense of EU competitors.'[65]

CURRENT THEMES, RECENT DEVELOPMENTS AND FUTURE CHALLENGES

The control of State aids has enjoyed a higher political profile since the start of the decade. This partly reflects the substance of the Lisbon agenda and its emphasis on economic reform, innovation and social cohesion, which followed on from the Stockholm Council commitment to less State aid spending overall and a reorientation of that expenditure towards 'horizontal objectives of common interest, including cohesion objectives'.[66]

Successive European Councils have added little substance to the means of achieving the 'less, but better' objective, at least in concrete commitments to reduce spending by the Member States. Nevertheless, political discussions have given an impetus to Commission action in the form of 'Scoreboards'[67] on State aid expenditure, cited earlier, a progress report on the reduction and reorientation of State aid[68] and, most recently, the State Aid Action Plan.[69]

Several important themes have emerged from recent Council conclusions and Commission reports: first, a consideration of the role of market failure in the justification for State aid; second, an emphasis on the efficiency and effectiveness of State aid and, related to this, a growing interest in evaluation and exchange of experience; third, a Commission commitment to consider the feasibility of developing economic criteria for assessing State aid impacts; and last, efforts to simplify, modernise and clarify the State aid rules.

Current Themes

Recent developments in State aid control have given greater prominence to market failure arguments in the justification for State aid. On the one hand, it has been stressed that State aids should be targeted at clearly identified market failures;[70] on the other, the Commission has emphasised the need to question whether State aid is always the most appropriate response to market failures – for example, it has argued that Member States 'ought to assess, on a case-by-case basis, whether existing market imperfections affecting SMEs would be better addressed through the provision of state aid, advisory and information services, the intensification of structural reforms, or a combination of these measures.'[71]

Related questions concern the efficiency and effectiveness of State aid. The Commission has procured external research which aims, inter alia, to draw up a list of criteria that make it possible to assess the circumstances in which aid is likely to be more or less effective.[72] For their part, at the November 2002 Competitiveness Council, the Member States undertook to improve the exchange of experience on a range of issues, including ex ante and ex post evaluations of State aid.

The role of economic analysis in State aid control is also rising up the Commission's agenda. Two main factors appear to underpin this. First, the Commission has been sensitive to criticism of its hitherto rather formalistic approach. The Director General of DG Competition has observed that 'there is the impression that we are simply applying rules which aim to curtail state aid as such rather than concentrating on controlling aid which really distorts the European single market'.[73] Second, the impact of enlargement on resources means that greater priority needs to be given to those measures that have the most impact on EU competition and trade.

There are two levels of analysis at which the role of economic criteria are relevant. First, there is the decision about whether a measure is caught by Article 87(1) at all. Does it, inter alia, distort or threaten to distort competition or affect trade between Member States? As mentioned earlier, it has been observed that the Commission interpretation of Article 87(1) almost amounts to a per se rule, but some recent cases have suggested a rather more reasoned approach. For example, in the Dorsten Swimming Pool case, which was highlighted as an instance in which the definition of aid was more tightly circumscribed (Monti, 2001), the Commission found that there was no aid because there was no effect on intra-Community trade.[74] As already mentioned, a similar conclusion was reached in the UK Brighton Pier case.

The second level of analysis concerns the severity of the distortion involved. This led the Commission to attempt to develop an economic basis for distinguishing between aid that is particularly harmful and aid that, although it falls within the scope of Article 87(1), does not significantly distort competition and trade;[75] this is sometimes referred to as a 'significant impact test'. The aim was that this distinction could be reflected in procedural reforms that might ease the burden of examining less significant cases and identify those where closer scrutiny was merited.[76] This approach underpinned the draft frameworks on lesser amounts of State aid (LASA) and aid with a limited effect on trade (LET). The objective of these frameworks was to enable the Commission to have a 'light touch' approach to the scrutiny of measures that complied with the LASA and LET criteria; in other words, there would almost be a presumption that aid meeting the conditions would be compatible with the Treaty.[77]

In practice, both proposals were dropped by DG Competition early in 2005. They failed to gain widespread support among the Member States, although the UK was an ardent supporter of a significant impact test approach. In addition, it seems probable that the legal services of the Commission had concerns about LASA and LET being open to challenge in the courts. It is unclear whether the Commission will revisit the significant impact test as part of the wider review currently underway; certainly there are no concrete proposals to do so in the State Aid Action Plan.

A number of steps have been taken, or are envisaged, with respect to the simplification, modernisation and clarification of the State aid rules. Commissioner Monti announced in 2003 that the Commission was reviewing existing State aid control instruments with a view to simplification and elimination of potential conflicts between the texts.[78] Also, the Commission has formalised its approach to complaints[79] and indicated that reimbursement of unlawful state aid will be subject to compound interest.[80] Together with the procedural Regulations adopted over the 1999-2001 period, these changes amount to a substantial reform package.[81] More generally, the State Aid Action Plan emphasises the role of the national authorities (courts and governments) and third parties in ensuring compliance.

Recent Developments

Against the backdrop of these themes and trends, a number of State aid frameworks are due for renewal before 2007, providing the Commission with: 'an unprecedented window of opportunity for a comprehensive review of the horizontal, and particularly Lisbon, objectives, and the new cohesion policy set out in the forthcoming Structural Fund regulations as well as to consolidate, and wherever possible simplify the rules.'[82] In addition to the new guidelines on rescue and restructuring aid and proposals on aid for SGEIs discussed earlier, DG Competition has also begun to formalise its approach to aid to innovation, to review the R&D aid guidelines and, of key importance given enlargement and the debate on EU cohesion policy post-2006,[83] to consider the future of regional aid control. Last, it is reviewing the environmental protection aid rules and the guidelines on aid to risk capital as well as a range of sectoral guidelines.[84]

DG Competition's current thinking on the reform of regional aid control post-2006 has been set out in two working papers[85] on the review of the Regional Aid Guidelines.[86] There are three main features of these proposals: first, that Article 87(3)(a) areas be defined on the basis of EU25 GDP (PPS) per head, rather than EU15 averages; second, that Article 87(3)(c) coverage be limited to so-called 'earmarked' regions,[87] rather than based on national population quotas as at present, and third, that all aid ceilings be reduced.

Overall, the proposals involve a very significant shift in the rules with sharp cutbacks in spatial coverage, most of which are borne by the EU15 Member States, and significant reductions in award values for eligible regions. The suggested cutbacks in total coverage within EU15 are dramatic – every country would be affected except Greece – but they are not uniform. There would be no assisted area coverage at all in Denmark, Luxembourg and the Netherlands or in mainland France. Coverage would fall by more than half in Austria, Germany, Ireland and the UK. The proposals virtually eliminate the possibility of conducting 'traditional' regional policy in many EU15 Member States. Even in countries with some coverage, such as the UK, Article 87(3)(c) areas would be designated on a 'top-down' basis and may only partially correspond to nationally-determined needs. If the current proposals are adopted, the UK assisted areas would comprise Cornwall and the Scilly Isles, West Wales and the Valleys, South Yorkshire, Merseyside and the Highlands and Islands – traditional priority regions like the central belt of Scotland or the North East of England would not be eligible for regional aid. It might be questioned whether it would be legitimate, on subsidiarity and proportionality grounds, for EU competition policy to dictate the substance and targeting of national regional policy in this way.

A more general concern is whether the reductions in assisted area coverage and rates might affect the EU's global competitiveness in attracting mobile investment. Some are sceptical about the capacity of incentives to offset locational advantages elsewhere,[88] but it is worth noting that the EU system of State aid discipline is unique; alternative locations are unlikely to display similar levels of self-restraint and are therefore often in a position to offer long-term tax and other advantages that may prove irresistible to mobile investors.

Future Challenges

The developments outlined in this chapter bear witness to a policy entering a new phase. The increased emphasis on the economic impact of State aids is surely to be welcomed as a genuine attempt to address the arbitrariness for which past State aid control policy has been criticised. Nevertheless, recent developments illustrate the incremental nature of policy development. Changes under the new rescue and restructuring guidelines are modest; the proposed LASA and LET guidelines have been dropped; and the failure of the Commission to adopt (under the Multisectoral Framework) a list of sectors with serious structural problems are all testament to the political sensitivities, the technical difficulties and the legal issues involved in altering the course of policy. In short, there are some very real challenges in trying to refocus State aid control.

Some important questions remain at a conceptual level. The definition of State aid is still fluid and the increasing complexity of public-private economic relations, especially in areas such as service or infrastructure provision, will not simplify the Commission's task in determining the existence of State aid. Moreover, the Commission's growing interest in examining measures relating to social security and taxation continues to raise difficult definitional issues; these seem increasingly likely to occur at the sub-national level, where trends to decentralisation may be difficult to reconcile with the Commission's approach to regionally differentiated taxation.

Further conceptual challenges arise from the growing interest in taking account of market failure in assessing State aids. Acceptance of market failure arguments is implicit in the Treaty provisions, but they do not explicitly require the identification of market failure in order for State aid to be justified; moreover, the identification of a market failure does not, of itself, justify an exception to the general ban. Article 87(3)(c), which has formed the basis for most policy allowing the use of aid, merely refers to 'aid to facilitate the development of certain economic activities or of certain economic areas, where such aid does not adversely affect trading conditions to an extent contrary to the common interest.' The identification of criteria to establish what is in the common interest remains elusive. Would evidence of market failure become a requirement for State aid authorisation? Would it be a necessary, but insufficient condition for allowing aid? Where would the burden of proof lie in market failure arguments for State aid? Would measures that in the Commission's view were ineffective be outlawed even in the absence of significant competition concerns?

Challenges also arise from the emphasis on policy linkages. In particular, the notion of 'cohesion' and how competition policy control of State aids can best contribute to it remains unclear. Since the early 1990s, the emphasis has been on competition policy enabling, or at least not frustrating, the adoption of coincident maps for national and EU regional policies. However, this is arguably a rather superficial preoccupation that conceals the need for a more fundamental debate about the appropriate articulation of spatial policy objectives at different tiers of government. Besley and Seabright (1999) consider the pursuit of coincident maps as 'a very significant flaw' in the Commission's market failure evaluation.

These conceptual issues spill over into and are difficult to disentangle from a range of technical issues. These are exacerbated by the combined effects of enlargement and the trend to decentralise responsibility for economic development to sub national levels. This creates an administrative imperative to focus Commission resources on priority cases. However, there are clear tensions between what is theoretically relevant and what is administratively feasible; between arbitrariness and relevance; and between transparency and politicisation.

The State aid control regime is easy to critique – there is excessive emphasis on formal aspects of policy and insufficient analysis of the real effects of aid on competition and trade. Moreover, State aid control policy as it has evolved is ill-suited to assess the increasingly sophisticated range of policy instruments being operated, or to consider those which it has not previously sought to address. However, critics should be under no illusions about the technical difficulties involved in addressing these issues. There are important gaps in the understanding of just how State aids affect competition and trade that are not answered by the academic literature in ways that are of practical relevance; even where the Commission has developed methodologies that sought to address competition issues more directly (for example, under the motor vehicle aid rules[89] or the 1998 Multisectoral Framework),[90] the absence of relevant, comparative and up-to-date statistical data at an appropriate level of analysis undermined the practical application of the methodologies concerned and damaged their credibility.

State aid control continues to face considerable political challenges. The role of the Council in State aid control has varied from the outset, with the Commission sometimes resisting Member State involvement and sometimes building on their apparent commitment to restraint. Recent developments suggest that State aid control is increasingly being considered within the context of broader macroeconomic policy, reflected in the growing interest in aggregate spending and the introduction of targets to limit expenditure. Whilst the Commission may welcome the support of the Member States as regularly expressed in Council conclusions, this support is less in evidence when national interests are at stake – for example when a major firm faces closure or the Commission seeks to exclude particular regions from eligibility for aid. The postponement of the publication of the heavily-trailed State Aid Action Plan until after the French referendum on the Constitutional Treaty illustrates continuing political sensitivities. Furthermore, in practice, Member State views on the matter are far from homogenous and the Commission may find increased Member State involvement in State aid policy formulation to be double-edged as countries float proposals that increase the Council's input into State control.

Looking forward, the control of State aid looks set to continue to face many challenges in accommodating the disparate interests of firms and policymakers across a Community with widely varying economic traditions and levels of economic development.

NOTES

1. Aid must be granted to individual consumers and not to undertakings.
2. L. Brittan, 'A bonfire of subsidies? A review of State aids in the European Community', address to the London Seminar on Competition Policy, London, 10 March 1989, mimeo.
3. The commitment made by the European Council in March 2000 was for the EU to become 'the most dynamic and competitive knowledge-based economy by 2010.' This was to be achieved by a series of goals in areas such as employment, innovation, enterprise, liberalization and the environment. 'Presidency conclusions', Lisbon European Council, 23 and 24 March 2000.
4. P. Sutherland, 'Competition policy in the EEC today', address to a delegation of Saarland, Bonn, 31 March 1987, mimeo.
5. See, for example, D'Sa (1998), but note that there have been several important procedural developments since this book was written.
6. See Commission Regulation (EC) No 794/2004 of 21 April 2004 implementing Council Regulation (EC) No 659/1999 laying down detailed rules for the application of Article 93 of the EC Treaty, OJ L140, 30 April 2004.
7. RAPID Press Release, 'Commission rules that France Télécom received illicit aid and orders that it be paid back to the state', IP/04/981, 20 July 2004.
8. RAPID Press Release, 'Commission refers Germany to Court of Justice for failure to recover illegal aid to Kahla', IP/05/189, 16 February 2005.
9. Distinct rules apply to agriculture, fisheries, transport and coal and the lead in implementing State aid policy in these sectors is taken by the relevant 'sectoral' directorates-general, as opposed to DG Competition.
10. Reflected in the growing body of aid codes, communications and frameworks covering a range of policy areas – see http://europa.eu.int/comm/competition/state_aid/legislation/.
11. Department of Trade and Industry (2004), 'European Community State aids: Guidance for all departments and agencies', European Policy Directorate.
12. The notion that firms should be entitled to assume that the award of State aid was lawful.
13. RAPID Press Release, 'British Aerospace repays State aid paid by the UK for its purchase of Rover', IP/93/405, 26 May 1993.
14. RAPID Press Release, N. Kroes, 'Reforming Europe's State aid regime: an action plan for change', Wilmer Cutler Pickering Hale and Dorr / University of Leiden Joint Conference on European State Aid Reform, Brussels, Speech/05/347, 14 June 2005.

15. European Commission (1999), XXVIIIth Report on Competition Policy 1998, Brussels, Luxembourg: OOPEC, p. 305.
16. European Commission, State Aid Scoreboard – Spring 2004 Update, COM(2004) 256 final of 20 April 2004, Brussels.
17. The Scoreboards and the later Surveys are available on the DG Competition website at: http://europa.eu.int/comm/competition/index_en.html.
18. European Commission, State Aid Scoreboard – Spring 2004 Update, COM(2004) 256 final of 20 April 2004, Brussels.
19. Case 30/59 *De Gezamenlijke Steenkolenmijnen in Limburg v High Authority of the European Coal and Steel Community* (1961) ECR 1.
20. Case 173/73 *Italian Government v Commission* (1974) ECR 709.
21. Commission Decision of 31 July 1991 concerning aid provided by the Derbyshire County Council to Toyota Motor Corporation, OJ L6, 11 January 1992.
22. Commission Notice on the application of Article 87 and 88 of the EC Treaty to State aid in the form of guarantees, OJ C71, 11 March 2000.
23. Commission Notice concerning aid elements in land sales by public authorities, OJ C209, 10 July 1997.
24. Commission Notice on the application of the State aid rules to measures relating to direct business taxation, OJ C384, 10 December 1998.
25. Commission Communication on State aid and risk capital, OJ C235, 21 August 2001.
26. RAPID Press Release, 'Commission approves regional venture capital funds for England', IP/01/785, 6 June 2001.
27. European Commission (1994), 'Public authorities' holdings in company capital', Bulletin of the European Communities, 9, Luxembourg: OOPEC, 3.5.1.
28. European Commission (2001), XXXth Report on Competition Policy 2000, Brussels, Luxembourg, OOPEC, point 312.
29. Case 730/79 *Philip Morris Holland BV v Commission of the European Communities* (1980) ECR 2671.
30. Community Guidelines on State aids for small and medium-sized enterprises (SMEs), OJ C213, 19 August 1992.
31. Council Regulation (EC) No 69/2001 of 12 January 2001 on the application of Articles 87 and 88 of the EC Treaty to *de minimis* aid, OJ L10, 13 January 2001.
32. Aids N 560/01 and NN 17/02 – United Kingdom – Brighton West Pier, C (2002) 942 fin., 9 April 2002.
33. See Bacon (1997) for a detailed treatment of this issue.
34. Commission Decision 80/932/EEC of 15 September 1980 concerning the partial taking-over by the State of employers' contributions to sickness insurance schemes in Italy, OJ L264, 8 October 1980.
35. Conclusions of the ECOFIN Council Meeting of 1 December 1997 concerning taxation policy, OJ C2, 6 January 1998.
36. The measure was clearly selective in that higher rates of taxation applied to services and agriculture.
37. Proposals for appropriate measures under Article 93(1) of the EC Treaty concerning Irish corporation tax (ICT), OJ C395, 18 December 1998.
38. This refers to 'market services which the Member States subject to specific public service obligations by virtue of a general interest criterion. This would tend to cover such things as transport networks, energy and communications' (European Commission, Services of General Interest in Europe, COM(2000) 580 final of 20 September 2000, Brussels).
39. C 280/00 *Altmark Trans GmbH Regierungspräsidium Magdeburg v Nahverkehrsgesellschaft Altmark GmbH.* (1993) ECR-I 7747. This case is attracting an expanding literature. See, for example, several articles in *European State Aid Law Quarterly* (3) 2003.
40. Including a proposal for a Community framework for State aid in the form of public service compensation, see http://europa.eu.int/comm/competition/state_aid/others/.
41. For example, postal services, broadcasting, audiovisual production, electricity, shipbuilding, transport, steel, agriculture and fisheries.

42. The various sectoral frameworks are not discussed further owing to their industry-specific nature; in many cases they merit a chapter in their own right.
43. See http://europa.eu.int/comm/competition/state_aid/legislation/.
44. Broadly, medium-sized firms are those with fewer than 250 employees and small firms those with fewer than 50. In addition, certain financial and independence criteria apply.
45. The current guidelines are Community framework for State aid for research and development, OJ C45, 17 February 1996.
46. N. Kroes, 'Towards a pro-active competition policy in favour of innovation', conference on Promoting Innovation and Competitiveness. A Transatlantic Dialogue, The Hague, The Netherlands, 27-28 April 2005, available at http://europa.eu.int/comm./competition/speeches/text/sp2005_006
47. Community Guidelines on State aid for environmental protection, OJ C37, 3 February 2001.
48. Commission Guidelines on national regional aid, OJ C74, 10 March 1998.
49. This is essentially the same as the definition of Objective 1 areas for the purposes of EU cohesion policy.
50. This ceiling was set on the basis that coverage should not exceed 50 per cent of the population, taking account of the then anticipated enlargement to 21 Member States.
51. National ceilings for regional aid coverage under the derogations provided for in Article 92(3)(a) and (c) [Article 87(3)(a) and (c)] of the Treaty for the period 2000 to 2006, OJ C16, 21 January 1999.
52. Typically, these range from 50 per cent to 20 per cent net grant-equivalent (NGE). NGE refers to the after tax value of assistance and is used by the Commission for comparing the value of all forms of regional aid.
53. Multisectoral framework on regional aid for large investment projects – rescue and restructuring aid and closure aid for the steel sector, OJ C70, 19 March 2002.
54. European Commission, XXXIIIrd Report on Competition Policy 2003, SEC(2004)658 final, 2004, point 389.
55. S. Cavallo and K. Junginger-Dittel (2004), 'The Multisectoral Framework 2002: new rules on regional aid to large investment projects', Competition Policy Newsletter, Spring, p. 82.
56. Invitation to submit comments pursuant to Article 88(2) of the EC Treaty, concerning aid C 39/99 (ex E 2/97) – English Partnerships (EP) under the Partnership Investment Programme (PIP), OJ C245, 28 August 1999.
57. Commission Decision of 22 December 1999 on aid scheme C 39/99 (ex E 2/97) United Kingdom English Partnerships (EP) under the Partnership Investment Programme (PIP), OJ L145, 20 June 2000.
58. House of Commons, Transport Local Government and the Regions Committee, The need for a European regeneration framework, Twelfth Report of Session 2001-2, HC 483-I of 31 July 2002, The Stationery Office, London.
59. European Commission letter to the UK government regarding rescue aid to British Energy plc, COM(2002) 4480 final of 27 November 2002, Brussels.
60. European Commission, State Aid Scoreboard – Autumn 2003 Update, COM(2003) 636 final of 29 October 2003, Brussels, p. 18.
61. Community Guidelines on State aid for rescuing and restructuring firms in difficulty, OJ C244, 1 October 2004.
62. Restructuring aid schemes for SMEs can be approved by the Commission.
63. Excluding Treuhandanstalt operations in the former East Germany.
64. European Commission, State Aid Scoreboard – Autumn 2003 Update, COM(2003) 636 final of 29 October 2003, Brussels.
65. London Economics, 'Ex-post evaluation of the impact of rescue and restructuring aid on the international competitiveness of the sector(s) affected by such aid', Final Report to the European Commission – Enterprise Directorate General, 2004, p. 120.
66. Presidency Conclusions, Stockholm European Council, 23 and 24 March 2001, point 21.
67. See http://europa.eu.int/comm/competition/state_aid/scoreboard/.
68. European Commission, Progress report concerning the reduction and reorientation of State aid, COM(2002) 555 final of 16 October 2002, Brussels.

69. European Commission, State aid action plan – less and better targeted State aid: a roadmap for State aid reform 2005-2009, COM(2005) 107 final.

70. 2467th Council meeting – Competitiveness (internal market, industry, research) – Brussels, 26 November 2002, 14365/02 (Presse 360).

71. European Commission, State Aid Scoreboard – Spring 2002 update, COM(2002) 242 final of 22 May 2002, Brussels, 2002, p. 8.

72. European Commission, Progress report concerning the reduction and reorientation of State aid, COM(2002) 555 final of 16 October 2002, Brussels.

73. P. Lowe, 'Introduction', EC Competition Policy Newsletter, 2003(1) Spring, p. 1.

74. Staatliche Beihilfe Nr. N 258/00 – Deutschland – Freizeitbad Dorsten, SG(2001) D/ 285046 of 12 January 2001.

75. P. Lowe, 'Introduction', EC Competition Policy Newsletter, 2003(1) Spring.

76. European Commission, Progress report concerning the reduction and reorientation of State aid, COM(2002) 555 final of 16 October 2002, Brussels.

77. For an overview of LASA and LET see Wishlade (2004).

78. RAPID Press Release, Mario Monti, 'Contribution of competition policy to competitiveness of European economy', Institute of European Affairs, Dublin, SPEECH/03/264 of 26 May 2003.

79. Form for the submission of complaints concerning alleged unlawful State aid, OJ C116, 16 May 2003.

80. Commission Communication on the interest rates to be applied when aid granted unlawfully is being recovered, OJ C110, 8 May 2003.

81. P. Lowe, 'Objectives of State aid policy in the European Union and in the international context', Information seminar for MPs of the Candidate countries on EU State aid policy, European Parliament, 26 May 2003.

82. European Commission, A proactive competition policy for a competitive Europe, COM(2004) 293 final, 20 April 2004, Brussels, p. 13.

83. European Commission (2004), Third report on economic and social cohesion, Luxembourg: OOPEC.

84. European Commission, State aid action plan – less and better targeted State aid: a roadmap for State aid reform 2005-2009, COM(2005) 107 final.

85. Review of the regional aid guidelines – a first consultation paper for the experts from the Member States, available at: http://europa.eu.int/comm/ competition/state_aid/regional/.

86. For an overview of the working paper and a more detailed assessment of its implications see Wishlade (2004) and Wishlade, F. 'Regional State aid and competition policy post-2006', Benchmarking Regional Policy in Europe, 2nd International Conference, Riga, April 2005.

87. 'Earmarked regions' are those losing Article 87(3)(a) status and sparsely-populated regions.

88. For example, in responding to the Commission proposals, the Italian authorities have expressed doubts as to whether incentives are really influential in the face of competition from, for example, the far east.

89. Community framework for State aid to the motor vehicle industry, OJ C279, 15 October 1997.

90. Both now superseded by the 2002 Multisectoral Framework.

10. Conclusions and Future Prospects

Roger Clarke and Eleanor J. Morgan

INTRODUCTION

The last few years have been an extremely eventful time in the development of UK and EU competition policy. The rapid pace of change can be seen in the amount of new legislation which has been put in place. There has also been a significant development in 'soft law', with numerous new notices offering detailed guidance on aspects of interpretation and implementation. The changes have affected the institutional structure, substantive assessment and procedures within both competition policy regimes as well as the allocation of responsibilities between the EU and the UK (and national authorities in other Member States).

In the UK, the two major legislative developments amount to a thorough-going reform of the competition policy regime. The Competition Act of 1998, in particular, and the Enterprise Act of 2002 have brought UK policy more into line with the approach in the EU. The Monopolies and Mergers Commission (MMC) has been restyled the Competition Commission (CC); monopoly investigations have been abolished and instead there are provisions for market investigation references; the old public interest test in merger policy has been formally replaced by one that focuses on a 'substantial lessening of competition', and ministers have been removed from the referral and decision-making phases in most areas so that the OFT and CC have become the determinative competition authorities. In addition, a leniency programme has been introduced in cartel policy, together with stronger investigative powers, and involvement in cartels by individuals has been criminalised. The Competition Appeal Tribunal (CAT), a specialised independent court, has been created to hear appeals and to review decisions made by the UK competition authorities.

The 1998 Competition Act also gave the regulators of privatised utilities new powers to enforce prohibitions on anti-competitive agreements and the abuse of dominant positions and they were subsequently empowered to undertake market investigations under the Enterprise Act. In addition, the structure of regulation of the utility industries in the UK is being altered by sector specific legislation (as, for example, in telecommunications through the Communications Act 2003) partly prompted by the need to transpose EU directives into UK law. This affects the work of the CC which has a potentially larger role in regulatory inquiries and appeals regarding licence modifications by the regulators although such activity to date has been much less than expected.

At the same time as these legislative changes have been taking place in the UK, there have been significant new developments in EU competition policy. Of these, the most important legislative reform was the adoption of a new Merger Regulation in 2004 which, among other changes, introduced a revised appraisal test giving greater prominence to effects on competition. This was accompanied by the publication of horizontal merger guidelines for the first time, alongside other new guidance notices. The system of block exemptions also began to alter in the late 1990s as part of the reform of Article 81; the 1999 block exemption on vertical agreements is a prime example of the move towards exemptions based on economic analysis rather than formal categories. In addition, leniency policy has been extended to help in detecting cartels. Alongside these developments, State aid policy has been evolving rapidly. The Commission's interpretation of the exceptions from the ban on State aid has led to a large body of soft law, and increasingly to actual legislation, as it attempts to exert more control over the levels and types of aid.

The liberalisation of the utility industries, where competition law on its own is insufficient to create a competitive environment, is another thrust of EU policy which has recently gathered some momentum. The sector specific legislation used to liberalise these sectors usually has precedence over competition law but the coexistence of the two types of policy has raised new issues.

Turning to the changing boundaries between the EU and national authorities, including the UK, recent legislative developments have shown the Commission's new willingness to transfer some of its earlier responsibilities to the national competition authorities. The Modernization Regulation of 2003 introduced significant changes to the enforcement of EU competition law by increasing the scope for Member States to investigate the abuse of dominance and cartel behaviour, and to impose remedies. It is still early on in this process which will eventually affect all of the national authorities within the EU. Some fine tuning of the referral provisions under the new merger regime has also taken place to facilitate the reallocation of cases to the authority best suited to deal with them. In the developing area of utility policy, national regulatory and competition authorities are expected to play their part by adopting policies agreed at EU level.

These and other changes detailed within the chapters of this book together amount to a wide ranging set of reforms to competition law both at UK and EU level. The actual impact of the legislative reforms, however, will depend not just on the new provisions but also on how they are interpreted and implemented. Much of the legislation is so recent that there is insufficient evidence to see how well it actually operates in practice; a full assessment can only be based on further experience of its application taking into account the effects of the accompanying soft law and internal reforms. With this caveat in mind, however, the next section looks at a selection of issues raised by the changes examined in the preceding chapters, placing particular emphasis on developments in the substantive assessment of competition cases. The book concludes by highlighting some of the more significant future challenges for UK and, particularly, EU competition policy.

CURRENT ISSUES

The main developments of policy towards monopoly and dominant firms have concerned the move towards an EU-based policy in the UK, the Modernization Regulation and the current review of policy in the EU. In the UK, the move towards EU policy has been accompanied by the introduction of market investigation references which widen the scope of UK policy in cases where a structural change in the market might be required or where no single firm holds a dominant position. The Modernization Regulation increases scope for devolution of powers to national competition authorities in Article 81 and 82 cases as well as creating a European Competition Network to consider the allocation of cases between the Commission and Member States. The review of Article 82 policy currently underway seeks to deal with a number of issues concerning the current operation of EU policy.

Two broad issues for future development of policy in this area can be distinguished. First, at UK level, the question arises whether the market investigation references introduced in the Enterprise Act will be effective in dealing with cases not captured by the Chapter I and Chapter II prohibitions. The policy is very new and no decisions have been reached at the time of writing[1] so its effectiveness remains to be seen. Some limitations of this policy, however, have been identified including the long time period allowed for investigations (up to two years) and the further time which may be required to deal with appeals to the CAT. In addition, it is not clear that the CC is best placed to implement the remedies it proposes but this remains to be seen. Second, at EU level, the main development in the immediate future is likely to be the possible reform of Article 82 policy in light of the current DG Competition review. At present only price based exclusionary abuses are being reviewed and a further review of other areas, in particular exploitative abuses, is expected at some time in the coming year. It is, therefore, difficult to assess at this stage exactly what changes will be made, although it seems likely that a provision will be included allowing efficiency gains to be considered in Article 82 cases to bring EU policy in dominant firm cases into line with other areas of competition policy, notably

Article 81 and merger policy. Problems may exist in introducing an 'as-efficient competitor' test in price based exclusionary cases, however, in so far as it is seen as a necessary condition for an abuse of a dominant position to be found, and whether this test will be introduced, and in what form, remains to be seen.

The Enterprise Act 2002 introduced the most substantial reform of UK merger legislation since its introduction in 1965. Although the 'substantial lessening of competition test' (which is similar to the test previously used in the US) formally replaced the 'public interest' test, this was not a new departure but usefully brought the law into line with existing policy. Indeed substantive merger policy remains largely unchanged; instead, the main changes to UK merger control are due to the accompanying institutional and procedural reforms (some of which have been referred to above). These have strengthened the hands of the competition authorities at the same time as significantly increasing transparency and accountability in this policy area.

The main substantive change introduced into EU merger policy is the introduction of a new test based on whether the transaction would significantly impede effective competition. The introduction of this effects-based test, a variant of the SLC criterion used in the US and more recently in the UK, is in line with economic theory and should move attention away from the focus on dominance under the previous test. It would have been simpler if all reference to dominance could have been removed, although the compromise wording in the regulation apparently reduces its role in the new policy. References to dominance also appear in various places in the horizontal merger guidelines. It therefore remains to be seen whether the changes to wording will influence actual practice sufficiently to meet the concerns about the attention given to dominance in previous merger policy.

Another key area of uncertainty under the new EU merger regime is the scope and likely treatment of non-coordinated ('unilateral') effects among oligopolists where there was an alleged 'gap' in merger control previously. The revised appraisal test opens the way for such effects to be controlled under the new regime and critics argue that this heralds a much more interventionist approach by the Commission as it potentially opens mergers below the traditional market share thresholds to challenge. It is hard to identify actual cases that might fit the guidelines on non-coordinated oligopolies, however, and it is debateable whether the extension of unilateral effects to oligopoly is worthwhile in view of the uncertainties that this introduces. In any case, the Commission's powers in this new area of enforcement have yet to be tested in the Courts. The Commission seems likely to proceed cautiously in view of recent Court setbacks in other aspects of merger policy which were so damaging to its credibility prior to the recent reforms.

The treatment of the small number of large conglomerate mergers is a controversial issue in the EU as the authorities have taken considerable interest in possible 'portfolio effects' according to which the market power due to owning a portfolio of brands may be greater than the market shares of the products taken individually and hence anti-competitive. The importance of these effects is disputed by economists who point to the very restrictive conditions under which conglomerate mergers might raise concerns. This is a particularly sensitive area of merger policy in the EU in the wake of the banned merger between GE and Honeywell. When the horizontal guidelines were introduced, the Commission promised guidelines on conglomerate (as well as vertical) mergers and this would be a welcome development. Such guidelines are expected to reflect the less interventionist stance towards conglomerate mergers demanded by the Court in its judgement on *Tetra Laval*, a stance that is already incorporated in the UK merger guidelines.

Important steps have been taken in recent years to strengthen policy towards cartels and horizontal restrictive practices in the UK and EU. It is widely accepted at both levels that hard core cartels are anathema to competition and need to be stopped. Leniency programmes have been developed to increase the scope for action and to bring about more successful investigations.

It is now necessary to allow the policy time to operate particularly in the UK, before assessing its effectiveness. Even at this stage, however, important issues need to be borne in mind. First, whether the policy is having an effect on larger cartels or whether it is just covering relatively small cases (such as the recent roofing contractor cases in the UK) where the economic impact is relatively limited. While small cases need to be considered, the effectiveness of the policy really needs to be evaluated in terms of its success in dealing with large hard core cartels, and an important goal of the competition authorities must be to uncover and successfully deal with such cases. Second, whether the penalties for operating cartels are sufficient and appropriate to deal with hard core cartels. One aspect of this, of course, is the role such policies play in deterring firms from setting up cartels. While fines can, in principle, have such an effect, whether they are now high enough to prevent cartels being formed remains an important issue. There is also the issue of individual responsibility in setting up hard core cartels, and whether individual criminal penalties, as operated in the US and now the UK, are appropriate. This needs to be examined at the EU level.

Finally, private class actions have been used in the US and are an important force in deterring firms from setting up hard core cartels so this raises the question whether a larger role needs to be given to such actions in the UK and EU. At present, the high costs of taking civil action and the risk that this action might fail are important deterrents to this branch of policy. This is also a current issue at both the UK and EU level.

Important developments in policy on vertical restraints have taken place in recent years, particularly in the EU. On the positive side, a new 30 per cent market share test has been introduced for non-hard core vertical restraints, below which anti-competitive effects are not now expected. Whilst this figure can be seen as essentially arbitrary, it captures the idea, prevalent in the literature, that vertical restraints are not expected to give rise to anti-competitive effects in the absence of market power. The new policy also adopts an 'effects-based' approach which replaces the earlier 'form based' approach to vertical restraints, and limits the possibilities for 'form shopping' between different combinations of vertical restraint. This will reduce the likelihood that firms can avoid the impact of policy in this area by adopting different forms of vertical restraint to like effect.

At the same time, however, some weaknesses exist in current EU policy. Most important amongst these is in the treatment of hard core vertical restraints for which a market share test will not apply. Whilst most economists would agree that minimum resale price maintenance is a hard core restraint tending to limit intra-brand, and possibly inter-brand, competition, it is less clear that other hard core restraints which mainly involve exclusivity conditions should be treated in the same way. At one level, since such agreements primarily affect intra-brand competition, there is a conflict between their hard core status and the overall Commission view that the main concern for policy should be restriction in inter-brand, not intra-brand, competition.[2] More substantively, the primary concern with exclusivity is that it gives rise to segmented markets and possibly third degree price discrimination. Since third degree price discrimination is not necessarily harmful and, in some circumstances, can increase economic welfare,[3] it is not clear that it is desirable to treat it as a hard core vertical restraint. The treatment of exclusivity reflects the political goal of the EU to create a single integrated market and this over-rides consideration of the net welfare gains that segmentation might provide. It could be beneficial to relax policy in this area, at least in some cases where segmentation might result in welfare gains.

Developments in the utility industries and competition policy are increasingly interrelated in the EU, and especially in the UK, reflecting the prevailing view that competition, where it can be achieved, will often be more efficient than direct regulation of privatised industries, which should only be used transitionally. This is a vast area raising many complex issues beyond the scope of this book but the UK evidence suggests that effective competition relies heavily on a carefully designed separation of the ownership of monopolistic network facilities from the provision of retail services (as in electricity and gas) rather than simply on making provision for open access through pricing arrangements. This raises questions about current EU policy, especially in telecommunications and energy where the main focus of recent directives has been on promoting the development of competition through opening third party access rather than vertical separation. The delays in agreeing policy at EU level and then in implementing the packages of directives and necessary secondary legislation in many of the Member States have perpetuated differing national frameworks and held up the implementation of other measures, such as market reviews, which are intended to bring the regulatory regimes of Member States closer together. Ensuring compliance nationally is a key issue alongside the appropriate design of policy; the proposed action against ten Member States which have not, as yet, complied with current energy directives suggests some tightening of approach.

Policy in the area of intellectual property rights (IPRs) has been guided by a number of decisions in the European courts. In the case of parallel imports, the European Court of Justice (ECJ) has taken the view that attempts to segment markets are not compatible with the EC Treaty but parallel imports from outside the EU are typically banned. The former viewpoint reflects the importance of the single market in the ECJ's thinking while the latter preserves the right of manufacturers to segment markets outside the EU. Decisions on licensing technical know-how have not shown a clear pattern, although the Court has recognised that such licensing may be required when an essential input is involved. This view was supported, in particular, in the *Magil* case where the ECJ ruled that the advantages of licensing outweighed any rights to the protection of IPRs. Decisions on copyright collectives have taken a relatively pragmatic approach, recognising the difficulties that individual owners have in collecting payments and allowing this to outweigh any possibility of infringement of Articles 81 or 82.

Of these issues, the tension that exists between the principle of supporting the single market and market segmentation in the case of parallel imports remains, perhaps, the most important issue. As in the case of exclusivity, the problem arises from the fact that market segmentation can have positive economic effects and hence it is not clear that it should be outlawed *per se*. Of the other issues, a fine line needs to be drawn between protecting IPRs on the one hand and the restriction of competition on the other. In this area, the ECJ has mainly adopted a fairly well reasoned approach allowing measures to support the protection of property rights in some cases and promoting competition in others, and it seems likely that this will continue in the years ahead. There is always scope for debate in this area, however, especially as new issues arise.

State aid policy is currently an important focus of attention in the development of EU competition policy. It is clear that an overly complicated set of rules, guidelines and exemptions has evolved over the years with cumbersome and lengthy procedures making it sometimes just as difficult to get approval for smaller aids as larger, potentially more distortionary ones. Deciding which State aid should be allowed basically should involve weighing any positive effects in terms of its contribution towards the recognised goals of State aid policy (such as cohesion or employment) against any detrimental effects on competition. Although there has been an emphasis in the past few years on 'less and better targeted' aid, actual changes to policy have amounted to incremental adjustments rather than a complete overhaul of the system. Among the problems of achieving the necessary reforms in practice are differing national circumstances and interests and, as with directives in the utility industries, Member States have enforced State aid rules to varying extents.

A more rigorous approach to the more distortionary forms of aid, especially those expected to create significant distortions of competition at EU level, is needed to help tackle the apparently continuing arbitrariness of State aid policy. This implies a firmer approach towards rescue and restructuring aid, especially restructuring aid to large companies. More extensive use of economic analysis could help to focus attention on areas where there is likely to be an important impact on EU competition and areas where any effect is likely to be small. The need for reform in this area of competition policy has become even more pressing with the recent enlargement of the Community. A number of frameworks are due for renewal before 2007 and consultations are now underway on an indicative road map for reforming the State aid provisions. This should provide an opportunity for far reaching reform of State aid policy to ensure it is better targeted and to consolidate and simplify the rules.

FURTHER ISSUES AND WIDER CHALLENGES

While a few areas of competition policy are in a transitional state, most notably EU policy towards State aids and dominant firms, many of the areas examined in this volume have been very substantially reformed in the past few years. After this period of rapid change on so many fronts, the main challenge facing the competition authorities internally in the shorter term is to consolidate the gains, ensuring that the legislation is applied in keeping with the spirit of the reforms and that the new competition tools are used as effectively and efficiently as possible. Their operation then needs to be assessed in the light of experience before making further fundamental changes.

Securing greater transparency has been one of the guiding principles of the recent new developments and while there have been important institutional and procedural reforms to facilitate these, there are still zones of discretion (as regards procedures in EU merger policy, for example). In any case, much depends on how every day practice develops around the revised procedures in the new institutional settings. Although some of the initial signs are encouraging, it remains to be seen whether a culture of greater transparency will become embedded in competition policy over time.

The publication of appraisal (and other) guidelines is a useful means of increasing transparency as well as helping to make policy more predictable. These can set out broad principles but cannot be applied mechanistically and their interpretation needs to be established in the decisional practice and case law. Economic theories change and analytical methods develop over time so guidelines will need regular updating to reflect changes in thinking and actual experience.

Another thrust of the recent reforms has been to increase the role of economic analysis in competition policy and to ensure that competition decisions are made on a sound analytical basis using up to date empirical methods. The increased level of staff expertise both in the EC Competition Directorate and in the UK (with a shift towards appointing more specialist members to the CC, for example) has been an important development.[4] There is some encouraging evidence of its initial effects but it will be a continuing challenge to ensure that the new expertise is appropriately deployed and received so that the relatively small changes in overall staffing can have the necessary overall impact on policies.

The degree of accountability has been another key issue in the recent reforms and more checks and balances have been introduced, including the new judicial review mechanism under the CAT in the UK and the emphasis on procedural reform in the EU. Increases in accountability, in turn, bring their own demands in ensuring that decision making in competition policy becomes sounder rather than overly cautious. Despite moves to increase accountability and transparency in the EU, there is still the fundamental question of the Commission's combined role as judge, jury and prosecutor and the relatively slow procedures for appealing against its actions. A major challenge for the Commission internally is to ensure that the impact of the recent reforms on its practice is sufficient to restore credibility and to prevent future calls for more far reaching institutional change at EU level.

These, then, are some of the many internal challenges facing the competition authorities in the UK and EU following the recent spate of reforms. There is also another important group of challenges, some of which are longer term, which can perhaps best be described as 'external'. Some are specific to the EU; others face competition policy makers around the world on a more general basis.

In the EU, the prospect of further enlargement is on the horizon. This will add to the case load, especially as regards State aids. There are already considerable challenges in accommodating the interests of consumers, firms and policy makers across the recently enlarged Community. These will be increased as and when additional countries, with varying economic traditions and levels of economic development, are brought into the EU. Each of the new Member States had to have its own functioning competition policy modelled on Articles 81 and 82 as a condition of accession and the newly established European Competition Network is providing a framework for cooperation among all the competition authorities within the EU.

There has also been an increased recognition in other parts of the world of the importance of protecting competition, as reflected in the considerable increase in the number of new competition regimes which have been established nationally or regionally in recent years. These differ in terms of their substantive features as well as their procedures and institutional contexts. This variety, together with the globalization of business, results in a number of problems. It makes it difficult for the competition agencies to cooperate in the investigation of possible anti-competitive merger proposals or behaviour which extend beyond the bounds of a single authority. It also adds to the burden on businesses which increasingly operate in various jurisdictions throughout the world and may face different obligations and penalties for similar behaviour under different regimes although it may allow firms to engage in transnational anti-competitive practices without effective sanctions. Antitrust authorities may lack the necessary instruments to deal with practices affecting competition in their territory which are organised elsewhere and the fact that action in some countries may be less rigorous than others may result in friction. It is unlikely that a set of international competition rules will be agreed in the foreseeable future,[5] so these twin challenges of proliferating competition regimes and the globalization of business have led to a continuing emphasis on developing mechanisms to improve and harmonize policies and on encouraging a consensus regarding appropriate approaches to international competition problems.

One approach to these challenges is to develop bilateral agreements. Such agreements enable cooperation to move further and more quickly between partners with similar approaches to key competition issues and substantive rules than would be possible in a multilateral context. So, for example, the EU has dedicated bilateral agreements with the US, with Canada and with Japan and there has been some convergence of policy in recent years. An important issue here is how far to go in bilateral agreements – are so called 'first generation agreements' allowing consultations and comity[6] enough or should confidential information be exchanged and enforcement activities be carried out on each other's behalf?

It is impossible for competition authorities to build bilateral cooperative relationships with all their counterparts globally and this means there is a need for multilateral cooperation. The Commission has played an important role in setting up and supporting the work of the International Competition Network (ICN), an informal organisation established in October 2001 where competition authorities can discuss competition policy issues and spread best practice. This network, which now has more than 80 members, has published a set of principles that competition authorities should respect when analysing mergers across several jurisdictions[7] which were influential in the recent reform of the EU merger regulation, for example. It is currently examining the problem of international cartels, building on work on hard core cartels already undertaken by the Organisation for Economic Cooperation and Development[8] with its more limited membership. Although the ICN's recommendations are not binding, they are helping to advance a growing body of accepted principles and best practice. These new developments reflect an important change in the international competition community. Up to about fifteen years ago, conflict rather than cooperation tended to characterise relationships among the relatively few established authorities; convergence would hardly have been recognised as an issue for debate and yet there have recently been important moves towards convergence, although these must not be overstated.

As well as the challenge of securing fair competition within the borders of the EU and more widely through effective competition policies and cooperation globally, there is the broader but related trade policy issue of the basis on which foreign companies compete in overseas markets. In the case of Europe, allowing more competition from beyond EU borders could also be an important means of enhancing competitiveness and promoting the Lisbon agenda. Difficult decisions need to be taken about opening EU product and service markets to further foreign competition as a complement to the advances in securing fair competition within the market through competition policy.

In conclusion, this book has shown the scale and richness of the new developments in UK and EU competition policy in recent years. The reform of competition policy, however, is never complete and much remains to be done to build on the recent reforms, to introduce changes in areas which have been less extensively altered – EU State aid policy, for example, where consultations are now underway – and grapple with new challenges as they emerge.

NOTES

1.   At a late stage in the preparation of this book , the CC reported on its first market investigation case (*Store cards*) on 7 March 2006. This found a lack of competition in the store card market and indicated a number of reforms the CC proposed to put in place to improve consumer awareness of the high interest rates charged in this market. See Competition Commission, *Store cards market investigation*, final report, 7 March 2006.

2.   Commission Notice – Guidelines on Vertical Restraints, OJ C291, 13 October 2000, point 119. As noted in Chapter 6, it is not clear that the Commission's view holds much water since intra-brand competition may be just as important as inter-brand competition.

3   It should perhaps be stressed, on the one hand, that it need not do so, especially where any increase in aggregate output is low. On the other hand, it will definitely increase welfare if it leads to a market being supplied which would not be otherwise.

4.   There are 20 economists with a PhD working in DG Competition, 10 of which are currently working in the office of the Chief Competition Economist. See L.-H. Röller, 'Using economic analysis to strengthen competition policy enforcement in Europe', European Commission, 21 March 2005 and also John Vickers, 'Law and Economics: the case for bundling', speech at the International Bar Association Conference, Brussels, 10 March 2005 for discussions of the trend towards using more economics and economists in competition policy.

5.   The EU has been a significant contributor to discussions on a possible multilateral agreement on competition in the World Trade Organisation (WTO). It has been included as an area for discussion in the WTO since 1996 and a working group has been created. The case for a multilateral framework to enhance the contribution of competition policy to international trade

and development was recognised at the Doha meeting of trade negotiators in November 2001 but no formal negotiations on a WTO treaty on competition were launched in Cancun in September 2003.

6. According to a 'positive comity' procedure, each party undertakes to investigate, upon request, anti-competitive activity in its own territory that adversely affects the interests of the other party.
7. See www.internationalcompetitionnetwork.org.
8. See OECD (2002, 2003).

References

Abreu, D., D. Pearce and E. Stachetti (1986), 'Optimal cartel equilibria with imperfect monitoring', *Journal of Economic Theory*, **39** (1), 251-69.

Aghion, P., N. Bloom, R. Blundell, R. Griffith and P. Howitt (2005), 'Competition and innovation: an inverted-U relationship', *Quarterly Journal of Economics*, **120** (2), 701-28.

Aghion, P., C. Harris, P. Howitt and J. Vickers (2001), 'Competition, imitation and growth with step-by-step innovation', *Review of Economic Studies*, **68** (3), 467-92.

Aghion, P., C. Harris and J. Vickers (1997), 'Competition and growth with step-by-step innovation: an example', *European Economic Review*, **41** (3), 771-82.

Alese, F. (2004), 'UK Merger review and Section 33: was the CAT not right?', *European Competition Policy Review*, **25** (8), 470-4.

Alonso, J.B. (1994), 'Market definition in the Community's merger control policy', *European Competition Law Review*, **15** (4), 195-208.

Anderson, S.P. and V. Ginsburgh (1999), 'International pricing with costly consumer arbitrage', *Review of International Economics*, **7** (1), 126-39.

Anestis, P., S. Mavroghenis and S. Drakakakis (2004), 'Rescue and restructuring aid: a brief assessment of the principal provisions of the guidelines', *European State Aid Law Quarterly*, **3** (1), 27-34.

Areeda, P. and D. Turner (1975), 'Predatory pricing and related practices under Section 2 of the Sherman Act', *Harvard Law Review*, **88**, 697-733.

Bacon, K. (1997), 'State aids and general measures', *Yearbook of European Law*, **17**, 269-321.

Bacon, K. (2003), 'The concept of State aid: the developing jurisprudence in the European and UK courts', *European Competition Law Review*, **24** (2), 54-61.

Baxter, S. and F. Dethmers (2005), 'Unilateral effects under the European Merger Regulation: how big is the gap?', *European Competition Law Review*, **26** (7), 380-9.

Bergman, L., G. Brunekreeft, C. Doyle, D.M.G. Newbery, M. Pollitt, P. Régibeau, M. Nils-Henrik and N.-H.M. von der Fehr (1999), 'A European market for electricity?', *CEPR/SNS Monitoring European Deregulation Series*, 2.

Besley, T., K., P. Seabright, K. Rockett and P.B. Sorensen (1999), 'The effects and policy implications of State aids to industry: an economic analysis', *Economic Policy*, **14**, no. 28, 13-53.

Bishop, S. and A. Lofaro (2004), 'A legal and economic consensus? The theory and practice of coordinated effects in EC merger control', *Antitrust Bulletin*, **49** (Spring), 195-242.

Bishop, S. and M. Walker (2002), *The Economics of EC Competition Law*, 2nd edition, London: Sweet & Maxwell.

Bolton, P., J. Brodley and M. Riordan (2000), 'Predatory pricing: strategic theory and legal policy', *Georgetown Law Journal*, **88**, 2239-330.

Bower, J. (2004), 'Electricity infrastructure and security of supply: should EU governments invest in transmission capacity?', Oxford Institute for Energy Studies, Oxford Energy Comment, March.

Brittan, S. (1984), 'The politics and economics of privatisation', *Political Quarterly*, **55** (2), 109-27.

Carlson, S.C. (1999), 'Patent pools and the antitrust dilemma', *Yale Journal of Regulation*, **16** (2), 359-99.

Carlton, D. and R. Gertner (2002), 'Intellectual property, antitrust and strategic behaviour', NBER Working Paper, no. 8976.

Carlton, D.W. and J.M. Perloff (2005), *Modern Industrial Organization*, 4th edition, Boston: Addison Wesley.

Clapham, J.H. (1922), 'Of empty economic boxes', *Economic Journal*, **32**, no. 127, 305-14.

Clarke, R. (1985), *Industrial Economics*, Oxford: Basil Blackwell.

Clarke, R., S. Davies and N. Driffield (1998), *Monopoly Policy in the UK: Assessing the Evidence*, Aldershot, UK and Brookfield, US: Edward Elgar.

Clarke, R., S. Davies, P.W. Dobson, and M. Waterson (2002), *Buyer Power and Competition in European Food Retailing*, Cheltenham, UK and Northampton, MA, USA: Edward Elgar.

Cohen, W., R. Nelson and J. Walsh (2000), 'Protecting their intellectual assets: appropriability conditions and why US manufacturing firms patent (or not)', NBER Working Paper, no. 7552.

Compt, O., F. Jenny and P. Rey (2002), 'Capacity constraints, mergers, and collusion', *European Economic Review*, **46** (1), 1-29.

Connor, J.M. (2001), *Global Price Fixing: Our Customers are the Enemies*, Boston: Kluwer Academic Publishers.

Coppi, L. and M. Walker (2004), 'Substantial convergence of parallel paths? Similarities and differences in the economic analysis of horizontal mergers in US and EU competition laws', *Antitrust Bulletin*, **49** (Spring), 101-52.

Crampes, C., A. Hollander and C. Macdissi (2004), 'On non-contractual means to curtail parallel trade', Université de Montréal, mimeo.

D'Sa, R. (1998), *European Community Law on State Aid*, London: Sweet and Maxwell.

Derclaye, E. (2003), 'Abuses of dominant position and intellectual property rights: a suggestion to reconcile the Community Courts case law', *World Competition*, **26** (4), 685-705.

Dobson, P.W. (2005), 'Exploiting buyer power: lessons from the British grocery trade', *Antitrust Law Journal*, **72** (2), 529-62.

Dobson, P.W. and M. Waterson (1996), 'Vertical restraints and competition policy', Research Paper no. 12, London, OFT.

Dunt, E., J.S. Gans and S.P. King (2001), 'The economic consequences of dvd regional restrictions', University of Melbourne, mimeo.

Encaoua, D. and A. Hollander (2002), 'Competition policy and innovation', *Oxford Review of Economic Policy*, **18** (1), 63-79.

Encaoua, D. and A. Hollander (2004), 'Price discrimination, competition and quality selection', Université Paris I, mimeo.

Encaoua, D. and D. Ulph (2004), 'Catching-up or leapfrogging? The effects of competition on innovation and growth', Cahier de la MSE, Serie Verte, 2000.97, revised version (2004).

Encaoua, D., D. Guellec and C. Martinez (2003), 'The economics of patents: from natural rights to policy instruments', Cahiers de la MSE, Serie Verte, 2003.124.

Evans, A. and S. Martin (1991), 'Socially acceptable distortions of competition: Community policy on State aid', *European Law Review*, **16** (2), 79-111.

Evans, J. and R. Green (2003), 'Why did electricity prices fall after 1998?', Cambridge Working Papers in Economics, CMI, no. 26.

Ewringmann, D. and M. Thöne with H. G. Fischer (2002), 'European aid control and environmental protection – evaluation of the new community guidelines on State aid', Berlin, Bundesumweltministerium, April.

Ficsor, M. (1990), *Collective administration of copyright and neighbouring rights*, Geneva, WIPO.

Fox, E.M. (2003), 'We protect competition, you protect competitors', *World Competition*, **26** (2), 149-65.

Gal, M.S. (2004), 'Monopoly pricing as an antitrust offence in the US and the EC: two systems of belief about monopoly?', *Antitrust Bulletin*, **49** (Spring), 343-84.

Gallini, N.T. and A. Hollis (1999), 'A contractual approach to the gray market', *International Review of Law and Economics*, **19** (1), 1-21.

Ganslandt, M. and K. Maskus (1999), 'Parallel imports of pharmaceutical products in the European Union', World Bank, Working Paper, no. 2630.

Geroski, P. and R. Griffith (2004), 'Identifying antitrust markets', in M. Neumann and J. Weigand (eds), *The International Handbook of Competition*, Cheltenham, UK and Northampton, MA, USA: Edward Elgar.

Gilbert, R. (2000), 'Antitrust policy for the licensing of intellectual property: an international comparison', *International Journal of Technology Management*, **19** (1/2), 206-23.

Gilbert, R. (2002) 'Antitrust for patent pools: a century for policy evolution', University of California, Berkeley, mimeo.

Gilbert, R. (2004), 'Convergent doctrines? US and EU antitrust policy for the licensing of intellectual property', University of California, Berkeley, mimeo.

Gilbert, R. and C. Shapiro (1996), 'An economic analysis of unilateral refusals to license intellectual property', *Proceedings of National Academy of Science, USA*, **93**, 12749-55.

Glachant, J.-M., U. Dubois, and Y. Perez (2004), 'Deregulating with no regulator: is Germany's electricity transmission regime institutionally correct?', ADIS Research Centre paper, University of Paris XI.

Glynn, D. and M. Howe (2003), 'Distribution: vertical restraints in UK and EU competition law', *Competition Law Insight*, July/August.

Goodman, S. (2003), 'Steady as she goes: the Enterprise Act 2002 charts a familiar course for UK merger control', *European Competition Law Review*, **8** (August), 331-46.

Goyder, D.G. (2003), *EC Competition Law*, 4th edition, Oxford: Oxford University Press.

Green, E.J. and R.H. Porter (1984), 'Noncooperative collusion under imperfect price information', *Econometrica*, **52** (1), 87-100.

Green, R.J. and D.M. Newbery (1992), 'Competition in the British electricity spot market', *Journal of Political Economy*, **100** (5), 929-53.

Grout, P.A. and S. Sonderegger (2005), 'Predicting cartels', Economic Discussion Paper, London, OFT.

Hall, B. and R. Ziedonis (2001), 'The patent paradox revisited: an empirical study of patenting in the U.S. semi-conductor industry, 1979-1995', *Rand Journal of Economics*, **32** (1), 101-28.

Hansen, M., A. Van Ysendyck and S. Zühlke (2004), 'The coming of age of EC State aid law: a review of principal developments in 2002 and 2003', *European Competition Law Review*, **25** (4), 202-33.

Hawk, B.E. and H.L. Huser (1996), *European Community Merger Control: a Practitioner's Guide*, Hague: Kluwer Law International.

Holmes, S. (2004), 'The environmental guidelines: black smoke or sustainable development?', *European State Aid Law Quarterly*, 17-25.

Horspool, M. and V. Korah (1992), 'Competition', *Antitrust Bulletin*, **37** (Summer), 337-85.

Hutchings, M. (2004), 'The competition between law and economics', European Competition Law Review, 25 (9), 531-3.

Irmen, A. (1998), 'Precommitment in competing vertical chains', *Journal of Economic Surveys*, **12** (4), 333-59.

Ivaldi, M., B. Jullien, P. Seabright and J. Tirole (2003), 'The economics of tacit collusion', IDEI, University of Toulouse, mimeo.

Ivaldi, M. and F. Verboven (2002), 'Quantifying the effects from horizontal mergers in European competition policy', IDEI, University of Toulouse, mimeo.

Jackson, P.M. and C.M. Price (eds) (1994), *Privatisation and Regulation: A Review of the Issues*, London: Longman.

Jacquemin, A. and M.E. Slade (1989), 'Cartels, collusion and horizontal merger', in R. Schmalensee and R.D. Willig (eds), *The Handbook of Industrial Organization*, Amsterdam: North-Holland.

Jenny, F. (1993), 'EEC merger control: economies as an antitrust defense or an antitrust attack', in B. Hawk (ed.), *Fordham Corporate Law Institute 1993*, New York: Transnational Juris Publications.

Katz, M. (1989), 'Vertical contractual relations', in R. Schmalensee and R.D. Willig (eds) *Handbook of Industrial Organization*, Vol. 1, Amsterdam: Elsevier Science.

Katz, M. and C. Shapiro (1985), 'On the licensing of innovations', *Rand Journal of Economics*, **16** (4), 504-20.

Kekelekis, M. (2004), 'The "statement of objections" as an inherent part of the right to be heard in EC merger proceedings: issues of concern', *European Competition Law Review*, **25** (8), 518-27.

Kolasky, W.J. and R. Elliot (2003), 'A North American perspective: the European Commission Notice on the appraisal of horizontal mergers', *Antitrust*, **17** (3), 64-9.

Korah, V. (2001), 'The interface between intellectual property and antitrust: the European experience', *Antitrust Law Journal*, **69**, 801-39.

Kunzlik, P.F. (2003), 'Globalization and hybridization in antitrust enforcement: European "borrowings" from the U.S. approach', *Antitrust Bulletin*, **48** (2), 319-53.

Kwoka, J. (1981), 'Does the choice of concentration measure really matter?', *Journal of Industrial Economics*, **29**, 445-53.

Lahiri, S. and Y. Ono (1988), 'Helping minor firms reduces welfare', *Economic Journal*, **98**, no. 393, 1199-1202.

Landes, W. and R. Posner (2003), *The Economic Structure of Intellectual Property Law*, Cambridge, MA: The Belknap Press.

Lerner, J., M. Strojwas and J. Tirole (2003), 'Cooperative marketing agreements between competitors: evidence from patent pools', University of Toulouse, IDEI Working Paper, no. 187.

Lerner, J. and J. Tirole (2002), 'Efficient patent pools', National Bureau of Economic Research, Working Paper, no. 9175.

Littlechild, S.C. (2000), *Privatisation, Competition and Regulation*, Institute of Economic Affairs, Occasional Paper no. 110.

Lowe P. (2004), 'Current issues of EU competition law: the new competition enforcement regime', *North-Western Journal of International Law and Business*, **24** (3), 567-84.

Lyons, B. (2004), 'Reform of European merger policy', *Review of International Economics*, **12** (2), 246-61.

Malueg, D. and Schwartz, M. (1994), 'Parallel imports, demand dispersion and international price discrimination', *Journal of International Economics*, **37** (3-4), 167-95.

Mathewson, G.F. and R.A. Winter (1984), 'An economic theory of vertical restraints', *Rand Journal of Economics*, **15**, 27-38.

Maurer, S. and S. Scotchmer (2004), 'Profit neutrality in licensing: the boundary between antitrust law and patent law', NBER Working Paper, no. 10546.

McGowan, L. (2005), 'Europeanization unleashed and rebounding: assessing the modernization of EU cartel policy', *Journal of European Public Policy*, **12** (6), 986-1004.

McGowan, L. and M. Cini (1999), 'Discretion and politicization in EU competition policy', *Governance*, **12** (2), 175-200.

Merges, R. (1999), 'Institutions for intellectual property transactions: the case for patent pools', University of California, Berkeley, mimeo.

Monti, M. (2001), 'Services of general interest in Europe', *Europäische Zeitschrift für Wirtschaftsrecht*, **6**, p. 161.

Morgan, E.J. (1996), 'The treatment of oligopoly under the European Merger Control Regulation', *Antitrust Bulletin*, **41** (Spring), 203-46.

Morgan, E.J. (1998), 'EU merger control reforms: an appraisal', *European Management Journal*, **16** (1), 110-20.

Morgan, E.J. (2001), 'A decade of EU merger control', *International Journal of the Economics of Business*, **8** (3), 451-73.

Morris, D. (2002), 'The Enterprise Act: aspects of the new regime', *Economic Affairs*, **22** (4), 15-24.

Motta, M. (2000), 'EC merger policy and the Airtours case', *European Competition Law Review*, **21** (4), 199-207.

Motta, M. (2004), *Competition Policy: Theory and Practice*, Cambridge: Cambridge University Press.

NERA (1999), 'Merger appraisal in oligopolistic markets', Research Paper 19, London, OFT.

Neven, D., R. Nuttall and P. Seabright (1993), *Merger in Daylight: the Economics and Politics of European Merger Control*, London: Centre for Economic Policy Research.

Neven, D., P. Papandropoulos and P. Seabright (1998), *Trawling for Minnows: European Competition Policy and Agreements Between Firms*, London: Centre for Economic Policy Research.

Newbery, D.M. (2002), 'Regulatory challenges to European electricity liberalisation', *Swedish Economic Policy Review*, **9** (2), 9-44.

Nicolaides, P. and M. Kekelekis (2004), 'An assessment of EC State aid policy on rescue and restructuring of companies in difficulty', *European Competition Law Review*, **25** (9), 578-83.

O'Brien, D.P., W.S. Howe and D.M. Wright, with R.J. O'Brien (1979), *Competition Policy, Profitability and Growth*, London: Macmillan.

OECD (2002), 'Fighting hard core cartels: harm, effective sanctions and leniency programmes', Paris: OECD.

OECD (2003), 'Hard core cartels: recent progress and challenges ahead', Paris: OECD.

Peeperkorn, L. (1999), 'The Commission's radical overhaul of EC competition policy towards vertical restraints', in J. Faull and A. Nikpay (eds) *The EC Law of Competition*, Oxford: Oxford University Press.

Phlips, L. (1995), *Competition Policy: A Game Theoretic Perspective*, Cambridge: Cambridge University Press.

Ramsey, F. (1927), 'A contribution to the theory of taxation', *Economic Journal*, **37**, no. 145, 47-61.

Rapp-Jung, B. (2004), 'State financing of public services: the Commission's new approach', *European State Aid Law Quarterly*, **3** (2), 205-16.

Rey, P. (2003), 'The economics of vertical restraints', in R. Arnott, B. Greenwald, R. Kanbur and B. Nalebuff (eds), *Economics for an Imperfect World: Essays in Honor of Joseph E. Stiglitz*, Cambridge, MA: MIT Press.

Rey, P. and J. Stiglitz (1995), 'The role of exclusive territories in producers' competition', *Rand Journal of Economics*, **26** (3), 431-51.

Rey, P. and J. Tirole (1986a), 'Vertical restraints from a principal-agent viewpoint', in L. Pellegrini and S. Reddy (eds) *Marketing Channels: Relationships and Performance*, Lexington, MA: Lexington Books.

Rey, P. and J. Tirole (1986b), 'The logic of vertical restraints', *American Economic Review*, **76** (5), 921-39.

Rey, P. and J. Tirole (forthcoming), 'A primer on foreclosure', in M. Armstrong and R. Porter (eds), *Handbook of Industrial Organization*, Vol. III, Amsterdam: Elsevier.

Ridyard, D. (2005), 'The Commission's new horizontal merger guidelines: an economic commentary', College of Europe, Brugge, Global Competition Law Centre, Working Papers Series 02/25.

Robert, G. and C. Hudson (2004), 'Past co-ordination and the Commission notice on the appraisal of horizontal mergers', *European Competition Law Review*, **25** (3), 163-8.

Scherer, F.M. and D. Ross (1990), *Industrial Market Structure and Economic Performance*, 3rd edition, Boston: Houghton Mifflin Co.

Schina, D. (1987), *State Aids Under Article 92 to 93*, Oxford: USC.

Scotchmer, S. (2004), *Innovation and Incentives*, Cambridge, MA: MIT Press.

Secrieru, O. (2004), 'The economic theory of retail pricing: a survey', Bank of Canada, Working Paper, no. 2004-8.

Shapiro, C. (2001), 'Navigating the patent thicket: cross licences, patent pools and standard setting', in A. Jaffe, J. Lerner and S. Stern (eds) *Innovation Policy and the Economy*, Vol. 1, Cambridge, MA: MIT Press.

Smith, M. (2001), 'How adaptable is the European Commission? The case of State aid regulation', *Journal of Public Policy*, **21** (3), 219-38.

Steiner, R.L. (1991), 'Intrabrand competition: stepchild of antitrust', *Antitrust Bulletin*, **36** (Summer), 155-200.

Stole, L. (forthcoming), 'Price discrimination and imperfect competition', in M. Armstrong and R. Porter (eds), *Handbook of Industrial Organization*, Vol. III, Amsterdam: Elsevier.

Subiotto, R. and F. Amato (2001), 'The reform of the European competition policy concerning vertical restraints', *Antitrust Law Journal*, **69** (1), 147-94.

Swann, D., D.P. O'Brien, W.P.Maunder and W.S. Howe (1974), *Competition in British Industry*, London: George Allen and Unwin.

Temple Lang, J. (2000), 'The principle of essential facilities in European Community competition law', *Journal of Network Industries*, **1** (4), 375-405.

Tichy, G. (2001), 'What do we know about success and failure of mergers?', *Journal of Industry, Competition and Trade*, **1** (4), 347-94.

Todino, M. (2003), 'International Competition Networks – the state of play after Naples', *World Competition*, **26** (2), 283-302.

Trogh, R. (2002), 'The international exhaustion of trade mark rights after Silhouette: the end of parallel imports?', University of Lund, Spring 2002, mimeo.

Utton, M. (2000a), 'Books are not different after all: observations on the formal ending of the Net Book Agreement in the UK', *International Journal of the Economics of Business*, **7** (1), 115-26.

Utton, M. (2000b), 'Going European: Britain's new competition law', *Antitrust Bulletin*, **45**, 531-51.

Valle, E. and K. Van de Casteele (2004), 'Revision of the rescue and restructuring guidelines: a crackdown?', *European State Aid Law Quarterly*, **3** (1), 9-15.

Verouden, V. (2003), 'Vertical agreements and Article 81(1) EC: the evolving role of economic analysis', *Antitrust Law Journal*, **71** (2), 525-75.

Verouden, V., C. Bengtsson, and S. Albæk (2004), 'The draft EU notice on horizontal mergers: a further step towards convergence', *Antitrust Bulletin*, **49** (Spring), 243-85.

Vickers, J. (2004), 'Merger policy in Europe: retrospect and prospect', *European Competition Law Review*, **25** (7), 455-63.

Vickers, J. (2005), 'Abuse of market power', *Economic Journal*, **115**, no. 504, F244-61.

Waterson, M. (1993), 'Vertical integration and vertical restraints', *Oxford Review of Economic Policy*, **9** (2), 41-57.

Werden, G.J. (2004), 'Economic evidence on the existence of collusion: reconciling antitrust law with oligopoly theory', *Antitrust Law Journal*, **71** (3), 719-800.

Whish, R. (2003), *Competition Law*, 5th edition, London: Lexis Nexis.

Wilks, S. (1999), *In the Public Interest: Competition Policy and the Monopolies and Mergers Commission*, Manchester: Manchester University Press.

Williamson, O.E. (1968), 'Economies as an antitrust defence: the welfare tradeoffs', *American Economic Review*, **58** (1), 18-31.

Wishlade, F. (2003), *Regional State Aid and Competition Policy in the EU*, The Hague: Kluwer Law International.

Wishlade, F. (2004), 'The beginning of the end, or just another new chapter? Recent developments in EU competition policy control of regional state aid', EPRC European Policy Research Paper, University of Strathclyde, Glasgow.

Wright, S., R. Mason, and D. Miles (2003), *A Study into Certain Aspects of the Cost of Capital for Regulated Utilities in the UK*, London: Smithers and Co.

Yvrande-Billon, A. (2003), 'Franchising public services: an analysis of the duration of passenger rail franchises in Great Britain', ATOM, University of Paris I Panthéon-Sorbonne, mimeo.

Index